EnGENDERing
Wealth and Well-Being

■

Latin America in Global Perspective

The fundamental purpose of this multivolume series is to broaden conceptual perspectives for the study of Latin America. This effort responds to a perception of need. Latin America cannot be understood in isolation from other parts of the world. This has always been so; it is especially true in the contemporary era.

Accordingly, the goal of this series is to demonstrate the desirability and the feasibility of analyzing Latin America in comparative perspective, in conjunction with other regions, and in global perspective, in the context of worldwide processes. A subsidiary purpose is to establish a bridge between Latin American "area studies" and mainstream social science disciplines, to the mutual benefit of both. Ultimately, the intent is to explore and emphasize intellectual challenges posed by dynamic changes within Latin America and in its relation to the international arena.

The present volume examines the impact of economic change on gender and on women's roles in Latin America and other parts of the world. The keynote volume for the series, *Latin America in Comparative Perspective: New Approaches to Methods and Analysis*, explores theoretical and methodological issues involved in the comparative analysis of Latin America. Other studies in this series will include:

Institutional Design in New Democracies, edited by Arend Lijphart and Carlos Waisman;

Domestic Politics and Global Environmental Policy, edited by Gordon MacDonald, Daniel Nielsen, and Marc Stern;

Civil-Military Relations After the Cold War, edited by David Mares;

Cooperation or Rivalry? Regional Integration in the Americas and the Pacific Rim, edited by Shoji Nishijima and Peter H. Smith.

This series results from a multiyear research program organized by the Center for Iberian and Latin American Studies (CILAS) at the University of California, San Diego. Principal funding has come from the Andrew W. Mellon Foundation.

EnGENDERing Wealth and Well-Being

■

Empowerment for Global Change

edited by

Rae Lesser Blumberg
Cathy A. Rakowski
Irene Tinker
Michael Monteón

Westview Press

BOULDER • SAN FRANCISCO • OXFORD

Latin America in Global Perspective

Copyright © 1995 by Westview Press, Inc.

Published in 1995 in the United States of America by Westview Press, Inc., 5500 Central Avenue, Boulder, Colorado 80301-2877, and in the United Kingdom by Westview Press, 12 Hid's Copse Road, Cumnor Hill, Oxford OX2 9JJ

A CIP catalog record for this book is available from the Library of Congress.
ISBN 0-8133-2106-9 — ISBN 0-8133-2107-7 (pbk.)

Printed and bound in the United States of America

The paper used in this publication meets the requirements
of the American National Standard for Permanence of Paper
for Printed Library Materials Z39.48-1984.

10   9   8   7   6   5   4   3   2   1

Contents

---■---

Acknowledgments

We begin by thanking colleagues, more than fifty in all, who have offered to us their insights and perspectives on the gendered impact of global economic change. Many of their suggestions and hypotheses have found expression in this book.

We wish to thank Peter H. Smith, director of the Center for Iberian and Latin American Studies (CILAS) at UCSD. We thank Deborah Ortiz, CILAS program coordinator, and Patricia Rosas, CILAS assistant editor, for their continuous support throughout our efforts.

We also thank the Andrew W. Mellon Foundation for support of our work on this project.

We close with expressions of gratitude and admiration for Barbara Ellington, our editor at Westview Press, whose insights and encouragement made this book possible.

Rae Lesser Blumberg
Cathy A. Rakowski
Irene Tinker
Michael Monteón

Acronyms

AD	Acción Democrática (Democratic Action)
AFL-CIO	American Federation of Labor and Congress of Industrial Organizations
AMAVEN	Asociación de Mujeres y Ambiente de Venezuela (Venezuelan Association of Women and Environment)
AMIGRANSA	Asociación de Amigos en Defensa de La Gran Sabana (Association of Friends in Defense of the Great Savannah)
CBI	Caribbean Basin Initiative
CESAP	Centro de Formación a Servicio de la Acción Popular (Social Movement Training Center)
CIPAF	Centro de Investigación para la Acción Femenina (Research Center for Feminism)
CONFEVECINOS	Coordinadora Nacional de Federaciones de Vecinos (National Coordinator of Neighborhood Federations)
COPAN	Comité Patriótico Nacional (National Patriotic Committee)
COWAN	Country Women Association of Nigeria
DR	Dominican Republic
ECLAC	Economic Commission for Latin America
EOI	export-oriented industrialization
EPZ	export-processing zone
FACUR	Federación de Asociaciones de Comunidades Urbanas (Federation of Urban Neighborhood Associations)
FORJA	Federación de Organizaciones de Juntas Ambientales (Federation of Boards of Environmental Organizations)

GAD	gender and development
GALS	guaranteed access levels
GDP	gross domestic product
GDR	German Democratic Republic
GEMA	Grupo de Estudio Mujer y Ambiente (Women and Environment Study Group)
GIDA	Grupo de Ingeniería de Arborización (Tree Engineering Group)
GNP	gross national product
GSP	Generalized System of Preferences
HABITAT	United Nations Center for Human Settlements
IDB	International Development Bank
ILGWU	International Ladies Garment Workers Union
ILO	International Labour Organization
IMF	International Monetary Fund
INCAP	Institute of Nutrition of Central America and Panama
ISI	import-substitution industrialization
KIP	*kampung* improvement projects
LDC	less developed country
LGA	Local Government Area
MAS	Movimiento al Socialismo (Movement to Socialism)
MNC	multinational corporation
NAFTA	North American Free Trade Agreement
NCHS	U.S. National Center for Health Statistics
NGO	nongovernmental organization
NIC	newly industrializing country
OAS	Organization of American States
OPEC	Organization of Petroleum Exporting Countries
PDVSA	Petroleos de Venezuela, Socios Anónimos
PRI	Partido Revolucionario Institucional
SAL	structural adjustment lending
SAP	structural adjustment program
SD	standard deviation
SPARC	Society for Promotion of Area Resource Centres
TNC	transnational corporation
UNCED	United Nations Conference on Environment and Development
UNCHS	United Nations Center for Human Settlements
UNDP	United Nations Development Programme
UNICEF	United Nations International Children's Emergency Fund
UNU/WIDER	United Nations University/World Institute for Development

USAID   U.S. Agency for International Development
WCED   World Commission on Environment and Development
WEDNET   Women, Environment, and Development Network
WHO   World Health Organization
WID   women in development

CHAPTER ONE

---■---

Introduction: Engendering Wealth and Well-Being in an Era of Economic Transformation

Rae Lesser Blumberg

THE DUAL GOALS OF THIS VOLUME ARE TO ANALYZE the gendered nature of economic transformation and to promote the understanding of this phenomenon in a cross-regional perspective, comparing trends in Latin America with developments in other world regions. All the chapters illustrate the ways in which economically empowered women engender wealth and well-being that radiate far beyond their own families.

To establish a historical and conceptual framework for approaching these interrelated issues, this introduction offers a three-part expedition through time, theory, and space. I begin by tracing the quarter century of intertwined gender and economic history since 1970. This period witnessed the rise and evolution of the field of women in development (WID), a great increase in the proportion of income-earning women around the globe, and sweeping changes in the world: its economy, its ecology, its political geography, and its population patterns.

In the second part, I will stress the relationship between women and income and I will argue that women's control of economic resources, especially income, is the most important predictor of the degree of gender equality. In addition I will also argue that women's control of income engenders not only their own empowerment but also the creation of wealth and well-being at levels ranging from the micro (family) to the macro (nation). In the third part, I will discusses the evolving field of women/gender and development, which has come to focus less on women's victimization by development policies and world economic trends and more on women's rising contributions to the economy and

1

welfare at micro- and macrolevels. A concluding comment projects these topics into the future by identifying gender issues for the next century. □

A QUARTER CENTURY OF GENDER AND GLOBAL CHANGE

An event-filled quarter century has passed since we began to consider that men and women play different roles in the process of development and are differentially affected by it. In 1970, when Danish economist Ester Boserup published her path-breaking book *Woman's Role in Economic Development*, the world was a far different place. The Cold War drove most decisions about which countries would receive international aid, and gender had not yet been imagined as a variable relevant for promoting economic or human development.[1]

Two historic "tipping points" took place in 1970. First, in the United States, the proportion of women in the labor force aged eighteen through sixty-four reached—and surpassed—50 percent.[2] This was a new phenomenon in Western industrial countries, and it coincided with the dramatic rise of a "second wave" women's movement that went far beyond the suffrage-oriented goals of the first wave and soon spread around the globe.[3] Second, multinational corporations (MNCs) overtook nation-states on the U.S. Library of Congress list of the 100 biggest entities in the world, 51 to 49.[4] With corporations measured in gross sales and countries in gross national product (GNP), this phenomenon was a harbinger of future global restructuring.

Boserup's book launched women in development (WID) as a new field. She focused on women, technology, population, and agricultural change, and her data indicated that these changes were more likely to marginalize women, whose workloads frequently rose but whose returns and resource bases also often eroded—especially where they previously had enjoyed more economic autonomy. Subsequent studies by WID scholars[5] and activists showed that women were, indeed, frequently hurt by development but also that women's productive labor was greater than anyone had suspected or than official statistics measured.

Now, some twenty-five years later, the Fourth World Conference on Women: Action for Equality, Development, and Peace, in Beijing in 1995, has been set in the context of a worldwide women's movement of substantial size and achievement. The major world axis is now North-South, between developed and developing nations, rather than East-West. Both the proportion of multinational corporations among the world's largest entities and the proportion of women in the labor force have risen further, functioning as lead indicators for two even more revolutionary developments—global restructuring and women's growing access to income.

First, with respect to global restructuring, capital, information, production, and even services have burst the bounds of nation-states. Corporations search the globe for the most advantageous place to produce products, or buy inputs, or declare earnings from transactions. Cheap, flexible labor is a key consideration.[6] Flexible labor means burgeoning informal sectors in most of the world,[7] rising ranks of temporary contract employees, and an intricate web of subcontracting that extends, for example, from poor Third World women working in their homes to slightly less poor ones working in export-processing zone (EPZ) factories.

Second, the proportion of the world's women who earn income has risen far faster than the proportion actually counted in labor force statistics, which primarily measure waged workers in the formal sector.[8] The growing legions of money-earning females are a truly revolutionary phenomenon. In general, regardless of how humble the amount or stressful the conditions under which it is generated, to the extent that women control that income it typically has multiple positive consequences, starting with women's greater self-esteem and stronger voice in household decision making.

As I have argued elsewhere, women's control of economic resources, especially income, relative to men is the single most important (although not the only) factor affecting the degree of gender equality at a variety of "nested" levels, ranging from the couple to the state.[9] A main theme of this book is the impact of the rising share of income under female as opposed to male control, from the microlevel of the household to the macrolevel of the state and even the globe. Increasingly, new evidence shows that women are contributing to the wealth and well-being of both their families and their nations as the transformations in the world economy over the last quarter century have increased the need to earn income to survive and have enhanced women's ability to generate that income.

Key Economic Trends

One major transformation began with the oil shocks of the 1970s. The price of oil at the wellhead quintupled in the wake of the 1974 oil embargo, then doubled again with the 1979 overthrow of the Shah of Iran. Hundreds of billions of new petrodollars flowed toward the members of the Organization of Petroleum Exporting Countries (OPEC). Following extant economic wisdom, the oil-producing countries deposited a large portion of their petrodollars in multinational banks. The banks then lent the funds to Third World countries, including the oil pro-

lity prices were generally high at the time, but during
rices of oil and other commodities dipped. The result
is. As their income dropped, many Third World debtor
...ule to keep up their interest payments.

under pressure from the World Bank and the International Monetary
Fund (IMF), those countries that could not keep up with their loan payments adopted neoliberal measures to stabilize their economies, which
cut back their public sector budgets and personnel, removed subsidies,
floated currencies, adjusted prices, and promoted exports. These "structural adjustment programs" (SAPs) are most prevalent in Africa, Latin
America, and the Caribbean, where the 1980s have been described as
"the lost decade of development." African economies shrank almost 3
percent a year in the 1980s, as fast as they had grown in the heady
postindependence period of 1965–1973.[10] Now thirty-five of forty-six
African countries have implemented SAPs.[11]

The economic crisis has driven more people into the informal sectors,
which are mushrooming in countries around the world. Since the public
sector and much of the formal private sector were shedding jobs—and in
most of the affected countries there is little or no government "safety
net" for the jobless or impoverished—the informal sector proved the best
refuge. But jobs in this sector are often precarious for both the self-
employed and their even more marginal workers (especially women):
except for some of the self-employed, income is usually lower than in the
formal sector and fringe benefits are almost nonexistent.

It is not just structural adjustment that is swelling the size of most
countries' informal sectors but also the process of global economic
restructuring itself. The rates of technological change and increases in
levels of "uncertainty" (situations too volatile and full of unknowns to be
able to assess) are accelerating worldwide. In response, both businesses
and people have become more mobile. Most countries have had to
abandon import-substitution industrialization (ISI), which dominated
development policy and practice in the post–World War II period. Under
ISI, a small number of privileged firms, sheltered by high tariff barriers,
with a tiny, often unionized, relatively well-paid, and overwhelmingly
male labor force, produced high-cost local versions of previously
imported products.

Instead, lured by the success of the newly industrialized countries
(NICs), especially the "four tigers" of Asia (Hong Kong, Singapore,
South Korea, and Taiwan), or prodded by SAPs, more and more countries have turned to nontraditional exports. Export-processing zones
have sprung up in scores of countries beyond the four tigers, although
most are concentrated in less than a dozen nations in Southeast Asia,
Latin America, and the Caribbean. In contrast to ISI male labor forces, the

workers in the EPZs are predominantly women—especially young, non-unionized women. Often they compete for rarely permanent and frequently tedious jobs. They tend to be better educated and better paid than young women doing similar jobs in domestic-oriented factories in their countries.[12] But by world standards, they are inexpensive and productive enough to attract an ever-growing number of firms. Export-oriented industrialization (EOI) is the latest development gospel for those promoting national income growth.

Women are also more likely to be employed in nontraditional agricultural exports, such as broccoli, spices, and flowers, than in such traditional export crops as bananas, cocoa, and sugar. The nontraditional agricultural export crops tend to be more labor-intensive or require more care in handling than traditional export crops, which is why the industry employs higher proportions of (lower paid) women. These new export crops are burgeoning, stimulated by SAPs and a growing global demand for healthy vegetables, unusual spices, and fresh flowers. It remains to be seen whether either export-oriented industrialization or nontraditional agricultural exports are viable strategies for large numbers of countries.

Meanwhile, the cash economy has penetrated to the most remote locations. Low-resource farmers increasingly sell part of their production out of dire financial need, and this means that millions more women and men enter or expand their involvement in the money economy. Due to the combined effects of the exploding informal sector, the jobs created by the "new international division of labor," and the spreading cash nexus, uncounted millions of women formerly in the subsistence sector have begun earning or increasing income. □

INCOME UNDER FEMALE VERSUS MALE CONTROL

A growing body of research supports the hypotheses of my theory of gender stratification and suggests that increased income under women's control enhances (1) their self-confidence, (2) their say in household decision making in the areas of fertility, economic decisions (such as buying, selling, or allocating major resources), and domestic decisions (such as the education of sons and daughters), and (3) their sway over other "life options" (such as marriage, divorce, and freedom of movement). Additionally, it is proposed that men spend income differently than women with provider obligations, who tend to hold back less for themselves and devote more to children's nutrition, health, and education.[13]

Elsewhere, I have argued that women contribute to the wealth of their nations (and families) by two intertwined chains, one based on production and the other on education.[14] In the first chain, women create wealth via their productive activities, especially those that result in income under their own control. Empirical studies now show the much greater share of national wealth created by women's production than is revealed in traditional analyses of national accounts statistics.[15] Other studies are demonstrating that women are more willing to take on extra work—even to the point of assuming workloads that approach physiological limits—if there is a monetary return they can control. The data indicate that women can approach or equal men's productivity in economic activities such as low resource farming and informal sector microenterprises even with smaller resource bases. For example, in findings from three studies in Africa, which statistically adjusted women's resources to equal those of men, women were consistently more productive.[16] An econometric study in Burkina Faso found the most spectacular difference: Women proved to be 600 percent more productive.[17]

Women often have greater unmet income needs and typically earn less than men. This means they have both greater incentives to earn money and lower opportunity costs (the value of their time for alternate income-producing uses). Therefore, they may also respond more strongly than men to a modest lowering of production constraints or a small rise in income. This was found, for example, in Jeanne Koopman Henn's study in Cameroon comparing the labor and income of men and women in two villages—one in which a new road was built connecting it to regional markets and one that remained isolated.[18] In the village with the new road, the women—who already worked over sixty hours per week (double the hours worked by men)—responded to the new access to markets by increasing their production and sale of perishable vegetable crops. This increased their workweek even more, but they averaged over 2.5 times more earnings from these crops than women in the village without a new road. The data also showed that men in the village with the new road barely increased the amount of time they spent in the cultivation of plantains and bananas, which became more marketable, even though these crops brought a significantly higher return than cocoa, their main cash crop. Henn offers no explanation for the men's less responsive market behavior.

It is also posited that women, to the extent possible, will attempt to reallocate their labor toward activities that put income or food under their direct control and away from activities that do not, even if the latter are somewhat more profitable to the husband or the household.[19] A good example is Christine Jones's quantitative random-sample study of the SEMRY I irrigated rice project in Cameroon.[20] The project could not cover its costs because farmers failed to cultivate enough of the available pump-irrigated fields. Women were expected to grow one rice plot as a marital obligation, but most wives would not grow a second plot of rice for their husbands. Jones's data show that the income from the SEMRY I project's harvests were given to husbands even though the wives had grown the crop. The husbands shared that profit with their wives, often paying them more than the women could have earned in other activities. Nevertheless, most women chose to cultivate their own sorghum, the planting and first weeding of which conflicted with the transplanting of rice.

As noted, once women with provider obligations gain control of income, evidence shows that they are more likely to spend that income on enhanced children's nutrition, health, and education and on family welfare. A variety of studies have found that income controlled by the mother is associated with better nourished children than is income controlled by the father. Current research also suggests a connection between income controlled by women and enhanced children's education—for girls as well as boys. For example, household survey data from Santiago, Chile, show that female household heads earned only half the income of male heads, but their children's rates of high school attendance lagged little behind the attendance rates of children in male-headed families: 3 percent less for girls, 11 percent less for boys.[21] In contrast, in male-headed households, boys were significantly more likely to attend high school—except when the wife earned more than her husband; in this case, there was no significant difference. If female-controlled income is also preferentially used for educating both girls and boys, we have an empirical link between the first chain (production-income) and the second chain (girls' education), whereby women contribute to the wealth and well-being of nations.

Education, or human capital formation, has long been documented as one of the most important factors stimulating development. Its role as a cornerstone of democracy is also increasingly recognized. Today, one of the first gender issues to be enthusiastically advocated by top development policy makers has been the importance of educating *girls*. Their level of funding for girls' education does not yet match their level of verbal endorsement, however. This is particularly unfortunate in view of the fact that matching every dollar spent educating boys with the same amount for educating girls generally has multiple payoffs: (1) a later age of marriage; (2) increased contraceptive usage; (3) lower fertility;[22] (4) dramatically reduced infant and child mortality; (5) improved child nutrition and general family health; (6) higher female participation in the modern wage labor force; (7) higher female earnings (which brings us back to the first chain); and (8) increased national development as measured by gross national product.[23]

The impact on national income growth stems from two sources: the human-capital effect of education and evidence that reduced fertility contributes to economic growth in less developed countries.[24] There is considerable evidence that income-earning women also have greater say in fertility. In most parts of the world, they use this leverage to *lower* it.

In sum, women's key contributions to world wealth and well-being—through production, through spending of the resulting income under their control, and through the consequences of their education—have come to provide an alternative view to women as victims of development.[25] □

THE EVOLUTION OF A PARADIGM: FROM "WOMEN AS VICTIMS" TO "WOMEN— NEEDED TO SAVE THE WORLD"

When the field of women in development emerged in the wake of Boserup's book, its initial focus was on how women were being disproportionately disadvantaged and marginalized by development and "modernization." Women were generally the sole focus of analysis, and they were viewed mainly as "victims" in need of advancement and assistance.[26] The 1970s emphasis was on "equity" and on integrating women of various countries, classes, and ethnicities into extant development efforts—which then almost always ignored or undermined them. Numerous empirical studies documented both women's major (albeit unsung) productive roles and the disasters that ensued from undercutting them.

The early 1980s saw the rise of conservative administrations (most notably Ronald Reagan's in the United States and Margaret Thatcher's in Britain), as well as the onset of the debt crisis. The major international donors of development aid—the World Bank and the U.S. Agency for International Development (USAID)—shifted from a focus on "development with equity" to an emphasis on the private sector, economic efficiency, and, as noted, the austerity and export-oriented policies of structural adjustment. The rhetoric of the growing WID field soon changed to accommodate the new realities. It stressed "efficiency" arguments: Planned development assistance better achieved its goals by incorporating women. For example, the largest-scale evaluation yet of the extent to which women were taken into account in a major donor's projects—and the consequences—concluded that the mainstream [USAID] projects that ensure women's participation in proportion to their roles and responsibilities within the project's baseline situation are more likely to achieve their immediate purposes and their broader socioeconomic goals than are projects that do not.[27]

One result of such findings was the emergence of "gender analysis" for development projects and programs. Although aimed at making sure that data on women are collected, gender analysis requires that information be gathered not only on women but also on women in comparison to men. A proper gender analysis looks at the gender division of: labor, resources and income, time, and other constraints, such as mobility. Gender analyses must also disaggregate by class, race, ethnicity, and, where relevant, by age or other significant planes of cleavage. These data must be related to the activities and benefits of the project. Ideally, the project then should be adapted to remove constraints on benefits to women.

By the mid-1980s, new rapid appraisal methodologies—including Rapid Rural Appraisal, Rapid Assessment Procedures, and Participatory Rapid Appraisal—were proliferating. They permit the quick and inexpensive collection of generally valid, reliable information on, inter alia, the gender analysis variables listed in the preceding paragraph. By the late 1980s, USAID and other development agencies adopted policies stipulating that all social indicators be disaggregated by gender and that projects incorporate a gender analysis. To date, these directives have met with only intermittent compliance, however.

Still, the emergence of rapid appraisal gender analysis and the fact that policy makers now pay at least lip service to the goals of promoting greater opportunities for women are significant advances. Moreover, in a 1990s version of the "development with equity" era two decades earlier, the policies of the Clinton administration once again stress that development must reach the disadvantaged. Combined with the Fourth World Conference on Women and the rise of a few "gender-sensitive" women and men into the upper-middle ranks of national and international bureaucracies, these trends should provide building blocks for a stronger, more gender-equitable foundation for development. Will gender finally come to be routinely taken into account in planned change during the remainder of the 1990s?

WID/GAD Perspectives

Meanwhile, the original WID paradigm continues to evolve. First, the emphasis is increasingly on *gender* rather than women (even if, empirically, the focus of practitioners and researchers continues to be mainly on women): Indeed, the field is now often called GAD—gender and development—rather than WID. Second, GAD stresses how gender is *socially constructed*, via the ways in which men and women participate in both production and reproduction. Third, what may be termed WID/GAD strongly challenges the picture of the household common to both mainstream and radical paradigms of development. These look at the household as a "black box," a monolithic unit that shares resources. For neoclassical economists, it does not matter who does the work or who receives income, information, or other forms of assistance; the household can be described by a single production function.[28]

By the late 1980s, WID/GAD researchers were widely contesting this view of the household. As they looked inside the black box, they found differential power and privilege based on gender and age. They discovered another gender-related reason that development assistance so often failed to meet its objectives: It *does* matter who works, who learns, and who gets rewarded. If the person who does the work is not the one taught about improvements or given a share in the benefits generated, that person is not likely to perform as hoped. In a disproportionate number of cases, the working person has turned out to be a woman.

A look inside the black box also revealed that women's relative control of income and property affected their degree of empowerment vis-à-vis family (and sometimes community) decisions. And because women devoted more of their income to children's nutrition, health, and education, these intrahousehold studies also indicated that directing development resource flows to women (as well as men) not only had a positive economic effect, it also enhanced indicators of well-being.

In short, the paradigm is shifting toward a view that women are needed by the world to solve its problems. This does not mean a shift to a worldview that things invariably are changing for the better for women. Rather, the new framing emphasizes the positive contributions of empowered women. Instead of focusing on "women needing help," the stress is now on how and why the "world needs women." The GAD paradigm provides a new lens to look at the economic transformations sweeping our globe—a gendered one. Analyses of the new international division of labor and global restructuring, as well as the debt crisis and structural adjustment programs, have been enriched by examining how gender makes a difference as a variable and how women make a difference in coping with economic crises. On the negative side, the studies show that many women—especially poor ones—are bearing the brunt of the crises.[29] They are disproportionately losing good public sector and formal sector jobs, moving into the precarious and often poverty-ridden informal sector, and substituting their own efforts for slashed spending on health, education, urban infrastructure, and other "social" commodities, even if it means adding to already brutal workloads. But there is also a positive side—including women's creative responses to the direst of circumstances.

Women disproportionately bear the responsibility of providing household supplies of water, fuel, and fodder, and they have a vested interest in the continued (or enhanced) availability of these resources. We are finding that women may be more responsive than men to conservation efforts. They may be more responsive to even modest incentives—or small decreases in constraints—that enable them to steward their resource bases from soils to plants to water. Accordingly, they could help lead the shift away from the extant growth-fixated development model that fails to adequately consider either the planet's or the people's well-being. □

GENDER ISSUES FOR THE NEXT CENTURY

What are some of the major issues for the future and what role will gender play? First, there can be little question that many of the most blatant forms of inequality, such as slavery and serfdom, have come under such strong international condemnation as to have been legally abolished everywhere although abuses continue in scattered countries. Other forms of exploitation, such as institutionalized racial and ethnic oppression, are censured almost everywhere, although they continue to occur widely. Still other forms, including the institutionalized subjugation of women, have been less universally denounced and in some places are increasing. Even so, there is overall progress. More than 100 nations, including some of the world's most patriarchal states, have signed the United Nations Convention on the Elimination of Discrimination Against Women. Some of these countries may not be enforcing the provisions of this document at present, but a foundation for future action has been laid.

Second, other recent, sweeping historical trends also seem to be moving us into a "techno-economic base."[30] Most frequently termed the information society, this new way of organizing production is furthest advanced in the United States. In an information society, knowledge is power. And knowledge is creating a more flexible form of power than military or even economic power. Worldwide, classes of the information-rich versus the information-poor may be emerging that do not coincide smoothly with existing forms of stratification.[31] But what is relevant here is that both the information workers and the managers cruising the emerging "information superhighway" have higher than average levels of education, and their ranks are more likely to include women than in the past.

Third, the issue of sustainable development is here to stay. The definition of development as unrestrained pursuit of national income growth at the expense of environmental health is coming under increasing condemnation. Women are heavily involved in the worldwide environmental movement and are actively promoting the idea that, as the principal household-level users of fundamental resources, they have the biggest stake in conservation. But those women must be recognized in their environmental protector role, their worldviews must be validated, and both their incentives and constraints must be addressed.

By placing women at the center of global restructuring and demonstrating women's centrality to wealth and well-being at both micro- and
macrolevels, this volume challenges everyone writing on social and economic change to utilize gender analysis. The chapters that follow paint a
composite picture of women as active agents of a form of development
that goes beyond economic growth as the ultimate goal. The authors,
documenting how women are empowered through control of wealth,
through education, and through organizing, reveal glimpses of a direct
relationship between these empowered women and a (lower fertility)
world of greater human and ecological well-being. □

NOTES

1. Ester Boserup, *Woman's Role in Economic Development* (New York: St.
Martin's Press, 1970).

2. Valerie Kincade Oppenheimer, "Demographic Influence on Female Employment and the Status of Women," *American Journal of Sociology* 78 (1973): 946–961.

3. Janet Saltzman Chafetz, *Gender Equity: An Integrated Theory of Stability and
Change* (Newbury Park, CA: Sage Publications, 1990).

4. Rae Lesser Blumberg, *Stratification: Socioeconomic and Sexual Inequality*
(Dubuque, IA: Wm. C. Brown, 1978), 95.

5. For example, Irene Tinker, "The Adverse Impact of Development on
Women," in Irene Tinker and Michele Bo Bramsen, eds., *Women and World Development* (Washington, DC: Overseas Development Council/American Association
for the Advancement of Science, 1976).

6. Guy Standing, "Global Feminization Through Flexible Labor," *World Development* 17, no. 7 (1989): 1079.

7. People working in the informal sector include those in nonprofessional self-
employment, workers in very small firms, unpaid family workers, and, in many
definitions, domestic service workers. This work is generally unregulated and
unprotected, and transactions do not usually enter into national accounts.

8. The formal sector's workers include self-employed professionals, employers, and workers in public sector and private sector firms and in legally registered
private sector firms whose transactions enter into national accounts. Some sub-
contract to the informal sector.

9. Rae Lesser Blumberg, "A Paradigm for Predicting the Position of Women:
Policy Implications and Problems," in Jean Lipman-Blumen and Jessie Bernard,
Sex Roles and Social Policy (London and Beverly Hills: Sage, 1976); Rae Lesser
Blumberg, "A General Theory of Gender Stratification," in Randall Collins, ed.,
Sociological Theory 1984 (San Francisco: Jossey-Bass, 1984); Rae Lesser Blumberg,
Gender, Family, and Economy: The Triple Overlap (Newbury Park, CA: Sage, 1991).

10. Stephen O'Brien, "Structural Adjustment and Structural Transformation in
Sub-Saharan Africa," in Christina H. Gladwin, ed., *Structural Adjustment and
African Women Farmers* (Gainesville: University of Florida Press, 1991); *World Bank,
Sub-Saharan Africa: From Crisis to Sustainable Growth* (Washington, DC: World
Bank, 1989).

11. "Bank Shifting Gears on Poverty?" *African Farmer* (October 1993): 40.

12. See, for example, Linda Lim, "Women Workers in Export Factories: Politics of a Cause," in Irene Tinker, ed., *Persistent Inequalities: Women and World Development* (New York: Oxford University Press, 1990).

13. I have synthesized these hypotheses and findings in several publications. See, e.g., "A General Theory of Gender Stratification," in Randall Collins, ed., *Sociological Theory 1984* (San Francisco: Jossey-Bass, 1984); "Income Under Female vs. Male Control: Hypotheses from a Theory and Data from the Third World," *Journal of Family Issues* 9, no. 1 (1988): 51–84; "Toward a Feminist Theory of Development," in Ruth A. Wallace, ed., *Feminism and Sociological Theory* (Newbury Park, CA: Sage Publications, 1989); "The Intersection of Family, Gender, and Economy in the Developing World," prepared for the International Year of the Family Occasional Paper Series, no. 9 (Vienna: United Nations 1YF Secretariat/1994); and Blumberg, *Gender, Family, and Economy.*

14. Rae Lesser Blumberg, *Making the Case for the Gender Variable: Women and the Wealth and Well-Being of Nations* (Washington, DC: Agency for International Development, Office of Women in Development, 1989).

15. Claudia Goldin, "The Female Labor Force and American Economic Growth," in Stanley Engerman and Robert Gallman, eds., *Long-term Factors in American Economic Growth* (Chicago: University of Chicago Press, 1986); see also Richard Anker, "Female Labour Force Participation in Developing Countries: A Critique of Current Definitions and Data Collection Methods," *International Labour Review* 122, no. 6 (November-December 1983): 709–723; Ruth Dixon, "Women in Agriculture: Counting the Labor Force in Developing Countries," *Population and Development Review* 8, no. 3 (1982): 539–566.

16. Peter Moock, "Managerial Ability in Small-Farm Production: An Analysis of Maize Yields in the Vihiga Division of Kenya," Ph.D. diss., School of Arts and Sciences, Columbia University, and Peter Moock, "The Efficiency of Women as Farm Managers: Kenya," *American Journal of Agricultural Economics* 58 (December 1976): 831–835; Rati Ram and Ram D. Singh, "Farm Households in Rural Burkina Faso: Some Evidence on Allocative and Direct Returns to Schooling, and Male-Female Labor Productivity Differentials," *World Development* 16, no. 3 (1988): 419–424; Kathleen Staudt, "Women Farmers and Inequities in Agricultural Services," *Rural Africana* 29 (Winter 1975–1976); and Kathleen Staudt, *Agricultural Policy Implementation: A Case Study from Western Kenya* (West Hartford, CT: Kumarian Press, 1985).

17. According to Ram and Singh (in note 16), yields from randomly selected plots were weighed and income data were intensively monitored. The marginal product for women's labor was 683 compared to 112 for men's labor at the sample mean in units of local currency.

18. Jeanne Koopman Henn, "Intra-Household Dynamics and State Policies as Constraints on Food Production: Results of an Agroeconomic Survey in Cameroon," in Susan V. Poats, Marianne Schmink, and Anita Spring, eds., *Gender Issues in Farming Systems Research and Extension* (Boulder: Westview Press, 1988).

19. Blumberg, *Gender, Family, and Economy.*

20. Christine Jones, "The Impact of the SEMRY I Irrigated Rice Production Project on the Organization of Production and Consumption at the Intrahouse-

hold Level," report prepared for the Agency for International Development, Bureau for Program and Policy Coordination, Washington, DC, 1983.

21. Rae Lesser Blumberg, Viviane Brachet-Marquez, Fernando Cortés, and Rosa María Rubalcava, "Women's 'Purse Power' in the Household: Reducing Favoritism Toward Boys' Schooling in Santiago, Chile," paper presented at the American Sociological Association meeting, Pittsburgh, 1992.

22. In some poor Third World countries, however, those with partial primary education have slightly higher fertility than those with no education, since fewer of their babies die.

23. Blumberg, *Making the Case for the Gender Variable*.

24. Peter Hess, *Population Growth and Socioeconomic Progress in Less Developed Countries: Determinants of Fertility Transition* (New York: Praeger, 1988).

25. Blumberg, *Gender, Family, and Economy*, and Chapter 10 by García and de Oliveira in this volume.

26. Rae Lesser Blumberg and Barbara Knudson, eds., *Gender Training Portfolio* (Santo Domingo: INSTRAW, 1993). For an alternate view of that evolution, see Irene Tinker, "The Making of a Field: Advocates, Practitioners, and Scholars," in Tinker, ed., *Persistent Inequalities*.

27. Alice Stewart Carloni, *Women in Development: AID's Experience, 1973–1975*, vol. 1, *Synthesis Paper* (Washington, DC: Agency for International Development, 1987), xiv.

28. Gary Becker, *A Treatise on the Family* (Boston: Harvard University Press, 1981).

29. Giovanni Andrea Cornia, Richard Jolly, and Frances Stewart, eds., *Adjustment with a Human Face*, vol. 1 (New York: UNICEF/Clarendon Press, 1987).

30. See Gerbard Lenski, *Power and Privilege* (New York: McGraw-Hill, 1966); Blumberg, *Stratification*. This would be the fifth major techno-economic base, or way in which people make a living from the planet, in human history. The other four were hunting and gathering, horticultural, agrarian, and industrial societies.

31. Alvin Toffler, *Powershift* (New York: Bantam Books, 1989).

PART ONE

An Overview of Gender
and Economic Transformation

Part One opens the discussion of economics and gender by looking at their relation in the broadest possible terms. The chapter by Valentine Moghadam considers the impact on women of contemporary economic change around the globe, and that of Michael Monteón reexamines current and historical data on economic crises in Latin America, expanding the understanding of these events through a gendered analysis. Each introduces issues that are treated in greater detail in later chapters, and both lay the groundwork for an explanation of why and how gender issues are related to larger patterns of change.

Moghadam provides an overarching view of contemporary economic change and its disproportionately negative effect on women. In so doing, she reframes many issues of gender and development in a broad, comparative context. She discusses global economic restructuring, which she characterizes as encompassing not only the globalization of production, the greater flexibility and mobility of labor, and the rapid growth of self-employment and small-scale enterprises in the informal sector but also the policies and impact of structural adjustment, the shift toward capitalism in Eastern Europe, and the rise of Islamist movements in the Middle East and North Africa. In discussing these changes, she demonstrates the numerous burdens that have fallen on women as formal employment declines for both women and men and as states cut their expenditures for social services. For example, she relates what it has meant for women in Eastern European countries to lose jobs and welfare provisions as those countries shift to market economies. And she makes the case that certain political and religious movements that seek to restrict women's mobility and employment can best be understood as social responses to cultural disruption brought on by economic and political change. Men in

15

power use control over women as a means to protect threatened cultural and religious identity.

Monteón compares the ways in which Latin America's experience in the debt crisis and the Great Depression affected women, and he finds both similarities and dramatic differences despite the paucity of information about the economic history of women earlier in this century. He emphasizes that the relation of economic crisis to women's empowerment is not a simple one, although each crisis has overlapped with an ongoing struggle by women for political and social change. The outcome in each instance has been uneven. But he suggests that, overall, Latin American women have achieved universal suffrage and also have made significant advances in reforming legal systems and gaining admission into the professions. Using his research as an example, Monteón argues that not only does an analysis of economic transformation benefit from a gendered perspective but also that gender studies could benefit from a stronger historical approach. Thus, he suggests the importance of a research agenda based on collaboration among women's studies scholars and economic historians.

Although both Moghadam and Monteón use economic crisis and transformation as their organizing theme, they remind us that struggles over employment and social services are also about social justice within a particular historical and cultural setting, including control over identities and values. They emphasize that the interrelatedness of socioeconomic change has profound consequences on gender relations.

CHAPTER TWO

————————— ■ —————————

Gender Dynamics of Restructuring in the Semiperiphery

Valentine M. Moghadam

IN RECENT YEARS, CONSIDERABLE ATTENTION HAS BEEN DIRECTED to three developments that have usually been analyzed separately: structural adjustment and the feminization of labor in developing countries; the transition to a market economy in Eastern Europe and the former Soviet Union; and the rise and expansion of conservative Islamist movements in the Middle East and North Africa. To examine the gender dynamics of these developments and to explore their commonalities, the World Institute for Development Economics Research of the United Nations University (UNU/WIDER) initiated a research program based on the following premises: (1) Restructuring is a global phenomenon, a fundamental feature of the world economy and not just of individual national economies; (2) marketization, structural adjustment, and Islamist movements are manifestations of the process of global restructuring; and (3) gender is an integral dimension of restructuring.[1] In this chapter, I will discuss some of my findings and provide a framework for understanding the relationship between gender and economic processes, including wealth and well-being. Following a review of some conceptual issues pertaining to economic restructuring, I will turn to the cases of, first, Eastern Europe and the former Soviet Union, and, second, the Middle East and North Africa. □

THEORETICAL GAPS AND NEW APPROACHES

In the late 1980s, perestroika in the Soviet Union and economic reform in Eastern Europe were widely analyzed in terms of the profound economic and political changes they heralded for the system of state socialism.

Today, much economic and sociological research focuses on the difficulties of the transition.[2] Although the prolific literature has drawn attention to interesting aspects of the problem, one category of analysis—gender—remains absent from most accounts, even those that study the social consequences of the reforms.[3] This oversight has occurred despite two decades of feminist scholarship, women in development research, and the more recent gender and development perspective, all of which revealed the unique impact of economic development, economic crisis, social breakdown, state formation, and juridical reorganization on women's productive and reproductive activities. In particular, a rich literature exists on structural adjustment and gender issues.[4]

In addition to the theoretical gap in most studies of economic reform, there has been a neglect of a comparative perspective, and as a result, certain outcomes of privatization and democratization that are regarded as "unexpected consequences" may, in fact, have been anticipated.[5] In particular, the Third World experience with revolutionary social transformation and with structural adjustment offered significant clues to the possible social, gender, and developmental consequences of rapid political and economic changes in Eastern Europe.[6] First, commonalities between restructuring of centrally planned economies and restructuring in developing countries include a shift from internally oriented to externally oriented growth and trade, from import-substitution industrialization to export-led manufacturing, and from large public sectors and nationalized industries to the privatization of enterprises and a contraction of the public sector wage bill. Second, the impact of restructuring on women ranges from retrenchment and mass unemployment to job opportunities in "flexible" labor markets, which include subcontracting and the revival of homework and of domestic and family labor systems. Such forms of unstable employment are characterized by low wages and the absence of social security. Third, a comparison of the early cases of Algeria and Iran with that of Poland finds that in each case "revolution" is tied to questions of cultural and religious identity. Patriarchal models of social transformation exalt women's role in the family and deny or downgrade women's reproductive and employment rights.

Like the study of structural adjustment and marketization, the rise of Islamist movements—usually examined in terms of intrinsic properties of Islam and Muslim societies—merits a macrosociological perspective and examination within the global process of economic restructuring. As will be shown later in this chapter, Islamist movements have emerged and spread in the context of economic failures and social disparities.[7] It is clear that the study of global restructuring is inadequate without attention to gender issues. But how should this analysis proceed?

An appropriate global and comparative approach for studying

restructuring processes is provided by world-system theory. Its basic premise is that there is a capitalist world economy that has integrated a geographically vast set of production processes into a single, worldwide division of labor across the three economic zones—core, periphery, and semiperiphery. (The semiperiphery includes the former Socialist economies as well as newly industrializing countries.) Thus, the multiple cultural systems of the world's people are part of a single, integrated economic system, for which global accumulation is the driving force. The capitalist world economy functions by means of a pattern of forty- to sixty-year business cycles, with upswing A-phases and downswing B-phases. These cyclical rhythms, known as Kondratieff cycles, or long waves, are a seemingly regular process of expansion and contraction of the world economy as a whole.[8] The world economy has been in the B-phase downturn since the mid-1970s. World-system theorist Christopher Chase-Dunn argues that the simultaneity and broad similarities of the deregulation and attack on the welfare state by the administrations of Reagan and Thatcher, the austerity socialism in much of Europe, the austerity and privatization policies in Brazil, Mexico, Argentina, and Chile, and the marketization in the former Socialist states are all related to the current downturn in the cyclical rhythm of the world economy.[9]

And what of class and gender in the world economy? According to Chase-Dunn: "The world class structure is composed of capitalists ... and propertyless workers. This class system also includes small commodity producers who control their own means of production but who do not employ the labor of others, and a growing middle class of skilled and/or professionally certified workers."[10] In many semiperipheral countries, it is precisely the numbers of self-employed and petty commodity producers that are growing, at the expense of regular wage and salary-earners, as labor market "flexibility" increases.

The place of gender in the world system remains undertheorized. However, at a very general level of analysis, one may begin to explain gender hierarchies and positions of women across the globe and within societies in terms of core, periphery, and semiperiphery locations. For example, in an early study, Kathryn Ward found that economic dependency led to greater inequalities—not only between countries and between classes within countries but also between men and women. Indeed, she found that dependency worsened women's status through limited job opportunities in the formal sector (jobs typically went to men), through women's relegation to unpaid work in the informal sector, and through increased childbearing. Fertility increases in the periphery either because women's socioeconomic position vis-à-vis men is lower and they have less control over that fertility or because children are needed as laborers or for old-age security.[11]

If peripheral status in the world system creates pressures for high fertility, a different logic operates for women in the semiperiphery and in the core. Most countries within the semiperiphery have seen dramatic declines in fertility, as more and more women have assumed nonagricultural employment in national and foreign-owned enterprises. In core countries, too, mass education, salaried employment, and social security programs have led to low birthrates. In turn, industrialization, capital accumulation, and the expansion of the public and private service sectors have been based on the utilization of female labor. Indeed, rapid industrialization and economic growth in the East Asian NICs and in the former centrally planned economies were almost certainly made possible by the massive incorporation of women into the labor force and the development process.

Ward and others have emphasized the role of women in the global economy, showing, in particular, the centrality of female waged and unwaged labor to new export-led strategies of industrialization.[12] More recently, Ward has been critical of world-system theory for what she perceives to be its overemphasis on exchange, accumulation, and class and its inability or unwillingness to theorize the gendered nature of production and the links between the formal sector and women's informal and housework labor.[13] Yet it cannot be denied that there *is* an accumulation process, at both national and global levels, and that this has class *and* gender dimensions. The accumulation process is predicated upon: (1) different forms of labor-capital arrangements, including informal and formal, large- and small-scale, salaried and unwaged, and self-employment; (2) different and changing forms of development strategies—import-substitution industrialization, export-oriented industrialization, oil or other commodity production for export, agricultural production, and trade and technology diffusion; and (3) both productive and reproductive work, as well as unproductive activities like banking, finance, insurance, speculation, and so on. Global accumulation as the driving force of the world system not only hinges on class and regional differences, it is also a gendered process. Similarly, global restructuring is gendered, as the following analysis suggests. □

THE GENDERED PROCESS OF GLOBAL RESTRUCTURING

A critical aspect of global restructuring is the "emergence of the global assembly line in which research and management are controlled by the core or developed countries while assembly line work is relegated to semiperiphery or periphery countries that occupy less privileged positions in the global economy."[14] By means of subcontracting and product differentiation, restructuring paradoxically concentrates control over increasingly dispersed production sites and decentralized organizations. This global assembly line approach to production "is attractive to transnational corporations (TNCs) and to employers seeking greater access to markets, diffusion of political and economic costs, improved competitive abilities, and product diversity. Within developing countries, restructuring is marked by growth of the service sector and specialization in export industries such as electronics, garments, and pharmaceuticals as a development strategy."[15] In the advanced capitalist countries, this process has taken the form of industrial restructuring, a shift from manufacturing to services, and the expansion of part-time and temporary jobs rather than stable employment.[16]

The centerpiece of global restructuring is the growth of the number of informal sector workers and the increasing use of female industrial workers in the informal sector, where pay and working conditions are unregulated by labor legislation. The existence of this sector is functional for capital inasmuch as it provides an alternative and cheap source of labor. By subcontracting industrial production to informal factories or home-based workers, employers can minimize competitive risks, wages, and the threat of unionization while maximizing their flexibility in hiring, their overhead costs, and their production processes.[17] In the United States, the growth of informalization has paralleled the increasing use of immigrant labor, drawing especially large numbers of Hispanic women into formal and informal arrangements in the garment and electronics industries of New York and California.[18] Temporary and part-time work, comparatively lower wages, and reduced membership in unions or other workers' organizations are additional characteristics of women's employment.[19] In the United States and Britain, international competition and declining profits in manufacturing led capital to break its social pact with labor. In Britain, "flexible workers" increased by 16 percent to 8.1 million between 1981 and 1985, and permanent jobs decreased by 6 percent to 15.6 million. Over roughly the same period, nearly one-third of the ten million new jobs created in the United States were said to be in the "temporary" category.[20] Although a U.S. Department of Labor publication states that "a key requirement in the future workplace will be *flexibility*— a managerial tool for employers as well as a time management tool for workers," the advantages of flexibility to capital, employers, and management seem clearer than those that could accrue to workers.[21]

The use of female labor has been especially striking in the export-manufacturing sector of semiperipheral countries, where export-processing zones have been set up to promote the textiles and clothing and electronics industries. Large EPZ operations exist in Hong Kong, South Korea, Puerto Rico, Singapore, Taiwan, Brazil, Haiti, Malaysia, and Mexico, where the incorporation of women has been significant. Indeed, observers—including Helen I. Safa, writing in this volume—note "the dispro-portionate access that women have to export manufacturing employment and their overwhelming importance as suppliers for the export manufac-turing sector."[22] Susan Joekes concludes that industrialization in the Third World has been as much female-led as export-led.[23]

Guy Standing hypothesizes that the increasing globalization of pro-duction and the pursuit of flexible forms of labor to retain or increase competitiveness as well as changing job structures in industrial enter-prises favor the "feminization of employment." But although women have been gaining an increasing share of many kinds of jobs, this change is occurring in the context of a decline in the social power of labor. More-over, women are still disadvantaged in the new labor markets (in terms of wages, training, and occupational segregation); and nonregular employ-ment is increasing.[24] In other words, new labor markets have made it much easier to exploit the labor power of women on a part-time and tem-porary basis and thereby substitute lower-paid female labor for that of more highly paid core male workers.

Standing's detailed study of Malaysia and the Philippines offers inter-esting findings with respect to the utilization and status of female labor.[25] Women workers are still concentrated in textiles and electronics and "other manufacturing"; men are concentrated in metals, minerals, and chemicals. However, some data suggest that sex-segregation may be declining in food-processing, wood products, paper products, and chemi-cals sectors. Among managers, there is a stated preference for men as pro-duction workers; women seem to have easier access to technical and professional categories. Moreover, women are better off in large firms rather than small ones. Export-orientation and female employment are positively correlated, and pay is higher in foreign firms for both men and women. The smaller the firm, the larger the male-female wage differen-tial. In larger firms, the pay gap is smaller, and the differential may be explained by the underrepresentation of women at the highest manage-rial and administrative levels. In Malaysia, the presence of a trade union is associated with higher relative wages for women. Certainly for coun-tries like Malaysia and the Philippines, flexible labor markets and export manufacturing will continue to rely on women workers, but work condi-tions and employment status leave much to be desired.

In summary, since the 1970s and especially during the 1980s, the worldwide economic crisis and the requirements of structural adjustment programs contributed to significant policy shifts in developing coun-tries.[26] Restructuring has been characterized by the shift from import-sub-stitution industrialization to export-led growth, from state ownership to privatization, from government regulation of prices and trade to liberal-ization, from a stable and mostly male-organized workforce to "flexible" and "feminized" labor, and from formal employment to the proliferation and expansion of informal sectors. This process is likely to continue through the 1990s. A world-system phenomenon, economic restructuring had spread to the former Socialist bloc by 1990. This process has had distinctive gender effects, as the following discussion shows. □

GENDER AND RESTRUCTURING IN EASTERN EUROPE AND THE SOVIET UNION

Because it entails political, juridical, and ideological transformations, the scope of restructuring in Eastern Europe and the former Soviet Union encompasses more than stabilization, price liberalization, and privatization. Economic reform changes production and social reproduction, and, because gender is embedded in those processes, women are profoundly affected by them.

The gender dimension of restructuring in the former socialist countries lies most obviously in the changes to women's status as workers. In a region of the world that once enjoyed the distinction of impressive human capital formation, the highest rates of female labor force participation and—most significantly—the largest female share of salaried employment, women now face unemployment, marginalization from the productive process, and the loss of previous benefits and forms of social protection such as maternity leaves and child-care facilities.

The specter that haunts post-1990 Eastern Europe is mass and long-term unemployment. This accelerating joblessness results from a constant fall in internal demand and real wages, the collapse of trade with the former Soviet Union, the closure of big state enterprises, and the sacking of thousands of civil servants. In all of Eastern Europe, women and young people have been among the hardest hit, often at a time when they are seeking their first paid employment. Throughout the region, income inequalities are growing, with the sharpest differences occurring along class, gender, and generational lines.[27]

With economic reform and the introduction of a competitive labor market, women have become particularly vulnerable to unemployment. In Poland, Romania, Croatia, Bulgaria, and Czechoslovakia, women constitute a significant proportion of the unemployed (see Table 2.1). They made up between 85 and 90 percent of those registered as unemployed in Romania in September 1990, and, in the former USSR, women made up 60 percent of those who lost employment between 1989 and 1991. When the state bureaucracy was streamlined during 1985 and 1987, women made up more than 80 percent of those laid off in the industrial sector.[28] According to a recent analysis of unemployment and poverty in Russia, women constituted more than 70 percent of the unemployed in 1992 and

TABLE 2.1   Official Unemployment Rates, Eastern Europe, 1990–1992
(in percentages)

	1990	1991	1992
Bulgaria			
Total	1.7	11.1	16.4
Male	–	–	13.7
Female	–	–	14.5
Croatia			
Total	8.0	14.0	15.0
Male	6.0	11.0	12.0
Female	11.0	16.0	18.0
Czechoslovakia			
Total	1.0	6.6	5.1
Male	0.09	5.9	4.7
Female	1.0	7.3	5.4
Hungary			
Total	1.7	8.5	12.3
Male	1.8	9.2	14.0
Female	1.4	7.6	10.5
Poland			
Total	3.5	9.7	13.3
Male	3.2	7.9	11.8
Female	3.8	11.8	14.9
Romania			
Total	–	3.0	8.4
Male	–	2.2	6.2
Female	–	4.0	10.7
Slovenia			
Total	4.7	8.2	11.5
Male	4.5	8.5	12.1
Female	4.8	7.9	10.8

Note: – indicates data are not available.
Source: ILO, *Yearbook of Labour Statistics 1993*, table 9A (Geneva: ILO, 1993).

1993: "The majority of them were previously employed in factory management and the scientific and technical subdivisions of enterprises of the state sector."[29] In the former German Democratic Republic (GDR), women's unemployment rates have risen much faster than men's. Between mid-1989 and mid-1991, they rose by 500 percent, compared with 300 percent for men. Furthermore, women in the former GDR have twice as high an unemployment level as do the men. According to a recent study, "There is a marked trend towards sex-related labor market segmentation, and women now account for two-thirds of the jobless; in the former GDR 84 percent of women of working age were in the labor force (compared with 53 percent in the west). Now standing at over 20 percent, official unemployment among women in the new federal states (i.e., eastern Germany), is almost double that of men. Women are also proportionally underrepresented on labor market programmes."[30]

In regard to layoffs, gender stereotypes presume that men will suffer more from unemployment than women; once fired, however, it is much more difficult for women to find jobs. There are fewer reemployment opportunities and fewer training or retraining programs for women. In the former Czechoslovakia, the International Labor Organization (ILO) found in 1991 and 1992 that women's unemployment level was higher than men's, it had grown faster, and it was higher in every region of the country except eastern Slovakia. Women were losing jobs in favor of men even in some formerly "female" branches, and there was a significantly lower integration of women in small business activities.[31] In eastern Germany, women in the educational sector lost jobs in large numbers for ideological as well as restructuring reasons. In the GDR, nine out of ten teachers were women, and almost one of every four researchers at the Academy of Science of East Germany was a woman. Now, however, the academy has been dissolved, and these women are lucky if they can get one of the 2,000 government-sponsored jobs in their field. The same process is occurring for managers. Though in June 1990, there were 200,000 male and 100,000 female executives in the GDR, a report by the German Institute for Economic Research in April 1992 showed that only 80,000 male managers were left—and almost no women.[32] Thus, there is institutional discrimination as well as overt discrimination in the economic transition.

There has been a tremendous decline in the textile industry in eastern Germany, where three-quarters of the industry's workforce were once women. Before reunification, the Saxony Spinning Company had 13,000 employees; its payroll is now expected to fall to 300. In the past, the mill was able to sell its yarns to thirty nations around the world, including former Socialist countries, and the region had sixteen mills run by one state corporation, with 80 percent of the work under contract to the Soviet

Union. But in the early 1990s, Eastern Europe disappeared as a market, and the strong German mark made the company's products expensive and thus uncompetitive. The Treuhand Commission, which was established to privatize former state companies, considered either selling the sixteen mills or liquidating them, due to the outdated machinery and rising value of the real estate. Not surprisingly, a 1992 poll in Brandenburg, a textile-producing state in the east, found that 82 percent of women surveyed believed that their lives were worse than they had been before unification and restructuring. Older and middle-aged women, in particular, have no training or experience relevant to the restructured economy and new technologies.[33]

Socialist countries traditionally facilitated the employment of women via extensive maternity and child-care leaves, rights to return to employment after such leaves, and company- or state-provided crèches and kindergartens. Prior to unification and restructuring, most GDR women had a secure job, and 92 percent had had at least one child by the time they turned twenty-three.[34] Following unification, when firms were privatized or found to be unprofitable, child care was the first benefit to be cut. Because of their legal concessions and leaves taken to care for children during illnesses, mothers in Hungary worked, on average, only 50 percent of the standard working hours. The direct costs of such provisions to the company in terms of direct expenditures as well as the indirect costs of, for example, keeping employment open during child-care leaves or work lost to care for sick children were of minor significance to a Socialist enterprise. In postreform conditions, however, such costs can no longer be borne by profit-maximizing enterprises, which will contract for the cheapest qualified labor.

With respect to Poland, Maria Ciechocinska found that in cities and towns with large numbers of child-care institutions, there was a low level of mothers on child-care leave.[35] Conversely, cities and towns with the fewest child-care institutions had the highest percentages of women workers on child-care leave. Thus, as privatization proceeds, one can easily predict a situation in which greater numbers and larger percentages of women will become "domesticated" as child-care institutions are either closed down or become prohibitively expensive. This is a major reason why, as Ciechocinska puts it, women "are paying a higher price for the transformations now taking place." The difficulties are also of a generational type, for older women are becoming redundant in the years prior to retirement. Employees who are considered to have the loosest attachment to the labor force are generally the most vulnerable. And this is invariably women, no matter what their stage in the life-course.

If the costs of providing the social benefits for women workers once borne by the state or Socialist enterprise are now to be assumed by private employers, this will likely reduce the demand for female labor, thereby limiting women's access to full-time employment and reducing their earnings in the formal sector. Why is this so? From a market point of view, female labor in Eastern Europe is more expensive than male labor—notwithstanding an earnings gap between men and women similar to that in Western countries—because of the costs involved in maternity and child-care provisions usually borne by enterprises. Certainly, female labor in the Socialist countries was of a different order from the "cheap and expendable female labor" of Third World industrializing countries, with their lax or nonexistent labor codes and social policies. This economic rationale, as well as gender bias, explains what has appeared to be a concerted effort to remove Eastern European women from the formal labor market in the context of economic restructuring. Although this may be profitable to employers, the consequences for women are dire. As Ruth Pearson observes, withdrawal of state support for working mothers in the former Socialist countries is likely to diminish the identification of women as both workers and reproducers and replace it with an exclusive ideology of reproduction.[36] In this way, not only are women among the principal losers in the restructuring process in the short term, but there may also be a strengthening of patriarchal concepts concerning men's and women's roles over the long term. □

GENDER AND RESTRUCTURING IN THE MIDDLE EAST AND NORTH AFRICA

In the Middle East since the 1960s, state expansion, economic development, and oil wealth have combined to create educational and employment opportunities favorable to women. For almost a decade after the oil price increases of the early 1970s, a massive investment program by the oil-producing countries affected the structure of the labor force within the relevant countries and, as a result of labor migration throughout the region, created what has been called a regional oil economy. For the OPEC countries, foreign exchange from oil revenues led to the accumulation of capital, and a modern manufacturing sector and an industrial labor force also emerged. Oil revenues and the strategy of import-substitution industrialization changed the structure of the labor force in Middle Eastern countries through the expansion of nonagricultural employment. In urban areas, the female labor force grew as women occupied paid positions as workers, administrators, and professionals in factories and offices. During this period, although all Third World regions saw a rise in the rates of female labor force participation, the largest increase was reported for the Middle East. Especially high increases occurred in Syria and Tunisia, where the female labor increase topped that of men.[37]

Women continued to enter the labor force during the 1980s, especially in the non-oil economies of Tunisia, Morocco, Syria, Turkey, and Egypt, and in most countries, the state or public sector became an important source of women's livelihood. Women's entry into public life has been facilitated by state-sponsored education and by job opportunities in the expanding government sector and public services. In Tunisia and Morocco, employment in the industrial sector accounted for much of the increase in the female labor force.[38]

Feminist concerns and women's movements also emerged, and by 1980 most Middle Eastern countries had women's organizations dealing with issues of literacy, education, employment, the law, and so on. These social changes have had a positive effect in reducing traditional sex segregation and female seclusion, in introducing changes in the structure of the Middle Eastern family, and in producing a generation of middle-class women who are not dependent on family or marriage for survival and status. Increased educational attainment and labor force attachment has created a stratum of highly visible and increasingly vocal women in the public sphere.[39]

State policies have been an important factor in women's economic and social status. In some countries, conservative state managers have done little to promote female employment or even mass literacy since gender equality and female empowerment rank low in their priorities. State policies in other countries, however, have facilitated female integration into public life. Egypt provides an example of how state policies have affected women's economic and social status in a positive way. In the late 1950s and during the administration of Gamal Abdel Nasser, Egypt's public sector expanded significantly through a series of Egyptianization decrees (1956–1959) that gave the government control of foreign-owned assets, such as the Suez Canal. This was followed in the early 1960s by the adoption of a highly centralized development policy approach and a massive wave of nationalizations of Egyptian-owned enterprises in industry, banking, trade, and transport. At the same time, the government embarked on an employment drive under which state-owned enterprises were forced to include among their annual targets the creation of significant numbers of new jobs. The administrative apparatus of the state was also expanded rapidly both at the central and local government level. Equally important was the objective of spreading health and education services in urban and rural areas, which brought a corresponding growth of government employment in these services.[40] The state's guarantee of a job to all high school and university graduates encouraged women, including women from working-class and lower-middle-class families, to take advantage of the free education provided by the state.

A distinctive feature of the Nasserist state was the political support it gave to the education of women and to their integration into national development. Labor Law 91 of 1954, over and above its guarantee of equal rights and equal wages, made special provisions for married women and mothers. Later, under Anwar Sadat, these provisions were expanded to facilitate women's participation in the labor market. This law was applied primarily in the public and government sectors, which made jobs in these areas particularly attractive to women. As a result, the state became the single most important employer of women.[41]

An issue that has been raised time and again pertains to why the Middle East has a smaller female labor force than other regions. Usually, notions of "culture" or "Islam" are offered as an explanation. But I believe the explanation lies in the region's political economy, its location within the world system, and its function as an oil-producing and oil-exporting region.

In the heyday of economic development, most of the large Arab countries, such as Egypt, Tunisia, Syria, and Algeria, embarked on an ISI development strategy. This was associated with an economic system characterized by central planning and a large public sector. WID specialists have noted that during the ISI period in Latin America and Southeast Asia, the bulk of the workforce was male, particularly in capital-intensive sectors such as steel, shipbuilding, and heavy industry.[42] The significant rise in female employment occurred with the shift from ISI to EOI—a pattern of industrialization that allowed Third World economies to compete in Western consumer goods markets, and that was largely based on the availability of cheap productive labor.

Political economists specializing on the Middle East point out that industrialization in the region, in contrast to Latin America and Southeast Asia, has been fairly limited. Robert Mabro notes that unlike Latin America, ISI in the Middle East did not evolve into manufacturing for export.[43] Because of oil revenues, governments chose to extend the import-substitution process, moving into capital-intensive sectors involving sophisticated technology.[44] One might add that, thus far, the function of the region within the world system has been to guarantee a steady supply of oil for foreign—especially core-country—markets, and to import industrial goods, especially armaments, mainly from core countries. One result has been limited industrialization and manufacturing for export; another has been limited employment opportunities for women in the formal industrial sector since capital-intensive industries and technologies tend to favor male labor.

Notwithstanding the limitations imposed on female employment as a consequence of the region's political economy and conservative state managers, there *was* a secular trend toward altering and improving women's work and lives. But this trend stalled in the 1980s in the context of a global economic crisis and a regional crisis of political legitimacy. The global oil market became very unstable at that time, leading to fluctuating and declining prices. The near-collapse of prices in 1986 (from $28 to $7 per barrel) had numerous repercussions through the Middle East: Austerity measures were introduced, the availability of development aid decreased, and major development projects were reevaluated or suspended. The Iraqi invasion of Kuwait in August 1990 raised the price of oil again, but the damage had already been done. In the 1980s, Arab countries experienced low or negative economic growth rates, declining state revenues, and high levels of indebtedness to foreign creditors. The most active Arab borrowers from the World Bank—Algeria, Egypt, Jordan, Morocco, Syria, and Tunisia—had to impose austerity measures on their populations as a result of World Bank and IMF structural adjustment policy packages, and several experienced "IMF riots."[45] Tough economic reforms, along with poverty, unemployment, and debt servicing—as well as political repression—have served to delegitimize "Western-style" systems and revive questions of cultural identity, including renewed calls for greater control over female mobility. In this context of economic failures and political delegitimation, Islamist movements are presenting themselves as alternatives. And, the combination of Islamist movements and economic failures has distinct negative implications for women's legal status and employment opportunities.[46]

An illustration of the impact of the economic crisis on women's employment is once again provided by Egypt. By the mid-1980s, the Egyptian government was faced with the difficult issue of how to reduce its commitment to job creation in the face of severe recessionary conditions in the economy. At the time, the country was experiencing a record 15.5 percent overall (open) unemployment, according to the 1986 population census (up from 7 percent in the 1976 census), and the prospects for either the domestic productive sectors or the Arab oil-rich markets to create significant job opportunities for Egyptian workers were poor. Moreover, high inflation effectively eroded the financial advantage of the white-collar workforce.[47] This has fueled social tensions—and led to the growth of Islamism, with its attendant ideological and social pressures on women. Many employed women now feel compelled to appear in *hijab* (Islamic modest dress) at work.[48]

Thus, even though many women have entered into previously male strongholds—universities, public administration, professions, industry, the business world, diplomacy, politics—the economic crisis in Egypt, and rapid demographic growth limit formal employment opportunities for women. A large majority of urban Egyptian women are engaged in the informal sector: They are street vendors and hawkers selling food and other wares, working at home as seamstresses, and generally engaged in a myriad of small-scale income-generating activities—though these activities are not reflected in official labor force statistics.

Another example of the gender effects of crisis and restructuring is provided by Algeria. Between 1967 and 1978, the Algerian government invested some 300 billion dinars to create over a million jobs and bring down unemployment from 25 percent to 19 percent of the active population. As a result of two national development plans, an industrial base was built that rested primarily on hydrocarbons, chemical and petrochemical industries, smelting industries, and construction and mechanical industries. Nonagricultural employment grew from 28 percent to encompass nearly 50 percent of the active population. However, in spite of its size and importance, the industrial base created in the 1970s employed only about 150,000 people, that is, about 4 percent of total employment or 11.6 percent of the active population. In the words of one analyst, "the planners opted for frontline technologies that are not large employers."[49] Nor are these technologies known to employ women in large numbers. Algeria's female labor force is not only small by world standards, it is also among the smallest in the Middle East/North Africa region.

In the 1980s, economic mismanagement, including an ever-growing importation of consumer goods, caught up with the Algerian government. The fall in the price of oil, from $30 a barrel in 1982 to $7 per barrel in 1986, led to a drastic reduction in state revenues, which were no longer large enough to service the debt and to import consumer goods or the intermediate materials required by industry. One consequence was a sharp growth in unemployment—rising to an estimated 22 percent of the active population in 1989.[50] In this context, the government decided to shift from an administered to a market economy in line with World Bank and IMF prescriptions. These policies have fueled considerable social discontent, leading to the growth and popularity of an Islamist movement. Because this movement opposed the government's new economic policies, its "populism" increased its social support. But on cultural and gender issues, the Islamists are extremely patriarchal. Algerian women, therefore, face added uncertainties in their already fragile and limited employment situation as a result of structural adjustment. And they face the formidable cultural, ideological, and political pressures of an increasingly violent Islamist movement.

Although more work needs to be done on labor market issues in the Middle East, recent studies show that the rate of unemployment is higher among women than among men,[51] especially in Jordan, Egypt, Algeria, and Iran, where educated women experience higher rates of unemployment than do educated men. This is clearly a result of gender discrimination: At a time of slack in the labor market, employers discriminate by hiring males, who are seen as the breadwinners of the household. Women may also be seen as more expensive labor because of legislation requiring child-care and maternity leaves, especially in the public sector and in large private enterprises.

In recent years, manufacturing for export, increased trade, and foreign investment have tended to encourage female employment in semiperipheral countries. In Tunisia, Morocco, and Turkey, export-oriented garment industries contributed to the growth of the female labor force during the 1980s. But much of this employment is home-based or in small unregistered workshops where wages are low and social security nonexistent. It is likely that as Middle Eastern countries continue to pursue economic liberalization in the context of global restructuring, women's employment will increase. However, the growth of job opportunities in small-scale manufacturing, as distinct from employment in large and modern firms or in the public sector, may not be in women's best interests. Thus, while middle-class Middle Eastern women face ideological pressures from Islamist movements, working-class women also face economic uncertainties and exploitative work conditions. □

CONCLUSION

The feminization of labor is a central feature of globalization, but the impact of economic restructuring on patterns of labor force participation varies across regions and economic zones within the world system. In many semiperipheral countries, including the Middle East and North Africa, female labor force participation has increased dramatically— albeit often under adverse working conditions. In post-Communist countries, on the other hand, female labor is apparently being marginalized in the context of economic restructuring.

Throughout Central and Eastern Europe, the transition to a market economy has caused much unemployment in a region where full employment was a central tenet of socialist doctrine. In 1990, when "shock therapy" was applied in Poland, unemployment surged, and output fell. The end of subsidies and price controls in Russia has resulted in severe hardships for citizens. As in developing countries undergoing IMF-prescribed stabilization and structural adjustment, restructuring in the former state Socialist countries entails austerity measures and belt-tightening. A striking feature of nearly all countries undergoing "economic reform" is the high proportion of females among the newly unemployed and the loss of free or inexpensive child care that invariably affects women workers more than their male counterparts. Although men have lost jobs, especially with the restructuring of industries and the contraction of state employment, women's unemployment is often greater. Gender bias and economic calculations seem to account for this.

In the Middle East, global restructuring has led to increases in female industrial employment in some countries, especially in the non-oil economies that have increasingly turned from ISI to manufacturing for export. In other countries, however, female employment remains relatively low due to the continuing reliance on oil revenues and due to patriarchal state managers and policies. Throughout the region, women have made steady progress in educational attainment, access to jobs and careers (especially in the public sector), and control over fertility. In the context of the current economic crisis, however, women must confront the deterioration of their employment environment, social position, and legal status. Job security is no longer guaranteed for either industrial workers or public sector employees; the real value of wages has declined in countries like Egypt; unemployment has grown; and Islamist movements are calling on women to revert to or remain in domestic roles.

Whether women will accommodate themselves to these developments or resist them remains to be seen. It should be noted that in the Islamic Republic of Iran, despite extraordinary ideological pressures on women to adhere to a patriarchal model of Islamic womanhood, about a million middle-class and working-class women have resisted this clarion call and stayed in—or joined—the labor force, whether out of choice or economic necessity. Even Islamist women in public positions—university lecturers, leaders of Islamic women's organizations, members of parliament—must be seen as subverting the patriarchal order, however unconsciously, by virtue of their insistence on their right to be in the public sphere.[52] No less can be expected of women in other Middle Eastern countries. Their task will be made easier if it can be shown empirically that economic growth is spurred by women's participation, that household and community welfare are enhanced by women's access to and control over economic resources and income, and that women's empowerment and national development are complementary.[53]

In both of these regions of the semiperiphery, policy makers must be made aware of the consequences that marginalizing or ignoring women will have on national development. They also must consider the benefits that accrue to women, their families, and ultimately their countries as a result of women's productive activities, especially those that generate income under female control. □

NOTES

1. The term restructuring refers to the reorganization of a system of production and may be used at the firm level, the national level, and the global level. In this chapter, *global restructuring* encompasses the array of liberalization and privatization policy shifts in developing countries and the transition to a market

economy in the former state Socialist countries; it also entails the increasing utilization of flexible labor markets.

2. See, for example, Olivier Blanchard, et al., *Post-Communist Reform: Pain and Progress* (Tokyo and Cambridge, MA: UNU Press and MIT Press, 1993); Anders Aslund and Richard Layard, eds., *Changing the Economic System in Russia* (London: Pinter Publishers, 1993); *Transition: The Newsletter About Reforming Economies* (World Bank, Socialist Economies Reform Unit, various issues since April 1990).

3. *Contemporary Sociology* has featured two symposia (May 1992 and January 1993) on the transformations in Central and Eastern Europe. None of the monographs reviewed address gender dynamics as part of the overall social analysis of causes and consequences of the transformation. But see *Feminist Review* 39 (1992); Valentine M. Moghadam, ed., *Democratic Reform and the Position of Women in Transitional Economies* (Oxford: Clarendon Press, 1993); Nanette Funk and Magda Mueller, eds., *Gender Politics and Post-Communism* (London: Routledge, 1993); Barbara Einhorn, *Cinderella Goes to Market: Citizenship, Gender and Women's Movements in East Central Europe* (London: Verso, 1993); and Monica Fong, *The Role of Women in Rebuilding the Russian Economy*, Studies of Economies in Transformation, Paper no. 10, World Bank, 1993.

4. See Guy Standing, "Global Feminization Through Flexible Labor," *World Development* 17, no. 7 (1989): 1077–1095; Commonwealth Secretariat, *Engendering Adjustment for the 1990s* (London: Commonwealth Secretariat, 1989); Ingrid Palmer, *Gender and Population in the Adjustment of African Economies: Planning for Change* (Geneva: ILO, 1991); Diane Elson, "Male Bias in Macro-Economies: The Case of Structural Adjustment," in Diane Elson, ed., *Male Bias in the Development Process* (Manchester: University of Manchester Press, 1991); Haleh Afshar, ed., *Women and Adjustment Policies in the Third World* (London: Macmillan, 1992).

5. But see Lance Taylor, "The Post-Socialist Transition from a Development Economics Point of View," paper prepared for the Conference on Transformation from a System of Central Planning to a Market Economy, Government of Finland and UNU/WIDER, February 6–7, 1992.

6. See Valentine M. Moghadam, "Bringing the Third World In: A Comparative Analysis of Gender and Restructuring," in Moghadam, ed., *Democratic Reform and the Position of Women in Transitional Economies*, 327–352.

7. Post-communist countries have similarly seen the emergence of patriarchal movements of religious and nationalist orientations. At the very least, this suggests a link between economic crisis and right-wing political agitation. In both Muslim and post-Communist countries, these movements have gender-specific implications: a conservative agenda for women that ties them to family, culture, and religion.

8. See Immanuel Wallerstein, "Long Waves as Capitalist Process," *Review* 4 (1989): 559–576; Terence Hopkins, Robert L. Bach, et al., *World-System Analysis: Theory and Methodology* (Beverly Hills, CA: Sage, 1982); Christopher Chase-Dunn, "The World-System Since 1950: What Has Really Changed?," in Charles Berquist, ed., *Labor in the Capitalist World-Economy* (Beverly Hills, CA: Sage, 1984); Thomas Richard Shannon, *An Introduction to the World-System Perspective* (Boulder: Westview Press, 1989). World-system researchers have correlated long cycles with

price rises and falls since 1790. For an overview and analysis, see Joshua Goldstein, *Long Cycles* (New Haven: Yale University Press, 1988).

9. Christopher Chase-Dunn, "Marxism and the Global Political Economy," paper presented at the annual meetings of the American Sociological Association, Washington, DC, August 1990.

10. Christopher Chase-Dunn, "The Kernel of the Capitalist World-Economy: Three Approaches," in W. Thompson, ed., *Contending Approaches in World-System Analysis* (Beverly Hills, CA: Sage, 1983), 73.

11. Kathryn Ward, *Women in the World-System: Its Impact on Status and Fertility* (New York: Praeger, 1984). Utilizing 1960s and 1970s data sets, this study found that "dependency"—measured by amount of foreign investment—worsened women's status and increased their fertility, an association that does not obtain today. It is true, however, that peripheral status is associated with high fertility.

12. Kathryn Ward, ed., *Women Workers and Global Restructuring* (Ithaca: ILR Press, 1990); M. Patricia Fernandez-Kelly, "Broadening the Scope: Gender and the Study of International Economic Development," in A. Douglas Kincaid and Alejandro Portes, eds., *Comparative National Development* (Chapel Hill: University of North Carolina Press, forthcoming).

13. Kathryn Ward, "Reconceptualizing World System Theory to Include Women," in Paula England, ed., *Theory on Gender: Feminism on Theory* (New York: Aldine, 1993).

14. Kathryn Ward, "Introduction and Overview," in Ward, ed., *Women Workers and Global Restructuring*, 1.

15. Ibid., 2.

16. Barry Bluestone and Bennett Harrison, *The Deindustrialization of America* (New York: Basic Books, 1982); David Harvey, *The Condition of Postmodernity: An Enquiry into the Origins of Cultural Change* (London: Basil Blackwell, 1989).

17. Ward, "Introduction and Overview," 2.

18. Saskia Sassen and Patricia Fernandez-Kelly, "Recasting Women in the Global Economy: Internationalization and Changing Definitions of Gender," in E. Acosta-Belen and C. Bose, eds., *Women in the Development Process in Latin America: From Structural Subordination to Empowerment* (Philadelphia: Temple University Press, 1992).

19. For statistical information on women's employment, see Women's Bureau of the U.S. Department of Labor, "Facts on Working Women," no. 93-2, June 1993. For information on changing patterns in U.S. unionization compared with West European countries, see *Dollars and Sense* (September 1988): 22. For information on women workers' progress on the issues of pay equity, sexual harassment, and fair employment practices in the public sector, see *WIN News* (1991): 72.

20. Harvey, *The Condition of Postmodernity*, 152.

21. See *Flexible Workstyles: A Look at Contingent Labor: A Conference Summary*, no. 93-2 (Washington, DC: U.S. Department of Labor, 1988).

22. Susan Joekes and Roxana Moayedi, *Women and Export Manufacturing: A Review of the Issues and AID Policy* (Washington, DC, ICRW, July 1987), 21.

23. Susan Joekes, *Women in the World Economy: An INSTRAW Study* (New York: Oxford University Press, 1987), 81.

24. Standing, "Global Feminization Through Flexible Labor."

25. Guy Standing, "Cumulative Disadvantage? Women Industrial Workers in Malaysia and the Philippines," in Valentine M. Moghadam, ed., *Trajectories of Patriarchy and Development* (forthcoming).

26. See the essays in Guy Standing and Victor Tokman, eds., *Towards Social Adjustment: Labour Market Issues in Structural Adjustment* (Geneva: ILO, 1991).

27. See *The Economist*, May 16, 1992, 29. See also Gyorgy Sziraczki and Jim Windell, "The Impact of Employment Restructuring on Disadvantaged Groups in Bulgaria and Hungary," Labour Market Analysis and Employment Policies Working Paper no. 62, Geneva, ILO, January 1993.

28. United Nations, *1993 Report on the World Social Situation*, advance version, January 1993, 206.

29. Natalia Tchernina, "Employment Deprivation and Poverty: The Ways in Which Poverty Is Emerging in the Course of Economic Reform in Russia," International Institute for Labour Studies Discussion Paper no. 60, Geneva, 1993, 10. Although the official unemployment rate in Russia is 2 percent, Guy Standing of the ILO estimates that it is actually at least 10 percent and rising.

30. M. Wiedemeyer, W. Beywl, and W. Hemlstadter, "Employment Promotion Companies in Eastern Germany: Emergency Measures or a Basis for Structural Reform?" *International Labour Review* 132, no. 5-5 (1993): 607.

31. See Liba Paukert, "The Changing Economic Status of Women in the Period of Transition to a Market Economy System: The Case of the Czech and Slovak Republics after 1989," and Monica Fong and Gillian Paull, "Women's Economic Status in the Restructuring of Eastern Europe," both in Moghadam, ed., *Democratic Reform and the Position of Women in Transitional Economies*.

32. *World Press Review*, April 1992, 11–12.

33. *News from IRENE* (Amsterdam), April 1992, 7, and *World Press Review*, April, 1992, 11–12.

34. Bettina Mussall, "Women Are Hurt the Most," *Der Spiegel* (Hamburg); reprinted in *World Press Review*, June 1991, 22.

35. This analysis is based on research findings prepared for the UNU/WIDER Conference on Gender and Restructuring and published in Moghadam, ed., *Democratic Reform and the Position of Women in Transitional Economies*, in particular: Maria Ciechocinska, "Gender Aspects of Dismantling the Command Economy in Eastern Europe: The Case of Poland," 302–326; Paukert, "The Changing Economic Status of Women in the Period of Transition to a Market Economy System: The Case of Czechoslovakia After 1989," 248–274; and Fong and Paull, "Women's Economic Status in the Restructuring of Eastern Europe," 217–247.

36. Ruth Pearson, "Questioning Perestroika: A Socialist Feminist Interrogation," *Feminist Review* 39 (Autumn 1990): 91–96.

37. ILO/INSTRAW, *Women in Economic Activity: A Global Statistical Survey (1950–2000)* (Santo Domingo: INSTRAW, 1985), 35.

38. For an elaboration, see Valentine M. Moghadam, *Modernizing Women: Gender and Social Change in the Middle East* (Boulder: Lynne Rienner Publishers, 1993), Chapter 2.

39. See ibid., chapters 4 and 8.

40. International Labor Oganization (ILO), *World Labour Report 1989* (Geneva: ILO, 1990), 52.

41. Homa Hoodfar, "Return to the Veil: Personal Strategy and Public Participation in Egypt," in Nanneke Redclift and M. Thea Sinclair, eds., *Working Women: International Perspectives on Labor and Gender Ideology* (London and New York: Routledge, 1991), 104–124.

42. See Ruth Pearson, "Gender Issues in Industrialization," in Tom Hewitt, Hazel Johnson, and David Wield, eds., *Industrialisation and Development* (Oxford: Oxford University Press, 1992), 222–247.

43. See Robert Mabro, "Industrialization," in Michael Adams, ed., *The Middle East* (New York: Facts-on-File, 1988), 687–696, and Alan Richards and John Waterbury, *A Political Economy of the Middle East* (Boulder: Westview Press, 1990).

44. Mabro, "Industrialization," 692.

45. Tim Niblock, "International and Domestic Factors in the Economic Liberalization Process in Arab Countries," and David Seddon, "Austerity Protests in Response to Economic Liberalization in the Middle East," both in Tim Niblock and Emma Murphy, eds., *Economic and Political Liberalization in the Middle East* (London: British Academic Press, 1993). See also Ziya Önis, "The Evolution of Privatization in Turkey: The Institutional Context of Public-Enterprise Reform," *International Journal of Middle East Studies* 23, no. 2 (May 1991): 163–176.

46. The socioeconomic backdrop to the rise of Islamist movements is explored in the introduction and in several chapters of V. M. Moghadam, ed., *Identity Politics and Women: Cultural Reassertions and Feminisms in International Perspective* (Boulder: Westview Press, 1994), and in V. M. Moghadam, ed., *Gender and National Identity: Women and Politics in Muslim Societies* (London: Zed Books, 1994). See also chapters 1 and 5 in Moghadam, *Modernizing Women*.

47. ILO, *World Labour Report 1989*, 52.

48. See Hoodfar, "Return to the Veil."

49. Lahouari Addi, "The Structural Crisis of the Algerian Economy," paper presented at the annual meeting of the Middle East Studies Association, Portland, OR (October 28–31, 1992), 2.

50. Ibid.

51. Sulayman Al-Qudsi, Ragui Assaad, and Radwan Shaban, "Labor Markets in the Arab Countries: A Survey," paper prepared for the Initiative to Encourage Economic Research in the Middle East and North Africa, First Annual Conference on Development Economics, Cairo, June 4–6, 1993.

52. For a discussion of Iran, see Moghadam, *Modernizing Women*, chapter 6.

53. Some studies on the Middle East are beginning to show this. See Elias Tuma, "Economic Costs of Ethnic and Sex Discrimination in Middle Eastern Society—An Exploration," paper presented at the annual meeting of the Middle East Studies Association, San Antonio, TX, November 10–13, 1990, and Nabil Khoury and Valentine M. Moghadam, eds., *Women and Human Development in the Arab World* (under review).

CHAPTER THREE

———————— ■ ————————

Gender and Economic Crises in Latin America: Reflections on the Great Depression and the Debt Crisis

Michael Monteón

SCHOLARS ANALYZING GENDER, PARTICULARLY WOMEN and development, have introduced new and important perspectives on the social consequences of economic calamity over the last fifteen years. Two elements, however, are missing from current discussion: a historical analysis of earlier economic crises and a reflection on the ways in which current research might pose new questions and lines of investigation about the past. Almost all research in the field of women's studies tends to focus on developments since World War II.[1] There is, as yet, very little that explicitly compares the evolution of work for women and men, nor is there very much on children and their participation in the economies of Latin America, even though forty million children under fifteen years of age are now working in the region.[2]

This chapter offers a reflection on two crises: the Great Depression of the 1930s and the debt crisis that has bedeviled Latin America since 1982. My purpose is to examine similarities and differences in their respective impacts on gender and on women's roles. Instead of comparing the social consequences of one economic crisis in different world regions, as is done in other chapters of this book, I present a longitudinal comparison of the social consequences of two different economic crises within a single world region. With allowance for historical context, this strategy provides a way of controlling for the potential effects of noneconomic factors. A first and necessary step for this approach is to identify the similarities and differences between these economic crises. I then move on to examine their respective impacts on gender and on women's roles in Latin America. □

TWO CRISES COMPARED

There are some important parallels between the Great Depression and the debt crisis. Neither, of course, began in the region: They were imported crises, which compounded problems within the area. Each began with financial instability and major changes in the prices of raw materials in the advanced industrial nations; the crisis was then transferred to Latin America through international lending and trade. Each caused severe political dislocations: Between 1930 and 1932, seventeen of the twenty-one governments in Latin America were overthrown (some more than once); the debt crisis led to a collapse of the military regimes and to a renewal of elected, civilian governments in the 1980s.

In each situation, the United States and its banking system played a major role in fomenting foreign loans. Each crash was preceded by a massive export of capital from the United States to nations that were borrowing money to sustain their imports and their governments. Of course, some borrowed more than others: Brazil and Chile faced unpayable debts in both crises. Venezuela, because of its oil resources, was the one nation that escaped the debt burdens of the 1930s, but no Latin American country has escaped the reversals of the 1980s. Both economic downturns hit Latin America with about the same degree of ferocity. In the early 1930s, when the terms of trade deteriorated and the capacity to borrow was exhausted, national incomes in Latin America fell 10 to 15 percent. Chile suffered the worst setback, an income collapse of 33 percent.[3] Fifty years later, at the height of the debt crisis, the per capita gross domestic product (GDP) of the region fell almost 10 percent; in Argentina, Uruguay, and Venezuela, it fell 15, 19, and 20 percent, respectively.[4]

There are, of course, important differences between the 1930s and the 1980s, both within the region and in the relationship of Latin America to the world economy. Latin America was still predominantly rural in the earlier decade; in many countries, financial institutions were at an initial stage of development; and the push to replace imported manufactures with domestically produced goods (the famous pattern of import-substitution industrialization) was introduced. The most striking difference vis-à-vis the world economy was that, in the 1930s, most Latin American nations (with the notable exceptions of Argentina, Cuba, and Venezuela) suspended their international debt payments for long periods. In the 1940s, Brazil, Chile, and Mexico wrote off many of their obligations, thus reducing the overall foreign debt burden on their governments and their economies.[5] They were able to do this with the cooperation of the U.S. government, which was anxious to promote regional stability. That was not the case in the 1980s, when the United States and other creditor governments put the preservation of international financial markets and their own banking systems ahead of the problems caused by Latin American indebtedness.

Latin America became a net exporter of capital as it met its debt obligations. One nation after another rolled over its debts, borrowing additional sums to keep payments current, until the region's total external indebtedness jumped from US$274 billion dollars in 1982 to US$445 billion a decade later.[6] Unable to pay these debts and cover current expenditures, governments have turned to the monetary printing press, causing repeated devaluations and hyperinflation. The debt crisis, by reducing the availability of credit within Latin American economies, forced the shutdown of entire industries, a sell-off of state-owned firms, falling real wages, and massive unemployment and underemployment. In the early 1980s, real wages in Mexico City dropped to 1938 levels.[7] In the relatively prosperous nations of Venezuela and Argentina, industrial jobs disappeared, and their middle classes shrank to percentages not seen since the 1930s. In Chile, often touted by free market advocates as a model for the rest of the region, 27 percent of the workforce is in the low-paid informal sector, and the minimum monthly salary had risen above US$100 only by 1992.[8]

These major differences are paralleled by important ideological contrasts as well. Governments in the 1930s deliberately abandoned liberal economic thinking, turning to ideas and policies being explored by Great Britain, France, Germany, and the United States. Latin American governments became economically more intrusive, actively promoting import-substitution industrialization—which boosted employment especially in the largest cities. This was the era of fixed prices and currency controls, of increased tariffs and numerous new regulations. In contrast, after an initial surge of regulations and financial controls, the debt crisis of the 1980s led to a drastic dismantling of regulatory mechanisms and a movement toward free trade. Mexico, famed in the 1930s for its revolutionary rhetoric and economic nationalism, became, by the 1990s, one of the leading proponents of free trade economics, recently signing the North American Free Trade Agreement (NAFTA). In Argentina, the Peronist president Carlos Menem, reduced the power of labor, accepted the U.S. dollar as a standard of monetary value, and in other ways abandoned the populist legacies of Peronism.[9]

Neither crisis was defined by policymakers in terms of gender or social structure. Government and financial leaders initially depicted both crises as a result of market difficulties that would soon be corrected. In

1930, there was optimism that the U.S. stock market would rebound and international prices would recover. In Chile, the government denied that any problem existed. In the 1980s, U.S. government officials and bank officers insisted that the crisis had to be handled on a case-by-case basis, resolving each shortage of hard currency as it occurred. There was a deliberate refusal to see it as something systemic or something more than a matter of economics.[10] In fact, the debt crisis reshaped every prospect of development and social change.

My reflection begins with a set of observations by Carlos Marichal, who noted the long-term impact of successive debt crises in Latin America. He cites at least three waves of boom and bust prior to the debt crisis of the 1980s: loans made as countries achieved independence, which ended in financial ruin in the 1820s; the railroad boom that began in the 1860s and collapsed in the Argentine panic of 1890; and the rush of loans in the 1920s that ended in the crash of 1929. Marichal concludes that these reversals accentuated the cyclical trends in Latin America's overall development and proved "critical junctures," periods of massive dislocation. The crises disrupted the flow of development capital into Latin America, often leaving the region as a financial pariah in the eyes of bankers in more advanced countries. The loss of capital was accompanied by a loss of European or North American markets, and the region's economic recovery after each crash took ten or more years. What he calls the "protracted nature" of the crises, as well as their repetitive, cyclical character, helps explain why the region has remained underdeveloped.[11]

Marichal never raises the issue of gender. But if it is true, as Joan Scott has argued, that gender relations are a reflection of power relations and that concepts of power are not always literally about gender, it then follows that each crisis delineated by Marichal must have altered gender roles. Yet apparently there was no group in the public sphere capable of articulating what was happening, at least none that has been consistently studied by historians.[12] We do not know how each crisis of the nineteenth century affected families or altered the role of women in the workforce. We do know, however, that patriarchy remained the dominant domestic ideology throughout the early decades of this century. Men exercised the *patria potestad*, complete and exclusive dominion over domestic property, wife, and children. This included the right, in many countries, to kill an adulterous wife. Women were seen as the receptacles of family honor, and protecting them was an essential task of manhood.

This ideal was difficult to achieve in the face of the Great Depression. Pay was too low to sustain a nuclear family on one wage. Not too surprisingly, widespread poverty and little social mobility created high rates of illegitimacy in the 1930s—as high as 30 percent in Chile and 45 percent in Lima, Peru.[13] Women tried to enter the workforce but found their options extremely limited. The most common employment of Latin American women outside the home was in domestic service and petty trading.[14] Well into the 1930s, the Brazilian census listed 80 percent of all women in the workforce as domestic servants. Although women had been admitted into universities in many countries, they were still effectively excluded from politics, law, and professional life.

Some changes were nonetheless taking place. Patriarchy was questioned in a first wave of feminism, which gained momentum when women in the United States and Britain won suffrage. By the 1920s, important women's movements were demanding the vote in Brazil and Cuba. In 1929, Ecuador was the first Latin American nation to grant suffrage to women; Brazil and Uruguay followed suit in 1932, as did Cuba in 1934. Only small numbers of women were involved in the effort to win these rights, however. Lynn Stoner's excellent study of early Cuban feminism, for example, reveals that probably no more than a thousand women were involved in the movement. Most of Latin America granted suffrage to women only in the late 1940s.[15]

The case of the 1930s suggests that economic crises in themselves are not necessarily transforming experiences for women. According to the limited scholarship that now exists, change for women in Latin America has been incremental, and it stems from an overall pattern of development that has been economically dependent upon more advanced countries, particularly the United States, and characterized by three interrelated phenomena: a population boom since World War II, rapid urbanization, and the rise of consumer-oriented, less religious societies. Economic crises usually have compounded problems and accelerated trends that were already in progress. In such crises, most women probably have been torn between social norms based on the patriarchal ideal and the need to work outside the household on extremely unfavorable terms. They often mobilized because the "patriarchal bargain"—the idea that women would be maintained in a decent life in the home—had broken down.[16]

But if women enter the workforce on terms decided by others, whether these others are men or multinational corporations, and if gender reflects the more general pattern of power relations in society, then women's prospects in any crisis turn on the extent to which power itself is being redefined. If this reflection is correct, the example of the 1930s indicates that the decisive moment regarding gender and development is likely to occur not at the peak of the crisis but during the subsequent phase of recovery, at a time when political actors, most of them men, are looking for new bases of support. That is the moment when women must insist on their place in politics: If they do not, a place will be assigned to them by default. □

THE 1930s AND THE PATRIARCHAL BARGAIN

Unfortunately, the precise impact of economic change during the 1930s on women in Latin America remains outside the purview of most existing scholarship. Asunción Lavrin, in discussing the role of women in the Latin American labor movements before 1925, argues that women won some victories but that change occurred slowly.[17] Well into the 1930s, only a small minority of women were in the workforce. Women made up approximately 15 percent or more of the U.S. labor force by the end of the nineteenth century and about 22 percent by 1930.[18] In contrast, most Latin American records claim that women were less than 10 percent of the labor force before 1930, although this varied widely from country to country and from urban to rural areas. Mexican data, for example, indicate that in 1930, women constituted less than 5 percent of the economically active population, and Cuban women made up about 10 percent; Chilean census data show that in 1907, women made up 28 percent of the workforce, dropping to 19 percent by 1930.[19]

It is more likely that these numbers reflected what was categorized as worth counting rather than reality. Women who worked in family shops or in agriculture often were not reported as being active in the labor force. In Chile, for instance, the wife and children of a tenant farmer worked under his contract at no additional pay. Commenting on a 1970s Mexican census report, which claimed that only 10 percent of women were working, Lourdes Arizpe calls the figure "laughable to anyone who knows rural Mexico." Noting the decline of women workers in Rio de Janeiro between 1900 and 1920, June Hahner wonders at her own findings and observes that "most lower-class families could not survive without female and child labor." Even the best-paid men of the period did not earn enough to support a family.[20]

Policy and Politics

In spite (or perhaps because) of women's contributions to economic production, one central aspect of Latin America's response to the Great Depression is indisputable. At the height of the crisis, women, children, and families were rarely taken into consideration in the design of government policies. The primary goal of the Latin American states from 1929 to 1933 was a resuscitation of the economy through an improvement in production and prices. Political leaders hoped this would lead to a recovery of male employment, which, in turn, would preserve families and social order. Neither the Chilean archives nor Mexican documents reveal policies designed to refinance the employment of women or to help women sustain their families.[21]

The impact of the Great Depression on women was expressed more in law than in issues of economic development. Women became active in reform movements, and in several countries, legislation was passed safeguarding women at work, reducing male control of the household, and recognizing women as rational beings capable of managing their own affairs. In 1934, the Chilean family code was altered to give married women the right to hold any employment (unless prohibited by court order at the request of the husband), to control her own earnings, to contract her own debts, to buy or sell her own property, and if a marriage was dissolved, to acquire the income and property she had earned or acquired during its duration. In Cuba, women's legal gains were even more impressive. In the home, men lost the right to murder adulterous wives, and in the event of divorce, they were forced to share property with their former wives and provide alimony and child support. In the factory, wages were tied to the task performed, not to the gender of the worker. Domestic servants acquired some legal protection, and a woman could not be fired just because she married. Women gained equal protection under the law in the 1940 constitution.[22]

Elsewhere in Latin America, however, legislation regarding working women enacted in the 1930s and early 1940s was strongly paternalistic, concentrating on prohibiting them, as one survey put it, "from working in occupations that are unhealthy and that contribute to immorality." Commonly, the laws granted women an eight-hour workday and forty-eight-hour work week, established contract conditions for home workers, allowed women in factories to nurse their infants, and restricted the grounds for dismissal. In Peru, for example, an employer could be fined for firing a woman three months before or after she gave birth.[23]

But what did such changes mean? We have yet to separate the various elements of law and social development, let alone disaggregate questions of labor reforms and gender issues in the first half of this century. But we do know that labor laws were selectively enforced. As far as we can tell, they had little impact on the countryside in either Chile or Cuba. The immediate effectiveness of domestic legislation has yet to be studied. But given the casual character of most urban male labor in the 1930s, it seems unlikely that women in working-class households could have expected much in any divorce. Nevertheless, there is evidence that laws had eventual consequences. In his classic study of Cuba, Lowry Nelson found that by 1950, divorce law had permitted couples to legalize already existing separations, and in the cities, he credits legal changes with the "emancipation of women," including their increased demands for improved social services.[24]

Participation in the Labor Force

Unfortunately, as a recent survey of Latin American labor history points out, there is as yet too little work that focuses on women.[25] The task of disaggregating the consequences of the 1930s crisis by gender involves both intellectual theory and sources of information. Theories in one subject (labor history or agrarian history) do not easily fit into another (women's history or gender studies). Moreover, the sources tend to be so disparate that it becomes difficult to accumulate information on questions relating to distinctive theories. In an exhaustive study of Chile's labor struggles in the 1930s, for instance, I encountered very few references to women, either at home or at work, and virtually none about children.

Two recent studies have successfully integrated women into working-class history during and after the 1930s. Using interviews as well as more traditional sources, Marjorie Becker has given us a new view of Mexican land reform during the populist administration of President Lázaro Cárdenas (1934–1940). She demonstrates that rural women in the state of Michoacán suffered divided loyalties when reform opened up economic possibilities accompanied by an official anticlericalism. Women knew that the attack on received, religious morality could have consequences for them far beyond what might be gained from a plot of land.[26] Specifically, women had to consider the overarching question of what would happen if social norms broke down in the face of the government's promotion of what it called "socialism." What would happen to the Catholic value structure in which they had been raised and with which they identified?

In her study of Brazilian coffee laborers, Verena Stolke traces the transformation of plantation labor from the *colonato* system (in which land was rented to tenant families) to a system of wage-paid laborers, working in groups or "gangs." She demonstrates that women's unpaid labor in the *colonato* (particularly the work they did growing food for the family) was essential to sustaining coffee production during the 1930s, when the product price fell precipitously. Plantation owners gradually gave up the *colonato* system, replacing it by the 1970s with gangs working solely for wages. The *colonato* regime had supported patriarchy, but the wage-labor regime separated families, sending women as well as men out to work in gangs and earn their own income. Men's position was often devastated by the change, for they lost control of the family and, as a result, lost self-esteem as well.

Stolke does not romanticize the past. Women were exploited under both labor regimes; and for many, the change led to a worse situation. Women responded not by joining labor unions or political parties but by demanding that their husbands become more successful providers. Their reaction endorsed "the very institutions which are at the root of their exploitation and subordination as women—i.e., marriage and family with a gender hierarchy and sexual division of labour within it."[27]

Taken together, these studies by Becker and Stolke suggest that economics alone does not explain either the persistence of patriarchal attitudes or the political behavior of women under conditions of economic crisis. In both situations, women seem to cling to the "patriarchal bargain" as well as the notion that men should be the primary providers even at the price of women's subordination. If this is true, it is not hard to understand why. Political movements in the 1930s did not offer women any real empowerment and certainly provided no ideal comparable to that of a secure family (however male-dominated). Joel Wolfe's work indicates that it took time to break down male chauvinist attitudes toward women as they entered mills and other factories created through import-substitution industrialization in Sao Paulo. Further, he quotes union leaders with strong anarchist backgrounds in the early 1930s who objected to women working in factories because they were perceived as taking jobs from men. Once women were in the factories, they tended to avoid unions not only because of leadership attitudes but also because, between job and housework, they had little time for union activities.[28] With the exception of Cuba and Brazil, wage parity without regard to gender was not established in law, and it existed nowhere in practice.

Similarly, we know that women participated in the early labor movements of Argentina, Bolivia, and Chile.[29] But they did not acquire a labor-based platform for their grievances. As one historian put it, women were victims of "union machismo."[30] A Sao Paulo union officer rationalized the absence of women in unions with this comment; "We protect the women, they don't need to struggle for their rights as workers."[31] This, of course, was not true. Women could be part of the struggle but not part of the vanguard for change.

Upturn and Recovery

The long crisis of the 1930s did not end in 1939. From the existing, albeit sketchy, evidence, it seems that the decisive changes for women took place not at the outset of the Great Depression but in the beginnings of a recovery in the late 1930s and early 1940s. Latin America benefited from the buildup to war and as a supplier to the Allies in World War II, and women gained as segments of the middle and working classes voiced demands for economic nationalism and a redistribution of income. New clientelistic arrangements would eventually result, but these crystallized at various times from the 1930s (the Cárdenas administration in Mexico) to the late 1940s (Peronism in Argentina) and the early 1950s (the Bolivian Revolution of 1952).[32] The benefits from such changes were unevenly distributed between cities and the countryside, between the middle class and the working poor, and between men and women.

A series of studies on women in Latin America by U.S. specialists in the early 1940s provides some descriptive information that indicates women in the late 1930s and early 1940s were entering the labor force in larger numbers at that time and undertaking new tasks; there was also a notable increase of women in universities. In Peru, for example, one report noted major changes in the last "ten or fifteen years." Before then, "work outside the home was not generally accepted for women of families in the middle and higher economic brackets." By 1940, however, women made up 35 percent of the workforce, 57 percent of all textile workers, and some 5,500 of the 9,600 teachers and public school administrators. Indeed, the rapid expansion of the textile industry was a decisive factor in women's increased visibility in the workforce, but women textile workers earned about half the wages paid to men in comparable situations. In 1939, women made up 32 percent of the Sao Paulo workforce; by 1943 that figure rose to 42 percent. They constituted a third of all office workers, although the majority labored in textile plants and canneries. Brazilian officials proudly announced that their labor laws were in accordance with recommendations of the International Labour Organisation.[33]

The studies make little reference to the roles of women in politics (which, of course, was not the immediate concern of the researchers), but all mention women's weak participation in unions.[34] Recent scholarship indicates that women in the textile industry became militant during the course of the 1940s, however, and emerged as important leaders in the labor fights of the early 1950s. They not only fought speedups and the rising cost of living but also demanded wages equal to those of men.

The first wave of feminism, from the turn of the century to the late 1940s, made only modest contributions to women's welfare. The movement was small, urban, and, above all, socially circumscribed. Yet it was also part of a more general phenomenon: the mobilization of the middle class. Hahner concludes that, like the men of the period, Brazilian feminist leaders were "classbound." They promoted government spending on health and education and favored labor reforms, but in the end, they had little to offer those beneath them socially. Heleieth Saffioti claims that Bertha Lutz, the great Brazilian feminist, identified "with the ideals of the middle layers of society." Summarizing the character of Cuban feminists, Stoner notes that most did not work for a living and "resisted a total commitment to political and social issues." She goes further and provides an epitaph for Latin American feminism of the era: Middle-class feminists gained "because they were empowered as political and social matriarchs. Other women … were not significantly more powerful than before."[35] In fact, the persistence and power of class differences found expression in a bitter paradox: To the extent that middle-class feminists achieved social reforms, they also raised the cost of hiring women, which may have succeeded only in reducing employment opportunities for women of the working class.[36]

The most concrete outcome of the postwar era was a brief revival of electoral politics and, with it, of women's acquisition of suffrage.[37] But once suffrage was won and the Cold War set in, the first wave of feminism lost its momentum. Women continued to demand legal and social reforms, but after the early 1950s, they subordinated their own agenda and leadership within male-dominated parties and unions. Organizations, national and international, based solely on women's initiative either disappeared or merged with male-dominated associations. Thus, though women became a section of the Peronist Justicialist Party, they had no real say in the development of party initiatives, and scholars note that the feminine ideal, espoused by Eva Perón, demanded that women subordinate themselves to male leadership.[38] When women were granted the vote in Mexico in 1953, their organizations were either disbanded or subordinated into a segment of the Partido Revolucionario Institucional (PRI). Moreover, as one historian noted, the groups that joined the party were first purged of any independent women leaders.[39] The Inter-American Commission of Women, formed at the initiative of women during the 1928 Inter-American Conference in Havana, succeeded in having the delegates at the 1938 conference in Lima include women's equal rights as part of the Inter-American principles. Eventually, a women's section emerged in the Organization of American States (OAS), formed in 1948.[40] Latin American women in international organizations demanded and won the inclusion of women's rights in the United Nations Charter in 1945, and they played a central role in organizing the 1975 International Women's Year Conference on the status of women. The changes that began in the 1930s thus carry forward into a more contemporary era, but so does the weight of patriarchy. □

THE 1980s AND WOMEN'S MOBILIZATION

The second wave of Latin American feminism appeared around 1970 and was strongly influenced by the revival of women's movements in Western Europe and the United States. It once again began in the more privileged social sectors,[41] but this second wave developed a far broader agenda and reached into elements of society that had not been touched by suffrage campaigns or earlier reforms. There are three notable differences between the first and second waves: (1) Contemporary feminist

ideology now relates gender to every aspect of Latin American development: technology, environment, race, class, ideology, religion, international setting, and so forth;[42] women in the poorer strata of societies—in
the countryside, shantytowns, and factories—have become deeply
involved today, and some have emerged as leaders of local and even
national movements; and (3) Latin American women have now gained
much more prominence in international settings, from the United
Nations to the media in advanced nations. The first International
Women's Year Conference in 1975 was followed by the UN Decade for
Women, and feminist symposia, called *encuentros*, have been held every
two years since 1981, drawing participants from throughout Latin
America. Women can now cite "international" norms in making their
arguments for local and national change.

Neoliberal Economics

The debt crisis of the 1980s prompted a return to pre-Depression points
of view in the form of neoliberal policy experiments. Countries with
aging industrial sectors, indebted governments, and negative capital
flows sought a revival of exports to rescue them. By the 1990s, Latin
America began selling not only minerals and foodstuffs but also manufactures produced for markets dominated by multinational corporations.
The region's fundamental export has become cheap labor, and women,
the cheapest laborers of all, have become central to the prospects of each
of these neoliberal models.

Like the Great Depression, the recent debt crisis occurred as a
segment of women were already reconsidering their options. We know
that, from the 1950s onward, the percentage of women in the labor force
of most Latin American countries was rising, although the reasons for
the increase varied widely from country to country. This trend was not
everywhere linear, however, for the percentage of women in the Chilean
workforce fluctuated considerably from the 1950s to the 1970s.[43]

One of the most notable changes since the 1930s has been in middle-
class women's prospects. By the 1990s, this group made up half of all
professionals and technicians in Chile and was a crucial component of
white-collar employment in every major Latin American city.[44] Although
a gender gap remains in education levels and literacy, it narrowed to
only 6 percent in the cities (compared to 12 percent in the countryside),[45]
and the vast majority of urban adult women are literate. In the 1930s,
women university graduates numbered a few thousand; now they
number in the millions. Furthermore, enrollment figures for women in
Latin American universities often exceed those for men. This has created
a demand for changes in the curriculum, with the result that women's

studies programs of considerable sophistication exist on many campuses.[46]

But there is a pronounced class difference in opportunities, and for most women, job prospects remain extremely limited. They are excluded from the better paid sectors in import-substitution manufacturing and in transportation and construction. But they are included in the relatively poorly paid export-processing zones. Contemporary policy rhetoric touts export processing and gendered change as though Latin America were entering an era of dramatic opportunities. But according to the United Nations, a working woman in the region is most likely to be single, in her twenties, and in domestic service. A recent study of provincial Peru demonstrates there are two main alternatives for women: entering petty trade or domestic employment. Most women who entered the workforce of Querétero, Mexico, in the 1980s made tortillas for a living. A survey of Brazilian women concluded their work almost everywhere was "subsidiary" to men's.[47] It is difficult to know if anything has changed in rural areas because women do not appear in much of the data. In fact, UN researchers had to look hard before they discovered that 40 percent of the coffee harvesters in Colombia were women, as were 70 percent of those picking fruit for Chile's booming export sector.[48]

The immediate impact of the debt crisis was on household income. Real salaries in Latin America fell 12 to 18 percent. And, women lost their jobs more often than men: Their unemployment rose substantially in the industrialized cities of Brazil, doubled in Venezuela, and quintupled in Bolivia. In industrial zones such as Sao Paulo and Montevideo, an increase in women workers was accompanied by a greater disparity between men and women's wages since women took jobs at salaries "well below those of men."[49] The impact on the gendered distribution of income was much more varied in other areas, but after twelve years of crisis, the gender gap remains wide. In Latin America, the wage differential ranges from a high point in Sao Paulo, where women are paid only 54 'percent of men's wages for comparable work, to a low point in Panama, where they earn 83 percent of men's wages.[50]

Political Activity

These dismal economic tendencies have coexisted with important political changes. The crisis in the 1980s, like that of the 1930s, seemed to intersect with—rather than cause changes in—women's labor participation and political behavior. On the broadest level, women were already responding to developments that had made their lives more difficult: the civil wars in Central America, the military governments of South America, and the effects of economic stagnation. The debt crisis was one of several events that galvanized many women to become politically involved.

The sheer quantity of women's organizations, the number of women in political and labor associations, and the roles that women play in social mobilization of all kinds are substantially different in the 1980s and 1990s. Women have not only established organizations, they also lead them. They have formed labor unions, producer and consumer cooperatives, professional associations, and political action groups. They have been central to the creation of communities devoted to the principles of liberation theology (which stresses that Catholic Christians must engage in social struggle to alleviate misery in the region).[51] And although women continue to have little direct voice or representation in governmental circles, they have a great deal more than in the 1930s, when their access to political power was virtually nil.

In the contemporary era all efforts at social organization and mobilization have been complicated by a prevailing consequence of the debt crisis: the spread of the informal economy. Casual work, petty trade, and domestic service have been among the most difficult activities to unionize at any time. And since women often dominate these sectors, it means that they have suffered disproportionately from impediments to collective organization.

As a price for their political activism, too, women have had to confront unprecedented levels of official violence. Torture and political murder are nothing new in Latin America, but the military regimes of the 1970s and 1980s discarded traditional constraints on the treatment of women and children. Women who mobilized under such regimes required unusual levels of commitment and courage, and as a result, they became both opponents of repression and symbols of resistance for everyone. There was nothing in the 1930s similar to the Chilean *juntas de madres* (mothers' committees) that ran the soup kitchens of Santiago in the face of the Pinochet dictatorship, or the Mothers of the Plaza de Mayo, who protested the disappearance of family members under the Argentine military regime of the 1970s and 1980s. And Rigoberta Menchú (an Indian victim of torture, who has won the Nobel Prize for her work on human rights) is something original in the history of Guatemala.[52] Women in the 1980s became essential to the political opposition of repressive regimes, at times, they even personified that opposition and its moral purpose. Sonia Alvarez, for example, has shown that in the early 1980s, Brazilian women's protest groups were a central force in the campaign to end military rule and to revive elected government.[53]

Nonetheless, the problem of social bias remains, even within political movements professing equality for women. No less a figure than Chile's Socialist president Salvador Allende remarked during the upheavals of his administration (1970–1973) "When I say 'woman,' I always think of the woman-mother." Studies sympathetic to revolutionary Nicaragua and Cuba note how hard it has been for women to gain equality of treatment at work, let alone in the home, even in regimes that pledge their support for such changes.[54] Well into the 1990s, men continued to control the formal mechanisms of the region's political economies, and those mechanisms—governments, political parties, labor unions, and professional associations—rarely reflected any link between the fate of women and the course of the region's development. Although a small fraction of women had gained employment in international agencies and gained access to professional careers, most women who were politically active found themselves in institutions that, at best, remained indifferent to women's issues or, in the case of unions, often were still profoundly sexist.

What Recovery?

Will women experience the resolution of the debt crisis as an improvement over the past? The current wisdom of international organizations is that recovery is under way. Data from the United Nations Economic Commission for Latin America and the Caribbean (ECLAC) indicate that in 1991, regional income went up for the first time in four years, so that per capita income in 1994 was at 1977 levels. Though this might serve as a statistical definition of "recovery," however, most Latin Americans are still reeling from what they have lost. What is one to say about a region so battered by inflation that ECLAC officials cheered the 1992 annual rate of 200 percent? By December 1993, inflation ran at about 15 percent per year—although the region's economy was growing at only 3.2 percent per year, a rate that is barely enough to absorb new entrants into the workforce and that cannot begin to address the "backlog of social deficiencies that has accumulated over the years."[55] The International Labour Organisation claims that eleven years after the start of the debt crisis more than 43 percent of all Latin American laborers are underemployed and 60 percent of all households are poor (defined as being without essential goods and services).[56] In the near future, Latin America must generate millions of new jobs since some 40 to 45 percent of the people of most countries are under the age of twenty.[57]

Even more troubling for any hope of economic renewal are the problems of the industrial democracies, especially in Japan, Western Europe, and the United States. Their capacity to import is supposed to drive Latin America's recovery, but they are suffering from high rates of unemployment, low rates of economic growth, or both. How will a slow advance in developed countries lead to a rapid or even modest gain by

Latin America? It is not clear that the process of restructuring economies to accommodate a neoliberal worldview will actually work, let alone that it can sustain democracy and civil rights in Latin America.

It is also unclear whether such a recovery, if it comes, will create the kinds of opportunities for women that emerged in the aftermath of the Great Depression. During the 1930s and 1940s, world conditions and import-substitution industrialization made it possible for political leaders in Latin America to broaden their social coalitions through populist policies; these strategies produced tangible benefits for women (as well as men) and encouraged the incorporation of women into politics. By comparison, prospects for the 1990s offer much less ground for optimism. Growth has given way to scarcity; expansion has surrendered to efficiency. The advent of democracy may have opened new channels for political participation by women, but the harsh realities of economic stringency are unlikely to yield a fair share of material benefits to women. Economic and social policies appear to confront a zero-sum situation, where one group's gain will have to be offset by someone else's loss. Under these conditions, less powerful groups, including women, will find it extremely difficult to prevail. If the pie is not growing, it is that much harder to obtain a decent slice. □

CONCLUSION

The rise of neoliberal economic policies in the 1980s and 1990s has overlapped with the surge in Latin American women's movements. How are we to interpret this conjuncture? Did the debt crisis represent a new turn of events for women and for the redefinition of gender relations, or did it signal a worsening of conditions despite the rhetoric of women's rights and concern for gender equality? Did it give women the chance to articulate new agendas, or will all such efforts founder on the rocks of global economic competition? The existing evidence is incomplete.

What has happened to Latin American women can be evaluated in a number of ways: across time, within the Third World, and in comparison with developed, industrial cultures. There is little doubt that they are generally better off than they were in the first part of this century. Most Latin American women born today can expect to live into their seventies, only a few years less than women in the United States.[58] And if we count general living standards, from access to potable water to literacy, the percentage and numbers of women who benefit have risen over the decades. But if changes for women are measured in relation to men and vis-à-vis the debt crisis, the record is mixed. As a UN survey put it, women were beginning to make some "significant gains according to indicators of health, child-bearing, education and economic, social and political participation" just as the debt crisis descended. But even then, measurable gains were largely limited to urban areas, and during the 1980s, there was a "serious macroeconomic deterioration ... as the decade progressed."[59]

These data indicate that although Latin American women lag behind those in "developed regions," they live in countries with generally higher per capita income than in most of Africa, Asia, and Oceania. But Latin American rates of female-headed households tend to be higher by 18 to 22 percent than in other parts of the Third World. Rates of political participation varied widely throughout Latin America, but seemed higher by the mid-1980s than most of the Third World and were higher in the region than they had been in the 1970s. Still, in most of the developed world, women hold 20 to 30 percent of all legislative seats; in Latin America, they hold only 5 to 15 percent.[60]

Women have entered public debates over power and social justice, but their hopes for effective equality are undercut by gender bias at every level of institutional arrangements—internationally, nationally, and in the home. In 1992, President George Bush's director of the U.S. Agency for International Development argued in favor of policies that raise women's income in underdeveloped regions because that would lead to greater family investment in nutrition, health care, and the overall welfare of children.[61] And international lending agencies have given priority to the extension of credit to women.[62] But surveys of development projects indicate that only a fraction of those funded in the 1980s directly involved women.[63]

Throughout this century, women's struggles in the political arena have involved national laws and personal customs. Basic changes have occurred, but they have been incremental and have not been tied to prospects for economic development. During the debt crisis and the subsequent collapse of military regimes in the 1980s, there was a political opening toward democratic norms. Within this space, women began to raise issues they had been privately voicing for ten years or more, and these issues went beyond the rhetoric that had accompanied the crisis of the 1930s.

Yet the corrosive effects of neoliberal policies have made it difficult for women to institutionalize changes. The logic of reform should have led women to either join unions or form their own labor associations, but unions, which had often been sexist and have been seen by many working women as irrelevant to their needs, are in decline.[64] Worse, it is extremely difficult to create new organizations at a grassroots level in the existing political and economic climate. How can anyone be expected to work long hours at low wages, look after an impoverished household, and also organize politically? One scholar surveying the efforts of poor women in Guayaquil to perform this "triple role" speaks of most of the women as "burnt out."[65]

Laws have changed, but the gender gap remains large. Women have statutory equality with men only in Cuba and Costa Rica; Bolivia, Colombia, and Venezuela give them equal status in controlling choice of residence, in demanding mutual fidelity, and in parental rights over children. Everywhere else, men have preferential rights in controlling family property and children. Moreover, women have yet to win basic medical care and control of reproduction.[66] And there is no doubt that the economic crisis was accompanied by intensified forms of domestic strife, the destruction of families, and the abandonment of thousands of children.

In sum, the historical record reveals a disheartening pattern: Gains for Latin American women have come at high cost. Greater political participation has been accompanied by greater violence—political, social, and domestic. Rising participation in the workforce has opened up the professions but left the majority of women in the lowest paying jobs. Greater media sensitivity and a change in the public discussion of women's problems has yet to be translated into legal equality in most of the region and into real equality anywhere. But each wave of feminist struggle, intersected as it has been by economic crisis, has pushed the agenda of social justice in new directions. We are now in the midst of the most broadly based struggle for women's rights and gender change that has ever occurred in Latin America. Seen from the ideal of equality, there is a long way to go; seen from the perspective of the last great capitalist crisis, the distance traveled is extraordinary. □

NOTES

I would like to thank Rae Blumberg, Pierrette Hondagneu-Sotelo, Christine Hunefeldt, Olivia Ruiz, Peter H. Smith, and Irene Tinker for their comments on this chapter.

1. My search on this subject utilized the MELVYL electronic library database system at the University of California, which reviewed some seven million titles on all campuses.

2. *San Diego Union*, February 15, 1993, 1.

3. Rosemary Thorp, ed., *Latin America in the 1930s: The Role of the Periphery in World Crisis* (New York: St. Martin's Press, 1984), appendices, 344.

4. Pedro-Pablo Kuczynski, *Latin American Debt* (Baltimore: Johns Hopkins University Press, 1988), 102–103.

5. Major works on Latin America and the Great Depression are: German D'Elia, *América Latina, de la crisis del 29 a la Segunda Guerra Mundial* (Montevideo: Ediciones de la Banda Oriental, 1982); Silvia Dutreniet Bielous et al., *El impacto político de la crisis del 29 en América Latina* (Mexico City: Alianza Editorial Mexicana, 1989); Angus Maddison, *Two Crises: Latin America and Asia, 1929–38 and 1973–*

83 (Paris: Development Centre of the Organization for Economic Cooperation and Development, 1985); and Thorp, *Latin America in the 1930s.*

6. Basic surveys on the 1980s include: Kuczynski, *Latin American Debt*; Jackie Roddick, *The Dance of the Millions: Latin America and the Debt Crisis* (London: Latin America Bureau, 1988); Barbara Stallings, *Banker to the Third World: U.S. Portfolio Investment in Latin America, 1900–1986* (Berkeley: University of California Press, 1987); Sue Branford and Bernardo Kucinski, *The Debt Squads: The U.S., the Banks, and Latin America* (London: Zed Books, 1988); Jeffry A. Frieden, *Debt, Development, and Democracy: Modern Political Economy and Latin America, 1965–1985* (Princeton: Princeton University Press, 1991); and Luis Vitale, *Historia de la deuda externa latinoamericana y entretelones de endeudamiento argentino* (Buenos Aires: Sudamericana/Planeta, 1986). Current debt information is from Chronicle of Latin American Economic Affairs, an electronic news service, from the Latin America Data Base (LABD), Latin American Institute, University of New Mexico, citing UN Economic Commission for Latin America and the Caribbean (ECLAC), "Panorama económico de América Latina 1991," and *Notimex*, December 16, 1991.

7. Jeffrey Bortz, "Wages and Economic Crisis in Mexico," in Barry Carr, ed., *The Mexican Left, Popular Movements and the Politics of Austerity* (La Jolla: Center for U.S.-Mexican Studies, University of California, San Diego, 1986), 45.

8. LADB, on industrial jobs, citing Agence France-Presse, October 1, 1992, and on the informal sector, citing Chilean National Statistics Institute, May 6, 1992.

9. *La Jornada* (Mexico City), November 11–22, 1993; *Los Angeles Times*, November 11–22, 1993; and LADB, June 3, July 22, and July 29, 1993.

10. C. Roe Goddard, *U.S. Foreign Economic Policy and the Latin American Debt Issue* (New York: Garland Publishing, 1993), 17–29, 45–52.

11. Carlos Marichal, *A Century of Debt Crises in Latin America: From Independence to the Great Depression, 1820–1930* (Princeton: Princeton University Press, 1989), 8–11, 239.

12. Joan Scott, "Gender: A Useful Category of Historical Analysis," *American Historical Review* 91, no. 5 (December 1986): 1059–1075, especially 1073–1075.

13. Dirección General de Estadística Chilena, *Estadística chilena* 18, no. 6 (June 1945): 117; the rate in Chile fell to about 22 percent in the 1940s. On Peru, see Laura Miller, "La mujer obrera en Lima, 1900–1930," in Laura Miller and Steve Stein, eds., *Lima obrera, 1900–1930* (Lima: El Virrey, 1987), 11, 29.

14. Latin American economic history is just beginning to include women. On the issue of domestic service, see such works as: Asunción Lavrín, ed., *Latin American Women: Historical Perspectives* (Westport, CT: Greenwood Press, 1978); Luis Vitale, *La mitad invisible de la historia: El protagonismo social de la mujer latinoamericana* (Buenos Aires: Sudamericana/Planeta, 1987); Sandra Lauderdale Graham, *House and Street: The Domestic World of Servants and Masters in Nineteenth-Century Rio de Janeiro* (Cambridge: Cambridge University Press, 1988); Donna J. Guy, *Sex and Danger in Buenos Aires: Prostitution, Family, and Nation in Argentina* (Lincoln: University of Nebraska Press, 1991); Rachel Soihet, *Condiçao feminina e formas de violencia: Mulheres probres e ordem urbana, 1890–1920* (Rio de Janeiro: Forense Universitaria, 1989); Hector Recalde, *Mujer, condiciones de vida, de trabajo y salud*, 2 vols. (Buenos Aires: Centro Editor de América Latina, 1988); and Elsa M. Chaney and Mary García Castro, eds., *Muchachas No More: Household Workers in Latin*

America and the Caribbean (Philadelphia: Temple University Press, 1989), especially the chapter by Elizabeth Kuznesof, "A History of Domestic Service in Spanish America, 1492–1980," 17–35.

15. On Brazil, see June E. Hahner, *Emancipating the Female Sex: The Struggle for Women's Rights in Brazil, 1850–1940* (Durham, NC: Duke University Press, 1990), 12, 144–169; on Cuba, see K. Lynn Stoner, *From the House to the Streets: The Cuban Woman's Movement for Legal Reform, 1898–1940* (Durham, NC: Duke University Press, 1991), 59–78; on suffrage, see Francesca Miller, *Latin American Women and the Search for Social Justice* (Hanover, NH: University Press of New England, 1991), 68–109.

16. Maxine Molyneux, "Mobilisation Without Emancipation? Women's Interests, the State and Revolution in Nicaragua," *Feminist Studies* 11, no. 2 (1985): 227–254; see also Deniz Kandiyoti, "Bargaining with Patriarchy," *Gender and Society* 2, no. 3 (1988): 211–290. The phrase is from Kandiyoti, but Molyneux discusses how gender interests can be defined in any given struggle.

17. Asunción Lavrín, "Women, Labor, and the Left: Argentina and Chile, 1890–1925," *Journal of Women's History* 1, no. 2 (Fall 1989): 88–116.

18. Ray Marshall and Beth Paulin, "Employment and Earnings of Women: Historical Perspective," in Karen Shallcross Koziara, Michael H. Moskow, and Lucretia Dewey Tanner, eds., *Working Women: Past, Present, Future* (Washington, DC: The Bureau of National Affairs, 1987), 8.

19. María del Carmen Elú de Leñero, *El trabajo de la mujer en México: Alternativa para el cambio* (Mexico City: Impresora Galve, 1975), 38; Stoner, *From the House to the Streets*, 39; Lucía Pardo V., *La participación de las mujeres en la fuerza de trabajo: Tendencias y características* (Santiago: Universidad de Chile, Departamento de Economía, 1988), 8.

20. Lourdes Arizpe, *La mujer en el desarrollo de México y de América Latina* (Mexico City: Universidad Nacional Autónoma de México, Centro Regional de Investigaciones Multidisciplinarias, 1989), 60; and Hahner, *Emancipating the Female Sex*, 106–107.

21. This included the records of the Ministry of Interior and Department of Labor in Chile and the presidential archival records at the Archivo General de la Nación of Mexico for the period 1920–1934.

22. Kathleen B. Tappen, The Status of Women in Chile (Washington, DC: Office of Inter-American Affairs, Research Division, June 1944), 4; Stoner, *From the House to the Streets*, 158–166, 179–184.

23. An excellent if brief source of information on women factory workers is the series of reports done by the U.S. Department of Labor, appearing in *Women's Bureau Bulletin*: "Women Workers in Argentina, Chile, and Uruguay," no. 195 (1942): quote on 9; "Women Workers in Brazil," no. 206 (1943); "Women Workers in Paraguay," no. 210 (1946); and "Women Workers in Peru," no. 213 (1947).

24. Brian Loveman, *Struggle in the Countryside: Politics and Rural Labor in Chile, 1919–1973* (Bloomington: University of Indiana Press, 1976), laws described on 197–200; Lowry Nelson, *Rural Cuba* (New York: Octagon Books, 1970, reprint of the 1950 edition).

25. Emilia Viotti da Costa, "Experience Versus Structures: New Tendencies in the History of Labor and the Working Class in Latin America—What Do We

Gain? What Do We Lose?" and June Nash, "Gender Issues in Latin American Labor," *International Labor and Working Class History* 36 (Fall 1989): 3–24, 44–50.

26. Marjorie Becker, "Lázaro Cárdenas and the Mexican Counter-Revolution: The Struggle over Culture in Michoacán, 1934–1940," Ph.D. diss., Yale University, 1988.

27. Verena Stolke, *Coffee Planters, Workers and Wives: Class Conflict and Gender Relations on Sao Paulo Plantations, 1850–1980* (Oxford: Macmillan Press, 1988), 63ff. and 240.

28. Joel Wolfe, *Working Women, Working Men: Sao Paulo and the Rise of Brazil's Industrial Working Class, 1900–1955* (Durham, NC: Duke University Press, 1993), 57, 80.

29. Sara Beatriz Guardia, *Mujeres peruanas: El otro lado de la historia* (Lima: Editora Humboldt, 1985), 77–92; Ximena Medinaceli, *Alterando la rutina: Mujeres en las ciudades de Bolivia, 1920–1930* (La Paz: CIDEM, 1989), 82–114; Lavrín, "Women, Labor, and the Left"; Miller, *Latin American Women*, 101–103.

30. Leonor C. Harispe, "La mujer y los sindicatos," Comisión Permanente en Defensa de la Educación (COPEDE), *Colección Ensayos* 2 (March 1987): 2.

31. U.S. Department of Labor, "Women Workers in Brazil," 32.

32. On labor and politics, see Ruth Berins Collier and David Collier, *Shaping the Political Arena: Critical Junctures, the Labor Movement, and Regime Dynamics in Latin America* (Princeton: Princeton University Press, 1991), chapter 2, especially 46–48; on populism, see Michael Conniff, ed., *Latin American Populism in Comparative Perspective* (Albuquerque: University of New Mexico Press, 1982); on Argentina and Bolivia, see Rodolfo Puiggros, *El peronismo, sus causas* (Buenos Aires: Ediciones Cepe, 1972), and Jonathan Kelley and Herbert S. Klein, *Revolution and the Rebirth of Inequality: A Theory Applied to the National Revolution in Bolivia* (Berkeley: University of California Press, 1981).

33. U.S. Department of Labor, "Women Workers in Peru," 2, 5–8, 23, 29, and "Women Workers in Brazil," 3, 23–25.

34. In addition to the articles of the *Women's Bureau Bulletin*, other useful surveys were done by the Office of Inter-American Affairs; see Kathleen B. Tappen, "The Status of Women in Brazil" and "The Status of Women in Chile" (Research Division, Social and Geographic Section, June 1944).

35. Hahner, *Emancipating the Female Sex*, 169, 179–180; Heleieth I.B. Saffioti, *Women in Class Society*, trans. Michael Vale (New York: Monthly Review Press, 1978), 211; and Stoner, *From the House to the Streets*, 74, 195.

36. See Saffioti, *Women in Class Society*, 185–189.

37. Wolfe, *Working Women, Working Men*, 165, 192–193; John D. French and Mary Lynn Pedersen, "Women and Working-Class Mobilization in Postwar Sao Paulo, 1945–1948," *Latin American Research Review* 24, no. 3 (1989): 99–125.

38. Sandra McGee Deutsch, "Gender and Sociopolitical Change in Twentieth-Century Latin America," *Hispanic American Historical Review* 71, no. 2 (May 1991): 271–274; see also Marysa Navarro, "Evita's Charismatic Leadership," in Conniff, ed., *Latin American Populism in Comparative Perspective*, and Julie M. Taylor, *Eva Perón: The Myths of a Woman* (Chicago: University of Chicago Press, 1979); Norma Sanchis, "Mujeres en la política ó política de mujeres? Un análisis de la experiencia de las mujeres peronistas, 1945–1955," in María del Carmen Feijóo, ed., *Nuestra*

memoria, nuestro futuro: Mujeres e historia, América Latina y el Caribe (Santiago: Isis Internacional, 1988).

39. Esperanza Tuños Pablos, *Mujeres que se organizan: El frente único pro derechos de la mujer, 1935–1945* (Mexico City: Miguel Angel Porrúa, 1992), 147–158.

40. Francesca Miller, "Latin American Feminism and the Transnational Area," in Emilie Bergmann, ed., *Women, Culture, and Politics in Latin America* (Berkeley: University of California Press, 1990), 18–24.

41. Nilsa M. Burgos Ortiz, Sara Sharratt, and Leda M. Trejos Correia, *La mujer en latinoamérica: Perspectivas sociales y psicológicas* (Buenos Aires: Editorial Humanitas, 1988), 47; on the origins of Latin American feminism, see also Nancy Saporta Sternbach, Marysa Navarro-Aranguren, Patricia Chuchryk, and Sonia E. Alvarez, "Feminisms in Latin America: From Bogotá to San Bernardo," in Arturo Escobar and Sonia E. Alvarez, eds., *The Making of Social Movements in Latin America: Identity, Strategy, and Democracy* (Boulder: Westview Press, 1992).

42. June Nash and María Patricia Fernández-Kelly, eds., *Men, Women, and the International Division of Labor* (Albany: State University of New York Press); Elizabeth Jelín, ed., *Women and Social Change in Latin America* (Atlantic Heights, NJ: Zed Books, 1990); Ximena Bunster and Elsa M. Chaney, *Sellers and Servants: Working Women in Lima, Peru* (Granby, MA: Bergin and Garvey, 1989); Janet Momsen and Janet Townsend, eds., *Geography of Gender in the Third World* (Albany: State University of New York Press, 1987); and Sarah A. Radcliffe and Sallie Westwood, eds., *Viva: Women and Popular Protest in Latin America* (New York: Routledge, 1993).

43. Catalina H. Wainerman and Zulma Recchini de Lattes, "Trabajadoras latinoamericanas: Un análisis comparativo de la Argentina, Bolivia y Paraguay," *Cuadernos del CENEP* 13/14 (June 1980): 55–56; Pardo V., *La participación de las mujeres en la fuerza de trabajo*, 31; Manuel Barrera, *La mujer en la estadística educacional y en la fuerza de trabajo chilenas* (Santiago: Universidad Católica de Chile, Programa Interdisciplinario de Investigaciones en Educación, 1976), 81–86.

44. Adriana Muñoz Dalborma, "Fuerza de trabajo femenina: Evolución y tendencias," in Centro de Estudios de la Mujer, *Mundo de mujer: Continuidad y cambio* (Santiago: Centro de Estudios de Mujer, 1988), 262; Ilse Abshagen Leitinger, "The Changing Role of Women in Latin America: A Descriptive and Theoretical Analysis of Six Countries, 1950–1970," Ph.D. diss., University of Denver, 1981, 149–160, and on the "double day," 331.

45. Nelly P. Stromquist, "Women and Literacy in Latin America," in Nelly P. Stromquist, ed., *Women and Education in Latin America* (Boulder: Lynne Rienner Publishers, 1992), 27; other chapters in this anthology warn that formal education alone does not eliminate gender biases.

46. Miller, *Latin American Women*, 65.

47. ECLAC (United Nations Economic Commission on Latin America and the Caribbean), *Los grandes cambios y la crisis: Impacto sobre la mujer en América Latina y el Caribe* (Santiago de Chile: ECLAC, 1990), 60; Florence E. Babb, *Between Field and Cooking Pot: The Political Economy of Marketwomen in Peru* (Austin: University of Texas Press, 1989), 64; and Sylvia Chant, "Family Structure and Female Labor in Querétero, Mexico," and Susan Cunningham, "Gender and Industrialization in

Brazil," both in Momsen and Townsend, eds., *Geography of Gender,* 278, and 278n, and 297, respectively.

48. ECLAC, Los grandes cambios, 98.

49. Ibid., 68.

50. Ibid., 66–71, 98.

51. The chapters in Radcliffe and Westwood, eds., *Viva,* are particularly good at demonstrating the range of women's organizations; see also Alicia Grandón, Betsey Valdivia, Cecilia Guerrero, and Patricia Ruíz Bravo, *Crisis y organizaciones populares de mujeres* (Lima: Pontificia Universidad Católica del Peru, 1987), 7–27.

52. On Chilean juntas, see María Elena Valenzuela, "The Evolving Roles of Women Under Military Rule," in Paul Drake and Ivan Jaksic, eds., *The Struggle for Democracy in Chile* (Lincoln: University of Nebraska Press, 1991); Catherine M. Boyle, "Touching the Air: The Cultural Force of Women in Chile," in Radcliffe and Westwood, eds., *Viva.* The symbolic importance of the Madres is discussed in Miller, *Latin American Women,* 8–13; Rigoberta Menchú, *I, Rigoberta Menchú, an Indian Woman in Guatemala* (London: Verso, 1984).

53. Sonia E. Alvarez, *Engendering Democracy in Brazil: Women's Movements in Transition Politics* (Princeton: Princeton University Press, 1990).

54. Georgina Waylen, "Rethinking Women's Political Participation and Protest: Chile 1970–1990," *Political Studies* 40 (1992): 309; on Cuba, see Deutsch, "Gender and Sociopolitical Change," 281–292, and Lois M. Smith and Alfred Padula, "Women in Socialist Cuba, 1959–1984," in Sandor Halebsky and John M. Kirk, eds., *Cuba: Twenty-Five Years of Revolution, 1959–1984* (New York: Praeger, 1984); on Nicaragua, see Helen Collinson, ed., *Women and Revolution in Nicaragua* (London: Zed Books, 1990).

55. LADB, citing ECLAC data, October 5, 1992, and ECLAC's executive secretary Gert Rosenthal, as quoted in *Latin American Weekly Report,* January 13, 1994, 11.

56. LADB, citing *Notimex,* August 23, 1991.

57. James W. Wilkie, *Statistical Abstract of Latin America* (Los Angeles: UCLA Latin American Center, 1992), Vol. 29, part II, 97–140.

58. Ibid.

59. United Nations, Department of International Economics and Social Affairs, Statistical Office, *The World's Women, 1970–1990: Trends and Statistics* (New York: United Nations, 1991), xv.

60. Ibid., 26–29, 40–41.

61. LADB, April 4–6, 1992, citing reports of Inter-American Development Bank's general meeting in Santo Domingo in the Spanish news service, EFE, and Agence France-Presse. The Bush official was citing Rae Lesser Blumberg, *Making the Case for the Gender Variable: Women and the Wealth and Well-Being of Nations,* Technical Reports in Gender and Development Series, no. 1 (Washington, DC: Office of Women in Development, Agency for International Development, October 1989). See also the special issue edited by Rae Lesser Blumberg, "Gender Stratification, Economy, and the Family," *Journal of Family Issues* 9 (March 1988): 1.

62. For example, the UNICEF effort in Bolivia, LADB, citing Inter Press Service, April 21, 1992.

63. Nuket Kardam, *Bringing Women In: Women's Issues in International Development Programs* (Boulder: Lynne Rienner Publishers, 1991), 23.

64. Rocío Londoño Botero, "Trade Unions and Labor Policy in Colombia, 1974–1987," in Edward C. Epstein, ed., *Labor Autonomy and the State in Latin America* (Boston: Unwin Hyman, 1989), 120; on attitudes of laboring women, see Margalit Berlin, "The Formation of an Ethnic Group: Colombian Female Workers in Venezuela," in Nash and Fernández-Kelly, eds., *Men, Women, and the International Division of Labor.*

65. Caroline O. N. Moser, "Adjustment from Below: Low-Income Women, Time, and the Triple Role in Guayaquil, Ecuador," in Radcliffe and Westwoods, eds., *Viva*, 194.

66. Margaret Schuler, assisted by Barbara Stob, "Women and the Law," in Rita S. Gallin, Marilyn Aronoff, and Anne Ferguson, eds., *The Women and International Development Annual*, vol. 1 (Boulder: Westview Press, 1989), 165. Since then, Ecuador has enacted (although not enforced) equal rights for women in all spheres. On rates of abortion in Brazil, see Alvarez, *Engendering Democracy in Brazil*, 67.

PART TWO

Engendering Wealth, Engendering Survival

The four chapters in Part Two reflect the critical importance of understanding how access to income and resources alters decision making and the well-being of women and men. This is true whether the experience is one of economic stability, economic growth, and increasing levels of production and efficiency or one of crisis, poverty, and the struggle for survival. The authors illustrate these contradictory trends through the life experiences of women and men in four different areas of the world. Helen Safa and Rita Gallin assess the feminization of labor-intensive export industries in the Caribbean and Taiwan; Claire Robertson and Behrooz Morvaridi look at people's responses to economic crisis and state policies in Kenya and Turkey, respectively.

Robertson's chapter presents a truly gendered study of over one thousand female and male traders in Nairobi. She gives voice to individual women who talk about defending their families' welfare in the face of great hardship, and she illustrates the toll the double day of trading and domestic work has taken on them. Comparing data from interviews conducted separately with women and men, Robertson reveals the gendered difference in access to resources and number of dependents, thus accounting for higher levels of male income. Interviews with women reveal how male dominance influences their trading strategies (including reliance on voluntary organizations and extended kin), how women successfully evade male controls and overcome landlessness and lack of access to capital and other resources, and how often men provide crucial support to wives and children.

Safa compares export-processing industries and the women who work in them in Puerto Rico and the Dominican Republic. She shows how women's different experiences are related to state labor and welfare policies, men's work, and remittances from family members who have

63

migrated to the United States. Drawing on diverse sources, including in-depth interviews with export workers, Safa makes the case that the nature of export processing and other economic changes affect not only the work opportunities and experiences of both women and men but also women's self-esteem and family relations. Women's autonomy is higher in Puerto Rico than in the Dominican Republic—a finding Safa relates to the erosion of the men's provider role, the length of women's employment, and higher income levels, fertility decline, and state welfare subsidies available to women in the former country.

Global restructuring brought export industry and commerce to the Taiwanese village studied by Gallin over the last two decades. In this case, patriarchal and industrial ideologies intersect to create efficient, successful enterprises that depend on the gender division of labor in the household. Gallin argues that this was a deliberate strategy directly responsible for the rapid rise of Taiwan as an industrialized economy. The Taiwanese case reveals, once again, how the critical role played by women's labor in these enterprises has broader implications for women's self-esteem, relative discontent, and family relations. Giving voice to women's feelings and aspirations, Gallin illustrates how seeds of change have been sown by the "ideological bonding" of production and family life.

Morvaridi contrasts the ways in which two ethnically different villages in Turkey have responded to the implementation of structural adjustment policies and cutbacks in state agricultural subsidies, especially for the production of sugar beets—the country's main cash crop. His case studies demonstrate that economic policies and programs can depend on male dominance in farming households. Thus, macroeconomic policies not only are implicitly gendered but can also become *explicitly* gendered when implemented by officials at the microlevel. In these villages, the struggle for survival under structural adjustment became a struggle for access to and control over productive resources—especially women's labor. In one village, men resorted to violence to assure women's labor, but women of both villages developed mechanisms of resistance, including elopement, migration, and strategic illnesses.

These chapters underscore the impossibility of ignoring the political, cultural, institutional, and personal dimensions of economic change. All show how macrolevel economic trends and policies create microlevel effects that interact with family systems to affect gendered work and power.

CHAPTER FOUR

■

Trade, Gender, and Poverty in the Nairobi Area: Women's Strategies for Survival and Independence in the 1980s

Claire Robertson

Kikuyu and Kamba women traders in the Nairobi area form the primary subject of this chapter, in which I will look at the implications for women's status of market trade in the 1980s. The stereotypical East African woman is a farmer, and development efforts involving such women usually focus on agricultural functions. However, Kikuyu women of central Kenya have been trading since at least the mid-nineteenth century, marketing foodstuffs in both local and long-distance trade, and Kamba women have also been involved in local trade since the nineteenth century.

The primary data used in this chapter are drawn from a survey of over one thousand female and male traders conducted in 1987–1988.[1] They allow for more gender analysis than the usual survey of African traders because one-third of the traders were male. From these data, we can closely test how differential access to resources governed by patriarchal societal norms affects the trading population.

The data were collected in sixteen trading locations (markets or streets) in and around Nairobi, a city of over a million people in 1990. Nairobi was founded in 1899 as a railway camp for the British Uganda railway and grew rapidly, becoming the capital of Kenya Colony in 1907. By 1988, it was a cosmopolitan, semi-integrated blend of many cultures, having lost some of its segregated character as a colonial city run for the benefit of white settlers. It increasingly reflected growing socioeconomic differentiation among a highly diverse population. Adding to its diversity was its status as a mecca for millions of tourists attracted by Kenya's wildlife. Thus, glaring contrasts of wealth and poverty are always present. This chapter is about the "other Nairobi" that tourists do not see, where most of the African population lives and works.

Nairobi is at the intersection of several ecological zones, which made it attractive for precolonial trade. Much of the long-distance commerce was carried out by Kamba men going to the coast with slaves and ivory in the nineteenth century and by Kikuyu women carrying foodstuffs to pastoral Maasai areas, in particular, to secure skins for clothing and cattle and goats to enrich their male relatives. As Nairobi grew, women naturally undertook to supply it with foodstuffs, and people in the nearby farming areas in Kiambu became involved in growing green vegetables to supply this market, especially from the 1940s onward.

This led to a struggle over women's control of their own labor, produce, and profits as men sought to enhance their own wealth.[2] Women's position in this struggle was undermined by a set of patriarchal societal structures that inhibited their trading activities. Both the Kikuyu and the Kamba were predominantly patrilineal and patrilocal, with polygyny practiced by wealthier men. Patrilocality, in which a woman at marriage joined her husband on his father's land and farmed a share of the husband's land, inhibited female relatives' cooperation in expanding businesses in the manner of West African coastal traders, for instance. The residential system promoted a division rather than a pooling of labor among co-wives or mothers and daughters-in-law. The women's right to control their own earnings was circumscribed by their lack of property rights. In theory, men had the right to control women's profits from selling foodstuffs because they were grown on male-owned and controlled land. In practice, however, this was contested terrain, with women sometimes able to control their own profits. The surest method to achieve control over their own labor, children, and profits was to leave home and go to Nairobi. During the twentieth century, the number of Kikuyu women choosing this option grew, especially when they were forced into it by divorce and landlessness. Trade in Nairobi thus became a survival strategy for women seeking independence from men. This chapter considers the merits of this strategy in the context of the 1980s. □

GENDER DIFFERENCES IN ACCESS TO RESOURCES

To analyze trade as a survival strategy, it is necessary to look at the resources women and men bring to it and the profits they get from it. Among these resources are level of education, property ownership, and networks of kin, friends, and coworkers, which are sometimes utilized to form self-help organizations. Nairobi-area data incorporating rural, suburban, and urban traders shed much light on the relative positions of women and men traders with regard to these resources. They also show that Kenya's increasing socioeconomic stratification is evident among the trading population, which differs not only by gender but also according to location and infrastructure. The trade locations surveyed varied greatly in nature, ranging from official, enclosed markets—with stalls constructed of cement block and tile roofs—to sprawling open-air markets to illegal street markets where sellers constantly flee police. Although this chapter will concentrate on gender differences, it is worth keeping such locational and infrastructure differences in mind as another facet of the trading hierarchy.

Gender differences in access to critical resources play a key role in convincing women to trade. Unlike coastal West Africa, where women's trade has a centuries-old history and an established role as the exclusive career for most uneducated urban women, in central Kenya women do not usually view trade as a preferred career. For most women and men, trade is a survival strategy adopted for lack of better alternatives. Those traders who began that way and then experienced success and developed a strong commitment to trade as an occupation are in the minority.

Access to Education and Property

Among the barriers to better opportunities are access to education and property. Women's lack of education limits their ability to secure reasonably well-paid jobs. Girls' education in Kenya expanded most in the 1970s, and the relatively older age of women traders logically puts them into the less-educated category. The mean average age of 686 women in the sample was 39.6, compared to 33.6 for the 331 men. The mean average number of years of education was 5.1 for women and 7.9 for men traders. Table 4.1 gives the breakdown for the sample (N = 1,018) according to sex and education level.[3]

Two facets of education level are worth noting. First, the most significant difference lies in the number of traders with no formal education, primarily older women. Fewer men in the sample fell into the age group encompassing those not likely to have gone to school. Second, this differential access to education carries over into the level of education attained by those in the sample who did go to school: 63.9 percent of the 465 women who had attended school received only a primary education, compared to 55.5 percent of the men. Only 24.4 percent of all of women traders reached Standard Six or Seven in primary school, compared to 32.9 percent of the men. To set these statistics in the context of the overall

TABLE 4.1   Education Level of Nairobi Area Traders by Sex, 1987–1988 (in percentages)

	No Education	Primary Standards 1–7	Middle Forms 1–4	Secondary Forms 5–6	Postsecondary Teacher Training, Vocational	Total
Women	29.3	43.4	24.9	0.1	2.3	100.0
Men	3.0	44.9	50.5	0.3	0.6	99.3

Note: N = 1,018.

Nairobi population, 27.2 percent of the women traders in the sample completed Form One or beyond, compared to 38.3 percent of the Nairobi women who were fifteen years of age and over in 1979. For men, 51 percent of the traders had completed at least Form One, compared to 43.9 percent of men fifteen and over in Nairobi.[4] Clearly, educational attainment is quite different for men and women traders. Women lack education as a result of a number of discriminatory factors, such as fewer and poorer schools, pregnancy terminating school attendance, parental reluctance to allow schooling because of the labor value of girls, and the poverty that forces that parental choice.[5] In contrast, men have had access to schooling—and male traders had above average access—but the chief difficulty they face is finding a job commensurate with that schooling. Many of the male traders were young job-seekers temporarily supporting themselves in the markets, often working as employees of more established traders.

Another critical resource is access to property—land in particular. The marital status of traders has particular implications for women's property rights. Kikuyu and Kamba women usually get access to land through a male relative, most often a husband. (Only five women in the survey—fewer than 1 percent—had purchased land themselves.) At marriage, a husband is expected to give his wife land to farm, which is often apportioned from his mother's share of his father's land. If the wife is later divorced, she loses that land and rarely gets anything from her father in compensation. Divorce thus means landlessness for women, even if they have sons entitled to their fathers' lands. In several cases, paternal uncles had taken land from nephews who were the sons of divorcees, even, in other cases, the sons of widows. In adjacent Kiambu and Murang'a, where most traders come from and where average household landholding size is below one acre, the fight over land is fierce.[6] Table 4.2 illustrates the marital status of traders by sex, and provides statistics for the Nairobi population age fifteen and over for comparison.

TABLE 4.2   Marital Status by Sex of Traders (T) in Sixteen Nairobi Areas, 1987–1988, Compared to Nairobi Population Age Fifteen and Over (N) (in percentages)

	Never Married		Married		Divorced or Separated		Widow or Widower		Total	
	T	N	T	N	T	N	T	N	T	N
Women	19.1	35.7	53.7	57.4	13.8	3.7	13.4	3.2	100	100
Men	41.7	38.6	57.4	60.3	0.9	0.8	0.0	0.3	100	100

Source: Republic of Kenya, Population Census 1979, vol. 3, pp. 24, 26.

These statistics show clearly that, although most women traders were married, divorced, or widowed, male traders were more likely to be unmarried and less likely to be single parents.

Data on landownership and number of dependents further document women's comparative lack of access to resources. The mean average number of acres farmed by women traders was 2.6, compared to 3 for men traders. A closer look at the most prosperous groups of traders yields a more accurate picture. A group of eight male storeowners—forty-eight years of age and older—at Nyamakima, a tough, inner-city neighborhood, had an average of 9.9 acres of land each, all of it worked by their wives and most of it owned rather than leased. A comparable group of seven women stallholders—aged forty-five and older—at Shauri Moyo, an official market, were not farming themselves (with one exception) and owned no land. One woman had access to thirty-five acres owned by her deceased husband and worked by her wife, who was acquired by woman-marriage (an occasional Kamba practice). Thus, even relatively prosperous women with a long trading history had not been able to buy land. Moreover, five out of seven of the women's spouses were not farming, so the women's earnings were not supplemented by crops grown for consumption or sale. The Nyamakima men, in contrast, often got income from cash crops sold by their wives.

Responsibility to Dependents

Dependency statistics illuminate not only the burden that forces women into trading but also some of the ideology regarding women's and men's earnings. The mean average number of people supported by women in the sample (N = 683) was 5.5, compared to 4.9 for the men (N = 330). The male statistic, however, is inflated because some men claimed that the wives were not assisting at all when, in fact, their children were living with their wives on a farm and being fed by them, and wives might or might not have been receiving remittances from their husbands. The ide-

TABLE 4.3   Occupation of Nonsupporting Spouses or Ex-Spouses of Traders (in percentages)

	Trade or Commerce	Farmer or Fisher	White-collar	Skilled or Service	Military or Guard	Day-laborer	House-wife	Unemployed	Other
Women	4.1	71.4	2.0	0.0	0.0	0.0	20.4	2.0	0.0
Men	11.7	26.2	11.7	31.0	4.8	4.8	0.0	7.6	2.1

Note: The definition of marriage used here includes common-law unions.

ology that views women's work in subsistence farming and feeding children as an extension of housework (and therefore of no value) and that defines cash as the only means of support worth mentioning comes into play here. A look at the occupations of spouses who were reported as not providing support validates this contention. Seventy-one percent of the male traders' wives were said to be farmers. (See Table 4.3.)

Since women do most of the farming, especially when the husband is in town, it is probable that most of the wives reported to be nonsupporters are supplying at least some food to the family. The same cannot be said for the nonsupporting husbands or ex-husbands who were farmers, however. Because it was humiliating for women to admit that their children's fathers were not contributing (several widows even claimed that their husbands were helping!), women may have overestimated the husbands' help and minimized any degree of estrangement. Therefore, when women said that their husbands were not assisting, I tended to believe them. One woman, franker than most, told me that her husband was farming. When asked if he was actually doing farmwork, she said no, he was "supervising"—"You know, that's what men do." She later said that he was elderly, disabled, and unable to work. Supervising was clearly a euphemism for not helping, couched in male-dominant terms. It is doubtful that the 26.2 percent of the male nonsupporters who were farmers were helping to any significant extent. The number of male nonsupporters who had skilled artisanal or service occupations is more noteworthy: 49.6 percent. They, like the women who were listed as housewives, were mostly urban residents.

The marital status of the nonsupporters is equally illuminating. Table 4.4 compares spouses or fathers of children according to their marital status and support role. Women clearly could count on more help from husbands than from lovers or ex-husbands, making it evident why some women stressed the importance of marriage beyond the concern of legitimizing the children. Most husbands who were still married were helping, as were the wives, especially when their understated role is taken into account.

TABLE 4.4 Spouses or Fathers of Children According to Marital Status and Support Role

	Never Married		Married at Present		Divorced or Separated	
	Help	No Help	Help	No Help	Help	No Help
% of Men or Husbands	1.9	98.1	80.5	18.5	4.6	95.3
(Number)	(105)		(359)		(86)	
% of Women or Wives	6.2	93.7	73.6	26.4	0.0	100.0
(Number)	(16)		(182)		(1)	

We also asked respondents to enumerate the people for whom they provide partial or full support. This question yielded the results shown in Table 4.5, broken down by age and sex of the respondent. Only 13.9 percent of the whole sample listed a spouse among those being supported—29.3 percent of the men and 6.5 percent of the women. However, wives who were being supported were usually listed as sharing in their own support, whereas husbands who were being supported were not. The 6.5 percent figure primarily includes elderly or disabled husbands living on farms. Women did not complain about having to support these men; when alcoholism was involved, however, they often divorced the husbands, who were likely to be abusive as well as nonsupporters. Women's role in supporting elderly husbands makes taking a younger wife a survival strategy for a man; in a smaller survey (N = 58 marriages), men were an average of seven years older than their spouses. Conversely, the chief reason for divorce given by women was nonsupport. Among 64 cases of divorce in the larger sample, 79.7 percent were said to have been sought by women (N = 51); of these, 76.5 percent were due to lack of support (N = 39).

The age data show that women generally began supporting dependents at a younger age than men, reflecting both women's younger age at marriage and unmarried motherhood. Children were by far the largest category supported. None of the never-married men in the sample reported supporting any children of their own, and no men were single parents. The few men who reported divorces had remarried, and if they had custody of children by a previous marriage, their second or subsequent wives were caring for those children. Child custody usually went to mothers, despite the law upholding paternal custody (most divorces were not taken to court). Levirate marriage, which was practiced in the past, has generally disappeared, and with it the responsibility of a hus-

TABLE 4.5   Mean Average Number of Dependents by Traders' Age and Sex
(N = 985)

	Age Group and Sex													
	15–19		20–29		30–39		40–49		50–59		60–69		over 70	
	F	M	F	M	F	M	F	M	F	M	F	M	F	M
Provides Most Support	0.4	0.0	0.6	0.3	1.8	1.1	1.9	1.7	2.3	4.1	1.9	3.8	0.7	4.0
Provides Partial Support	2.5	3.3	3.3	4.4	4.7	4.4	4.2	6.0	3.5	5.4	5.0	4.5	4.0	8.0
Total Dependents	2.9	3.3	3.9	4.7	6.5	5.5	6.1	7.7	5.8	9.5	6.9	8.3	45.7	12.0

band's lineage to support the children of a deceased male member. Coresidence was a critical factor in support; children not living with a male parent were far less likely to be supported by him whatever the status of the union that produced them. There were, however, a few cases in which mothers supported sons and daughters who were living away from home by paying their rent; this was especially true for sons, whose right to a separate residence was widely recognized. Unmarried adult daughters were more likely to live with their mothers.

It is clear that a prime survival strategy involved sharing the burden of support. Both sexes reported sharing support for more people than they supported alone. Members of the family of origin—mothers, fathers, sisters, and brothers—were the next most frequently supported category after children. Female respondents were also supporting significant numbers of relatives by marriage, usually their husbands' mothers and sisters and sometimes their co-wives' children. Men reported supporting a much narrower range of relatives. They shared support for more of their siblings than women did, but they supported far fewer of their relatives by marriage. Only one man reported supporting a grandchild, compared to ninety-five grandchildren supported by women. Women were also more likely to be providing most of the support for dependents. They shoulder most of the burden of support for dependents in 27.9 percent of the cases, compared to only 15.2 percent for men.

The overall differences in the dependency burden are clear: Women traders are providing more support for more people than are men traders, and more men traders are younger with no dependents. Women began supporting others at a younger age and peaked earlier in their support pattern, but men, though reporting more dependents in their older years, supported fewer people altogether.[7] In the markets, there were few older men traders, most of them in their sixties, but many older women sixty years of age or older. Furthermore, the usual minuscule earnings of elderly women traders contrasted sharply with those of the older men, who were likely to be proprietors of the few businesses of some scale, long-time urban residents, and sometimes governors of the market. Elderly women, in contrast, were more likely to be recent urban immigrants whose rural destitution forced them to relocate to avoid burdening their children. There were also a few well-established women traders who fit more into the male profile mentioned earlier, but most of them were younger than comparable men—in their forties and fifties and still possessed the strength required for active wholesaling. As one woman said, "Your profits depend on the strength of your back." The time women must put into trading activities militates against farming, but prosperous men have wives who farm for them. The one woman-marriage case mentioned previously involved a mother of daughters who was, first, seeking to secure a male heir for her deceased husband and, second, labor for working her husband's land; her daughters were either married and farming their husbands' lands or helping her trade. □

INDIVIDUAL COPING STRATEGIES

In addition to statistics, it is helpful to look at the coping strategies of individual women to see how they managed to eke out a living, for the most part on extremely limited resources. Five abbreviated life histories—two from very poor women, one rural and one urban, and three from middling to prosperous traders in urban and suburban markets—are illustrative.[8] The following life histories are derived from interviews with these women.

Wanjiku

In 1988, Wanjiku, a wiry, nervous forty-seven-year-old trader, had three teenage children and was selling beans at Gitaru Market, located about twenty kilometers from Nairobi near a main highway. She had never married and therefore had no land, but she made do by farming a quarter of an acre of poor quality government land, which was too small to grow maize, the chief staple. To help support her children, she had also joined two women's associations. For one, she made sisal bags that are much in demand on the international market; a wholesaler, a woman from Meru, bought them at a low price for resale. The other association was a cooperative farmwork group composed of church members. Wanjiku's efforts in these activities plus selling her produce two days a week in the market were not sufficient to earn a living, however. Her nineteen-year-old daughter was helping her farm, but her two sons were, respectively, unemployed and underemployed. Wanjiku was therefore doing casual farm labor five or six days a week for Ksh20 per day in wages (approximately US$1.18). Her employer wanted to reduce these further by giving her a monthly salary, but Wanjiku refused because she could neither afford to take less in pay nor to wait for her wages. At one point, she was employed digging ditches for the Nairobi City Council, but that job paid even less.

Wanjiku worried a good deal about how her family would survive. She did not blame the father of her children for his nonsupport, for her reputation was impaired when she was interned at age thirteen during the Emergency in the 1950s: Girls in that situation were routinely molested by Homeguards, although Wanjiku said that this did not happen to her because her breasts had not developed at that point. Her future lover was instrumental in putting her in touch with her parents after she was summarily removed to the camp, and he remained her faithful friend until they later became lovers. But he was poor, and her parents disapproved of the liaison; she therefore had to devise various pretexts to meet him and never spent a whole night with him. Eventually, they had a disagreement over her joining the Anglican Church, and he married another woman. He never paid bridewealth for this "wife" either, so both his unions remained in common-law status only. He had four more children with his wife and never gave Wanjiku or her children any support. Meanwhile, her younger brothers had too many children themselves to help her, so she soldiered on, perforce on her own. She said, "I will do anything to get money."[9]

Wambui

Wambui was thirty-seven years old in 1987, selling beans on the street at Nyamakima in downtown Nairobi. The careers she had undertaken to feed herself and her five children moved from the legal to the illegal. She began trading by selling vegetables at Wakulima, the mostly wholesale vegetable market in downtown Nairobi. At that time, she had moved to Nairobi from Murang'a when her husband, who was selling secondhand clothes, sold his farm with her house on it. She and the three children were literally starving. She considered herself to be divorced, and, in any case, felt her husband had betrayed her by not telling her before they married that he had had another wife, who ran away because of ill treatment.

Upon coming to Nairobi, she was supported for some time by liaisons with men, especially one long-term relationship that produced two children; so that by 1987, she was supporting five children aged nineteen to five years. She took up residence in a huge squatter settlement area now recognized by the government, Mathare Valley. When her Wakulima business failed she turned to beer-brewing, a risky but sometimes profitable occupation. In this case, it worked for three years before she was arrested and jailed, effectively ending her business and putting her children's welfare in jeopardy. When she emerged after six months, she began selling beans at Nyamakima, a job that lasted for two years. In November 1987, the police were raiding that location at least once a week, confiscating the traders' commodities or fining them, with the encouragement of the adjacent dried staples storeowners.

Wambui formed part of a tough, youngish group of traders in a centrally located slum, for whom illegal activities were a way of life and a necessity for survival. Her battle made her a strong believer in birth control, at least for other women: She felt that women should have only one or two children because of the difficulty of supporting them. Her older daughter, at age nineteen, was unemployed; her fifteen-year-old son sold vegetables at Wakulima. Her twelve-year-old daughter stayed home, but the eight-year-old was in school. None of the children had gone past Standard Four in school. Wambui stressed both the importance of educating the children and the severe strain brought on by her fourth pregnancy, which also bore the stigma of illegitimacy. "I almost committed suicide because of the pain I was feeling. But I said I won't abort and persevered ... and again with the fifth child. I actually cried ... I knelt down and prayed to God not to give me another child. ... From that time God heard my prayers. I have never conceived again. Maybe it is God who helped after hearing my prayers."[10]

Despite their divergent backgrounds, Wanjiku and Wambui shared not only their poverty but also some characteristics that contributed to that poverty. Both had little or no formal education; Wanjiku was taking adult education classes to learn to read, and Wambui had no schooling at all. Both were without a male partner who helped with support; the men involved in their lives did not take responsibility for their children in any major way, although Wambui's husband occasionally gave money for food and clothes. He also had paid bridewealth, and the union had been sanctioned by her parents. Nonetheless, the marriage had ended after eight years, and Wambui said that his irresponsibility had persisted for most of that time.

These women adopted various strategies to earn a living. Both grew up in rural areas and had worked as farmers and in Nairobi (Wambui farmed until the land was sold). They worked very hard at their occupations—more than sixty hours a week, excluding domestic work. But despite their labor, they and their children were at risk. None of the children had progressed past Standard Six in school, and as a result, the women had unemployed grown children to support; in the daughters' cases, this posed the risk of having to support grandchildren, too. Their move to the Nairobi area also signaled the beginning of the formation of multigenerational female-headed households.

Contrasting the experiences of the two women, it is clear that Wanjiku had a slight edge over Wambui. Although it is often said that most of Kenya's poverty is rural, Wambui was worse off because of her complete landlessness, her greater burden (she was also helping to support her mother in Murang'a), and her sole dependence on a marginal trade perpetually vulnerable to police harassment. Her income was, in fact, substantially below that of Wanjiku, who herself was one of the poorest in the sample.

We also need to look at individuals who were somewhat better off and whose earnings were in the middle to higher ranges among traders. Florence, whose story follows, enjoyed great advantage of having an official market stall; her history represents a version of the rags-to-riches story (relatively speaking).

Florence

Florence, an attractive, slim, and vigorous woman, left her husband when he lost out in a land dispute with his younger brother. She was forty-five years old in 1987 and the mother of nine children, running a restaurant in a newish downtown Nairobi official market and had several employees. She had been in Nairobi for seventeen years, working her way up from selling green maize at Wakulima and peddling fresh vegetables from home to home. This activity was interrupted by a bout with tuberculosis in 1984, at which point the Nairobi Senior Medical Officer intervened and requested city officials to provide better housing for her and her family. A large loan was given for the purpose of building a house at Dandora, a self-help housing scheme, to replace the family's paper shack at Mathare. In 1987, Florence was living there with six of her children and three grandchildren by her second daughter, who had not married. The two-room house had no door because some of the money had gone to set up the business.

Three of Florence's children had reached Standard Seven, and her eldest daughter was pursuing adult education and sewing classes. Florence herself had been to Standard Four. Three of the children— two sons and a daughter—had acquired skills enabling them to get jobs, and one daughter was also trading. The youngest four children, aged fourteen to eight, were in school at levels appropriate for their ages. Florence said that none of her grown daughters (aged twenty-seven, twenty-four, and nineteen) had married because her own experience was so bad. Her in-laws had harassed her, her husband had abused her, and none of them had provided any support. She left her husband partly because she wished "to have the freedom to rear her children." She preferred not having her daughters help her in the business because she saw a conflict between the roles of daughter and employee. Since the older daughters all had children (an average of three apiece), she felt that it was cheaper and more sensible for them to stay with their children to avoid child-care problems.

Florence's tuberculosis was cured, but she said that she could not work as hard as she previously had. Nevertheless, she had great plans for the business—plans that would require capital. She hoped to divide the stall and make part of it into a shop for selling canned goods. She also wanted her daughters to have their own businesses. "I can make my own way," she said. "A husband is good for what?"[11]

Caterina

Caterina was a fifty-year-old Kamba woman selling chickpeas and millet in downtown Nairobi, at an illegal market located on private land in an Indian neighborhood. She had six living children in 1987, four others having died of measles. She and her husband were farming at Embu, and that met their needs until the 1984 drought. At that point, their cattle died, and her husband asked her if she could do something to earn cash to help with the children's school fees. They adopted a new strategy: He would look after the children in Embu while she traveled to Nairobi to sell dried staples. She began trading with the help of her coworkers, who taught her how to do sums so she would not lose money. First, she hawked from door to door and gradually worked up to selling larger quantities on credit to other hawkers. Soon, she was buying in rural areas and transporting goods to Nairobi for sale, doing small-scale wholesale and some retail business. Caterina's earnings were used for food, clothing, and school fees for the children and occasional support for her husband's sister and her five daughters.

The strategy seemed to be paying off with regard to paying school fees, helped along by Caterina's membership in two women's groups. She boasted, "My daughter has never been sent home from middle school because fees are not paid." The oldest daughter reached Form Two, the next son completed Form One and was still continuing, and so were the younger children. But the life was strenuous and exhausting for Caterina. She would spend six weeks in Nairobi, sleeping at a carpentry shop in a large market at a cost of Ksh1.50 (US$0.09) per night, and then two weeks at home. Her husband did not cook for the children, so she relied on her eldest daughter to do so. Caterina was adamant about her helping. Once when she was sick, her daughter was helping her and complaining about how tiring the work was. Caterina said, *"That's* what you eat."[12]

The theme of cooperation between husbands and wives is expressed most strongly in the next history, which shows not only how men can help but also how a reduced dependency burden, even if temporary, can facilitate prosperity.

Nyokabi

Nyokabi, a tall, imposing woman, lived and worked at Wangige, on the outskirts of the city in an area rapidly succumbing to the expansion of Nairobi. She and her husband married when Nyokabi was just sixteen and pregnant with their only child, a daughter. Somewhat unusually for a woman of fifty-nine, Nyokabi had gone to Standard Four, and her husband to Standard Six. Both Nyokabi and her husband were devout churchgoers, and Nyokabi was an active member of the Anglican Mothers' Union. The ideology of Christian marriage had made a strong impact on Nyokabi, who attributed some of her husband's steady qualities to his devoutness. She noted proudly that, unlike his cohorts, he never stayed out drinking beer and running around with women. His Christian devotion, however, did not prevent him from taking a second wife when Nyokabi proved to be subfecund, a move of which Nyokabi approved. In 1986 her co-wife deserted them, leaving six children to be supported. They also had taken on the support of four of her husband's nephews and nieces. But Nyokabi and her husband did not find this support as onerous a burden as it might have been because they were already established economically.

Cooperation among family members served them very well. Nyokabi and her husband began with four acres of land he had inherited, on which they grew coffee and marketable garden crops, while Nyokabi traded and belonged to two women's groups. They prospered and built a three-room house for rental purposes, purchasing nineteen more acres of land divided between four locations. In 1988, they had begun building an eight-room rental house in cooperation with his patrilineal relatives through the formation of a mutual savings association. Their own house was built of stone and timber and had a metal roof, unlike the usual mud-and-wattle construction.

Although Nyokabi was selling bananas, dried staples, and milk from their cow two days a week at Wangige Market, a legal outdoor market, it was clear that more income came from their joint landholdings. Her husband hired labor to farm cash crops for the most part. They had managed to send their daughter to Form Four; at age forty-three, she was married with children and self-sufficient as a primary teacher. The four nieces and nephews had enough training to secure jobs and were living independently. Nyokabi's eldest stepson had also gone to Form Four and was in training to be a welder, and the other four stepchildren were in school in grades appropriate to their ages. Nyokabi reported that she and her husband shared money impartially, giving cash to each other as needed, and that she was very happy with her husband's support. They also shared ownership of the land that was purchased. "We are united," she said.[13]

A solid marriage with shared property is one survival strategy that women adopt. Sharing of property in marriages is quite unusual in Kenya, but it clearly is pursued in some Christian communities. Another Anglican woman at Wangige was in despair because her husband was drinking, abusing her, and running around with other women, but she convinced him to go to church with her, and he experienced a born-again Christian conversion. She credited faith with remedying their problems and creating mutual devotion.[14]

These histories show that the most economically secure women are those who have husbands with earnings who contribute to the household. Women therefore place a high priority on marriage, occasionally to the point of paying their own bridewealth. But the goal is difficult to achieve. In this sample, 45.3 percent of the women traders had no husbands, while 6.7 percent had husbands who were dependents themselves. An additional 2.6 percent of the women had husbands who were not helping to support their families. Of 686 women, a total of 54.6 percent could not rely on spouses for support, nor did they get substantial help from relatives, who were struggling with their own burdens.

Most women traders, then, are forced to be self-reliant. Indeed, they pride themselves on it—a fact made apparent in many conversations about support. A few examples show the depth of women's belief in the value of self-sufficiency. For example, a ninety-four-year-old Kamba woman, who was eking out a very meager living by hawking, said, "I don't get anything from my children, and I don't like to take anything from anybody, unless one of these women here gives me rice to go and cook. No, I have never spent a night under somebody else's roof."[15] A younger (forty-three years of age) woman, when asked from whom she would get money if she needed it, said, "There is no one whom I can ask.

I would just use my mind. I come and sell something here so that I can get the Ksh100, but I can't go get it from anyone."[16] A sturdy independence was the ideal for many women, expressed succinctly by a fifty-four-year-old trader at Kawangware, a suburban market. Asked if there was anyone who should be helping her, she replied, "I don't get any assistance, and I also don't want that assistance. Everybody has his or her own problems."[17] A thirty-five-year-old woman, who had an alcoholic husband, and who was struggling to pay school fees for her two children said that getting money or help from her childless elder sister, a wholesaler and landowner, would be difficult: "She might say that if we just waste our money on my husband, we shouldn't bother her. You know, it's not usual for Kikuyus to support others."[18] Another woman, who had access to fifteen acres and thus could look forward to self-reliance, said, "When I get old, I will just go home and work on that farm. I won't rely on anybody."[19] The strongest statement about self-reliance came from a fairly successful bean trader at Kiambu Town Market, some twenty kilometers north of Nairobi: "I have four children. The boy became a thug and joined a band; he started drinking beer, which I don't like because if I joined hands with him he would wreck my business. ... Whatever money he gets, let him help himself. Each of the girls has her husband, so they should use their brains to support themselves. I won't ask them to help me, and, in return, I won't help them."[20]

If many women made economic independence a matter of pride and were reluctant to accept help even from their children, many also interpreted their own economic responsibilities broadly. A woman in her seventies at a village some thirty kilometers from Nairobi had decided to trade because her husband liked the cash she earned and because they needed to feed their children but had very little land. She said, "Children don't ask their fathers for food, do they? They ask their mothers. The responsibility is hers."[21] Many women go even further. A forty-five-year-old woman at Gikomba, the largest illegal market in Nairobi, explained, "You see, in Ukambani when a girl gets married, they don't bother about you any more. My brothers are able to help me support my children, but, you see, I am married; I have to look after my own."[22] Nevertheless, this woman was assisting her brothers financially whenever they came to Nairobi, and she viewed that as part of her responsibilities.

We have already seen that more women than men were helping relatives by marriage. One forty-seven-year-old widow said that her husband's mother and brothers were not helping her and added that "out of the realization that they will never help, if I had problems I would never go to anybody." Though making claims on no one, she claimed responsibility herself, saying that her daughter "can work and get money to clothe her children, but I am responsible all the same."[23] One of the most extreme cases in which women claimed responsibility for supporting grandchildren was that of Njoki, a forty-seven-year-old wholesaler with eleven dependents, including two grandchildren fathered by two of her unmarried sons. The unwed mother of one of these brought the granddaughter to Njoki, asking that she care for her. Another of her sons refused to marry the mother of his own son, but, Njoki said, after "he went there and found that the child was going to die because the mother didn't care for him," he brought the boy to Njoki so she could look after him. Meanwhile her unmarried twenty-eight-year-old daughter had two children and was trading in the same market, and Njoki's nineteen-year-old daughter, Muthoni, was pregnant, which was going to add yet another dependent. Njoki said, "Muthoni does try, but she doesn't really know the value of children like I do because she's also still a child. So it's my responsibility."[24]

However, some women (like Wambui who contemplated suicide) were finding the dependency burden overwhelming. Njoki was separated from her husband, but she eagerly accepted added dependents to be supported from a thriving urban wholesale business. Njeri, forty-six, was trying to support four daughters ranging in age from twenty to twelve on a small, rural retail dried staples business, she said, "If my daughters had children I would accept them. I pray to God to help my children so that we can help each other. I pray to Him every day so that He can change my husband's heart, so he will come back to me. I pray to God also to help my daughters get husbands and that they will stay together. And I always pray to God that these children will not have children to add to my burden. I don't think I can manage an extra burden."[25] Nejeri's husband had divorced her because of her conversion to Christianity. Like a number of other men, he strongly resisted the effort to reform his behavior that is encouraged by that religion.

Women took up trading at a fairly late age—30.6 years on the average—at which point they were likely to have four or five children to support. The average age for beginning trade among men, by contrast, was 25.1, when many had not yet married. Aside from a few very old women, some of these young men were the only people in the sample with no dependents. However, most were helping parents support siblings. Furthermore, women undertook trade in order to meet family needs, such as school fees, not because they viewed trade as a career they might enjoy. Some had come to enjoy their trading, but many said that they would do any other work if it were more profitable, which shows a weak commitment to trade as an occupation. In other words, trade was a strategy, not a commitment, albeit a strategy that absorbed most of the women's time.

Another strategy—membership in voluntary associations—is linked to women's participation in trade (and farming), and it enhances women's resources. These associations, often conducted on the principle of a tontine, are called "rotating savings associations" in the literature. Members receive pooled money on a "share basis" (ownership of one share means one contribution and one turn at getting the pool per rotation, ownership of two shares means two daily or weekly contributions and two turns per rotation, and so forth). Such associations have a long history among West African traders, who typically used profits from the association for investment in trade or for urgent family expenses. But the Nairobi-area traders showed some interesting differences in this regard. Associations were not usually family-based but were composed, instead, of coworkers, whom traders saw as their most important resource for help in times of crisis. Many of the associations were targeted in their purpose: The pooled money was to be used to buy land that would be worked cooperatively by members or to buy roofing for members' houses. So common is this second purpose that such associations in Kenya are sometimes called "roofing societies." Personal uses, such as paying for funerals, were less often mentioned (astonishingly, paying school fees was not even cited), and women did not talk about investment in business as a goal. Of course, when the moneys were not targeted (and most were not), women could use the funds as they wished. Of the women surveyed, 3.6 percent belonged to *harambee* (self-help) groups that often perform communal labor, building schools and other projects, and 14.2 percent belonged to church groups that perform a variety of aid functions.

Women traders relied more heavily than men on voluntary associations; 56.6 percent of the women held memberships compared to only 22 percent of the men. Moreover, women belonged to more associations than men did, an average of 1.1 apiece, compared to .4 for men. Male associations also tended to be less numerous, narrower in focus, and somewhat larger in membership, averaging thirty people, compared to twenty-three for women's groups. The men's dues were larger, too: Those who belonged paid an average of Ksh413 per month to their associations, compared to Ksh342 for women. The priority women gave to memberships in these associations is apparent when ratios are computed comparing mean average earnings for female and male traders to the amount paid in dues. The ratio for women was 121.4, compared to 734 for men, indicating that many women found associations to be an essential strategy in mitigating poverty, and they therefore invested a higher proportion of their earnings in them. There was a negative correlation between the amount of profits earned for all traders and the amount put into savings associations, chiefly because women earned less than men and invested more. It is possible that the very fragility of women's businesses, especially when illegality was involved, militated against such investments.

It is also clear that in certain markets, membership in voluntary associations was not just an economic strategy but also a dimension of female solidarity, sometimes with ethnic or political overtones. Kamba women, in particular, led a number of dance associations at Gikomba and Ngara. Members of such associations demonstrated strong loyalties and performed for pay on special occasions. On state holidays, it was usual for these women to be asked to perform for President Daniel Arap Moi. One small market was even shut down temporarily for the purpose of dance rehearsals.

Having looked at traders' access to critical resources, dependency burden, and strategies in relation to trade, I will now consider the relative success of women and men traders by looking at their starting capital and profits. In accordance with women's lack of access to critical resources such as land, education, and wage jobs, the mean average starting capital for women traders who used cash was Ksh836.39 (approximately US$50) compared to Ksh2,352.91 (approximately US$139), for men traders, a difference that is significant at the .00 level (N = 1,064 businesses).[26] The ratio of men's average start-up capital to women's start-up capital was 281.4, a figure that was exceeded by the ratio of average male profits to female profits of 292. Table 4.6 shows the mean average differences by age and sex for profits made on good and bad days of selling (N = 835 for a good day and 828 for a bad day). On both good and bad days, men's average profits were more than twice those of women. These differences would have been even greater had the older and generally well-established male storeowners at Nyamakima been willing to release profit data. The reasons for men's greater profits include their higher starting capital, which allowed them to deal in such commodities as fresh vegetables (they have greater unit value than dried staples, a women's commodity) or on a larger scale. Men also had lighter domestic work obligations, which allowed them to stay longer in the market. Men spent an average of 66.9 hours selling each week compared to 50.6 for women, and also spent more days selling per week (6.3, versus 5.1 for women). Some of this difference is accounted for by women's stronger presence in two-day suburban or rural markets; however, many women traders circulated among two or three different two-day markets, a strategy that enabled them to sell daily. The lower average age of male traders, as well as the higher incidence of wage employment in the market among young male sellers, also made them likely to spend more time trading (in part because, as employees, they often had less discretion about their hours than women did). Family obligations weighed heavily on women, not only in reducing their selling hours, but also in forcing them to withdraw capital from the business. Table 4.6 shows that their earnings dropped off sharply when women were in their forties, mainly because they took out

TABLE 4.6   Gross Profits of Traders, Good and Bad Days, by Age and Sex (in Ksh)

	15–19 years	20–29 years	30–39 years	40–49 years	50–59 years	60–69 years	70+ years	Average
Women Traders								
Good Days	153.6	140.4	151.8	120.0	114.8	97.8	105.1	132.9
Bad Days	90.0	45.4	46.6	40.4	28.0	24.7	35.0	41.5
Men Traders								
Good Days	274.0	363.8	254.8	346.5	57.8	116.3	128.0	318.1
Bad Days	74.5	106.9	64.8	113.4	11.9	50.8	55.6	93.3

capital to pay school fees, which increased as children got older. For men, the indicators are less certain because of the incidence of missing data in the older and usually more successful age groups.

Aside from the question of gender differences in profits, how did the traders' profits meet standard-of-living requirements in Nairobi in 1987–1988? After subtracting the costs of doing business, net profits are approximately 12 percent of the gross profits given in Table 4.6, according to information given by traders. On this basis, the mean average daily earnings of women traders were Ksh10.45 (approximately US$0.61), compared to Ksh24.70 (approximately US$1.45) for men; both of these figures were well below the minimum daily wages in Nairobi—Ksh30.80 (approximately US$1.81) in June 1987. The 1987 *Statistical Abstract* for Kenya defined households with poor incomes as earning less than Ksh700 (US$41.18) per month (middle was Ksh700 to 2,499, up to US$147, and upper was Ksh2,500 and above, over US$147).[27] Male traders were earning an average of Ksh669.12 (US$39.36) per month compared to Ksh229.12 (US$13.48) for women, who less often had household income supplemented by other earnings.[28] Of course, these averages disguise the great variations between urban and rural women and between commodities. Urban traders were likely to work more days per week at daily markets, while rural traders were more likely to have supplemental income from casual labor done on nonmarket days, as in Wanjiku's case, or from farming some land. But we have already seen that women generally were likely to be supporting more dependents than men did, especially dependents for whom they bore primary financial responsibility. Profit results clearly show that women had to meet those obligations with lower earnings. The overall picture in terms of profits, then, was a gloomy one, which explains the almost universal willingness of traders—so frequently expressed—to do any type of work that was more profitable. □

CONCLUSION

Women traders and their children are for the most part a population in jeopardy. They are at high risk of homelessness, malnutrition, illiteracy perpetuated in their children, disease, and all the other effects of destitution. Furthermore, children are not usually getting the training, either at school or in trade, to escape poverty. A rough estimate puts this trading population at 40,000 in the Nairobi area alone. And yet, women traders are the working poor, often putting in sixty or more hours per week supplying the Nairobi area with essential foodstuffs; some even grow the foodstuffs they sell. They perform an essential role in feeding Nairobi, but while carrying out that role, they are often persecuted by police, whose loose interpretation of rules and regulations is used to extort bribes from the women.

The desperation of the women traders' plight has led to their increasing militancy, documented elsewhere.[29] In 1989 some 300 women traders demonstrated at Nairobi City Hall protesting police persecution. Much of the ongoing struggle centers around achieving legal permanent selling space, which would alleviate much of the harassment. Ever since the famous 1972 International Labor Organization report that pointed out the possibilities for economic development inherent in the informal sector, the Kenya government has maintained that it is working to foster such enterprises.[30] However, those measures have chiefly benefited the exclusively male manufacturing component of the informal sector, which has been given permanent business space and allowed to construct stalls. In contrast, when 400 female dried staples sellers at Gikomba got together in 1988 and had handsome sheds built to shelter themselves and their goods from the elements, the police came within days and tore down the construction, even maliciously destroying metal roofing pieces to prevent their reuse.

Male dominance, then, has had multitudinous effects on women traders' lives. It has forced them into trade through landlessness; divided the dependency burden unevenly when men do not fulfill support obligations toward women and children; reduced women's profits through a lack of access to capital and other critical resources and an uneven gender division of labor; failed to provide women traders with legal urban selling space; and subjected some of them to intense police persecution. One effect of such domination is that its victims will attempt to escape it. Urban trade thus represents both a survival strategy and a bid for independence. New residential patterns are emerging out of both the urban and rural experiences: multigenerational, female-headed households that are usually poor. Some women, however, have been able to take advantage of their independence to build businesses of substance.

In a widely misunderstood quotation, Engels said that "the first condition for the liberation of the wife is to bring the whole female sex back
into public industry [which will] in turn demand the abolition of the
monogamous family as the economic unit of society."[31] Trade for these
women has both caused and resulted from changing marital and residential patterns. For women, it does represent an opportunity that they
value, but it must be made more profitable in order for it to become a
career. Meanwhile, women are beginning to maximize their chances by
understanding the value of reduced fertility and by rejecting inegalitar-
ian marriage. Marriages that work most successfully are like that of
Nyokabi, who negotiated more equality. But many young women reject
marriage altogether, in favor of securing the right to their own profits
and children. It is clear, then, that for these women, economic and social
strategies are inextricably linked with strategies to evade patriarchal controls and that this evasion is so critical to their survival that it will continue to grow. □

NOTES

1. These surveys were conducted while I was in Nairobi on a Fulbright Fellowship.

2. This argument forms the core of my forthcoming work, *Healing Together
Gave Us Strength: Women, Men and Trade in the Nairobi Area, 1890–1990.*

3. A census of all traders in sixteen trade locations included more than 6000
individuals. At these same locations one out of six traders was then selected
randomly to participate in a longer survey of over 1,000 men and women.

4. Republic of Kenya, Central Bureau of Statistics, *Population Census of Kenya:
Urban Population* 3 (1979), 24–25.

5. Republic of Kenya/UNICEF, Central Bureau of Statistics, *Situation Analysis
of Children and Women in Kenya*, Section 3 (1984), 51–77.

6. Ibid., Section 1, 30.

7. It is probable that the relatively few older male traders who reported having
nonsupporter wives with many children in rural areas skewed the statistics
unduly, since those wives were likely, in fact, to be supporters.

8. To protect the identities of the informants, their names have been changed,
and letters or numbers assigned to informants.

9. Interviews no. 728, August 3, 1988; August 17, 1988.

10. Interviews no. 114, November 27, 1987; January 7, 1988.

11. Interview no. 26, October 16, 1987.

12. Interviews no. 71, October 29, 1987; December 1, 1987.

13. Interviews no. 450, May 16 and 25, 1988.

14. Interviews no. 465, May 19, 1988; June 1, 1988.

15. Interview no. 77, November 11, 1987.

16. Interview no. 142, January 15, 1988.

17. Interview no. 559, June 22, 1988.

18. Interview no. 108, November 18, 1987.

19. Interview no. 253, April 8, 1988.

20. Interview no. 808, October 19, 1988.

21. Interview E, July 12, 1988.

22. Interview no. 149, April 26, 1988.

23. Interview no. 133, December 15, 1987.

24. Interview no. 112, November 23, 1987.

25. Interview no. 847, October 13, 1988.

26. Cash starting capital is, in itself, a sign of greater resources; many women had to launch their businesses by using their own produce.

27. Republic of Kenya, Central Bureau of Statistics, *Statistical Abstract*, 257, 260ff.

28. This calculation factors in the lower average number of days worked per month by women as compared to men, cited earlier. It also assumes the lower profit margin associated with the dried staples traders, who were the most numerous in the sample and almost universally female. It therefore understates the earnings of men and women dealing in more profitable commodities.

29. Claire Robertson, "Traders and Urban Struggles: The Creation of a Militant Female Underclass in Nairobi, 1960–1990," *Journal of Women's History* 4, no. 3 (Winter 1993): 9–42.

30. International Labor Organization, *Employment, Income and Equality* (Geneva: International Labor Organization, 1972).

31. *The Woman Question, Selections from the Writings of Marx, Engels, Lenin and Stalin* (New York: International Publishers, 1951), 40.

CHAPTER FIVE

— ■ —

Gender Implications
of Export-Led Industrialization
in the Caribbean Basin

Helen I. Safa

EXPORT-LED DEVELOPMENT STRATEGIES have become increasingly popular in Latin America and the Caribbean since 1980, especially in the manufacturing sector. The Border Industrialization Program in Mexico is the best known and most important in terms of exports to the United States, but other countries also have turned to export as a way of earning foreign currency and alleviating the debt crisis.

Ever since the smaller countries of Central America and the Caribbean were incorporated into the world economy in colonial times, export has been their primary development strategy. Starting in the 1960s, traditional agricultural exports such as sugar, coffee, and bananas were supplemented by an increase in manufacturing (following the example set by the "industrialization by invitation" strategy initiated by Puerto Rico a decade earlier). Import-substitution industrialization, which was designed in the postwar period to stimulate domestic industry in Latin America, never achieved great success in the countries of the Caribbean Basin. This was due to the lack of capital and technology in these countries, which was more acute than in Latin America. Moreover, the viability of an internal market, critical for import substitution, was hampered by the small size of these countries, combined with their low purchasing power. Therefore, to gain access to foreign markets, capital, and technology, Caribbean countries have become increasingly dependent on multinational corporations.

In recent years, spurred on by the debt crisis and growing unemployment, the competition among Latin American and Caribbean countries for foreign investment in export manufacturing has been intense. Governments attempt to encourage foreign investment by lifting trade barriers, by offering tax holidays, and in some countries, by allowing unrestricted profit repatriation. Special export-processing zones are constructed at public expense for export-manufacturing plants, complete with water, electricity, roads, and other amenities. The state's major role in fostering export manufacturing often has been supported by the U.S. Agency for International Development (USAID), which adopted this as a development strategy for Latin America and the Caribbean in the 1980s.[1] USAID financing and advertising of free trade zones has recently come under sharp attack and been subjected to some restrictions by the U.S. Congress as a result of U.S. labor unions' investigations into these practices and their consequent job loss for U.S. workers.[2]

In addition to providing costs benefits to U.S. manufacturers, export manufacturing was seen by Washington as a way of improving the stagnant economies of the Latin American and Caribbean countries and of promoting political stability in the region.[3]

Special tariff programs such as items 806.30 and 807 of the U.S. Tariff Codes and the Generalized System of Preferences (GSP) were instituted to promote the relocation of labor-intensive phases of manufacturing abroad. U.S. government support for export manufacturing in the Caribbean Basin was enhanced by the 1983 enactment of President Reagan's Caribbean Basin Initiative (CBI). Although textiles and garments have been excluded from the CBI, due to opposition from U.S. labor, certain Caribbean countries have been granted special import quotas by the United States through the Guaranteed Access Levels (GALS) program, sometimes referred to as 807a. Apparel imports to the United States under the GALS program have grown by 76 percent annually since 1987, but they are limited to garments manufactured entirely from fabric made and cut in the United States.[4]

Partly in response to these tariff incentives, U.S. investment in the Caribbean Basin between 1977 and 1982 grew faster than in any other world region. The composition of U.S. investment in the region also changed dramatically after 1984, largely due to sharp cuts in traditional commodities such as sugar in the Dominican Republic, bauxite in Jamaica, and petroleum in Trinidad. Mining and mineral products constituted over half of all U.S. imports from Caribbean Basin countries in 1984, but manufacturing surpassed them by 1990. Between 1984 and 1990, manufacturing's share of U.S. imports from the region increased from 22 percent to 50 percent, or, in real terms, from US$1.94 billion in 1984 to US$3.76 billion in 1990.[5]

The shift toward export manufacturing in the Caribbean Basin countries implies a profound restructuring of their economies away from traditional commodities into a source of cheap labor for U.S. industry. Unlike import-substitution strategies, export manufacturing lessens the need to develop an internal market. However, effective international competition requires the reduction of production costs, principally wages, which helps explain why women hold most jobs generated through export manufacturing. In contrast, under import-substitution manufacturing, women represent only a small percentage of the industrial labor force. The bulk of these export workers are employed in Asia, with an increasing percentage in Latin America and the Caribbean.

This chapter will focus on the gender implications of export-led industrialization in two countries of the Hispanic Caribbean, Puerto Rico and the Dominican Republic. These countries share similar historical and cultural patterns but differ substantially in state policy. Puerto Rico's Operation Bootstrap, begun in the 1950s, served as a model for export-oriented industrialization under CBI as well as earlier strategies of "industrialization by invitation," although this has seldom been acknowledged publicly.[6] Despite its unique status as a "colony" of the United States, the Commonwealth of Puerto Rico offers important lessons on the limitations of this model. The Dominican Republic, on the other hand, is a classic case of recently initiated export manufacturing, with a total in December 1992 of 140,000 workers employed in 404 firms located in special free trade zones.[7] About 60 percent of the jobs are held by women, and about half of the 140,000 workers are still employed in the three original free trade zones created before 1980. This study centers on those three zones.

The Dominican Republic has become the leading source of exports under CBI, with exports totaling US$516.9 million in 1988—2.6 times more than the total from all other CBI countries for which data was available.[8] This sharp increase is directly attributable to currency devaluations mandated by the International Monetary Fund, which lowered the cost of labor and other expenses in the Dominican Republic to one of the lowest levels in the Caribbean. The number of workers increased dramatically starting in 1986, precisely when structural adjustment measures were being implemented. Due to manufacturing, the value of exports increased by 12.8 percent annually between 1983 and 1988, despite the sharp decline of Dominican sugar exports in response to reduced U.S. import quotas.

In this chapter, the emphasis is on the region's garment industry, which, along with electronics, has been the area of greatest growth in export manufacturing in the Caribbean Basin. In 1987, it accounted for approximately one-fourth of all imports to the United States from the Caribbean.[9] Most of the growth in garment imports from the region falls under items 807 and 807a, which specifically limit non-U.S. inputs. In

1988, garments represented 78 percent of all manufacturing exports from the Dominican Republic, with a total value of US$183.8 million, an increase of 333.4 percent since 1981. In fact, the Dominican Republic is now the leading source of garment manufacture in the Caribbean Basin.[10]

However, unlike the situation in East Asia, export-led industrialization in the Dominican Republic and Puerto Rico has not led to self-sustained growth capable of generating more indigenous and capital-intensive forms of industrial production. The reasons lie fundamentally in two factors: First, state industrial policies favored foreign investment in export manufacturing over domestic industry and, second, import restrictions in the United States limited export-led industrialization to assembly operations.

Employment in sugar production, involving primarily men, declined in the Dominican Republic starting in the 1980s and in Puerto Rico as early as the 1940s. But export manufacturers requiring cheap, unskilled labor preferred to hire women workers. This restructuring of the labor force has profound gender implications at the household level in both countries. Incorporation of women into the industrial labor force, although they work in dead-end, low-paying jobs, has given Dominican and Puerto Rican women more economic responsibility and authority in the household. Men have been increasingly marginalized, either through unemployment in Puerto Rico or through rising informalization in the Dominican Republic. Thus, it is not only the increasing employment of women but also the decreasing formal employment and wages of men that are making women major contributors to the household in both countries.

These household-level changes will be examined through data from two surveys. I conducted the first survey in 1980, and it involved 157 women workers in three Puerto Rican garment plants. The second study, a 1981 survey of 231 women workers in the three oldest export-processing zones of the Dominican Republic, was conducted by the Centro de Investigación para la Acción Femenina (CIPAF), a private Dominican women's research center. In addition, I conducted in-depth interviews in 1986 with a subsample of women working in the garment industry in both countries, which also enabled me to examine the effects of the economic crisis in the intervening period. The analysis focuses on the impact of export manufacturing on differential rates of male and female labor force participation and on changing gender roles in the household. □

STATE POLICY AND EXPORT-LED INDUSTRIALIZATION

Garment and textile manufacturing has commonly represented the first stage of industrialization in both advanced industrial and developing countries. This is true whether we are referring to earlier forms of industrialization in the nineteenth century or the more recently initiated export manufacturing. Developing countries have a comparative advantage in labor-intensive industries such as garment manufacture because they require relatively low levels of capital and technology and an abundance of cheap labor, provided chiefly by women. However, the enclave pattern of export-led industrialization in the Caribbean, combined with low levels of investment in research and development and tariff regulations requiring the use of U.S. materials, has resulted in little skill or technology transfer to these developing countries. It has also dampened rather than stimulated domestic production.

The Puerto Rican and Dominican garment industry's heavy dependence on U.S. capital, technology, and markets, plus the lack of linkages to the domestic economy in all areas except labor, significantly reduces the ability of these countries to generate capital and more indigenous and capital-intensive forms of industrial production. Unlike the Asian experience (where state power was strong and guaranteed domestic linkages), export-led industrialization in the Caribbean has increased dependence on the United States while contributing little to the general economic development of these small and open economies.

In the Caribbean, the state's principal role in export manufacturing is to create a favorable climate for foreign investment through investment incentives and the control of wages and labor. Most workers in Caribbean export-processing zones operate on a piece-rate system and are entitled to the minimum wage only if they meet their production quotas. Hourly wages vary considerably between countries, with a high in 1988 of $4.28 an hour in Puerto Rico (where the federal minimum wage applies) to a low of $.55 an hour in the Dominican Republic (Table 5.1). Labor control can be achieved through outright repression or prohibition of unions in free trade zones, as in the Dominican Republic, or through co-optation of labor, as in Puerto Rico. Both repression and co-optation lead to a weak and fragmented labor movement. This increases the vulnerability of women (and men) workers in both countries.

Both labor and the state were further weakened by the economic crisis that hit most of the Caribbean in the mid-1970s and 1980s. Rising prices of oil, a decline in traditional exports such as sugar and nickel (resulting from the international recession of 1980–1982 accompanied by a severe cut in the U.S. sugar quota for the Dominican Republic), and deteriorating terms of trade and foreign exchange earnings brought on this crisis.[11] Caribbean countries are now even more dependent on export promotion to ease the decline in their balance of payments, to service their debts, and to reduce growing unemployment. Many of the Caribbean and Latin American states have been forced to adopt IMF structural

TABLE 5.1   Hourly Wages in the Caribbean, 1988 (in US$)

Dominican Republic	.55
Haiti	.58
Jamaica	.88
Trinidad-Tobago	1.80
Barbados	2.10
Puerto Rico	4.28
U.S. Virgin Islands	4.50

Note: Hourly wages include fringe benefits; the data are for semiskilled labor in export-processing industries.
Source: Carmen Diana Deere, Peggy Antrobus, Lynn Bolles, Edwin Meléndez, Peter Phillips, Marcia Rivera, and Helen I. Safa, *In the Shadows of the Sun: Caribbean Development Alternatives and U.S. Policy* (Boulder: Westview Press, 1990), 149. Based on data from The Bobbin Consulting Group (Columbia, SC), 1988.

adjustment policies that involve reduction in control over their economies and cuts in government services and personnel. Labor has also been weakened by structural adjustment measures that generally resulted in higher levels of unemployment and lower real wages.

State policy toward export-led industrialization has differed somewhat in Puerto Rico because, as a commonwealth affiliated with the United States, its economy is totally controlled by Washington. Although this assures Puerto Rico free access to the U.S. market, the federal government restricts the range of permissible economic and political activities and state economic policy is very dependent on federal transfer payments to sustain an increasingly impoverished economy. U.S. corporations located in Puerto Rico pay no federal income tax but are subject to a 10 percent Puerto Rican tollgate tax unless some of their profits are reinvested in the island.

The Dominican Republic has greater political autonomy but is increasingly dependent on U.S. market forces to sustain its economy. State economic policy was set by a "predatory state" established by the dictator Rafael Trujillo, who ruled the country from 1930 to 1961. Despite elections and lip service given to increasing democratic participation, the state has continued to serve the interests of the agrarian and industrial elite, with little attention directed to the needs of the poor. In both cases, export-led industrialization has intensified dependence on the United States and failed to generate self-sustained growth. It has also contributed to a marginalization of male labor, which has weakened men's authority in the household. □

THE RISE AND DECLINE OF OPERATION BOOTSTRAP

Puerto Rico's export-led industrialization program—Operation Boot-strap—started earlier than those in most other countries due to its free access to the U.S. market. It was part of an ambitious program started in the late 1940s designed to move the economy away from monocrop sugar agriculture and to improve the standard of living through increased employment and heavy investment in housing, health care, and education. In the mid-1960s, Operation Bootstrap changed from a labor-intensive to a capital-intensive focus, and, in the mid-1970s, it entered a third stage of high-tech industrialization. Though different in emphasis, no one stage eclipsed the other, so that labor-intensive indus-tries such as apparel continued to be the major source of female employ-ment in manufacturing in the 1980s. Although the industrialization program was initially designed to provide employment to men displaced from agricultural work, women became the primary workforce in the labor-intensive factories, such as the apparel and food-processing sectors that arrived in the program's first stage.

Although growth in manufacturing output more than tripled from 1950 to 1980, it still could not offset the enormous declines in agriculture over this period. In 1940, agriculture employed 44.7 percent of the labor force, manufacturing employed only 10.9 percent: In 1980, agriculture had declined to a mere 5.2 percent, and manufacturing nearly doubled to 19 percent. Some of this surplus labor was absorbed in services and par-ticularly in public administration, but many people migrated to the United States. Migration peaked in the 1950s, precisely when Operation Bootstrap was taking off. It continued at high levels until 1970, encom-passing about 605,550 people in this twenty-year period—a figure equiv-alent to 27.4 percent of the 1950 population.[12] Despite this "safety valve," unemployment rates continued to hover around 12 to 15 percent from 1950 to 1970, and increased considerably in 1980, when they quadrupled for men and doubled for women (Table 5.2). Unemployment rates con-tinue to be higher for men than for women, and, in our sample survey of garment workers, 90 percent said it is easier for a woman than for a man to find a job. In addition, male labor force participation rates declined about 20 percent between 1950 and 1980 (Table 5.2). This reflects the pre-cipitous decline in agricultural employment, declining net out-migration, and increasing levels of higher education, which kept young men (and women) out of the labor market. However, women were affected less negatively than men, and after an initial decline from 1950 to 1960, their participation rates rose again, reaching 31.4 percent in 1990. Women were absorbed into export manufacturing, the public sector, and the growing service industry. With rising rates of unemployment, men (and later women) migrated; some withdrew entirely from the labor force.

Growing male unemployment, higher wages, and the increasing cost of transportation prompted the inauguration in the mid-1960s of the second stage of industrialization. This stage focused on capital-intensive industries such as petrochemicals and pharmaceuticals, which employed more men.[13] Higher wages reflected the rising cost of living as well as efforts on the part of U.S. unions to close the wage gap between the mainland and the island. In 1950, the average hourly wage in manufacturing was only 28 percent of the U.S. wage, but the full extension of U.S. minimum wage laws to Puerto Rico in 1981 considerably reduced wage differences. In apparel, for example, the differences ranged from 35 percent of U.S. earnings in 1955 to 75 percent in 1983.[14] Despite these increases, however, the apparel industry remained the lowest paid industry on the island, with an average hourly salary in 1985 of $3.95 an hour.

TABLE 5.2   Rates of Labor Force Participation and Unemployment for Females and Males in Puerto Rico, 1950–1990

	Females		Males		
	Ages 14 +	Ages 16 +	Ages 14 +	Ages 16 +	Both
Labor force participation rates:					
1950	30.0		79.8		54.6
1960	20.1		71.5		45.5
1970		28.0		70.8	48.0
1980		27.8		60.7	43.3
1990		31.4		61.6	45.4
Percent of the civilian labor force unemployed:					
1950	13.1		15.3		14.7
1960	10.4		12.7		12.1
1970		10.2		11.0	10.7
1980		12.3		19.5	17.1
1990		10.7		16.2	14.2

Note: These figures rely on sample population surveys conducted by the Puerto Rican Department of Labor but are generally deemed more reliable than the census.

Source: Estado Libre Asociado de Puerto Rico, Departamento del Trabajo y Recursos Humanos, 1991, Serie Histórica del Empleo, Desempleo, Grupo Trabajador en Puerto Rico, 1947–1990 (San Juan, Puerto Rico, Department of Labor and Human Resources, 1991).

Capital-intensive industries were adversely affected by the oil crisis, which hit Puerto Rico and the United States in 1974 and virtually eliminated Puerto Rico's petrochemical industry. These capital-intensive industries employed more men than women, but the total number of jobs generated was small due to a higher capital-labor ratio, and the indirect employment effects were also minimal.[15]

In an attempt to attract more stable industries catering to a highly skilled and better paid labor force, Puerto Rico initiated the third stage of industrialization during the 1970s. It focused primarily on high-tech industries such as electronics and scientific instruments. However, at this stage, manufacturing played a secondary role to the growing service sector, and industrial incentives were extended to include export-service industries such as investment banking, public relations, insurance, and computer services. Puerto Rico's role as the leading financial, administrative, and trade center for the Caribbean was reinforced in 1976 by Section 936 of the U.S. Internal Revenue Code, which granted tax-free privileges to firms that kept their profits in Puerto Rico for at least five years before repatriation to the United States. Section 936 made Puerto Rico into a major tax haven for manufacturing multinationals within the United States, including for profits derived from production elsewhere.[16] But this continued dependence of Puerto Rican export manufacturing on U.S. investment failed to generate self-sustained growth, despite the move into capital-intensive and high-tech industries.

Each of these stages in the industrialization process affected female employment. Women constituted the primary labor force in the early stages of labor-intensive industrialization. More than half of all new jobs created between 1960 and 1980 went to women, and in 1980 they still constituted 44 percent of all workers in the manufacturing sector.[17] They were also attracted to better paying, white-collar jobs, particularly in the government, which became the principal source of employment in Puerto Rico by 1980. It seems that Puerto Rican women now may be experiencing a bifurcation in the labor force, with younger, more educated women entering these newer, white-collar professions, while older, less educated women remain in declining manufacturing industries and low-paid service jobs.[18] This is reflected in the age profile of our Puerto Rican sample: Over 75 percent of the women garment workers were over thirty, and two-thirds were married.[19] This contrasts sharply with the profile of women workers in export manufacturing, most of whom are young (as in the Dominican Republic) and single.

Relatively high educational and low fertility levels among the Puerto Rican women in our sample were partly the result of conscious state policies to upgrade the labor force and reduce population growth. In 1980, when this survey was conducted, 39 percent of all Puerto Rican women were high school graduates, which corresponds to the percentage in our sample, and fertility rates had declined to 2.8 births per woman, again approximating the rates in sample.[20]

Both higher educational and lower fertility levels contributed to an improvement in women's occupational profile and to their greater rates of participation in the labor force. Women are also working more because of the rising cost of living and the increasing unemployment and declining real wages among men, which make it necessary for both husband and wife to contribute to the household economy. In our sample of female Puerto Rican garment workers, nearly three-fourths claimed their families could not survive without their income. In fact, the woman's salary never represented less than 40 percent of the total annual family income, even among single women, and it was usually higher among married women and especially female heads of household.[21] As noted, Puerto Rico's export-led industrialization has provided more jobs for women than for men. It also has contributed to the weakening of the man's role as primary breadwinner in many households, thus leading to new patterns of authority and changing gender roles.[22]

The majority of married women in our sample maintained that they shared household decision making with their husbands, and that husbands no longer had exclusive budgetary control, as was common when the man was the sole breadwinner. Most husbands had accepted that their wives worked and no longer considered it a threat to their authority because they realized it was impossible to live on a single wage. A divorced mother of teenage children who had worked for several years in the garment industry commented on how authority patterns have changed now that both husband and wife are working: "A person who works has rights. ... Now he [the husband] is obliged to let her give orders, because she is contributing. ... Now it is both of them, before it was one. ... Well, in that sense, the woman is better off."

However, the increasing incorporation of women into the labor force could not meet the economic needs of many of the Puerto Rican poor, particularly during a time of high unemployment and rising living costs. The percentage of households headed by women also increased from 16 to 19 percent between 1970 and 1980 and to 23.2 percent in 1990.[23] This was due, in part, to the high divorce rate, which may have been affected by the marginalization of men. As a result, many poor families, including the working poor employed in low-wage industries such as apparel, became increasingly dependent on transfer payments to support themselves. These transfer payments, primarily federal funds in the form of social security and food assistance, grew from 12 percent of personal income in 1950 to 30 percent by 1980. Food stamps, or *cupones*, as they are known in Puerto Rico, were used by 58.4 percent of the population in

1980.[24] In our 1980 sample, only 19 percent of the households received food stamps, chiefly large families with many young children or families with female heads. Though seen as subsidies to workers, these transfer payments are also aids to low-wage industries like apparel that do not pay an adequate wage and might otherwise leave the island because of wage increases or a shortage of cheap labor.

By providing alternative or supplementary sources of income, transfer payments reduce the dependence on wages for both sexes and may help explain declining male labor force participation rates. These payments also reduce a woman's dependence on a male wage and, combined with the modest growth in female employment, give a woman greater economic autonomy. However, transfer payments together with migration of working-age adults also have contributed to a low overall activity rate, so that by 1983, over one-half of all Puerto Rican families were without any resident wage earner.[25]

In addition to ambitious government programs in housing, education, and health, these social support measures helped to underwrite the costs of social reproduction for the working class and to contain class conflict. State policy also was directed at co-opting the labor movement rather than repressing it, as was done in the Dominican Republic and other Latin American and Caribbean countries. Industrialization led to a profound recomposition of the working class and, paradoxically, to a weakening of the labor movement. The strength of the militant sugarcane workers' union was sapped by the decline of the industry and increasing fragmentation and diversification of the industrial labor force. Fragmentation and competition between labor unions was accentuated by the rapid growth of American Federation of Labor and Congress of Industrial Organizations (AFL-CIO) affiliates, in which the International Ladies' Garment Workers' Union (ILGWU) played a leading role. Though unionized, most women workers in our sample regarded the ILGWU as a company union that did little to defend their interests or invite rank-and-file participation. The union's primary interest has been in containing worker demands in order to retard the flight of garment plants to cheaper wage areas, but it has not been very successful. The proportion of unionized workers in Puerto Rico as a whole dropped from 20 percent in 1970 to 6 percent in 1988, which can be partially blamed on union neglect of women workers.[26]

The final blow to the labor movement and to the industrialization program came with Puerto Rico's loss of its comparative advantage as a source of cheap labor. In the 1960s, many countries such as Mexico, Jamaica, the Dominican Republic, and the newly industrializing Asian nations began to copy Puerto Rico's export-led industrialization strategy. Most Caribbean countries acquired duty-free access to the United

States in 1983 through the CBI. And rising wages eliminated Puerto Rico's one remaining competitive advantage—cheap labor. Puerto Rico has tried to counter this competition in manufacturing with the establishment of twin plants, utilizing funds accumulated under Section 936. These plants are similar to those along the U.S.-Mexican border. More skilled stages of manufacturing are carried out in Puerto Rico, with the initial assembly work taking place in the Dominican Republic, Haiti, and other Caribbean islands.

As Puerto Rico's percentage of total manufacturing employment decreased from 25 percent in 1977 to 21 percent in 1984, there was a concomitant decline in the garment industry.[27] This has been particularly difficult for older women workers who have worked in the garment industry for twenty years or more and have no alternative sources of employment. For example, one fifty-nine-year-old woman worker, who had been employed by the same garment firm for twenty-two years, claimed she was only hoping she could hold out until she reached the legal retirement age of sixty-two before the firm closed and she could collect her monthly union pension of $100. The plant in which she originally worked had shut down, and she was forced to commute to one of their rural branches to retain her job. Workers in our sample were aware that production was being moved elsewhere, particularly to the Dominican Republic, where most of the labor-intensive operations for this firm are already located and where wages are very low. This woman noted: "You know that there they work for sweet potato peel; they say that they pay women there a little more than fifty cents [an hour], right?"

As the garment industry declined, the structure of production also shifted from transnational to local capital, often subcontracted to larger U.S. firms. In 1983, 50 percent of garment plants were locally owned. They were usually smaller and less capitalized than U.S. plants, employing 31 percent of the total labor force in the garment industry. It was estimated that, by 1983, $50 million—or one-fourth of the value of local production—was manufactured in *marquesina*, or "carport operations," that is, small workshops in the underground economy.[28] Women are the principal workers in these illegal operations, and, in the early 1980s, they often were paid as little as $1 an hour. They also receive no fringe benefits. However, since much of this income is unreported, it may be more easily combined with transfer payments such as public assistance, unemployment insurance, or social security, and it is not subject to taxation. As in the United States, these underground sweatshops lower both the labor and the infrastructure costs of production. Symptomatic of the decline in the established garment industry, they may contribute to that decline through additional competition.

Despite its problems, Operation Bootstrap transformed Puerto Rico from an agrarian to an urban, industrial economy, with a tenfold increase in per capita GNP between 1950 and 1980.[29] With its transformation into an increasingly important financial center, Puerto Rico is now totally integrated into the U.S. economy. External investment has shifted from sugar plantations to manufacturing and, more recently, to banks and other commercial institutions. But even with massive migration and transfer payments, Operation Bootstrap failed to provide sufficient income or jobs to sustain the population. Gross inequalities in income remain: In 1990, for example, 55 percent of working families were below the poverty level.[30] This was principally a result of the lack of jobs and high unemployment—factors that are, as noted, more marked in Puerto Rico among men than women. Although female labor force participation increased, the percentage of families without wage earners also rose. These families became dependent on transfer payments and probably unreported income from the informal sector. And with the lessening dependence on male wages, there has been an increase in marital instability and a rise in female-headed households. In both Puerto Rico and the Dominican Republic, export-led industrialization has contributed to women becoming major contributors to the household economy. □

THE DOMINICAN REPUBLIC:
EXPORT MANUFACTURING AND THE ECONOMIC CRISIS

Although both countries underwent a rapid transformation from an agrarian to an industrial economy, the development process in the Dominican Republic differed considerably from that of Puerto Rico. The Dominican Republic remained dependent on agricultural exports, principally sugar, until the early 1980s, when the United States drastically cut its sugar quotas. Industrialization started much later in the Dominican Republic than in Puerto Rico, and it focused largely on import substitution until the massive and rapid expansion of export manufacturing in the 1980s. This expansion resulted largely from the reduction in the cost of labor due to the economic crisis and currency devaluation (the peso was first devalued in 1984, under strong pressure from the International Monetary Fund). Manufacturing exports grew 307.4 percent between 1981 and 1988 to US$502.1 million, with textiles and garments averaging 35.8 percent of exports during this period.[31]

Though the three original free trade zones studied here started in the early 1970s, the impetus for export manufacturing in the Dominican Republic in the 1980s came from the economic crisis and structural adjustment measures mandated by the IMF. These increased the country's need for foreign exchange and resulted in rising unemployment rates, inflation, and lower real wages. Unemployment peaked at 27 percent in 1985, and underemployment in 1980 was estimated at 43 percent.[32] Despite several increases in the minimum wage, the real hourly wage in the Dominican Republic (adjusted for inflation) declined 62.3 percent from 1984 to 1990.[33] The steady reduction in U.S. sugar quotas from the Dominican Republic starting in the early 1980s aggravated the need for foreign exchange and resulted in increased unemployment, particularly among men. Although the Dominican Republic accounts for roughly half the U.S. sugar quota from the Caribbean Basin, the amount dropped from an average annual 1.6 million tons in 1979–1981 to 268,000 tons by December 1987. Though export manufacturing was designed to compensate for the loss of employment and foreign exchange in sugar production, it actually contributes less to GDP since the value-added component of sugar is estimated to be as high as 90 percent; in garments assembled from cloth made and cut in the United States, it averages, at most, 27 percent.[34]

Export manufacturing was attracted by the abundance of low-cost female labor in the Dominican Republic. There women have higher unemployment rates than men and are paid less. In 1983, the average monthly wage for women was DR$165 (Dominican pesos) compared to DR$291 for men.[35] Female labor force participation rates in the Dominican Republic quadrupled from 9.3 percent in 1960 to 38 percent in 1990 (Table 5.3).[36] Several factors in the development process favored this dramatic increase, including urbanization, the growth of the tertiary sector, and the growth of export processing. At the same time, changes were taking place in the female population that made women more employable, including improvement in educational levels and a marked decline in fertility.[37] The increase in female labor force participation rates was much greater than male rates, which, since 1960, have stabilized at around 72 percent (Table 5.3). Overall activity rates have also increased, contrary to the situation in Puerto Rico, where there has been a sharp decline. It would appear that with the onset of the economic crisis and the decline in sugar production and import-substitution industrialization in the 1980s, an increasing number of both sexes are entering the informal sector, which now employs more men than women and is the principal source of employment for men.[38]

Male unemployment and informalization, lower wages for both genders, and rising inflation increased the pressure on women to work to supplement the household income. By 1981, women constituted 40 percent of the workers in the non-sugar manufacturing sector, most of them concentrated in free trade zones.[39] Due to the increase in these zones since 1980, export manufacturing now constitutes the second most

TABLE 5.3   Female and Male Labor Force Participation Rates in the Dominican Republic

	1960	1970	1981	1990
Female	9.3	25.1	28.0	38.0
Male	75.9	72.6	72.0	72.2
Both	42.8	48.8	49.5	54.6

Source: Nelson Ramírez, Isidoro Santana, Francisco de Moya, and Pablo Tactuk, *República Dominicana: Población y Desarrollo, 1950–1985* (San José, Costa Rica: CELADE, 1988), 41, Table 11.18. Based on the National Office of Statistics, 1966, 1985, and unedited tables from 1970 census. 1990 figures from Clara Baez, "Mujer y Desarrollo en la República Dominicana: 1981–1991," unedited report prepared for the Inter-American Development Bank (Santo Domingo: 1991), 13.

important source of urban employment for women, after domestic service. Garment firms employing a largely female labor force have always predominated in the Dominican free trade zones, and they constituted 67 percent of all firms in 1992.[40] Although the percentage of women compared to men working in these zones has declined somewhat since the mid-1980s, export manufacturing clearly remains a key component of Dominican development strategy and has had a major impact on women's incorporation into the labor force. As a result, working women have become major economic contributors to the household. In our sample of women workers in export manufacturing, 38 percent considered themselves to be the primary breadwinner (Table 5.4).

In 1986, Juana Santana, for example, sustained her family of three children on her weekly salary of DR$57 (about US$20), which covered food, rent, and the cost of a baby-sitter as well as her own expenses such as transportation and lunch. Her partner earned some money driving a taxi owned by his family, but like many of the men living with the women interviewed in 1986, he did not have a stable job. With three children to support, her husband's unstable income, and the high cost of living, Juana knew she had to continue working. As she noted: "Anyway, I have to work, either in the zone or in a private home [as a domestic], because I cannot be dependent on my husband. ... what he earns is not enough, to help my family and to help me here at home."

Juana's situation remains typical—many women workers in the free trade zones still face low wages, poor working conditions, lack of inexpensive and adequate child care, limited job alternatives, partners who offer no or limited assistance, and an increasingly high cost of living. Export manufacturers have shown a preference for women workers because they are cheaper to employ and less likely to unionize and are

TABLE 5.4   Women Workers in the Free Trade Zones of the Dominican Republic
by Marital Status and Principal Provider (in percentages)

Principal Provider in Household		Marital Status		
	Single	Married [a]	Widows, Divorced, and Separated	Total
Woman worker	19.6	26.3	74.2	37.7
Spouse	–	58.4	1.6	30.3
Parent(s)	35.3	0.8	11.3	11.2
Other	45.1	14.5	12.9	20.8
Total	100.0	100.0	100.0	100.0

[a] Includes consensual unions.

believed to have greater patience for the tedious, monotonous work of
assembly operations. Like most women workers in export manufacturing worldwide, Dominican women in our sample were young, rural
migrants (75 percent were under thirty), and two-thirds had no previous
work experience, which increases their vulnerability. However, contrary
to global patterns, more than half of the Dominican women workers
sampled were married, and over one-fourth were female heads of household, carrying the heaviest financial responsibility since most were the
sole economic provider. As in Puerto Rico, the percentage of Dominican
female heads of household is increasing, it reached 24.1 percent by
1984.[41] Again, this may be partially attributed to the marginalization of
men. The inability of men to fulfill their role as economic provider may
contribute to marital instability in both countries.

Why do the workers not protest? Many factors contribute to the lack
of worker solidarity in export manufacturing: the youth of the workers,
their constant turnover, their recent entry into industrial employment,
family responsibilities, high unemployment, and the lack of job alternatives. However, the principal obstacle to greater labor solidarity in the
Dominican Republic has been outright government repression. Popular
discontent is expressed in turnover or eventual withdrawal from the
workforce, rather than through labor organizing. In fact, there are few
officially recognized unions operating in the Dominican free trade
zones, although they are not legally prohibited. Workers are simply fired
and blacklisted with other plants if any union activity is detected. Hilda,
for example, was fired several years ago along with sixty other women
for trying to organize a union in the same factory where she and Juana
worked. As the manager told them when they were fired: "Whoever gets

involved in unions here knows she will lose her job and will no longer work in the free trade zone because, as you know, the big fish eats the little fish." Women workers who have tried to take complaints of mistreatment or unjust dismissal to the Ministry of Labor generally have been rejected, and preference has been given to management.

Although they are relatively weak at the level of the workplace and the polity, Dominican women workers in the free trade zones have begun to assume more authority in the family. As in Puerto Rico, the majority of the married women we surveyed maintained that they shared household decisions with their partners and that men no longer had exclusive budgetary control. Their authority in the home was derived from their increased economic contribution to the household, which took on major significance in light of increased male unemployment and declining wages. In short, the data indicate that it is not simply a question of whether women are employed or not but also the importance of their contribution to the household economy that gives women a basis to resist male dominance in the family.[42]

A thirty-eight-year-old supervisor in the free trade zones who now lives alone, although she has had eight children in three consensual unions, says she would not quit working even if she found another man because, "They think that if the woman works, she will rule too much, because that's the way it is here in Santo Domingo. That when a woman works, they think she is liberal, a little too liberal, that they can't mistreat or abuse her. But for many men when the woman isn't working, the woman is obliged to wait, to have a bad time, to put up with many things from a man. But when the woman is working, then things change because we are both working." This supervisor clearly expressed the subordination that lack of paid employment imposes on Dominican women.

Most women workers agreed that paid employment had given them greater legitimacy to negotiate with their husbands, even though 80 percent of the married Dominican women sampled still considered the man to be the head of the household. In general, more egalitarian relationships were found among couples where both were working, were better educated, had lived in the city longer, had not married very young, and were legally married rather than living in consensual unions. Although less marked than in Puerto Rico, most of the changes in Dominican household authority patterns came about through a gradual process of negotiation, in which women used their economic contribution to the household to bargain for greater autonomy and authority. Compared to the Puerto Rican sample, the Dominican women workers who were sampled were younger and had more children to support, which increased their dependence on men's wages. The rate of consensual unions also was much higher among Dominican than Puerto Rican women, and this affected household stability. Furthermore, Dominican women had not been working as long and enjoyed less protection on the job. These factors, coupled with the pressures of the economic crisis, heighten insecurity and the fear of challenging male dominance.

Despite the spectacular increase in export manufacturing in the Dominican Republic, this sector's contribution to economic development is questionable. Though export manufacturing was designed to alleviate unemployment and to produce badly needed foreign exchange, neither goal has been achieved adequately. Jobs created in the free trade zones have primarily gone to women and have contributed to an increase in their labor force participation. But these jobs have failed to reduce male unemployment, and the wages paid women workers tend to be extremely low and generate few demand linkages to the rest of the economy. Dominican export manufacturing is an increasingly inefficient generator of foreign exchange, and, between the 1970s and 1988, the value added from free trade zone exports dropped from 45 to 25 percent of foreign exchange between the 1970s and 1988. As a result, despite the fivefold increase in the total value of exports from the Dominican free trade zones between 1980 and 1988 (from $117 million to $517 million), the economy remained virtually stagnant with average GDP growth rates of only 1.1 percent per annum.[43] The fundamental reason can be found in U.S. trade policies, which reduced export manufacturing in the Dominican Republic (and throughout the Caribbean Basin) to assembly operations with very few domestic inputs. □

CONCLUSION

Four main actors appear to have played critical roles in the promotion of export-led industrialization: the state, foreign capital, local capital, and labor—including an increasing proportion of women. In the Caribbean, as in Latin America generally, foreign capital has played the dominant role. Multinational corporations have long been the main source of capital inflow.[44] Part of the explanation for this lies in the hegemonic role U.S. capital has historically played in the region, even in the export of primary commodities such as sugar in the Dominican Republic. U.S. economic hegemony also weakened the local industrial elite, particularly in the Caribbean, where small size and low purchasing power sharply weakened the domestic market. The state and labor were weakened further by the economic crisis and structural adjustment measures, whereby the IMF largely determined the terms of trade, wage increases, currency exchange rates, and even state development policy. As Barbara Stallings notes, "In its extreme version, the issue at stake is whether the state's choice of development strategy determines the role of foreign capital or whether foreign capital determines development strategy."[45]

A comparative analysis demonstrates that East Asian countries, such as Taiwan and South Korea, have opted for the first strategy and that the Caribbean and Latin America have fallen victim to the latter. Though East Asian countries are often presented as models of development, the export-promotion strategies they follow are quite different from those in the Caribbean, and they point up the importance of state policy in determining the growth potential of export-led industrialization.[46] Policies in Taiwan, South Korea, and Singapore have relied heavily on state intervention in the economy, including control over foreign capital and technology, and they are not examples of free market principles, as some have suggested. East Asian states have led the shift toward more capital-intensive forms of export-led industrialization, including heavy investment in research and technology and in manpower training programs. They have not allowed assembly industries to dominate, as has been the case in Puerto Rico and the Dominican Republic. Use of domestic inputs in export-processing zones in South Korea and Taiwan also rose substantially as early as the 1970s,[47] but in the Dominican Republic in a 1987 survey, only 4 percent of local costs were spent on raw materials.[48]

In this way, East Asian states—unlike Latin America and especially the Caribbean—avoided dependency on the United States. Consequently, they were able to move into the second stage of high-tech and more capital-intensive, export-led industrialization. Between 1980 and 1987, South Korea and Taiwan maintained average annual growth rates of 8.6 and 7.5 percent, respectively,[49] much higher than the average GDP growth rate of 1.1 percent per annum in the Dominican Republic.

In Puerto Rico (as in South Korea and Taiwan), rising wages as well as competition from cheaper wage areas required changes in development strategies toward more capital-intensive and high-tech industries, but the scope of this industrialization was insufficient to reduce male unemployment, and the country continued to depend on U.S. investment. Despite these changes in development strategy, the Puerto Rican economy failed to generate self-sustained growth and is now heavily dependent on transfer payments provided by the U.S. government to sustain its population. Even the tax-free privileges granted to U.S. corporations operating in Puerto Rico under Section 936 have come under increasing attack from the U.S. Congress. This underlies Puerto Rico's vulnerability. The Dominican Republic, for its part, fears that the North American Free Trade Agreement will reduce its competitive advantage vis-à-vis Mexico and hamper growth of U.S. investment in export manufacturing.

Labor in both the Caribbean and East Asia is under strong state control to ensure the political stability needed for foreign investment and

economic growth. It could be argued that a weak labor sector is necessary for success in export-led industrialization. Cheap wages and labor's
quiescence are critical components for international competition.[50] This is
one of the reasons why women are favored as wage earners in both
regions. However, full employment in the more developed East Asian
countries, such as Taiwan and South Korea, has contributed to greater
domestic demand and to some improvement in workers' bargaining
power, wages, and working conditions.[51] The success of these strategies
can be seen in the increasing labor shortages in the more fully developed
Asian countries, particularly in low-wage industries. In the Caribbean
Basin, however, export manufacturing has not led to any reduction in
surplus labor. These surpluses have led to massive migration and the
marginalization of men in both Puerto Rico and the Dominican Republic.

The East Asian emphasis on capital-intensive industrialization for the
domestic as well as the export market has maintained the incorporation
of men into the labor force, enabling them to retain their economic
control over the household to a considerable degree. But in both Puerto
Rico and the Dominican Republic, women have become major contributors to the household economy. The women workers who were sampled
claimed to have greater authority over budgets and other household
decisions as a result of their increased economic contribution. And, in
general, there has been a weakening of the man's role as principal breadwinner, although this is more marked in Puerto Rico than in the Dominican Republic. The industrialization process is much older in Puerto Rico,
leading to more extensive proletarianization and erosion of male authority in the household. The Puerto Rican women workers studied here
proved less dependent on a male wage than Dominican women, due to
the demographic reasons outlined earlier and to transfer payments and
other forms of social support, which are virtually nonexistent in the
Dominican Republic. Standing suggests that this pattern of "global feminization" of labor—with increased female labor force participation and
declining male participation—extends far beyond the Caribbean region
and is due to increased international competition and the growth of
export manufacturing, labor deregulation, and structural adjustment
measures that have weakened workers' bargaining power in both
advanced industrial and developing countries.[52]

Failure to generate self-sustaining growth through export manufacturing limits the possibility for male employment and increases dependence on female labor in both countries. This failure can be attributed
partially to different state policies in the Caribbean and East Asia. These
policies reflect the weak state in Puerto Rico, the Dominican Republic,
and the Caribbean generally, as well as a tradition of dependence on the
United States. The promotion of assembly operations over more complex

forms of export manufacturing also reflects conscious U.S. trade policies aimed at maintaining control over production and skilled jobs in the United States, designed, in part, to appease domestic labor interests. U.S. success in promoting this policy throughout the countries of the Caribbean Basin will only accelerate their conversion into sources of cheap labor for U.S. entrepreneurs while decreasing their capacity for self-generating growth. Finally, at the level of the region's households, the promotion of labor-intensive assembly manufacturing will also contribute to the increasing marginalization of men, the increased dependence on women's wages, and the change in gender roles. □

NOTES

I wish to acknowledge the financial support of the National Institute of Mental Health for collection of the Puerto Rican survey data, and the Wenner Gren Foundation for collection and analysis of the in-depth interviews in both Puerto Rico and the Dominican Republic. Several institutions and individuals assisted me in this endeavor. Foremost thanks go to Magaly Piñeda, Director of the Centro de Investigación para la Acción Femenina (CIPAF), for supplying me with their data on Dominican women workers and to Frances Pou, for her assistance in the collection of the in-depth interviews. I am also indebted to Lorraine Catanzaro, Quintina Reyes, and Milagros Ricourt for their assistance in the analysis of the Dominican data. I also wish to thank Carmen Pérez Herrera, who conducted the survey interviews with Puerto Rican women in 1980, and Clifford Depin (now deceased), who as Director of the ILGWU in Puerto Rico facilitated access to the factories and data from their own files. Finally, thanks to all my colleagues for their critiques of earlier drafts of this paper

1. Susan Joekes and Roxanna Moayedi, *Women and Export Manufacturing: A Review of the Issues and AID Policy* (Washington, DC: International Center for Research on Women, 1987).

2. Keith Bradsher, "Conferees Agree to Restrict Projects by AID," *New York Times*, October 4, 1992, 5.

3. Carmen Diana Deere, Peggy Antrobus, Lynn Bolles, Edwin Meléndez, Peter Phillips, Marcia Rivera, and Helen I. Safa, *In the Shadows of the Sun: Caribbean Development Alternatives and U.S. Policy* (Boulder: Westview Press, 1990), 154.

4. Carmen Diana Deere and Edwin Meléndez, "When Export Growth Is Not Enough: U.S. Trade Policy and Caribbean Basin Economic Recovery," *Caribbean Affairs*, 5, no. 1 (1992): 61–70.

5. Ibid., 70.

6. Emilio Pantojas-García, "The U.S. Caribbean Basin Initiative and the Puerto Rican Experience: Some Parallels and Lessons," *Latin American Perspectives* 12, no. 4 (1985): 105–128.

7. Consejo Nacional de Zonas Francas de Exportación, Secretaría de Estado de Industria y Comercio, *Evaluación zonas francas industriales* (Santo Domingo: Ministry of Industry and Commerce, 1993).

8. Andréa Dauhajre, E. Riley, R. Mena, and J. A. Guerrero, *Impacto económico de las zonas francas industriales de exportación en la República Dominicana* (Santo Domingo: Fundación Economía y Desarrollo, 1989), 97.

9. Deere et al., *In the Shadows of the Sun*, 166, 167.

10. Dauhajre et al., *Impacto Económico de las Zonas Francas Industriales de Exportación en la República Dominicana*, 39–40, 98.

11. Deere et al., *In the Shadows of the Sun*, 26.

12. James Dietz, *Economic History of Puerto Rico: Institutional Change and Capitalist Development* (Princeton: Princeton University Press, 1986), 258, 286.

13. Palmira N. Ríos, "Export-Oriented Industrialization and the Demand for Female Labor: Puerto Rican Women in the Manufacturing Sector, 1952–1980," *Gender and Society* 4, no. 3 (1990), 321–337.

14. Carl Priestland and Smiley Jones, *Problems Facing the Local Apparel Industry of Puerto Rico* (San Juan, Puerto Rico: Economic Development Administration, 1985), 26.

15. Dietz, *Economic History of Puerto Rico*, 254.

16. Emilio Pantojas-García, *Development Strategies as Ideology: Puerto Rico's Export-Led Industrialization Experience* (Boulder: Lynne Rienner Publishers, 1990).

17. Alice Colón, Marya Muñoz, Neftali García, and Idsa Alegría, "Trayectoria de la participación laboral de las mujeres en Puerto Rico de los años 1950 a 1985," in *Crisis, sociedad y mujer: Estudio comparativo entre países de América (1950–1985)* (Havana: Editorial de la Mujer, Federación de Mujeres Cubanas, 1988), table 2, 24.

18. Luz de Alba Acevedo, "El desarrollo capitalista y la nueva división del trabajo: El empleo de la mujer en los servicios en Puerto Rico," paper prepared for the XV Congress of the Latin American Studies Association, Miami, 1989, 12.

19. The older age represented in our Puerto Rican sample may be overstated since we deliberately drew a larger sample of women who had worked ten years or more in the same firm in order to examine the effects of long-term employment on women's status. Longer-term workers would naturally tend to be older.

20. Harriet B. Presser and Sunita Kishor, "Economic Development and Occupational Sex Segregation in Puerto Rico: 1950–1980," *Population and Development Review* 17, no. 1 (1991): 60–61.

21. Helen I. Safa, "Female Employment in the Puerto Rican Working Class," in June Nash and H. I. Safa, eds., *Women and Change in Latin America* (South Hadley, MA: Bergin and Garvey Publishers, 1985), 103.

22. Helen I. Safa, "Women and Industrialization in the Caribbean," in Sharon Stichter and Jane Parpart, eds., *Women, Employment, and the Family in the International Division of Labor* (London: Macmillan, 1990), 72–97.

23. U.S. Bureau of the Census, *General Characteristics of the Population* (Washington, DC: U.S. Bureau of the Census, 1990).

24. Dietz, *Economic History of Puerto Rico*, 297.

25. Teresa L. Amott and Julie Matthaei, *Race, Gender, and Work: A Multicultural Economic History of Women in the United States* (Boston: South End Press, 1991), 278.

26. Carlos Santiago Rivera, "Industrial Reconversion and Economic Restructuring: The Challenge for the Puerto Rican Labor Movement," *Radical America* 23, no. 1 (1989): 93.

27. Priestland and Jones, *Problems Facing the Local Apparel Industry of Puerto Rico*, table 1.

28. Ibid., tables 2 and 3, 20.

29. Dietz, *Economic History of Puerto Rico*, 244

30. Colón et al., "Trayectoria de la participación laboral de las mujeres en Puerto Rico," table 4, 26; U.S. Bureau of the Census, *General Characteristics of the Population*.

31. Dauhajre et al., *Impacto económico de las zonas francas industriales*, 38–39.

32. Nelson Ramirez, Isidoro Santana, Francisco de Moya, and Pablo Tactuk, *República Dominicana: Población y Desarrollo, 1950–1985* (San José, Costa Rica: CELADE, 1988), 44–47.

33. Fundación APEC de Crédito Educativo (FUNDAPEC), *Encuesta nacional de mano de obra* (Santo Domingo: Inter-American Development Bank and FUNDAPEC, 1992), 32.

34. Deere and Meléndez, "When Export Growth Is Not Enough," 63–66.

35. Clara Baez, "Mujer y desarrollo en la República Dominicana: 1981–1991," unedited report prepared for Inter-American Development Bank, Santo Domingo, 1991, 20.

36. As in Puerto Rico, labor force participation rates in the Dominican Republic show a great deal of variability, depending on the source. These figures are drawn from national household surveys conducted by the National Statistics Office and (for 1990 only) by the Central Bank of the Dominican Republic, which are deemed more accurate than the census. The figures given are for the population ten years and older, while in Puerto Rico or the United States, only people sixteen years of age and over are considered to be in the labor force.

37. Isis Duarte, Clara Baez, Carmen J. Gómez, and Marina Aríza, *Población y condición de la mujer en República Dominicana*, Study no. 6 (Santo Domingo: Instituto de Estudios de Población y Desarrollo, 1989).

38. Baez, *Mujer y Desarrollo en la República Dominicana: 1981–1991*, 19. These informal sector estimates are based on a 1983 household survey in Santo Domingo (the capital) by the National Statistics Office and the National Planning Office. In that survey, informal sector workers were distinguished from those working in the government, modern, and domestic sectors, and they were counted in labor force participation rates. However, the informal sector is undoubtedly less important in Puerto Rico due to the alternative of transfer payments, and even those working in carport industries constitute a small fraction of the population and are probably not counted in labor force participation rates.

39. Duarte et al., *Población y condición de la mujer en República Dominicana*, 124.

40. Consejo Nacional de Zonas Francas de Exportación, *Evaluación zonas francas industriales*.

41. Carmen Julia Gómez, *La problemática de las jefas del hogar* (Santo Domingo: CIPAF, 1990), 227.

42. Rae Lesser Blumberg cites similar evidence in Blumberg, ed., *Gender, Family, and Economy: The Triple Overlap* (Newbury Park, CA: Sage Publications, 1991), 97–127.

43. Deere and Meléndez, "When Export Growth Is Not Enough."

44. Even in the larger and more advanced industrial economies of Argentina, Brazil, and Mexico, the share of foreign firms in manufactured exports is greater than in South Korea and Taiwan. See Rhys Jenkins, "The Political Economy of Industrialization: A Comparison of Latin American and East Asian Newly Industrializing Countries," *Development and Change* 22 (Newbury Park, CA: Sage Publications, 1991), 197–231.

45. Barbara Stallings, "The Role of Foreign Investment in Economic Development," in Gary Gereffi and Don Wyman, eds., *Manufacturing Miracles: Paths of Industrialization in Latin America and East Asia* (Princeton: Princeton University Press, 1990), 80.

46. Gary Gereffi, "Paths of Industrialization: An Overview," in Gary Gereffi and Don Wyman, eds., *Manufacturing Miracles: Paths of Industrialization in Latin America and East Asia* (Princeton: Princeton University Press, 1990); Jenkins, "The Political Economy of Industrialization."

47. Patricia Wilson, *Exports and Local Development: Mexico's New Maquiladoras* (Austin: University of Texas Press, 1993), 23.

48. Alfonso Abreu, Manuel Cocco, Carlos Despradel, Eduardo García Michael, and Arturo Peguero, *Las zonas francas industriales: El éxito de una política económica* (Santo Domingo: Centro de Orientación Económica, 1989), 145.

49. Gereffi, "Paths of Industrialization," 11.

50. Frederic Deyo, "Industrialization and the Structuring of Asian Labor Movements: The 'Gang of Four,'" in M. Hanagan and C. Stephenson, eds., *Confrontation, Class Consciousness and the Labor Process* (Westport, CT: Greenwood Press, 1986).

51. Linda Lim, "Women's Work in Export Factories: The Politics of a Cause," in Irene Tinker, ed., *Persistent Inequalities: Women and World Development* (New York: Oxford Univesity Press, 1990), 113.

52. Guy Standing, "Global Feminization Through Flexible Labor," *World Development* 17, no. 7 (1989): 1077–1095.

CHAPTER SIX

■

Engendered Production in Rural Taiwan: Ideological Bonding of the Public and Private

Rita S. Gallin

THE RESTRUCTURING OF THE GLOBAL ECONOMY that began in the 1960s has stimulated a burgeoning literature on forms and patterns of women's employment in the Third World.[1] Much of this work has focused either on family supply factors that propel women into the labor force or on state and industry demand factors that can either draw them into or expel them from the workforce.[2] Much of the literature has also highlighted the ubiquitous presence of ideology in these forces of supply and demand.[3]

Some writers, for example, have demonstrated how women are disadvantaged as workers by a private sphere ideology, which proposes that these women are a labor input into the household economy (i.e., that they "work for the family" rather than for themselves).[4] Others have shown the way in which women's position in the labor force is shaped by a public sphere ideology—be it state *or* industry—that emphasizes the notion of separate domains and contends that men are workers and women are housekeepers.[5] Few researchers, however, have explored how family, state, *and* industrial ideologies converge to subordinate women in the workplace.[6] My purpose in this chapter is to address this gap by discussing how the ideological bonding or intersection of the public and private engenders production in rural Taiwan.

This chapter is based on data collected in Hsin Hsing, a village whose economic system has changed between the late 1950s and 1980s from one primarily based on agriculture to one predominantly dependent on off-farm employment.[7] I will begin by describing development in Taiwan and discussing the traditional Chinese family in order to establish the

113

context for the material that follows. I will then describe development in Hsin Hsing, examine production and reproduction in the village, and discuss ways in which the intersection of gender ideologies encoded in family conventions, state policy, and managerial practices shape patterns of production in the local area. In the concluding section, I will consider the implications of the Taiwan case within the context of recent analyses of global economic restructuring and employment generation. □

DEVELOPMENT IN TAIWAN

When the Chinese Nationalist government retreated to Taiwan in 1949, it found the island to be primarily agricultural, with conditions that were not consistently favorable to development. To spur economic growth, the government initially strengthened agriculture to provide a base for industrialization, briefly pursued a strategy of import substitution during the 1950s, and then, in the 1960s, adopted a policy of industrialization through export. The latter policy produced dramatic changes in Taiwan's economic structure. The contribution of agriculture to the net domestic product declined from 36 percent in 1952 to only 7 percent in 1986, and that of industry rose from 18 to 47 percent over the same period. Trade expanded greatly, increasing in value from US$303 million in 1952 to US$64 billion in 1986. The contribution of exports to the volume of trade also rose dramatically, from US$116 million (38 percent) in 1952 to US$40 billion (63 percent) in 1986.[8]

Similar changes can also be documented for other Third World countries that adopted policies of labor-intensive, export-oriented industrialization (e.g., Singapore). In contrast to such developing countries, however, Taiwan's planners did not depend primarily on direct foreign investment to stimulate development; rather, they relied on capital mobilization within the domestic private sector and on an elaborate system of subcontracting to spearhead the growth of manufactured exports. Indeed, subcontracting is so thoroughly institutionalized on the island that one foreign executive remarked that Taiwan "is not an exporting nation ... [but] is simply a collection of international subcontractors for the American market."[9] This assessment notwithstanding, Taiwan's industrial structure is based on and sustained by vertically integrated and geographically dispersed small-scale businesses.

As early as 1971, for example, 50 percent of the industrial and commercial establishments and 55 percent of the manufacturing firms in Taiwan were located in rural areas.[10] Most such businesses are small- and medium-sized operations that produce for domestic and international markets; more than 90 percent of the island's enterprises employs fewer than thirty workers each[11] and in 1987, these small businesses employed almost three-quarters (74.2 percent) of Taiwan's labor force.[12] Further, these small businesses are the mainstay of the island's trading economy, accounting for 65 percent of exports in the late 1980s.[13]

The predominant form of these enterprises is the family firm. In fact, 97 percent of all businesses owned by Taiwanese are family-organized.[14] Taiwan's economy, in sum, is sustained by a multitude of small- and medium-sized family firms that are located across the island and that provide income for the majority of the population—a population in which wealth is increasingly becoming unequally distributed.[15] □

THE TRADITIONAL CHINESE FAMILY

The economic family, the *chia*, is the basic socioeconomic unit in China. This family can take one of three forms: conjugal, joint, or stem. The conjugal family consists of a husband, wife, and their unmarried children; the joint family adds two or more married sons and their wives and children to this core group. The stem family—a form that lies somewhere between the conjugal and joint family types—includes parents, their unmarried offspring, and one married son with his wife and children.

Life within the family is shaped by China's patrilineal kinship structure, which recognizes only male children as descent-group members with rights to family property. In the past (and, to a large extent, today) residence was patrilocal; when a woman married, she left her natal home to live as a member of her husband's family and severed her formal ties with her father's household. Parents considered daughters a liability; they were household members who drained family resources as children and who withdrew their assets (domestic labor and earning power) when they married. Sons, in contrast, contributed steadily to the family's economic security during its growth and expansion and provided a source of support in old age. Not surprisingly, parents strongly preferred male children.

Traditionally, all members of the family lived under one roof, except for a few who worked outside to supplement or diversify the group income. Ideally, the family functioned as a single, cooperating unit in all activities. Men and women performed different tasks as members of a cooperative enterprise in which all property belonged to the family as a whole, except for the jewelry and cash brought into the household by a woman as part of her dowry. Others in the family had no rights to this "private property" (*sai khia* [Taiwanese]; *sz fang chien* [Mandarin]), which a woman could augment with any money she might be allowed to retain during her married life.

An authoritarian hierarchy based on gender, generation, and age dominated life within the family. The eldest male had the highest status; a woman's status, although it increased with age and with the birth of sons, was lower than that of any man. Women's desires were subordinated to those of men, just as the wishes of the young were subjugated to those of the old. Even though women's work was necessary for the maintenance of the household, family members took women's labor for granted. In short, women had no real control over their own lives; social and economic marginality marked their experience. □

DEVELOPMENT IN HSIN HSING

Hsin Hsing is a nucleated village approximately 125 miles southwest of Taipei, Taiwan's capital city, and is located beside a road that runs between two market towns, Lukang and Ch'i-hu. Its people, like most in the area, speak Hokkien (Minnan), and their ancestors migrated from Fukien, China, several hundred years ago. In 1958, the registered population of the village was 609 people, living in ninety-nine households or economic families. About four-fifths of the people were between one and forty-four years of age, and slightly less than half were male. Conjugal families predominated, accounting for 66 percent of all village families (56 percent of the population). In contrast, only 5 percent of households (10 percent of the population) were joint families, and the remaining 29 percent of households (35 percent of the population) were stem families (see Table 6.1).

During the 1950s, when no significant industries or job opportunities existed locally, land was the primary locus of production. Almost all families derived most of their livelihood from producing two rice crops per year, raising marketable vegetables, and, in some cases, earning wages from farm labor.[16] Men worked in the fields while women managed the house and children, worked as an auxiliary farm labor force, raised poultry, and, in their "spare time," wove fiber hats at home to supplement the family income.

Hsin Hsing began to change in the mid-1950s and early 1960s as population pressure on the land created problems of underemployment and made farms too small to support family members. Increasing numbers of men began to migrate to the larger cities of the province to seek jobs and supplemental income.[17] As the stream continued throughout the 1960s, labor shortages became acute, farm profits dropped, and agricultural production declined. (In Taiwan as a whole, agricultural production leveled off and varied by only a small amount from year to year in the late 1960s.)[18] The stream of migration and the decline in rural production might well have continued in Hsin Hsing but for certain national and international developments in the 1970s.

TABLE 6.1   Population of Hsin Hsing Village by Period and Age

	1958		1989	
	Number	%	Number	%
1–15	269	44.2	137	30.0
16–44	235	38.6	194	42.5
45–64	90	14.8	77	16.8
65 and older	15	2.5	49	10.7
Total	609	100.0	457	100.0
Sex Ratio (males per 100 females)	95		93	

Note: Although the data in Table 6.1 have different sources, correlations with other statistical materials confirmed the accuracy and comparability of the two data sets.
Source: 1958 Household Record Book, Pu Yen Township Public Office; 1989 Field Survey.

The government's policy of export-oriented industrialization brought about rapid urbanization and migration from rural areas to cities during the 1960s. Large segments of the rural population were absorbed by urban industry, and, by 1972, the value of a farmer's production was only one-fifth that of a nonagricultural worker.[19] In 1973, to stem the stagnation of agriculture, the government guaranteed the rice price and established the Accelerated Rural Development Program.[20] The implementation of these policies created a climate in which farmers believed they could derive profits from cultivating their land, and it accelerated industry's move to the countryside—a process that had begun in the 1960s.

These attempts to invigorate agriculture were followed by the oil crisis of 1974 and the world recession and inflation of 1974–1975. The pace of industrialization in Taiwan's cities slowed,[21] and more than 200,000 urban workers lost their jobs when some factories shut down and others cut back production.[22] The city lost its aura of opportunity and the country-side began to look more promising.

A comparison of the population structure of Hsin Hsing in 1989 and in 1958 suggests one of the outcomes of these developments. By 1989, the village population had declined to only 457 people in 76 households versus 609 people in 99 households in 1958 (see Table 6.1). Fewer than three-quarters (72.5 percent) of the 1989 population was forty-four years of age or younger (versus 82.8 percent in 1958), and the proportion of men had increased to 52 percent. This increase partially reflected a decline in male emigration and a rise in the migration of unmarried women to urban areas. It also reflected the return of male out-migrants to the village in search of business opportunities and work.

Further examination of the data suggests another way in which the villagers responded to change in the macroenvironment—they delayed family division, choosing to maintain more complex units. By 1989, conjugal households no longer predominated in Hsin Hsing; they comprised only 38 percent of all families (29 percent of the population), down from 66 percent in 1958. Fully 12 percent of households (16 percent of the population) were of the joint type, up from only 5 percent in 1958. The remaining 50 percent of families (55 percent of the population) lived under the stem arrangement, compared to only 29 percent in 1958. The reasons for this increase in complex families have been described in detail elsewhere.[23] Here, it is sufficient to note that the villagers believed this form of family organization provided a mechanism for achieving socioeconomic success in a changing world. A family that included many potential nonagricultural workers, as well as other members who could manage the household, supervise children, and care for the land, was able to diversify more easily than a small family.

The success of this strategy could be seen throughout the local area. Labor-intensive factories, service shops, retail stores, and construction companies blanketed the local terrain. By 1989, forty-seven enterprises had been established in the village, and resident families derived 85 percent of their income from off-farm employment. Nevertheless, fully 84 percent of all village households continued to do some farming, and families engaged in both farming and off-farm work were by far the most common.[24]

The transformation of the village economy thus altered the class structure of the community. In 1958, all but ten of the village families were owner-farmers; by 1989, the community was economically differentiated. It included members of the proletariat, who were protected by government labor codes and received wages determined by contract, and members of the subproletariat, who, because they were not benefiting from government legislation, received casual rather than protected wages. The community also included members of the petite bourgeoisie and the bourgeoisie: Each group owned the means of production, but the petit bourgeoisie did not hire wage labor, and the bourgeoisie had control over labor power. The multiple reasons for a specific family's location in this hierarchy defy easy generalization, but clearly, women's and men's roles in production and reproduction were integral to the hierarchy's formation. □

PRODUCTION AND REPRODUCTION IN HSIN HSING

One travels by bus from Lukang to Hsin Hsing on a cement road flanked by clusters of village houses, farmland, and more than fifty factories. These labor-intensive companies, which produce for foreign and domestic markets, include large establishments that manufacture mirrors and venetian blinds, medium-sized enterprises that produce furniture and clothing, and small factories and family workshops that either operate as subcontractors for larger firms or produce directly for the domestic market. In addition to the factories along the road, the area is dotted with other establishments that also produce commodities for foreign and domestic consumption. Many are located in or next to their owners' homes.

This was the case for all of the eleven factories and two workshops and for 89.5 percent of the nineteen sales and service shops owned by Hsin Hsing villagers.[25]

The diversity of these enterprises can be seen in Table 6.2, as can the tendency for these enterprises to be controlled on the basis of gender. Fully four-fifths of the village enterprises were owned by men, who also tended to operate businesses, that were larger in scale and more highly capitalized than those of women. Only one woman, the producer of sport-shoe tongues, owned a firm of a caliber comparable to those owned by men.

Nine of the factory owners produced for export. Eight were subcontractors whose production represented a subprocess in the creation of a final product for export, and one—the toy and novelty manufacturer—produced a complete product, which he exported with the help of a trading partner. Seven factory owners employed wageworkers, and one owner was the woman who produced shoe tongues. All these employers paid their male workers monthly wages and their female workers by the piece. "Women's hours are uncertain," one male employer explained, "sometimes they arrive late and leave early to take care of housework." Four of the factory owners also employed outworkers, supplying them with raw materials and paying them on a piece-rate basis at levels lower than the minimum wage (US$290 per month in 1989–1990).

Regardless of whether men employed outsiders, most were assisted in their businesses by family members, predominantly their wives. Indeed, only ten of the men operating businesses (25.6 percent) did so without waged or non-waged workers. Five of these men (the three itinerant vegetable sellers, the juice vendor, and the farm labor broker) worked outside the village, and four others were involved in gambling ventures. In one case, this latter undertaking was so successful that the man's wife had retired from her factory job to become a housekeeper.

TABLE 6.2   Enterprises Operated by Hsin Hsing Villagers, 1989–1990

	Number		Number
Factories and Workshops		*Sales and Services*	
Toys and novelties[a,b]	1	Grocery store[c]	4
Auto mirrors[a,b]	1	Barber shop[c]	1
Auto oil seals[a,b]	1	Beauty parlor	1
Decorative pillows	1	Motorcycle repair and sales	2
Umbrella frames[a,b]	1	Tailor shop	1
Nylon athletic rope finishing[a]	1	Chinese medicine shop	1
Suitcase construction	1	Pinball parlor[c]	1
Sport shoe tongues[a,b,c]	1	Pesticide shop	1
Metal finishing[a,b]	2	Betel nut vending[c]	3
Custom iron springs[a,b]	1	Taxi service	1
Wire sealing[a]	1	Interior design and decoration[c]	1
Puffed rice candy and cereal	1	Fried chicken vending[c]	1
	13	Juice vending	1
Percent of total	27.7%		19
		Percent of total	40.4%
Agriculture Related			
Intinerant vegetable sales	3	*Other*	
Rice mill	1	Construction and masonry[b]	1
Grape farm	2	Gambling (numbers games)	4
Pig farm	1		5
Duck farm	1	Percent of total	10.6%
Vegetable farm	1		
Farm Labor Brokerage	1		
	10		
Percent of total	21.3%		

[a] The owners of these factories produced for export. With the exception of the man producing toys and novelties, all were subcontractors.

[b] With the exception of one metal finisher, the owners of these enterprises hired waged labor.

[c] With the exception of three grocery stores operated by men, these enterprises were operated by women.

Note: Total number 47 (100%).

The only other man who worked alone owned a tiny grocery store, and his wife was a full-time factory laborer. Women entrepreneurs, in contrast, tended to manage their businesses single-handedly. Seven (87.5 percent) of the eight women owning businesses operated small-scale enterprises, which they ran by themselves.

Because village enterprises tended to be owned by men, it was not surprising to find that over one-quarter (28.4 percent) of the married men in the village identified themselves as entrepreneurs (and farm marketers) in comparison to fewer than one-tenth (6.7 percent) of the married women (see Table 6.3).[26] Similarly, it was not surprising to find that married women were four times more likely than men to be workers in a family business and to report that they were working without wages.

Only two (10.5 percent) of the nineteen women working in family businesses were paid for their efforts; both were newly married women who worked for their fathers-in-law, and each received US$75 per month for her labor. Three of the five men working in family businesses (60 percent), in contrast, were paid for their efforts; one was an unmarried son who, his father reported, "needed money for entertainment," and the other two were married men who were partners in a business with their married sister. Because the sister was no longer a member of her birth family—having severed formal ties with her father's household at marriage—the three siblings divided their profits and paid themselves salaries.

Women who worked without wages frequently voiced dissatisfaction with the arrangement. For some, dissatisfaction was rooted in the knowledge that others were paid for performing similar work and often for working fewer hours. As one forty-seven-year-old woman said: "I work eight hours a day and if we're busy I ... might work until one or two in the morning. When you export, you must meet deadlines. The only difference between me and the workers is that I don't get a wage." Other women were dissatisfied because, as the women just quoted observed, their husbands were withholding a resource that they believed gave a woman a degree of control over her life and a measure of self-respect. Still other women who worked without wages (as well as women who worked for wages) resented the inequitable division of labor imposed by the arrangement. As one thirty-six-year-old woman reported, "Women have two jobs—work and housework. A husband only has one job. It's not fair."

Although this woman's analysis of the gender division of labor in the village was correct, few married women identified themselves as housekeepers since such tasks fell within the traditionally accepted purview of wives and mothers. Indeed, only one-fifth (22.5 percent) reported that they did housework.[27] This was because most women had entered what traditionally was considered men's spheres of production—the agricul-

TABLE 6.3   Primary Occupation of Married Hsin Hsing Villagers by Gender,[a]
1989–1990

	Male		Female		Row Totals	
	Number	%	Number	%	Number	%
Wage worker	39 (35.8%)[b]	40.6	57 (47.5%)	59.4	96	41.9
Entrepreneur	11 (23.8%)	76.7	8 (6.7%)	23.5	34	14.8
Worker in family business	5 (4.6%)	19.2	21 (17.5%)	80.8	26	11.4
Farmer/Marketer	5 (4.6%)	100.0	–	–	5	2.2
Farmer	27 (24.8%)	71.1	11 (9.2%)	28.9	38	16.6
Soldier	2 (1.8%)	100.0	–	–	2	0.9
Housekeeper	–	–	13 (10.8%)	100.0	13	5.7
Retiree	5 (4.6%)	33.3	10 (8.3%)	66.7	15	6.5
Totals	109	47.6	120	52.4	229	100.0

[a] In addition to the married villagers, the figures include five widowed men and twenty-one separated women and widows.

[b] Figures in parentheses represent column percentages.

tural and industrial sectors. Men and women, however, tended to occupy different economic spaces in these sectors.

For example, women were less likely than men to report that they were farmers; rather, they identified themselves as auxiliary farm workers.[28] Women, however, were one-and-one-half times more likely than men to say that they worked for others. (If women who worked without wages in family firms were included, this ratio would increase to two to one.) Moreover, the types of jobs men and women held were different (see Table 6.4).

Twenty-six women identified themselves as domestic-based outworkers, in comparison to only one man, a widower without adult children in the village. More women than men also reported that they held jobs that were classified as unskilled, and men were six times as likely as women to be white-collar workers and more than three times as likely to be skilled blue-collar workers. For example, although three women and four

TABLE 6.4 Type of Off-Farm Employment of Married Hsin Hsing Villagers Working for Wages, by Gender, 1989–1990 [a]

	Male		Female		Row Totals	
	Number	%	Number	%	Number	%
Factory	19 (48.7%)[b]	42.2	26 (45.6%)	57.8	45	46.9
Other blue collar[c]	11 (28.2%)	78.6	3 (5.3%)	21.4	14	14.6
White collar work[d]	8 (20.5%)	80.0	2 (3.5%)	20.0	10	10.4
Homework	1 (2.6%)	3.7	26 (45.6)	96.3	27	28.1
Totals	39	40.6	57	59.4	96	100.0

[a] Includes five widowed men and twenty-one separated women and widows.

[b] Figures in parentheses represent column percentages.

[c] This category includes construction workers, artisans, and line supervisors in factories.

[d] This category includes practical nurses, clerical, workers and minor officials in banking and government.

men worked in construction, the men were, as one woman explained, "masters" (bricklayers and plasterers), but the women were "helpers" (brick and sand carriers). This difference in classification may, in part, explain why women were paid less than men. "They make less money," in the words of a forty-six-year-old factory worker, "because they do lighter work. If more strength is needed to do the job, then the worker will get more pay." Although this woman did not complete her syllogism, its logical conclusion was that strong men accordingly made more money than weak women. This explanation, however, sidesteps the contexts in which village men and women lived. □

POLITICAL, SOCIAL, AND ECONOMIC CONTEXTS OF PRODUCTION AND REPRODUCTION

Because the economy of Taiwan is inextricably linked to the world capitalist system, it depends heavily on foreign trade and is extremely vulnerable to international market fluctuations. Accordingly, to ensure its advantage in the world economy, Taiwan's government has striven to maintain a favorable investment climate, including political stability and low wage rates, in order to discourage domestic and foreign investors from seeking a low-cost labor force elsewhere.[29] This policy has had profound effects on the political, social, and economic contexts in which villagers existed.

Political Context

The government has passed a series of laws to restrict workers' rights.[30] The Labor Union Law, for example, includes provisions that severely limit the right to organize and bargain collectively; the Labor Dispute Law prohibits strikes. The Labor Standards Law, in contrast, guarantees workers' rights, such as minimum wages, pensions, benefits, pay equity, and occupational safety and health. But this law covers only a small proportion of the island's workers, primarily because it exempts workplaces with fewer than thirty employees. Moreover, passage of the law in 1984 did little to improve workers' conditions. The minimum wage it mandates per month is less than the amount needed to maintain a minimally adequate standard of living, and the benefits it guarantees apply only to workers and not to their dependents.

Provisions for pay equity and pensions included in the Labor Standards Law are rarely enforced. The Taiwanese government relies on management's voluntary compliance, imposing only extremely light fines for infractions of the law. Further, the government grants industry considerable latitude in choosing strategies that will encourage productivity and discourage labor unrest.[31] In combination, government regulations and guidelines erect powerful barriers to equitable labor relations, thereby creating an attractive investment environment.

Other laws and policies enhance the attractiveness of Taiwan's business environment by affirming the ideological precepts of traditional Chinese culture. For example, equal rights for women are incorporated in the constitution, but family law places women at a decided disadvantage.[32] Women's rights are subordinated to those of men, and a woman has no legal claim to a share in family decisions. This subordination is reinforced through the ideological messages delivered by the educational system and the media. Public discourse defines a woman's primary roles as wife and mother and a man's as husband and worker. The law and the government's ideological apparatus, in short, create conditions necessary for molding women (and men) into the kind of workforce that the political economy requires.

Social Context

In Taiwan, this formative process is borne by the family, and mothers and fathers in Hsin Hsing were eminently qualified to discharge the responsibility. Imbued with the patriarchal prejudices of the traditional Chinese family, they taught their daughters by word and deed that they were subordinate to men, and they socialized their sons to believe that they were superior to women. Moreover, they anticipated that the women who entered their households as the brides of their sons had received similar training, and they expected them to conform to traditional definitions of "proper womanhood."

Mirroring a saying of Confucius, villagers often remarked that a proper woman's main virtues are "obedience, timidity, reticence, [and] adaptability."[33] In addition, they believed a proper woman accepted the presumption that, as one thirty-four-year-old man claimed, she would be "the first to rise and the last to go to bed" and that her interests would be subjugated to the success and requirements of her husband and her children. A proper woman, in short, acquiesced to the "shoulds" and "oughts" considered a natural counterpart to female existence and acknowledged that her life was marked by "compromise, compromise, compromise," as a twenty-nine-year-old woman declared. Village men and women had thoroughly internalized these norms, as their definitions of a "good wife" illustrated. Domestic work was women's work, and men were unwilling to accept responsibility for it. Rather, they identified productive labor as their primary role, as one twenty-eight-year-old man confirmed: "Men aren't willing to do housework. If you asked ten men, you wouldn't find three willing to do housework. I wouldn't do it. I don't have the patience to do it. [Why?] In the old days, the men farmed and the women took care of the house. If I stayed in the house, I would think I was inferior. Women have to do housework. It's the traditional way. It's *natural* for a man to earn money. I would not stay home."

Domestic work was also women's work because, as this young man illustrated, villagers believed that society was constructed in such a way that it was "natural" for women, as wives and mothers, to assume all responsibility for the maintenance of the household and family. Nevertheless, although reproduction was an integral part of the wife and mother roles, neither women nor men disassociated these roles from the work role. Working was central to the wife-mother role, and a good wife, according to a twenty-nine-year-old factory worker, "helps her husband with whatever he needs. If a husband can't do something, then the wife has to help. [Help?] Work and make money. Everyone agrees that you should make money. Women don't have to ask their husbands when they go out to work. If they have small children, they do piecework at home to earn money. There's no need to discuss going to work since you work to make money. The money is for family living." Working off-farm, then, fell within the definition of "proper wifehood" and also was seen as necessary, legitimate, and an integral part of caring for the family.

Cash was required to care for the family because the rural economy was highly commoditized. The money that entered the household in the form of husbands' earnings, however, often was not adequate to pay for the wide range of household expenditures incurred monthly by village families. Women therefore had to work to secure a basic standard of living for the family, education for their children, or long-term security. Women, moreover, usually had to assume responsibility for managing the family budget.[34] Administration of this treasury, however, did not imply control.[35] Women consistently reported that their husbands decided not only what was necessary but also what was basic—and that men's definitions of what constituted basic expenditures were considerably different from women's definitions. As a result, many women echoed the complaint of one forty-three-year-old wage laborer, who noted that managing the budget was "a big worry—really a big responsibility. A woman has to be very smart to handle this responsibility. She has to know what the family needs most. A man doesn't really know if the family needs something or not. If there's not enough money she must figure out how to get it. If the family needs something desperately and there is not enough money, she must borrow money."

Perhaps because they had to borrow money or spend their own earnings to cover cash shortages, many women said they did not have *sai khia*, or private money. Nevertheless, a few village women, because of their families' relatively stable economic conditions, were able to retain their earnings.[36] These caches of funds served two important functions: They enabled women to create a minimum space for control over their lives, and they helped them to gain a measure of self-respect. These functions are illustrated well in the following quotes. One woman entrepreneur, thirty-four years of age, noted that "When a woman has *sai khia*, she can have her own opinion. She can speak louder. If she wants something, she can say, 'I'm using my own money!'" Similarly, a twenty-nine-year-old woman who worked in a family business but received no wages, stated that "if you have *sai khia* you don't have to ask your husband for money. You can have self-esteem. You don't have to be raised—like a child—by your husband."

Work for wages, then, gave some women control over money, offering them the means to negotiate certain male prerogatives embedded in the conjugal relationship. Although other women were unable to realize this benefit, their waged work nonetheless improved their chances to attain their goals—subsistence, the well-being of the household (particularly that of their children), and long-term security. In both women's and men's view, women's productive labor was critical to the maintenance and viability of the family and was central to the wife-mother role.

Economic Context

Women and men carried these ingrained understandings about female and male roles to the workplace. In addition, they brought with them very different personality traits that gave men, but not women, a decided advantage in their dealings with employers. A sixty-two-year-old factory worker illustrated this difference well. I had visited the mirror factory where she was employed and had seen her and a male coworker laboring together to transfer very large and heavy mirrors from the floor to a hoist. When I visited with her later, she offered the following explanation for men's and women's assignments to different positions in the labor force and their different wage rates. "Men get more money because they ask for more money. If they didn't get more money, they would change their jobs. Men are stronger and therefore can move things [countering what I had seen earlier]. There's a division of labor: Men do big jobs; women do small jobs. There's no way [to change the division of labor and unequal wage rates]. It's useless to ask for a raise. They won't pay attention if I ask for a raise. Also [and she smiled], it saves money to let women do certain work." This woman clarified how the socialization process plays itself out in adult behavior and how capital benefits from women's low-cost labor.

In addition, she suggested yet another possible reason why women's wages were lower than those of men. By indicating that employers meet men's demands and ignore those of women, she proposed a gender logic that employers used to suppress women's wages relative to those of men. This "gender logic" refers to the tactics managers use to promote hierarchy in the workplace, thereby controlling and dividing workers.[37] Local managers were authorities in this strategy. They consistently invoked and reinforced existing ideas about women's roles and subordinate position, encoded in public and private ideologies, to explain the organization of business in the area. For example, employers used villagers' understandings of men's and women's capacities to assign them different responsibilities. "Women are weaker than men and can't do big and heavy jobs," one manager offered in explaining job segregation in the factory.[38] Another reported that "women are better than men at jobs which require patience," an ability critical to the successful completion of work in the venetian blind factory that he managed.

Managers, however, paid women who had this skill less than they paid men who did not. On the one hand, they paid women less than men because they believed that "men have to raise families" and thus required higher wages than women. On the other, they paid women less because they regarded women's primary roles to be those of the wife and mother, even when women were full-time workers. Accordingly, managers assumed that women worked to supplement their husbands' incomes, and they used this presumption to justify paying women low wages.

Managers were also able to hire women at low wages because they played on women's own consciousness as wives and mothers. Women entered the off-farm labor force with the ideology of "proper woman-hood" thoroughly internalized. Managers therefore could pay them less than men because women did not identify themselves primarily as workers; rather, they saw themselves as wives and mothers who were caring for the family. Although the women of Hsin Hsing invariably spoke to the unfairness of the female-male wage disparity, they accepted it as their fate. They did not expect that women would be paid the high wages that men received.

In sum, managers "gendered" the workplace through job segregation and separate wage rates. They used existing gender ideology to depict women as "weak" and tractable and men as "strong" and demanding, thereby legitimating the organization of work and its different rewards. Women and men workers rarely challenged these ideas: Men benefited from them, and women expected to be treated differently because they were women. This situation, however, resulted in deskilled and lower paying jobs for women and skilled and higher paying jobs for men. □

CONCLUSION

In this chapter, I have examined the ways in which the intersection of gender ideologies encoded in family conventions, state policy, and mana-gerial practices shapes patterns of production at the local level. This study revealed that in Taiwan, women and men were incorporated into the labor process in different and unequal ways. Further, the gender divi-sion of labor masked important aspects of the relations of production— relations were "engendered" on the basis of crucial assumptions about women and men. The government of Taiwan actively encourages gender ideology based on female domesticity to promote its comparative advan-tage in the global economy, families teach and impose this ideology to ensure their survival or mobility, and management appropriates this ide-ology to reap the rewards of industrial capitalism. I have argued that this ideological bonding of the public and private has systematically con-strained women's options while expanding those of men.

Nevertheless, strands in the interview excerpts I have quoted suggest that the incorporation of women into the labor process also brings with it the possibility of change. Money can be a mechanism that imposes and reproduces hierarchical structures. However, it can also be a mechanism that modifies gender relations within the family. Although only a few women—primarily young women—controlled their earnings in the village, their access to an income provided them with an extremely important base from which to challenge absolute financial dependence on their husbands—a dimension of the conjugal relationship they judged oppressive. Women's control of their earnings thus has the potential to erode traditional ideology and its norms of behavior and to provide women with the resources necessary to create an autonomous space.[39]

Is it possible to generalize from the Taiwan case presented here? Unique historical and cultural factors were responsible for the Taiwan "miracle." Nevertheless, recent analyses of global economic restructuring and employment generation resonate with images of the Taiwan experience.[40] "There is a global trend to reduced reliance on full-time wage and salary workers earning fixed wages and fringe benefits. ... [The quest for] flexible low-cost labor has encouraged industrial enterprises everywhere to reduce their fixed wage labor force, make payment systems more flexible and use more contract workers, temporary labor and out-sourcing through use of homeworking or subcontracting to small informal enterprises that are not covered by labor or other regulations."[41] Informalization and fragmentation of the labor process in both industrialized and industrializing nations have spurred the rapid growth of low-wage female employment.[42] And as the Taiwan case shows, the incorporation of women into areas of production that lack the capacity for developing skills and accumulating of capital is not accidental.

The feminization of labor reflects the desire to have a more disposable or flexible labor force with lower fixed costs. Women have very specific characteristics that make them vulnerable and that allow companies to enforce their own demands. Women's compliance with these demands is generated through complex processes in which they learn to accept an image of themselves as less important than men. This image, reproduced within the family and imposed by state institutions and managerial practices, is an effective form of control that is difficult—but not impossible—to contest. □

NOTES

Research for this chapter was carried out in collaboration with Bernard Gallin, whose insights helped me immeasurably. We acknowledge with thanks the organizations that provided financial assistance over the years and made possible our field trips to Taiwan. Specifically, funding was provided by a Foreign Area Training Fellowship (Ford Foundation), Fulbright-Hays Research Grants, the Asian Studies Center at Michigan State University, the Mid-West Universities Consortium for International Activities, the American Council of Learned Societies, the Social Sciences Research Council, and the Pacific Cultural Foundation. We are also grateful to the Chiang Ching-kuo Foundation for funding (1992–1994) to analyze our data and to our graduate assistants, Ross Gardner and Chun-hao Li, for their invaluable help.

1. See, among others, Lourdes Benería and Shelley Feldman, eds., *Unequal Burden: Economic Crises, Persistent Poverty, and Women's Work* (Boulder: Westview Press, 1992); Lourdes Benería and Martha Roldán, *The Crossroads of Class and Gender: Industrial Homework, Subcontracting, and Household Dynamics in Mexico City* (Chicago: University of Chicago Press, 1987); Sharon Stichter and Jane L. Parpart, eds., *Women, Employment, and the Family in the International Division of Labour* (Philadelphia: Temple University Press, 1990); Kathryn Ward, ed., *Women Workers and Global Restructuring* (Ithaca: ILR Press, 1990).

2. For a review, see Sharon Stichter, "Women, Employment, and the Family: Current Debates," in Stichter and Parpart, eds., *Women, Employment, and the Family in the International Division of Labour.*

3. Here ideology is taken to mean an active formulation of specific aspects of worldviews that (1) incorporate values, norms, and knowledge, and (2) are assertions of what people consider important and natural, honorable and good, and dishonorable and bad. Ideologies legitimate action and are involved in the formation of personal identity.

4. Alison MacEwen Scott, "Informal Sector or Female Sector? Gender Bias in Urban Labour Markets," in Diane Elson, ed., *Male Bias in the Development Process* (New York: St. Martin's Press, 1991); Sallie Westwood, "Gender and the Politics of Production in India," in Haleh Afshar, ed., *Women, Development and Survival in the Third World* (New York: Longman, 1991).

5. John Humphrey, "Gender, Pay, and Skill: Manual Workers in Brazilian Industry," in Haleh Afshar, ed., *Women, Work and Ideology in the Third World* (London: Tavistock, 1985); Kuniko Fujita, "Gender, State, and Industrial Policy in Japan," *Women's Studies International Forum* 10, no. 6 (1987): 589–597.

6. For an exception, see Helen I. Safa, "Women and Industrialization in the Caribbean," in Stichter and Parpart, eds., *Women, Employment, and the Family in the International Division of Labour.*

7. The research covers the period from 1957 to 1990. The first field trip, in 1957–1958, involved a seventeen-month residence in the village. This was followed by two separate studies, in 1965–1966 and 1969–1970, of out-migrants from the area. Subsequent field trips to the village spanned two months in 1977, six months in 1979, one month in 1982, and eight months in 1989–1990. During these visits, colleague Bernard Gallin and I collected data using both anthropological and sociological techniques, including participant observation, in-depth interviews, surveys, and collection of official statistics contained in family, land, school, and economic records.

8. Min-jen Lu, "Promotion of Constitutional Democracy Government's Goal," *Free China Journal*, October 5, 1987, 2.

9. Douglas Sease, "U.S. Firms Fuel Taiwan's Trade Surplus," *Asian Wall Street Journal*, June 8, 1987, 1.

10. Samuel P.S. Ho, *The Rural Non-Farm Sector in Taiwan*, Studies in Employment and Rural Development no. 32 (Washington, DC: International Bank for Reconstruction and Development, 1976). Ho explains the dispersal of industry to

the countryside as a product of industry's desire to be near the sources of low-cost labor and raw materials. Though this is true, the government encouraged the movement by refraining from protecting agricultural land until the goal of industrialization had been achieved and farm productivity had declined. In November 1975, the government promulgated a law barring the use of certain agricultural land (i.e., grades 1–24) for purposes other than farming. Before the passage of this law, only land grades 1–12 had been regulated and protected.

11. Walden Bello and Stephanie Rosenfeld, *Dragons in Distress: Asia's Miracle Economies in Crisis* (San Francisco: Institute for Food and Development, 1990), 219.

12. Directorate-General of Budget, Accounting and Statistics (DGBAS), *Yearbook of Manpower Statistics, Taiwan Area, Republic of China* (Taipei: Executive Yuan, 1988), 116–117. The definition of size varies in the literature on Taiwan. Ho, "The Rural Non-Farm Sector in Taiwan," defines a small business as one with fewer than ten workers, a medium business as one with ten to ninety-nine workers, and a large business as one with 100 workers or more. In contrast, Richard Stites, "Small-Scale Industry in Yingge, Taiwan," *Modern China* 8 (1982), 248, defines a small business as having 100 or fewer workers, and Thomas Gold, *State and Society in the Taiwan Miracle* (New York: M.E. Sharpe, 1986), 141, note 16, defines a large business as one with more than 300 workers. For the purposes of this chapter, a small business is defined as one with fewer than thirty workers (such businesses are not protected by government regulations), a medium business is defined as one with thirty to ninety-nine workers, and a large business as one with 100 workers or more.

13. Bello and Rosenfeld, *Dragons in Distress*, 241.

14. Susan Greenhalgh, "Microsocial Processes in the Distribution of Income," paper prepared for the Taiwan Political Economy Workshop, East Asia Institute, Columbia University, New York, December 18–20, 1980, 13.

15. "Hard to Slow a Rich Man Down in the ROC," *Free China Journal*, August 11, 1988, 3; Wey Hsiao, "Changes in Class Structure and Rewards Distribution in Postwar Taiwan," in Robert V. Robinson, ed., *Research in Social Stratification and Mobility*, vol. 6 (Greenwich, CT: JAI Press, 1987); Diana Lin, "Real Estate Divides Rich From Poor," *Free China Journal*, June 4, 1993, 4.

16. Despite implementation of the Land Reform Program and changes in the tenancy to ownership ratio, most families cultivated small farms: 45 percent of village families cultivated less than 0.5 hectare, and 84 percent cultivated between 0.5 and 1.0 hectare (1 hectare equals approximately 2.47 acres). For a detailed description, see Bernard Gallin, *Hsin Hsing, Taiwan: A Chinese Village in Change* (Berkeley: University of California Press, 1966).

17. Bernard Gallin and Rita S. Gallin, "The Integration of Village Migrants in Taiwan," in Mark Elvin and G. William Skinner, eds., *The Chinese City Between Two Worlds* (Stanford: Stanford University Press, 1974).

18. Council for Economic Planning and Development (CEPD), *Taiwan Statistical Data Book* (Taipei: Council for Economic Planning and Development, Executive Yuan, 1979), 59.

19. Shu-min Huang, *Agricultural Degradation: Changing Community Systems in Rural Taiwan* (Washington, DC: University Press of America, 1981), 3.

20. Terry Y.H. Yu, "The Accelerated Rural Development Program in Taiwan," in *Industry of Free China, Council for Economic Planning and Development* (Taipei: Council for Economic Planning and Development, Executive Yuan, 1977).

21. CEPD, *Taiwan Statistical Data Book*, 78.

22. Huang, *Agricultural Degradation*, 163.

23. Bernard Gallin and Rita S. Gallin, "Socioeconomic Life in Rural Taiwan: Twenty Years of Development and Change," *Modern China* 8 (1982): 205–246; Bernard Gallin and Rita S. Gallin, "The Chinese Joint Family in Changing Rural Taiwan," in Sidney L. Greenblatt, Richard W. Wilson, and Amy Auerbacher Wilson, eds., *Social Interaction in Chinese Society* (New York: Praeger, 1982); Rita S. Gallin, "The Entry of Chinese Women into the Rural Labor Force: A Case Study from Taiwan," *Signs* 9 (1984): 383–398; Rita S. Gallin, "Mothers-in-Law and Daughters-in-Law: Intergenerational Relations in the Chinese Family in Taiwan," *Journal of Cross-Cultural Gerontology* 1 (1986): 31–49.

24. The change in the villagers' mode of production was not simply a response to rural industrialization. Despite implementation of new policies, agriculture remained an unprofitable venture; on the average, Hsin Hsing farmers realized less than US$50 from the rice they grew on 1 hectare of land in 1989. Nevertheless, they continued to cultivate the land because (1) it was a source of food (rice); (2) the mechanization and chemicalization of agriculture obviated the need for either a large or a physically strong labor force; and (3) the decreased size of family farms—in 1989 the average acreage tilled per farming household was 0.63 hectares—required less labor. For Taiwan as a whole, the average acreage tilled was 0.79 hectares, see "As Taiwan Modernizes, Agriculture's Face Wrinkles," *Free China Journal*, August 9, 1990, 3.

25. The fried chicken and juice vending businesses were operated outside the village.

26. The number of entrepreneurs in Table 6.3 and the number of enterprises in Table 6.2 do not correspond because several men operated more than one business. For example, a man involved in a gambling venture also operated one of the grocery stores and the Chinese medicine shop. Another was a subcontractor for both the umbrella frames business and the nylon athletic rope finishing operation.

27. In addition to the thirteen women who identified housekeeping as their primary activity, fourteen others reported it as their second activity. To determine the occupations of villagers, we asked two questions: What do you do most of the time? What else do you do?

28. All farmers were, with one exception, over fifty years of age. The exception was a thirty-four-year-old man who operated a gambling venture and whose wife identified herself as a housekeeper. Farming was the work of older villagers because young people, as one woman reported, "don't like to work in the fields. Therefore, the older villagers must do it. Their daughters-in-law are busy with their work and so [older villagers] must do it."

29. Wages have been rising in Taiwan, reaching US$494 per month on August 13, 1993, and many local manufacturers have "gone offshore" to decrease their wage bill. The increase in wage rates, however, has not slowed foreign investment in the island. Presumably, the population's high levels of education, relative to that of people in other countries in Asia, have been more important to capital than

the cost of labor. The government was well aware of the links between education and development when it made junior high school free and "compulsory" in 1969.

30. Until July 15, 1987, Taiwan was under martial law on the grounds that the province was engaged in civil war against the mainland People's Republic of China. The lifting of "emergency controls" and changes in labor laws, however, have not altered "the basic pattern of industrial relations"; see Marc J. Cohen, *Taiwan at the Crossroads* (Washington, DC: Asia Resource Center, 1988), 128.

31. Rita S. Gallin, "Women and the Export Industry in Taiwan: The Muting of Class Consciousness," in Ward, ed., *Women Workers and Global Restructuring.*

32. Lan-hung Nora Chiang and Yenlin Ku, *Past and Current Status of Women in Taiwan,* Women's Research Program Monograph no. 1 (Taipei: Population Studies Centre, National Taiwan University, 1985), 12–21.

33. Cited in Olga Lang, *Chinese Family and Society* (New Haven: Yale University Press, 1946), 43.

34. The allocation of the earnings of a woman and her husband took one of three basic patterns: pooling, the housekeeping allowance, and the joint family budget; see Gallin and Gallin, "The Chinese Joint Family in Changing Rural Taiwan." In all three patterns, however, husbands often deposited or turned over only a portion of their earnings, retaining indefinite amounts for their personal use.

35. See also Lydia Morris, *The Workings of the Household* (Cambridge: Basil Blackwell, 1990), 106; Ursula Sharma, "Public Employment and Private Relations: Women and Work in India," in Stichter and Parpart, eds., *Women, Employment, and the Family in the International Division of Labour,* 241.

36. Although married women "owned" their *sai khia* (husbands have no rights to their wives' private money), most used it either for family living expenses or to provide venture capital for their husbands' (rather than their own) enterprises. Only two of the women entrepreneurs in the village—the owner of the beauty parlor and the woman who produced sport-shoe tongues—had used their *sai khia* to establish their businesses. In the latter case, the woman's father-in-law bought the land on which she erected her factory.

37. Karen J. Hossfeld, "Their Logic Against Them: Contradictions in Sex, Race, and Class in Silicon Valley," in Ward, ed., *Women Workers and Global Restructuring,* 157.

38. Workers sometimes used this logic to obtain release from a task they did not want to do. One women reported, "We say 'You can't ask us to do this. We're too weak to do this.'"

39. Rae Lesser Blumberg, "Introduction: The Triple Overlap of Gender Stratification, Economy, and the Family," in Rae Lesser Blumberg, ed., *Gender, Family, and Economy: The Triple Overlap* (Newbury Park, CA: Sage Publications, 1991).

40. Arthur MacEwan and William K. Tabb, eds., *Instability and Change in the World Economy* (New York: Monthly Review Press, 1989); Nanneke Redclift and Enzo Mingione, eds., *Beyond Employment: Household, Gender and Subsistence* (Oxford: Basil Blackwell, 1985).

41. Guy Standing, "Global Feminization Through Flexible Labor," *World Development* 17, no. 7 (1989): 1079.

42. Alejandro Portes, Manuel Castells, and Lauren Benton, eds., *The Informal Economy: Studies in Advanced and Less Developed Countries* (Baltimore: Johns Hopkins University Press, 1989); Priscilla Connolly, "The Politics of the Informal Sector: A Critique," in Redclift and Mingione, eds., *Beyond Employment*; Lourdes Benería, "Subcontracting and Employment Dynamics in Mexico City," in Portes, Castells, and Benton, eds., *The Informal Economy*; Standing, "Global Feminization Through Flexible Labor."

■

CHAPTER SEVEN

Macroeconomic Policies and Gender Relations: The Study of Farming Households in Two Turkish Villages

Behrooz Morvaridi

HOUSEHOLD-LEVEL DYNAMICS IN FARMING FAMILIES reflect both established patterns of gendered power relations and the impact of macroeconomic policies on resource allocation and use. Therefore, two inextricably related levels of analysis are essential to conceptualize changing gender relations in farm households. The first is the analysis of intrahousehold relations: how men and women negotiate, how decisions on the economic and social aspects of household life are made, and how resources are distributed among and controlled by household members. The second is the analysis of the impact of macroeconomic policies on household relations. In this chapter, I will apply this dual analysis to a comparative study of farming households in two Turkish villages and of the impacts of macroeconomic policies implemented by the state Sugar Corporation. The analysis considers linkages between structural adjustment and household dynamics, especially how the gender division of labor, local culture, and systems of power relations mediate household responses to changes in the wider economy. □

MACROECONOMIC POLICIES, STRUCTURAL ADJUSTMENT, AND GENDER RELATIONS: FRAMEWORK FOR ANALYSIS

If policymakers attempt to integrate women into development, it is typically as a resource for development. However, for the most part, development plans and macroeconomic policies ignore the issue of gender, even when policies target household resource allocation and use. Although apparently gender neutral, plans and policies actually incorporate stereotypes and assumptions regarding gender roles. As a result, their impact is different for men and women. Structural adjustment policies provide a good example.[1]

Structural adjustment refers to a package of restrictive monetary and fiscal policies, such as cutbacks in public expenditure and the promotion of exports to service national debts and to ease balance-of-payments problems. Reforms in agriculture include changes in agricultural pricing policies, reduction or elimination of certain agricultural input subsidies, and the gradual phasing out of state marketing boards in favor of market liberalization. Moreover, structural adjustment has a direct—and gendered—impact on farming households and leads to changes in working conditions.[2]

The literature on macroeconomic reforms and structural adjustment shows that some attention has been paid to the role of gender issues in structural adjustment policy making. A number of World Bank documents, for instance, stress how women shift from one sector to another under structural adjustment in ways that increase economic efficiency. Some documents discuss the need for improved access to education, training, and technology to expand women's opportunities in the market. Other documents of the World Bank and the United Nations International Children's Emergency Fund (UNICEF) consider the "human face" of adjustment and support redressing the negative side of policies by ameliorating their impact on the poor. Identified effects include declining living standards, child malnutrition, and greater work burdens for women. Proposals to alleviate poverty and negative impacts tend to target women and extremely poor households during the period of adjustment.[3]

Nonetheless, this show of concern over structural adjustment's impact on women fails to address the fact that plans and policies affect women at the intrahousehold level and through the division of labor. How households respond to policies and how women are affected also depend on intrahousehold gender relations, not just on economic and cultural factors outside the household. For instance, in settings where structural adjustment policies add to the pressures on small farming households for accumulation and survival, the burden of achieving greater efficiency and economizing often falls on women. Some policymakers recognize this and explicitly value women's role in ameliorating the impact of structural adjustment because of women's "ability to devise and implement survival strategies for their families, using their unpaid labor to absorb adverse effects of structural adjustment policies."[4]

But since structural adjustment and other macroeconomic policies "are not explicitly conceptualized in terms of the operations of households ... the economists engaged in this know little or nothing about household ... processes."[5] After all, knowledge of the internal workings of the household does not inform neoclassical economics.

There is an additional obstacle to developing gender-sensitive macroeconomic and structural adjustment policies. Economists have tended to treat the household as a single unit in analyzing decision-making behavior. The assumption is that household members subordinate their individual needs to the pursuit of common household goals. Resulting policies ignore the reality that the behavior of individuals within the household reflects specific gender and age differences and that these are the essence of hierarchical, unequal intrahousehold dynamics. Taking the household or the family as a single unit obscures conflict and inequality in the home and the power relations implicit in the gender division of labor.[6]

In most farm households of developing countries, the ideology of patriarchy sustains the division of labor between men and women in the production process. (By definition, patriarchy is understood here to mean the material and ideological domination of women's sexuality and labor both in the home and at work).[7] For instance, in many settings, the eldest male household member is, by definition, the household head. He dominates access to capital, land, and other means of production and organizes and directs agricultural production. This gendered authority structure can be reinforced by external agencies and by state marketing boards and credit institutions that deal with him alone, even when other household members are critical participants in agricultural production. The result is limited access to resources by other household members and increasing pressures on male household heads to exploit other family members. This has been the case in Turkey and is the subject of this chapter.

The Turkish Case Studies

The Turkish case studies presented in this chapter highlight state agency practices in the commercialization of small family farms, the implementation of structural adjustment programs, variation in gender relations across rural communities, and their combined outcome on farming households. I collected the data in 1983 and 1990 in eastern and western Turkey. The two villages selected show cultivation and landholding patterns representative of their respective regions (all villages in those regions were visited).

In conducting household surveys, both structured and unstructured interviews were carried out, collectively and with individual household members. Most adult men in the villages were interviewed, but because of cultural restrictions, fewer women were interviewed. Women interviewed were identified through a referral process. After households were grouped by land-holding size, ten households were randomly selected from each village for more detailed study.

Background

Since 1961, state planning in Turkey has attemped to transform agriculture from subsistence to market production. By 1980, thirty-two agricultural products received subsidies and by the early 1980s, many family farms in Turkish villages had commercialized their farming, assisted by these subsidies and by credit facilities provided by government agencies. But many problems have plagued the transformation of agriculture, including late payment of subsidies from state agencies to farmers, late credit payments, and partial or delayed crop payments. In some cases, farmers have been forced to sell their crops at low prices to the private sector rather than to the higher paying state marketing board. Further, both state agencies and farmers have suffered from high rates of inflation, which averaged 50 percent per annum in the 1980s and as much as 70 percent per annum in the early 1990s.[8]

Financial difficulties, among other causes, led to a shift from import-substitution to export-oriented strategies as structural adjustment was initiated in the mid-1980s. This included an emphasis on the export of manufactured goods. However, the commercialization of agriculture continues to be an integral part of Turkey's overall economic strategies in the 1990s. Now, however, the goal is the full integration of farms into the market and the easing of their dependence on state subsidies and assistance. Subsidies and price support mechanisms have been cut back— perhaps prematurely. (For example, the number of subsidized agricultural commodities has been reduced from thirty-two to eighteen.) These actions have had an unfavorable effect on production and have threatened household income in many farming areas. Meanwhile, the government has been unsuccessful at cutting the budget deficit. These factors have exacerbated inflation, eroded real wages and farm earnings, worsened income distribution, and led to a squeeze on markets and credit. For many small farms, restricted access to credit has meant reduced access to inputs such as fertilizers and machinery on which production and income rely.[9] The consumption of capital inputs such as fertilizers, for instance, remained stable at 7 to 8 million tons between 1984 and 1990, despite the fact that the area cultivated actually increased from 16.6 million hectares in 1984 to 19 million hectares in 1990.[10]

Gender and Restructuring

The national economic plan and government programs that have transformed Turkish agriculture make little or no mention of their impact on women's work and welfare. This lack of recognition of women—often the predominant labor force in agriculture—reflects prevailing attitudes. Today, gender inequality persists, particularly in rural areas, despite the fact that Kemal Ataturk, the founder of modern Turkey, introduced major reforms including secularism and a Western-style civil code in 1921. These led to the abolishment of polygyny, increasing the minimum marrying age to fifteen for women and seventeen for men, and an amelioration in the inequality of divorce and inheritance laws. However, a woman still must live where her husband chooses and still must have her husband's permission to work outside the household. If she does not financially contribute to the household expenses, she is required to perform domestic chores. According to state law, therefore, the husband or father is the legal household head. It should come as no surprise, then, that according to the 1985 Turkish Population Census, men constituted 96.8 percent of all household heads (defined as the person responsible for the earnings, expenditures, and management of the household). Even in rural areas where women are major contributors to agricultural production, men still constitute 94.9 percent of all household heads.

Women made up 53.8 percent of the total labor force in agriculture, and 92 percent of women worked as unpaid family labor. An estimated 65 to 70 percent of all agricultural employment can be categorized as nonwaged, reflecting the importance of unpaid family labor in rural production. Some 30 to 35 percent of the wage labor is made up of people— both men and women—who are landless or are small landowners who hire themselves out to other farms in the peak seasons.[11]

Since women are rarely designated as household heads with the authority to directly influence and take advantage of changes in the production process, it is primarily through internal household relations that they influence and are affected by macroeconomic changes. Thus, when the state encouraged small farms to adopt a more intensive cropping system, cultural norms of patriarchal control led to a generalized attempt to increase the exploitation of unpaid female labor. This process is played out at the household level, with important differences between regions.

Intrahousehold Consequences
of Macroeconomic Transformation

Households are not independent arenas for mediation, exchange, and negotiation. National factors, such as family law and national economic plans, as well as regional factors contribute to the nonuniform impacts of structural adjustment policies and development plans across households. Among the most important mediating factors are regional and village-level characteristics, such as the level of development and degree of government intervention, ethnic and religious differences, local history and demographic characteristics, ecological factors, and so forth. For this reason, analyses of intrahousehold dynamics benefit from a comparative approach. These critical differences are reflected in the two villages compared in this chapter: Kahve Tepe is located in western Turkey, the country's most developed region, and Ak is located in eastern Turkey, the least developed area. Their infrastructural, demographic, economic, religious-ethnic, and cultural differences are outlined in the following sections. □

KAHVE TEPE

The village of Kahve Tepe is located in Biga Province. In 1990, it consisted of 250 people and 62 households, with an average of 4 members each. Although the inhabitants of Kahve Tepe are Turks, their ancestors originated in Circassia, north of the Caucasus Mountains on the Black Sea. Their descendants have preserved their Circassian culture and language, but they practice Sunni Islam, the official religion of Turkey. Infrastructure is well developed in this village: For example, farms use water pumps, and houses are built of cement and have plumbing.

In 1990, the total cultivated area of the village was 1,645 donum (10 donum = 1 hectare). Sugar beets, corn, beans, sunflowers, and wheat were Kahve Tepe's major crops. Development programs started in the village in the 1950s, and the state Sugar Corporation, which buys and markets sugar beets, was well established in the region. However, agricultural production in Kahve Tepe remained diversified, reducing dependence on the main export crop—sugar beets—and on the corporation as well. But then and now, the amount of area under sugar beet cultivation depends on the Sugar Corporation's strategy and on supply and demand factors.

In general, agricultural production is highly mechanized, and advanced technology is used for diverse crops and during all stages of the agricultural cycle in Kahve Tepe. There were six tractors and 1 combine-harvester in the village, and two farms had hoeing machines; farmers who did not own machinery hired equipment from others when necessary. A modern irrigation system and a good road to transport produce to market have favored agricultural programs in the village.

Gender Division of Labor in Kahve Tepe

Men are involved in plowing, preparing the land, irrigation, applying fertilizers and dealing with merchants and state agencies. Each household had at least one cow, usually milked by the mother of the family, and some milk was sold to merchants; women often had control over the money from the sale of this milk.[12] Although hoeing is, technically, a "woman's job," most families used a hoeing machine (which can be rented by the day) instead of female labor. Some households employed female labor from other villages, and in the poorest households, female members were pressured to work in the fields, although men sometimes joined in the hoeing and harvesting in peak seasons.

Women's status in Kahve Tepe is quite high by the standards of rural Turkey. No domestic violence was detected there, and before marriage, single girls were only expected to help their mothers in domestic work such as cooking. Furthermore, young women were mobile as long as they were unmarried. They could talk to boys and walk freely within and outside the confines of the village, and it was not unusual for girls and single women to have male friends. In a conversation with a group of women aged eighteen to twenty-two, I was told that

> we do not marry immediately. It takes a long time for us to choose our future husband. A marriage is unlikely without the girl's consent, but it is also difficult without the father's. If we see a boy, we ask to be introduced, and then we talk together. If, at the end of the day, we do not like each other, we remain just friends, and there is no obligation for marriage. Do not misunderstand us—we do not get close to them, we only talk so that we can get to know each other. We do not marry a boy because of his money but for his beliefs, and that is why it is important to take time to know each other. We can walk in the village together and talk about anything the boy asks. People who are not Circassian do not understand our culture. They gossip about us and think because our young girls talk to boys they are easily available. This has sometimes caused confrontation. We do not let them come to our weddings.

Life changes once a woman is married because men become more patriarchal toward their wives and significantly restrict their freedom of movement. Indeed married women cover their faces in public and cannot go anywhere unless accompanied by their husbands. They also dress in black as a sign of devotion to their husbands. And though unmarried women are not obliged to work on the farm, this also changes after marriage. If their labor is needed, married women are expected to work in agricultural production and in milking the cows, as well as in cooking and rearing children. In poorer households, married women might hoe the land, and they are the main source of labor for harvesting sugar beets and sunflowers. However, this only occurs if the family cannot hire daily female waged labor from other villages.

The cutbacks in subsidies and increases in the costs of agricultural inputs under structural adjustment programs have made it more difficult to rent a hoeing machine or hire waged labor. The labor of married women has become more important in farming, and women's burdens have increased. Some parents have turned to their unmarried daughters to meet their farm needs, which has resulted in serious confrontation and a transformation of household relations. One male head of household, complaining that he did not have power over his daughters, illustrated both the conflict that arises and the impact of local cultural norms regarding unmarried women's status and duties. He revealed that household heads "convince," rather than command compliance: "All our young girls do is make us a cup of tea. But if you ask them to help with the hoeing, they wouldn't. I am now in financial trouble because the merchants and the Sugar Corporation paid my crop money late. I asked my own daughter to finish hoeing 2.5 donum of my land. After hours of reasoning, she accepted, but it took four days to finish the hoeing, and this was with the help of four of her friends and some younger children. Two women could finish that piece of land in two days without difficulty."

Given the increased hardship in Kahve Tepe, many young people move away from the village to cities where they have relatives. During the 1980s, forty-two household members migrated to Istanbul and Izmir, and in particular, the number of unmarried women who choose to live in the cities has increased. A few families have migrated to Germany and then returned to the village to find wives for their sons. Young people, especially women, prefer to work outside the household and reject farming tasks.

Declining incomes linked to structural adjustment policies had other gender impacts. The late 1980s, for instance, saw an increase in the number of "kidnappings" of women (with their consent) by future husbands. One explanation for this is that the cost of the traditionally lavish wedding is increasingly high relative to income: Parents often cannot afford weddings. As one father explained: "In this day and age when our income is low and the prices of everything are high and getting higher, how could we afford to marry our children properly? They run away from the expenditure, and when they return, they visit the father of the bride, kiss his hand, and pay him $150 [as of 1991] as bride-price. The father then spends this money on their welfare. Before our incomes dropped, we did not have to worry about these things." Other reasons for kidnap marriages may include a young woman's desire to avoid farming tasks in poorer households in favor of marriage into a more prosperous household. □

THE VILLAGE OF AK

The village of Ak is located in the district of Igdir in Kars Province. The people are Azeri Turks, and they practice Shi'i Islam, similar to the religion practiced in Iran. The Shi'i are very conservative, and in their culture, religion, family, and community are very closely intertwined. At the time of this 1990 study, approximately 600 people resided in 105 households in Ak, with an average of 5.7 members per household. About 51 percent of the population was male, and most households were made up of extended families of brothers with their wives and children. Their elderly parents and unmarried sisters lived in a separate house on the same plot of land. Infrastructure is poorly developed, and houses are constructed of mud and hay and have flat roofs.

The village is highly stratified, with wealth concentrated among fewer families than was the case in Kahve Tepe. These few families control great tracts of land and have a monopoly over tractors and threshers. With the exception of the sons of wealthy families who go to cities to study, there was very little migration out of Ak. Although four families were landless at the time of the study, land was available for new farmers.

Farmers with low income from their own land frequently find jobs in and around the village at different points in the agricultural cycle. Some poor farmers engaged in seasonal temporary migration to work in the construction industry, and a few farmers left the village in the 1960s and early 1970s, migrating to Germany. The few who returned have set up small businesses in the village. The village was targeted by the Sugar Corporation under the Turkish government's 1980 policy to identify the most underdeveloped agricultural regions for assistance.

In 1990, the total cultivated area in Ak was 6600 donum, of which 850 donum was devoted to sugar beets and 500 donum to cotton. There were twenty-two tractors in Ak village in 1990, belonging to 30 percent of the farm households (some households formed small cooperatives to purchase tractors jointly). Households that could afford to do so rented tractors when needed. Because only men from the households that own the tractors are permitted to drive them, there are periods when some farmers are idle and unable to farm due to lack of machinery. There were no hoeing machines or combine harvesters. Irrigation is done through a canal system owned by the state water authority, which charges a different fee for each type of crop; rates for cash crops and vegetables are higher than for subsistence crops (this also was the case in Kahve Tepe).

Sugar beets were introduced to this area as part of the government regional development program. Both cereal (wheat and barley) and cash crops (sugar beets and cotton) constitute the main agricultural production of the area. Since income per donum is higher for sugar beets than for other crops and since the Sugar Corporation is an important source of credit and technical assistance, most farmers rely on sugar beets for their income, and it has consequently become the dominant crop in the village.

Unlike Kahve Tepe, the women's movement in the village of Ak is restricted, illustrating the patriarchal control of both unmarried and married women. (When interviewing women in Ak village, I was always accompanied by the youngest male member of the household.) As an eighteen-year-old from a middle-sized household said:

> We can't talk to a man from the village in public, let alone a strange man from the city. I will only talk to you here under these trees because no one can see us and you came with my brother, but still it is considered very bad. If someone sees us talking to each other, the next hour everybody in the village would know, and they would gossip. You never see a girl talking to men. Immediately, a stamp would be stuck on her forehead. That would be the end of that girl's life—nobody in the whole region would marry her. In our village, if a boy pushes a girl or takes her scarf off in public, that girl belongs to the one who pushed her or has taken the scarf off. If the father refuses to give his daughter, then the girl remains at her father's house; the father of the household usually gives permission in the end because otherwise it brings bad luck.

The Gender Division of Labor

Agricultural tasks are strictly gender-specific. Men plow and sow the seeds of all crops (wheat, barley, sugar beets, and cotton). Hoeing and harvesting are done by women, although men helped harvest wheat and barley. The division of labor by gender gives women the most labor-intensive jobs—in particular, the hoeing of cash crops such as sugar beets.

The adoption of new technology in Ak has been selective and relates to the specific nature of the gender division of labor. Agricultural tasks, traditionally the responsibility of men, became capital-intensive, but women's work has tended to remain labor-intensive. Furthermore, both the unequal distribution of machinery in different periods of the agricultural cycle and the expansion of the area under cultivation in the village as commercialization has increased have changed the pattern of demand for labor, especially female labor.

With the exception of the wealthiest families, farm households seldom used herbicides or machinery because they cannot afford the cost of inputs: It is cheaper to use a female wage laborer or members of their own households. In fact, male farm heads argued that women do a better job of hoeing than do machines. (On the other hand, an extension agent commented that farmers did not know how to operate the machine, which theoretically can hoe in ten hours a tract that would take a woman seventy hours to complete. The agent also believed that 20 to 30 percent of the crop is lost because of the inefficiency of female labor.)

The male head of household organizes the production process and controls female labor. Both unmarried and married women performed vital work in the fields as unpaid family labor, but women were excluded from control of household farming resources and decision making on resource use and were not considered suited for assuming responsibilities beyond their household domestic and farming duties. They received no payment for their work and were dependent on men. If women work as wage laborers, men control their earnings. Village men argued that women are incapable of organizing the production process or of dealing with external agencies such as the Sugar Corporation and merchants.

Women who worked in sugar beet and cotton fields complained about their working conditions, but since they are controlled by the men in their family, they cannot force changes in these conditions:

> We have told the men many times about the hard conditions of work in the field. We neither sit nor stand but have to bend with hoes in our hands in order to dig the weeds out, with all our force. At the same time, we have to be careful not to damage the crop. ... All the domestic work is also done by us women, preparation of dung for the winter, taking care of children. In the winter period we don't stop working at home, milking the cows, washing, making yogurt and cheese, but these are not considered work in comparison to what we do during the hoeing period.

The women also complained about the lack of consideration for them and their productive needs. As one woman noted, "Our weeding tools are not sharp enough, and we need to work longer hours and harder to get rid of the weeds. We have asked my father to change them many times, but he has refused, saying he is too busy. We are not allowed to go to the town to buy new tools ... but most of the jobs are done by women."

Women's complaints reflected the extreme stress they are under because of poverty and the sugar beet development program. Yet they are expected to avoid speaking out in front of men about their problems and about everyday happenings. This creates insecurity for women and makes it difficult for them to communicate their hardships. As a result, they report resorting to passive resistance, such as "taking ill" or refusing to cook because of exhaustion.

Men show little understanding or tolerance for women's situation. A group of mostly married men, interviewed collectively in a coffeehouse, expressed little respect for the village women, and some freely admitted using force and violence to maintain patriarchal authority within the household. One household head who spoke on behalf of the group summed up the attitudes that prevail in the village: "A man must demonstrate his manhood and behave like a man. We all know that women work both day and night. But it is essential to beat them once or twice a week. If we don't beat them, they will do what they want. If we are soft with our women, they will take over."

The dynamics of domestic violence as a form of coercive control is intimately connected with the household's accumulation and survival process. It is perpetuated by social relations within the household and has intensified under structural adjustment and agricultural change. When farmers in Ak encounter financial or production difficulties, they use any "acceptable" means, such as violence or coercion, to make women work.

Women's situation appears to be worst in middle-strata households. In the poorest households, men and women often hire out their labor for wages or men may join women in the field; wealthy households hire laborers or use the machinery they owned. But for middle-income households, the costs of machinery and hired hands have become increasingly prohibitive, so they turn instead to their own household members for labor. In this group, violence is most common, and the daughters' age of marriage is rising. That is, fathers delay their daughters' marriages in order to make use of their labor for a longer period. Furthermore, having a marriageable daughter has become a money-making opportunity. The bride traditionally has received a dowry of gold and ornamental bedding to take into marriage. More recently, the groom also must compensate the future father-in-law for the loss of female labor and perhaps provide the future wife with gifts of household items. This reflects the increasing value of the labor of women.

Data from the two villages I studied provide a sketch of the different types of intrahousehold response to economic crisis and the hardships ensuing from the implementation of structural adjustment programs. Specific responses varied by ethnic-religious factors and by relative economic prosperity. However, additional factors intensified the exploitation of women in Ak—factors that merit further attention: the presence of the Sugar Corporation and the village's increasing dependence on sugar beet production.

State Agencies and Unpaid Family Labor

As stated earlier, the expansion of commodity relations in Turkey's rural areas is mediated by state agencies through price-support policies and subsidies. These usually take the form of capitalist legal contracts, which bind farms to sr̞ ‑cific productive conditions. Through the pressures created by such contracts—both on the household and on state agencies—macroeconomic policies are transformed into microlevel programs, with dramatic consequences for gender relations within the household. Because Ak is in a less developed region, it receives more government attention than better-off Kahve Tepe and because of the higher levels of poverty there, government incentives and subsidies have had a greater impact on agricultural transformation in Ak than they had in Kahve Tepe. More importantly, because the corporation also faces a crisis situation—declining budget and greater demand from farms for assistance—it has increasingly incorporated, implicitly or explicitly, knowledge of intrahousehold relations into its decision-making process.

In recent decades, sugar beets have been a popular crop among Turkish cultivators, in great part because of guarantees such as the assurance of crop sales and subsidies provided by the Sugar Corporation. Furthermore, data on crop yields suggest that, given the right conditions, sugar beet production is more profitable for small farms than are other cash crops, such as cotton.

Under structural adjustment, the support offered to farmers by the Sugar Corporation has changed. Credit facilities are more restricted, inputs are less freely distributed, and subsidies to farms have been reduced. The restricted access to inputs has threatened household income in traditional beet-farming areas, as was illustrated in the case of Kahve Tepe. There, however, a diversified cropping system softened the blow. The Sugar Corporation itself has encountered cash-flow problems under structural adjustment, which has resulted in inefficiency in paying farms for crops (often, payments are made in installments instead of up front) and loans. For instance, farm heads reported that the Sugar Corporation typically delays payment for their sugar beet crops for six months, which places smaller farms under severe financial pressure. (Larger farms get around this by borrowing at high interest rates.) In general, increases in the price of agricultural inputs, such as fertilizer, have resulted in higher costs of production for cash crops and have reduced income per donum. Thus, the increased cost of production together with the late payment for crops can place small farms in a permanent state of debt.

In Ak, where farms on average are smaller and less financially stable than those of Kahve Tepe, these pressures have affected gender relations within the household both directly and indirectly. These gender relations are influenced not only by logistical problems described earlier, but also by administrative features of the Sugar Corporation. For instance, the corporation generally deals only with men, even though sugar beet production depends on female labor (especially when mechanization is low). In selecting clients with which to work, the corporation assesses the ability of men to guarantee unpaid female labor, and it pressures men to exploit female labor through the "sugar beet contract" that is signed by the corporation and the male head of household. Certain rules specified by the corporation and obligatory for the cultivators are outlined in the contract, including the expected levels of production, the costs of inputs, and the purchase price for the crop. A local corporation manager and two agricultural engineers then supervise the production process and the distribution of subsidies and other supports to the farms. They also provide the corporation with information on the gendered division of labor, which is then incorporated into the contract, and they guarantee compliance with the terms established in that contract.

One important subsidy that the corporation has given to male heads in advance of the harvest is money for wages. This practice was intended to enable farms to employ wage labor for hoeing, a traditionally female task. However, with the implementation of structural adjustment, the corporation manager introduced tighter controls on the distribution of wage money. He encouraged a greater use of unpaid (and in hoeing, presumably female) family labor, to maximize profit by increasing total yield per donum and reducing the cost of production. Furthermore, encouraging unpaid family labor lowers the corporation's costs and financial risks. The manager identifies specific households who supply their own family labor, and each head who signs a contract has to provide the corporation with details on landholdings, number of children by age and sex, and household assets. Allocation of contracts favors households with their own supply of family labor. As the manager explained: "Frequently the farms spend the wage money, which is paid by us in order to employ wage labor, on personal needs. That is why I have to know how many children a family has, how many of them are female, and how many of them are male. ... We know what they cultivate, how much they are in debt, and to whom." This shows that household structure and gender relations within the household, as well as its economic status, influence a household's relationship with state agencies responsible for motivating the integration of farms into the market. In sugar beet production, despite the "official ignorance" of gender issues in macroeconomic policies, the potential for exploiting female labor has, in fact, become an economic requirement for access to state assistance programs based on those policies.

Therefore, the financial problems and economic crises that small farming households in Turkey have encountered under adjustment (e.g., reduction of government support policies) are only the factors leading to the intensification of women's work. Agency policies and traditional, gender-based productive techniques are others. In this case, the unintended pattern of "structural adjustment on the backs of women," detected by studies in Latin America and Africa, has been transformed into official state policy by its representatives in Turkey's Sugar Corporation.

But women do not have an infinite capacity for absorbing increasing demands on their labor. Their responses, cited earlier, include passive resistance in Ak and elopement, migration, and verbal complaints in Kahve Tepe. Furthermore, the process of mechanizing agriculture has favored traditionally male tasks over women's tasks, freeing up men's labor time. So entrenched are gender roles and relations within the household, however, that men resist increasing their labor inputs even when mechanization of their tasks permit it. This is especially true if the new task is identified as a "woman's job," as revealed in the following quote from an Ak farmer:

> My father used to say that the luckiest people are those who have lots of sons, but I say that the more girls you have, the luckier and wealthier you are. ... To cultivate more cash crops, one needs women and cash. I do not have either. My wife can't work because she has become ill again. ... You ask me why I don't weed. Well, every person in our household has a task. Hoeing is a woman's task, and while hoeing is going on we [the men] take a rest. I would not weed even if you threatened to kill me. ... One year, because I couldn't afford to hire a female wage laborer, I worked one day hoeing sugar beets, and afterwards I stayed in bed for four days. ... Worst of all, when after four days I managed to walk to the coffeehouse, the men made insulting remarks, "Are you a woman doing woman's work?"

This trend could be reversed if the corporation paid as much attention to changing men's perception of gender-appropriate tasks as it does to guaranteeing a supply of female labor for production. □

CONCLUSION

This chapter illustrates that macroeconomic policies and practices affecting the Turkish farm household—in particular, the process of commoditization and agricultural transformation—are inextricably linked to gender relations within it.[13] As revealed by the case studies, the implementation of macroeconomic policies made use of the gendered division of labor, even when gender was not "officially" addressed in those policies. At the same time, changes in state agricultural policies and practices created pressure to intensify patriarchal control within the household. The example of the Sugar Corporation shows how an apparently gender-neutral organization acknowledges, for its own convenience, the role that women's labor plays within household production cycles yet continues to deal exclusively with men and to base agricultural assistance on the exploitation of unpaid family labor—especially female labor in hoeing. The chapter also shows how variations in cultural norms and economic prosperity are related to different strategies to utilize or replace female labor with varying degrees of success. The case of Kahve Tepe illustrates that where gender relations are more liberal, women have chosen to move away from farm work and from the village in times of crisis, leaving small and less financially viable farm households in decline. In contrast, where gender relations are more rigid and where women have been severely restricted by men and forced to increase their work burden—as happened in Ak—household income has not (at least in the short term) declined as rapidly as it might have in households without a female labor supply.

The idea of engendering macroeconomic policies by taking account of women as a source of production may acknowledge the value of women's labor. But at the household level, women's position and the conditions of their work are likely to worsen unless there are changes in both intrahousehold social relations and state agency practices, which currently rely on and reinforce the patriarchal control of female labor. □

NOTES

I would like to thank the Eastern Mediterranean University for its financial support for this research. I also am very grateful to Cathy Rakowski for her constructive comments and to Shirley Parks.

1. Caroline O. N. Moser, "Gender Planning in the Third World: Meeting Practical and Strategic Gender Needs," *World Development* 17, no. 11 (1989): 1799–1825; Diane Elson, *Male Bias in the Development Process* (Manchester: Manchester University Press, 1991); Haleh Afshar and Carolyne Dennis, eds., *Women and Adjustment Policies in the Third World* (London: Macmillan, 1992); Lourdes Benería and Shelley Feldman, eds., *Unequal Burden: Economic Crises, Persistent Poverty, and Women's Work* (Boulder: Westview Press, 1992).

2. Afshar and Dennis, eds., *Women and Adjustment Policies in the Third World.*

3. World Bank, *Women in Development: Issues for Economic and Sector Analysis,* Working Paper no. 269 (Washington, DC: World Bank, 1989); Giovanni Andrea

Cornia, Richard Jolly, and Frances Stewart, eds., *Adjustment with a Human Face*, vol. 1 (New York: UNICEF/Clarendon Press, 1987).

4. Elson, *Male Bias in the Development Process*, 57.

5. Diane Elson, "From Survival Strategies to Transformation Strategies: Women's Needs and Structural Adjustment," in Benería and Feldman, eds., *Unequal Burden*, 30.

6. Nancy Folbre, "Hearts and Spades: Paradigms of Household Economies," *World Development* 14, no. 2 (1986): 245–255; Naila Kabeer and Susan Joekes, "Researching the Household: Methodological and Empirical Issues," *IDS Bulletin* 22, no. 1 (1991); Rae Lesser Blumberg, "Income Under Female Versus Male Control," *Journal of Family Issues* 9, no. 1 (1988): 51–84.

7. Michelle Barrett, *Women's Oppression Today* (London: Verso, 1980).

8. State Planning Organisation, *Planning in Turkey: Consortium Report on the Second Five-Year Development Plan* (Ankara: SPO, 1978), 51; Ustun Erguder, "Agriculture: The Forgotten Sector," in Metin Heper, ed., *Strong State and Economic Interest Groups: The Post–1980 Turkish Experience* (New York: Walter de Gruyter, 1991).

9. It has become increasingly difficult for small farms to obtain credit through the banking system since the Agricultural Bank specifies lending conditions that relate to household income. Only large landholders, who have suffered less under structural adjustment, are in a position to fulfill the requirements for receiving credit. Conditions attached to credit from the Agricultural Bank for purchasing machinery have also become more strict. Until 1984, credit at an interest rate of 22 percent was available to farmers with 12.5 hectares of land for buying tractor, provided that the borrower deposited 40 percent of the machine's total cost. The bank accepted a group application, allowing small farmers access to credit, as long as the farmers together mortgaged 12.5 hectare of land. The bank's policy changed in 1984. Credit is now given at high interest rates only to those who individually own 12.5 hectares of land, and shared purchasing of tractors is no longer accepted. See Behrooz Morvaridi, "Gender and Household Resource Management in Agriculture," in Paul Sterling, ed., *Culture and Economy: Changes in Turkish Villages* (Huntingdon: Eothen Press, 1993), 87. See also Bahaftin Aksit, "Studies in Rural Transformation in Turkey, 1950–1990," in Sterling, *Culture and Economy*, 189. Thus, in the era of structural adjustment, farmers who possess large areas of land have more access to circulating capital and are consequently in a better position to benefit from new technology.

10. Gulten Kazgan, "Current Trends and Prospects in Turkish Agriculture," *Studies in Development* 19, no. 3 (1992): 317–336.

11. State Institute of Statistics, *Population Census* (Ankara: SIS, 1986).

12. Throughout Turkey, women accumulate gold as an investment; this gold is a woman's primary asset and private property. The greater the amount of gold, the greater the security and status of the woman; so to the extent possible, women attempted to invest their milk money and other income into gold. See also, Carol Delaney, "Traditional Modes of Authority and Co-operation," in Sterling, *Culture and Economy*.

13. For further information, see Behrooz Morvaridi, "Gender Relations in Agriculture: Women in Turkey," *Economic Development and Cultural Change* (April 1992); Behrooz Morvaridi, "The Strategies of Households in the Production of Cash/Food Crops," in Terry Marsden and Jo Little, eds., *Political, Social and Economic Perspectives on the International Food System* (London: Gower Publications, 1990); Behrooz Morvaridi, "Cash Crop Production and the Process of Transformation," *Development and Change* 21 (1990): 4.

PART THREE

Engendering Well-Being

The contributors in Part Three take a closer look at family well-being, emphasizing that the connections among income, economic crisis, and well-being are neither simple nor straightforward. The four authors use economic crisis and restructuring as the backdrop against which they highlight women's roles as active agents in enhancing well-being in the household and community. Patrice Engle looks at the creation of well-being by parents who earn income in Guatemala and Nicaragua. Kenna Owoh analyzes women's efforts to secure improved health care in Nigeria. Brígida García and Orlandina de Oliveira study women's attitudes and perceptions of well-being across two class groups in urban Mexico.

Engle's quantitative study of urban Guatemala and Nicaragua provides evidence of the relative importance of women and men's earnings for children's nutritional status. She finds a complex relationship: How much women earn is a critical factor for children's well-being but so, too, is the amount men contribute to the household. She explains why findings vary somewhat between countries, and by type of family (for instance, when the father is present or absent) and raises intriguing policy issues concerning well-being. Should overburdened women be encouraged to work even harder to provide sustenance for their families? How can fathers' commitment to children be encouraged so they will contribute more?

Owoh presents two health-care experiences as examples of alternatives to the state-versus-market approach that infuses structural adjustment policies. In Nigeria, neither the state nor the market have been able to meet health-care demand; in particular, both ignore the needs of poor, rural women and of certain ethnic groups. Yet Nigerian women, like their counterparts in other countries, find their health declining due to economic hardship and increased burdens under structural adjustment. In response, Nigerian women organized to control health-care services—

153

in one case through their new identity as paying consumers and in another through efforts to establish alternative services. However, as Owoh explains, factors beyond their control—such as credit regulations and a shortage of nurses—created obstacles that must be addressed at the policy level.

García and de Oliveira's qualitative study of well-being and gender relations among married Mexican women is unique because it explores the *perceptions* held by women of different classes about their work, roles, and relationships. The themes of commitment to work and satisfaction with their contributions to the family are important to both middle- and working-class women, but variables of education and age are related to important differences in women's attitudes and experiences. Younger and more educated women, for example, aspire to more egalitarian relationships, and middle-class women also had more say in children's education than did working-class women. Through their in-depth interviews, García and de Oliveira show how women's employment translates into greater decision-making power in childbearing, higher self-esteem, and more egalitarian relationships.

All three chapters illustrate the ways in which women's contemporary actions, choices, and decisions are structured by their identities (as workers, as mothers and wives, as patients or consumers, as members of a specific class or religious group, and so forth). They show women not as victims of crisis or male dominance but as agents of change. Thus, they further our understanding of the important relationships between gender, income, well-being, and relative power—linkages that were introduced in preceding chapters—and they set the stage for the discussion of empowerment strategies that follows in Part Four.

CHAPTER EIGHT

■

Father's Money, Mother's Money, and Parental Commitment: Guatemala and Nicaragua

Patrice L. Engle

SINCE THE 1980s, RESEARCHERS HAVE BEEN FINDING evidence that supports the hypothesis that mothers prioritize the use of income differently than men. A number of authors suggest that when women have control of income, funds are more likely to be used to meet the immediate needs of children. Given the consistency of these findings, we are left with a policy dilemma: Should women be encouraged to work even more than they already are in order to improve the nutritional status of their offspring? Or should men be encouraged to change their spending priorities? There is ample evidence from numerous cultures that women are working many more hours than men and that their workloads increase with larger families, though men's workloads do not.[1] Yet evidence from countries that have systematically tried to increase the male role in child care suggests that men have made only slight changes in their home production contribution.[2] In some cultures, it is assumed that women will take full responsibility for the feeding and care of children.[3] The emerging data suggesting that women's work can have benefits for young children's health and nutritional status must not be seen as an excuse to institute policies to further limit paternal responsibility for offspring. More information is needed to determine why maternal income seems to have relatively greater positive effects than that of fathers and to understand factors that limit the contributions of fathers to their children's well-being.

One policy strategy is to encourage an increase in wage rates for women and to develop improved systems of child care. A second

155

approach is to change men's spending priorities to increase the proportion of their income directed to children's basic needs, as Judith Bruce and C. B. Lloyd have recommended.[4] To attempt the second approach, we must understand differences among men in regard to their paternal commitments. I address this issue here, but as in many investigations, because too little information on fathers' beliefs and attitudes was collected, the data are derived from interviews with women.

This chapter has four related purposes. The first is to explore what happens when women improve their relative economic power in the household. Empirical studies on urban Chile and periurban Guatemala and household expenditure data from Brazil demonstrate that such improvement leads to women's greater decision-making in the home and to improved child welfare.[5] This supports Rae Lesser Blumberg's gender stratification model: As women earn more income, they have greater status in the household, and this means that they are more influential in decision making.[6] Relative economic power thus becomes the most important of the major independent "power variables" affecting overall gender stratification. The greater a woman's economic power, the greater her control within the family.

The second purpose is to explore mechanisms through which maternal work for earnings could positively aid children's well-being. Once the mother has decision-making power, why would she preferentially allocate resources to offspring? Psychological theory suggests that women are more attached to their children than are men because they spend more time caring for them.[7] Women's purported greater responsiveness may be due to cultural norms that ascribe responsibility for child nutrition to the mother (and lead her to invest greater amounts of time to child care), rather than to some innate psychological predisposition.[8]

A third purpose is to test the hypothesis that the more committed a father is to the welfare of his children, the greater the physical growth of those children will be. The relative significance of the mothers' control of income might also be due to male spending patterns for nonproductive goods such as alcohol or cigarettes. A recent careful analysis of expenditure patterns by men and women in the Ivory Coast, for example, suggests that men spend a higher proportion of their income on restaurants, alcohol, and cigarettes than do women.[9] The factors that may be associated with the individual differences in spending patterns among the fathers was not examined in those studies, but they are investigated here.

A fourth purpose is to compare the relative importance of the mother's income and the father's income for the anthropometric status of children in two settings that differ in terms of marital unions and amount of paternal support. In one—Managua, Nicaragua—the proportion of women in unions is low, as is paternal support; in the other—peri-urban Guatemala—there is a higher percentage both of couples who reside together and of paternal support. Several arguments suggest that the mother's income may be more important for children's well-being than is that of the father, when other factors are eliminated.[10] Yet since children raised without paternal support lack a significant source of money, it appears that they should be poorer. These two lines of thought must be reconciled. To isolate factors behind findings relating income generation to children's nutritional status, this chapter uses two groups of children, twelve months to nineteen months of age—ninety from peri-urban Guatemala and eighty from Managua, Nicaragua. Maternal income generation and child undernutrition are common in both groups.

For women's income to be particularly beneficial for children's health or nutritional status, the women must have some independent control over income; that is, not all of the family income should be pooled. This condition seems to exist in many Third World settings. In the analyses supporting this perception, researchers adjust for prior differences in wealth or education of families when examining the effects of maternal control of income. This adjustment isolates the effects of maternal income from the possibly greater relative poverty of working women. Women who work for income are often poorer or less likely to be married than women who do not work.[11] But though this strategy of "adjusting" or "controlling" for confounding variables is to be recommended, it is also important to examine differences without making these adjustments. Even if a mother's income has a relatively greater effect on her children than income from the father, when a family in which the mother is working is much poorer, children will suffer.

In the study examined here, three hypotheses concerning the influences of maternal versus paternal incomes on children's nutritional status are addressed: Women's income earning is more likely to be associated with better nutrition for young children than is men's support; these effects are greater in societies where men's relative contribution to the family is lower; and there is variability among men in terms of their contributions to household expenses. □

THE NICARAGUAN STUDY

Location

As part of a larger UNICEF-funded study of factors related to poor nutrition, data were collected in poor neighborhoods surrounding Managua, Nicaragua.[12] The houses were generally of poor quality, income was at the poverty line or below, and there was little agriculture. Half of the dwellings had dirt floors, but almost all had electricity. The research site was less impoverished than some Latin American shantytowns since each family had a plot of land and a house. Under the Sandinistas, residents were receiving titles to this land.

Subjects

Eighty children between the ages of twelve months and nineteen months were randomly sampled from ten barrios where nutritional status had been identified as low. The mean age of the children was fifteen months, and half of the subjects were girls. Over 27 percent of the children would be classified as undernourished by World Health Organization (WHO) standards, and they were more than two standard deviations (SDs) below the U.S. National Center for Health Statistics (NCHS) standards of height for age (see Table 8.1.).[13]

Instruments and Procedure

The study was conducted during the months of July through October 1989. We attempted to contact one house per block to assure a representative sample. If the family agreed to participate, the observer entered the home and interviewed the caregiver about household composition, family support systems, and maternal employment. All children under age four in the family were weighed and measured. The observer then quietly observed the family in the home for an average of three hours. In addition eating behavior and activity patterns were measured during both the first visit and an additional one. Details of this study are reported elsewhere.[14]

Variables

Nutritional status was assessed by measuring the children's height to the nearest millimeter and weight to the nearest tenth of a kilogram, following World Health Organization recommendations. Children were measured in the horizontal position.[15] Weight was measured on a Salter Scale, and height was measured on a board marked in centimeters that was specifically constructed for this study. All height and weight measures were transformed into z-scores, based on NCHS normative data. This transformation provides an age-and-gender standardization, with a mean of zero and a standard deviation of 1. The three measures used were *height for age, weight for height,* and *weight for age.* Height for age generally reflects early and long-term undernutrition (stunting), weight for height reflects short-term deficits (wasting), and weight for age in younger children reflects a combination of both factors.

TABLE 8.1   Characteristics of Sampled Nicaraguan and Guatemalan Families with Children Twelve Months to Nineteen Months of Age

	Nicaragua (N = 80) %	Guatemala (N = 90) %
Legally married	22	52
Single	26	7
Father always or mostly lives at home	64	90
Father provides no support	26	4
Women work	56	48
Women worked in week prior to interview	56	40
Mother's occupation [a]		
Domestic work	7	28
Informal work	48	33
Formal or skilled work	43	39
Mothers employed outside home	80	68
Hours worked per week for women		
1 to 8 hours	18	37
9 to 24 hours	15	30
25 to 40 hours	13	9
40+ hours	34	25
Percent of children malnourished		
less than 2 standard deviations for ht/age	27.5	41
less than 2 standard deviations for wt/age	21	23
less than 1 standard deviation for wt/ht	28	24
Living in extended families	41	27
Female-headed household	10	6
Mean years of education of mother	4.94	4.61
standard deviation	(3.44)	(4.17)
Mean number of children living	1.23	2.95
standard deviation	(1.99)	(1.86)
Mean nuclear family size	4.75	4.72
standard deviation	(2.02)	(1.77)

[a] Percent of all workers.

Mother's Work and Father's Support

Mothers were coded according to whether they were currently involved in earning income. Mothers reported whether the child's father lived in the house and whether he provided no, partial, or full support for the child. The father's age, schooling, literacy, and occupation were also coded. However, for many women not currently in a relationship, no information on the baby's father was available. Frequencies are shown in Table 8.1.

Control Variables

Three variables aside from maternal employment or paternal support were used to adjust for differences between families that could influence the children's nutritional status: mother's education, gender of the child, and a wealth indicator, determined by observations of the quality of the house (including materials in the walls, floor, and roof) and of services and facilities available. □

THE GUATEMALAN STUDY

Location

The two towns in the study, located in an industrial area south of Guatemala City, had a combined population of approximately 5,000 in 1987. The towns were relatively rural until recently when the city crept closer, bringing in a number of new industries. Residents worked in these industries' factories or in Guatemala City, a twenty-minute bus ride away. The towns were less economically homogeneous than the barrios of Managua, and the residents were primarily wage earners. Only 15 percent of the families reported planting corn and beans, but 42 percent raised chickens for eggs and an occasional meal.

A few residents owned a truck or car. Renting was the most common pattern of tenancy, with rents ranging from 15 to 100 quetzales (about $6 to $40) per month (at the time of the study, a quetzal was equivalent to $0.37).

Sample

One child per family was included in the study—the youngest child within the age range of eight months through forty-seven months.[16] For comparison with the Nicaraguan study, only the subjects in the same age range (twelve months to nineteen months) were analyzed (N = 90). However, the total sample consisted of 294 children, and some analyses using the entire cohort will be discussed here. All of the descriptive data refer to the 90 subjects in the subsample. The women in the sample were *ladino* (Spanish-speaking) and of mixed Mayan and European descent. At the time of the study, mothers had an average of 2.95 children, the average family size was 4.72 members, and 73 percent of the women interviewed lived in nuclear families (see Table 8.1).

Patterns of Work

Almost half of the mothers (48 percent) had earned some income during the preceding twelve months. Of these, 40 percent had worked in the previous week (versus 56 percent in the Nicaraguan sample). Among the Guatemalan working mothers, 25 percent worked at least 40 hours per week, 52 weeks of the year. One quarter (28 percent) were domestics, primarily ironing and washing on a daily basis for more wealthy patrons in the same town. Thirty-three percent were informal workers: door-to-door saleswomen, day laborers in agriculture, and tortilla-makers. Factory workers, clerks or waitresses, women with a trade (such as seamstresses), and women with their own small businesses—formal sector workers—composed 39 percent of the economically active women.

Instruments and Procedures

The height and weight of all children under forty-eight months of age were assessed using a Salter Scale for weight and a horizontal infant board for length (height). The interviewers-anthropometrists were four Guatemalan teachers familiar with the town, trained in interviewing and assessing of nutritional status by the Institute of Nutrition of Central America and Panama (INCAP). Each woman was interviewed in her home regarding her work, child-care patterns, family relationships, feeding practices, and knowledge of child development. In most cases, the husband was not present during the interview, particularly for sections relating to intrahousehold relationships. If he was present, the questions concerning him were asked last, after he had left the room in most cases.

Variables

All height and weight measures were transformed into z-scores based on normative data from the NCHS norms as in the Nicaraguan sample.[17] Two measures of paternal support were collected. The first was based on the mother's statement of how much the father earned and how much he contributed to the food expenses, with the interviewer calculating the percent of his income that he contributed. Using these numbers, we also calculated the percent of the family income that the father earned. The same four variables were created for the woman, and each was transformed into an indicator of income per month per nuclear family member.[18] Finally, a measure of full, partial, or no paternal support was constructed based on whether the father provided all of the family income, some of it, or none of it, according to the mother's report. All the income information about fathers was obtained from the mothers. All women in unions were able to report the husband's earnings, and possibly the mothers' reports were fairly accurate.

Control Variables

As in the Nicaraguan study, we controlled for house quality, mother's education, and gender of the child and assessed the effects of paternal support and maternal waged work on the anthropometric status of children. For analyses using continuous measures of income as independent measures, additional control variables were used: age of child, birth order, and adult and sibling help in child care. □

COMPARISON OF THE GUATEMALAN AND NICARAGUAN SAMPLES

Table 8.1 compares the two samples for the dimensions of marital status, maternal employment patterns, paternal support, and child nutrition. The two samples were similar in terms of mother's years of schooling and family size, but there were striking differences in marital relations and father support. Far fewer Nicaraguan mothers were legally married (22 percent versus 52 percent). Instead, they were more likely to be single or separated (26 percent versus 7 percent) or living less than half the time with the spouse (36 percent versus 10 percent). Moreover, they were more likely to receive no support for the child from the father (26 percent versus 4 percent). The Nicaraguan women were also more likely to be living in extended households (41 percent versus 27 percent) but were equally likely to be female heads of household (10 percent versus 6 percent).

More Nicaraguan women were in the labor force, compared to Guatemalan women, and a higher percentage were working, particularly when the calculation was restricted to those working in the week previous to the interview (56 percent versus 40 percent). Domestic work was far less common in Nicaragua than in Guatemala (7 percent versus 28 percent), and Nicaraguan women were more likely to work away from home (80 percent versus 68 percent). Moreover, on average, women were working more hours per week in the Nicaraguan sample (see Table 8.1). Unfortunately, because of the economic situation in Nicaragua, no income data were collected, so that actual salaries could not be compared between groups. However, it appears that Nicaraguan women generally received

less support from their husbands and spent more time in income generation than did Guatemalan women. Children in both samples showed
similar levels of nutrition for weight for age and weight for height;
however, there was a higher percent of stunted (low height for age) children in the Guatemalan sample.

Effects of Mother's Work on Child Nutritional Status

Table 8.2 shows the association of remunerated work with child height
for age, weight for age, and weight for height (after controlling for the
three socioeconomic variables of wealth, mother's education, and gender
of child). In Nicaragua, employed women had children with significantly
higher weights for height, as compared to children of unemployed
women. The difference was also significant (although less so) without the
controls. For Guatemalan women and children, none of the differences in
nutritional status as a function of work status were significant, regardless
of whether we controlled for house quality, mother's education, and
gender of child.

Effects of Paternal Support on Child Nutritional Status

Table 8.3 shows the effects of paternal support on children's height for
age, weight for age, and weight for height (controlling for the three
socioeconomic factors). In Nicaragua, children who received full
support from the father were taller than those who did not. However,
when the variables of house quality and mother's education were controlled, the relationship between the level of paternal support and child
height disappeared.

In Guatemala, controlling for the three socioeconomic variables, the
amount of father support had a marginal effect on children's height for
age; after adjusting for the three controls of wealth, mother's education,
and gender of child, the effect became significant (see Table 8.3). Surprisingly, post hoc comparisons revealed that the best-nourished children
were those raised with *no support* from the father. This small group of
children (N = 10) were significantly taller than those who relied on the
support of both mother and father, although not taller than those who
relied solely on support from the father.

The interpretation of these results can be facilitated by examining
income variables associated with the degree of father support. There was
no difference in the overall expenditures for food among the three household types (mother and father both support the family, only father supported the family, no support received from father) (F = .56; p =
nonsignificant). Half the women who were female heads of household
lived with extended family members, and half lived alone, and they did
not earn significantly more than working mothers with partners. There-

TABLE 8.2   Analysis of Variance of Mother's Employment on Anthropometric Status

| | Nicaragua (N = 80) | | | |
	Nonworking Mother (N = 35)	Working Mother (N = 45)	F_{model}	F_{work}
Without Controls				
Height/age	−1.34	−1.62		1.16
Weight/age	−1.38	−1.27		0.48
Weight/height	−0.72	−0.34		1.94[a]
Controlling for Wealth, Maternal Education, and Gender				
Height/age	−1.36	−1.60	2.85[a]	1.00
Weight/age	−1.43	−1.23	3.13[a]	0.87
Weight/height	−0.77	−0.29	3.00[a]	5.98[a]

| | Guatemala (N = 90) | | | |
	Nonworking Mother (N = 42)	Working Mother (N = 43)	F_{model}	F_{work}
Without Controls				
Height/age	−1.68	−1.85		.44
Weight/age	−1.31	−1.46		.44
Weight/height	−0.37	−0.39		.01
Controlling for Wealth, Maternal Education, and Gender				
Height/age	−1.68	−1.85	3.00[a]	.47
Weight/age	−1.31	−1.46	4.13[a]	.42
Weight/height	−0.37	0.39	0.39	.01

[a] $p < .05$ (significant at the .05 level).

Note: All anthropometric scores are standardized with a mean of zero and a standard deviation of 1 using NCHS norms.

TABLE 8.3 Analysis of Variance of Anthropometric Status by Degree of
Support from Father

		Anthropometric Measures		
		Height/Age	Weight/Age	Weight/Height
	Category N	Nicaragua (Total N = 80)		
		Without Controls		
Father provides				
None	23	−1.88	−1.56	−.48
Partial	14	−1.67	−1.31	−.38
Full	43	−1.23	−1.19	−.56
F value		3.21[a]	1.06	.24
		Controlling for Wealth, Maternal Education, and Gender		
Father provides				
F value		1.88	0.40	0.23
	Category N	Guatemala (Total N = 90)		
		Without Controls		
Father provides				
None	10	−1.08	−0.96	−.33
Partial	46	−2.00	−1.56	−35
Full	38	−1.65	−1.33	−.42
F value		2.56[a]	0.02	.40
		Controlling for Wealth, Maternal Education, and Gender		
Father Provides				
None	10	−1.06	−0.96	−.33
Partial	46	−2.01	−1.52	−.35
Full	38	−1.62	−1.31	−.42
F value		3.40[a]	1.37	.07

[a] $p < .05$ (significant at the .05 level).

Note: F is a statistic used to determine the level of statistical significance in analysis of variance.

fore, it is plausible that these single mothers allocated more funds to children and that this accounted for their better growth.

Variability Among Fathers

Table 8.4 presents data for both Nicaragua and Guatemala, relating characteristics of the father (e.g., whether he lived in the household) with the amount of support that he provided. As hypothesized, levels of support varied among fathers. In Nicaragua, over one-quarter of fathers provided no support, 18 percent gave some support, and 54 percent provided full support. Further, residency was highly associated with the level of support: All of the 39 fathers living in the home on a full-time basis paid at least partial child support; indeed, 85 percent of the resident fathers paid full support. The 20 fathers who were involved with the family but not present in the home full-time were almost equally divided between the no support, some support, and full support categories. Few households with uninvolved fathers reported any support.

In Nicaragua, fathers who gave support were significantly more likely to be legally married to the child's mother. Indeed, marital status was highly associated with the likelihood of the father providing full support: 94 percent of married men, 61 percent of men in consensual unions, and only 5 percent of single fathers provided full support. Women receiving no support from the child's father were most likely to be living with their parents, and those receiving full support lived either with their husbands only or with their husbands and extended families. Almost half of the families were extended rather than nuclear. Women who reported that the child's father provided full support were less likely to work themselves, although a substantial number still worked. How much support the father provided was not associated with either the number of young children or the household's wealth. In fact, the noncontributing fathers had, on average, 2.6 children under five, compared to 2.0 for the contributing fathers.

In the Nicaraguan sample, data on schooling and age were available for only a few of the noncontributing fathers. There were no differences in father's literacy or years of schooling by his level of child support. However, the fathers providing full support were significantly older than the other fathers. (In this case, $F = 4.16$; $p < .05$; means = 23, 28, and 33 years, respectively for men providing no support, partial support, and full support.) Among employed fathers, whether they provided full or partial support was not affected by occupational status ($x^2 = .13$, df = 2). However, fathers who were present but not contributing were more likely to be unemployed ($x^2 = 11.9$; $p < .05$, df = 4) than were contributing fathers.

TABLE 8.4 Association of Father Support (full, partial, or none) by Mother's Work, Father's Place of Residence, and Marital Status

| | Amount of Father Support | | | |
	None	Partial	Full	X^2
	Nicaragua *(N = 80)*			
Mother's work				
Yes	26%	36%	56%[c]	5.2[a]
No	74	64	44	
Father's residence				
Not involved	83%	7%	2%[c]	61.7[b]
Absent	17	50	21	
Present	0	43	77	
Marital Status				
Single	90%	5%	5%[d]	60.1[b]
Consensual	9	29	61	
Legal	0	6	94	
	Guatemala *(N = 90)*			
Mother's work				
Yes	40%	19%	72%[c]	51.4[a]
No	60	86	0	
Father's residence				
Absent	60%	11%	0%[c]	13.8[a]
Present	40	89	100	
Marital Status				
Single	50%	50%	0%[d]	13.7
Consensual	8	43	49	
Legal	8	57	34	

[a] $p < .05$ (significant at the .05 level).
[b] $p < .01$ (significant at the .01 level).
[c] Numbers shown are summed down the column to 100%.
[d] Numbers shown sum across the row to total 100%.

Guatemalan fathers also varied in amount of support, with 11 percent providing minimal or no support (4 percent provided absolutely no support), 51 percent providing partial support, and 38 percent providing full support. As Table 8.4 shows, the level of support also varied by residence pattern, marital status, and work status of the mother, just as it did in Nicaragua. There was, however, a marked difference between the Guatemalan and Nicaraguan samples in terms of the percent of women receiving full support who nevertheless worked. Fully 44 percent of such women continued to work in Nicaragua, whereas none did so in Guatemala.

Unlike their Nicaraguan counterparts, Guatemalan men who provided partial support had significantly more children ($F = 4.47$; $p < .01$), and were significantly older ($F = 3.22$; $p < .05$) than those providing either total support or no support. These differences suggest that the life course of work and childbearing varied somewhat in the two settings. In Guatemala, the more common pattern for women was to begin to work when the children were old enough to share in caregiving. Thus, older fathers tended to provide partial support because their wives had begun working. □

INCOME ANALYSES IN GUATEMALA

Given the more extensive information on incomes in Guatemala, it was possible to examine the effects of parental income on children's nutritional status using figures reflecting actual earnings.[19] In the overall sample, I examined the relationships between the eight per capita income measures (four for the mother, four for the father) and total income earned, total money spent on food, and children's height for age, weight for age, and weight for height.[20] Sample sizes varied depending on whether the correlation was with the mother's income ($N = 133$) or the father's income ($N = 253$).

Multiple regressions were performed separately for each of the ten income measures for each anthropometric indicator (see Table 8.5). For each regression, I selected one income variable while controlling for all potentially confounding variables. The results suggest that the father's total income was less related to the child's nutritional status than was his contribution to the household food budget. Specifically, the father's contribution was significantly associated with the child's weight for age, but total paternal income was not. On the other hand, for mothers, total income was associated with both the height for age and the weight for age of their children, and the amount contributed was associated with their weight for height. In other words, the father's total income was less related to the child's nutritional status than the percent of income contrib-

TABLE 8.5 Slopes of Adjusted Income Variables (per capita per month) on Children's Nutritional Status

		Nutritional Status Indicators					
		Height for Age		Weight for Age		Weight for Height	
Income Measures	N	$R^{2(c)}$	b	$R^{2(c)}$	b	$R^{2(c)}$	b
Total family income	293	.19[b]	.0003	.16[b]	.0007	.06[a]	.0008
Food expenses	292	.18[b]	.006[a]	.16[b]	.003	.06[a]	−.0006
Mother's income	133	.26[b]	.013[b]	.23[b]	.011[b]	.10	.005
Father's income	254	.19[b]	.001	.17[b]	.002	.08[b]	.001
Mother's contribution	122	.18[b]	.007	.19[b]	.010	.16[a]	.010[a]
Father's contribution	254	.19[b]	.005	.17[b]	.005[a]	.08[b]	.003
% of mother's income contributed	113	.17[a]	−.003	.16[a]	−.0003	.14	.002
% of father's income contributed	254	.22[b]	.008[b]	.21[b]	.009[a]	.09[b]	.004[a]
% of family income mother earns	133	.29[b]	.013[b]	.28[b]	.013[b]	.13[a]	.007[a]
% of family income father earns	253	.21[b]	.007[a]	.19[b]	.007	.08	.002

[a] p<.05 (significant at the .05 level).
[b] p<.01 (significant at the .01 level).
[c] Statistical significance indicators following the R^2 refer to the significance of the model, whereas those for the b values refer to the the significance of the named variable.

Note: Adjusted for age of child, maternal education, house quality, birth order, gender of child, sibling help with child care, and adult help with child care.
b = slope.
p = significance.
R^2 = proportion of variance explained.

Source: Patrice Engle, "Influences of Mothers' and Fathers' Income on Children's Nutritional Status in Guatemala," Social Science and Medicine 37, no. 11 (1993): 1303–1312.

uted, and the percent of the father's income contributed was significantly associated with all three anthropometric measures. This association is striking since total paternal income was unrelated to any of the measures.

For the mothers in the large sample, the percent of income contributed was unrelated to any of the nutritional status measures, possibly because in poorer families, mothers tended to contribute a higher percent of their incomes. In contrast, total maternal income was related to both the height for age and weight for age of the offspring.

To determine the most important income variables, a separate analysis was conducted in which the three income variables (total income, contribution to household expenses, and percent of income contributed) and potentially confounding variables were entered into one regression for fathers and into another for mothers earning an income. The results for fathers showed that the only income measure related to nutritional status was percent of income contributed, which was significant for the children's weight for age (b = .008; p <.05) and weight for height (b = .008; p <.05). For mothers, none of the income measures were related to nutritional status when all were entered into the equation—in other words, when one looks for the *net* effect of each income variable. Thus, the father's percent of income contributed was a better predictor of the children's nutritional status than was his total income, although there was no difference for mothers.[21]

Finally, regression analyses suggested that the percent of the family income earned by mothers was significantly associated with all three nutritional status measures at or beyond the .05 level, even after controlling for confounding variables. Conversely, the percent of family income earned by the father was unrelated to the child's nutritional status when I controlled for other income variables.

Patterns in the Subsample

These analyses were repeated in the subsample, which consisted of children from twelve months to nineteen months of age. The same regressions on the ten income variables were performed as with the larger sample (see Table 8.6). Fewer income measures were associated with child nutritional status, controlling for the confounding variables since the subsamples were less than a third the size of the overall sample. The percent of family income earned by the mother continued to be significantly associated with the child's height for age. In a separate analysis, when all the maternal income measures were entered into a single regression, only the percent of family income earned by the mother continued to be significantly associated with height for age (b = .016; p <.01) and weight for age (b = .001; p <.10), which is similar to the findings for the entire sample. In addition, the percent of family income earned by fathers was significantly associated with children's height for age, also as in the larger sample.

It might appear contradictory that both mothers who earned the higher percent of the family income and fathers who earned the higher percent of the family income had children with less stunting (height for age). For example, if the father was earning more than half the income

TABLE 8.6 Slopes of Adjusted Income Variables (per capita per month) on Children's Nutritional Status: Guatemalan Subsample (N = 90)

		Nutritional Status Indicators					
		Height for Age		Weight for Age		Weight for Height	
Income Measures	N	R^2	b	R^2	b	R^2	b
Total family income	90	.25[b]	−.0001	.20[b]	.001	.05	.001
Food expenses	90	.27[c]	.010	.23[c]	.012	.06	.006
Mother's income	45	.40[c]	.008	.31[a]	−.002	.61	−.008
Father's income	80	.28[c]	.002	.24[c]	.003	.07	.002
Mother's contribution	40	.37[b]	.006	.30	.028	.16	.036[a]
Father's contribution	83	.34[c]	.0003	.24[c]	.002	.06	.002
% of mother's income contributed	40	.37[b]	−.002	.28	−.003	.17	−.002
% of father's income contributed	80	.28[c]	.005	.22[b]	.004	.05	.0006
% of family income mother earns	45	.50[c]	.014[b]	.34[b]	.007	.09	−.002
% of family income father earns	80	.35[c]	.017[c]	.26[c]	.011[a]	.06	−.003

[a] p<.10 (significant at the .10 level).
[b] p<.05 (significant at the .05 level).
[c] p<.01 (significant at the .01 level).

Note: Adjusted for age of child, maternal education, house quality, birth order, gender of child, sibling help with child care, and adult help with child care.
b = slope.
p = significance.
R^2 = proportion of variance explained.
Statistical significance indicators following the R^2 refer to the significance of the model, whereas those for the b values refer to the the significance of the named variable.

earned by the pair, the mother would have to be earning less than half, and vice versa. However, the samples are different. In the case where the mother's percent of family income earned was important, the sample consisted only of mothers who were working, including those who were female heads of household and earning *all* of the parental income. It is the children of female household heads who appeared to be growing best. Inspection of the scatter plot indicates that there are no outliers (deviant results that are essentially "off the graph"); the response is consistent, although the sample size is small. The analysis of fathers, on the other hand, included only those families with a father present. Therefore, the ten children growing most adequately were not included since they lived in father-absent households. When the father was present, children were doing better if their fathers were earning all the household income. However, as the analyses reported earlier indicate, the food expenditures of these families was no greater per child than in households where the father provided only partial support, nor did these families differ in overall income. □

CHARACTERISTICS OF CONTRIBUTING FATHERS

It is important to understand the characteristics of the fathers who contributed to the welfare of their children by giving a higher percent of income or a higher amount to daily food purchases. Data suggest that fathers who contributed more earned less overall, and in cases where the mother worked, wives earned a relatively higher percent of the family budget.[22] Table 8.7 shows the correlations of the various income measures with several measures of socioeconomic status in Guatemala—number of children; amount of time mother worked; quality of the house; father's age, occupation, and education—for the entire sample of 294 families.

Men who contributed a higher percent differed from others primarily in the number of children they supported; the more children, the higher the percent of income contributed. Fathers who contributed a higher percent were less educated and had lower-level occupations, suggesting that they were earning less income, as noted earlier. The percent contributed was unrelated to the father's age. It appears that fathers who contributed a higher percent of income had lower incomes and more children, in keeping with Engel's Law.[23]

If we use the previous measures of full, partial, or no support, it appears that, in *both* Nicaragua and Guatemala, fathers who contributed full support were more likely to be legally married, living in the home, and to have nonworking wives. However, the Nicaraguan fathers who failed to pay support were significantly younger; this was not found in Guatemala. Nonsupporting Guatemalan fathers did not differ significantly in age and education, although the sample was very small. The fathers who paid partial support (whose wives earned some income) were older and had more children. These findings point to differences between the two cultures in terms of family formation. □

CONCLUSION

The results from Nicaragua support the hypothesis that in households with income-generating mothers, children aged twelve months to nine-

TABLE 8.7 Correlations of Selected Income Measures with Socioeconomic
Status Indicators: Full Guatemalan Sample (N = 294)

Income Measures	Number of Children	Mother's Education	Hours of Work	Father's Age	Father's Education
Father's income					
per person per month	$-.31^b$	$.45^b$	$-.02$	$-.07$	$.40^b$
Mother's income					
per person per month	$-.40^b$	$.43^b$	$.33^b$	$-.21^a$	$.46^b$
Amount father gives					
per person per month	$-.34^b$	$.48^b$	$.10$	$-.07$	$.46^b$
Amount mother gives					
per person per month	$-.27^b$	$.28^b$	$.40^b$	$-.11$	$.44^b$
Percent father gives					
per person per month	$.17^b$	$-.04$	$-.03$	$.00$	$-.15^b$
Percent mother gives					
per person per month	$.20^b$	$.00$	$.25^b$	$.15$	$-.03$
Percent of total family					
income mother earns	$-.08$	$-.06$	$.34^b$	$.16$	$-.09$

[a] p<.05 (Significant at the .05 level).
[b] p<.01 (Significant at the .01 level).

Note: Data for mothers' income are only presented for women who worked (N =
133). Data for fathers are presented only for couples with a resident father (N =
254).

teen months will be better nourished than children in households where
the mother does not work (controlling for socioeconomic status indicators). For the Guatemalan sample of children aged twelve months to
nineteen months, anthropometric status was not associated with whether
the mother worked; however, the percent of family income earned by the
mother was important. These results suggest that maternal income can
be important for nutritional status during this age period, particularly if
contributions from the father are relatively low.

These findings are similar to those of other studies, suggesting that
for children beyond the infancy period, the net effect of the mother's
work on children's nutritional status is positive, when controlling for the
family's wealth.[24] Most of these studies also report that women who
work for income tend to be *poorer* than those who do not. Therefore,
without additional income from the mother's employment, it is likely
that these children would be even more malnourished.

In the Guatemalan case, the percent of family income earned was the most predictive of the maternal measures: The higher the percentage, the better nourished the children were (controlling for confounding variables). This was true both in the overall sample and in the subsample.[25] This finding supports Blumberg's gender stratification theory, which suggests that as women's earning power in the family increases, children's welfare will also improve and that economic power is a key factor.[26]

The father's income is associated with better nutritional status in both Guatemala and Nicaragua. In Nicaragua, children raised without the father's income were significantly shorter than were those who benefited from paternal income, although these effects vanished when controlling for house quality and mother's education. In Guatemala, the higher the father's income, the greater the child's nutritional status, but as in the Nicaraguan case, these effects vanished when controlling for socioeconomic status variables. Perhaps these controls were too stringent since house quality may be a function of paternal income.

In contrast, the relatively small group of Guatemalan children raised in female-headed households were taller for their age than the children whose fathers provided partial support. This finding held true both initially and after controlling for socioeconomic status variables. It is possible that these children, because of the greater allocation of income under the control of mothers, did the same or better than children in situations where fathers contributed partial support.

The two studies varied in patterns of father support. In Guatemala, only 4 percent of families had no paternal financial support compared to 26 percent in Nicaragua. There, fathers who did not provide any support tended to be younger, but in Guatemala, there was no age effect. In contrast, the Guatemalan fathers who provided only partial support tended to be older and have more children. The Nicaraguan pattern reflects the risk inherent in early and unwed pregnancies, which was not evident in Guatemala where permanent relationships begin at the first pregnancy.[27]

Variability in father support existed in both cases. In Nicaragua, more support appeared to be associated with living in the home, legal marriage, the older age of the father, and the father's employment. These variables seem to reflect both economic realities (being able to support children) and the nature of the relationship with the wife, a variable that has emerged in a number of studies of variations in paternal commitment.[28]

Analyses of the larger Guatemalan data set of 294 children indicated that the amount the father contributed and, more importantly, the percent he contributed were significantly associated with the nutritional status of the children.[29] The slopes (b values) generated in the analyses can be used to calculate the effect a change in the independent variable will have on the child's nutritional status. For example, to increase the child's height for age by half a standard deviation, it would be necessary to increase the salary of the mother by $11.40 per person per month. To achieve a similar change by manipulating the father's income would require his salary to increase by $166.

These data suggest that some fathers are more committed to their offspring than others, a finding reflected in the percent of income allocated to children. We need much more information on this subject. Existing studies are limited to anecdotal evidence about alcoholism and misuse of family funds,[30] and even these anecdotes rely on mothers' reports of fathers' behavior and may be methodologically compromised as a result. The current literature on this subject indicates that paternal commitment depends on cultural norms, the father's ability to support a family, the nature or warmth of the father-mother relationship, and male psychological characteristics. Despite its shortcomings, the literature demonstrates that, in most cultures, men do not perform much child care, but that they can attend to their children as warmly and responsively as do women.[31]

The literature on male parenting does not provide a clear ranking of factors affecting paternal commitment to children. In some Third World cultures—the Cameroons, for example—cultural factors are obviously important since they encourage fathers to stay removed from offspring.[32] In Chile, the combination of cultural change and economic crisis (the decline of male privilege and church authority, the increase in television viewing, and women working outside the home) has led men in urban, lower-class households to shirk familial responsibility.[33] In the United States and other developed nations, men are also abandoning their family responsibilities, and the combination of rising divorce rates and increasing numbers of children born out of wedlock are dramatically augmenting the number of female-headed households.[34]

A few programs have attempted to increase paternal responsibility, among both intact families and families with nonresident fathers. The majority have been introduced in developed countries, but efforts are beginning in Jamaica, Lesotho, Bangladesh, Colombia, and elsewhere. The more successful programs have increased the amount of father-child contact and paternal child support payments. Fathers who have had the experience of extended infant caretaking tend to become more aware of their children's needs, even if the reason for their nurturing may have been economic rather than a desire to expand their parenting role. Becoming "attached" to a child, which occurs during early caregiving, appears to be a significant factor in long-term father-child bonds.[35]

We still know very little about the factors that influence the paternal commitment to children. Despite the messages of the "new fatherhood" and images that present a committed and involved parent, the reality is that fewer fathers are taking responsibility for the economic support of their children than ever in the past. Social movements are demanding more of men, while their status in the home is simultaneously being undermined. Successful strategies for improving child welfare not only must provide opportunities for both men and women to work but also must encourage a pattern of paternal commitment to children. □

NOTES

1. Judy McGuire and Barry Popkin, "Helping Women Improve Nutrition in the Developing World: Beating the Zero-Sum Game," World Bank Technical Paper, no. 114 (Washington, DC: World Bank, 1990).

2. Nancy Folbre, "The Black Four of Hearts: Towards a New Paradigm of Household Economics," in Daisy Dwyer and Judith Bruce, eds., *A Home Divided: Women and Income in the Third World* (Stanford: Stanford University Press, 1988). Folbre cites Nicaraguan data.

3. See, for example, B. A. Nsamenang, "Perceptions of Parenting Among the Nso of Cameroon," *Father-Child Relations: Cultural and Biosocial Contexts* (New York: Aldine de Gruyter, 1992): 321–344.

4. Judith Bruce and C. B. Lloyd, "Beyond Female Headship: Family Research and Policy Issues for the 1990s," paper prepared for the project on Family Structure, Female Headship and Maintenance of Families and Poverty, sponsored by the Population Council and the International Center for Research on Women (1992).

5. Mayra Buvinic, J. Valenzuela, T. Molina, and E. Gonzales, "The Fortunes of Adolescent Mothers and Their Children: The Transmission of Poverty in Santiago, Chile," found that women in urban Chile with a higher percent of control over their own income had children who were better nourished (*Population and Development Review* 18 [1992]: 269–297). In periurban Guatemala, I examined effects of the percent of income contributed by men and women on children's nutritional status and found that the higher the percent of maternal income, the greater the control over decision making about purchases, and the better the child's nutritional status. Mothers who contributed anything to the family purchases contributed a higher percent of their incomes to household expenses than did fathers (Patrice L. Engle, "Influences of Mothers' and Fathers' Income on Children's Nutritional Status in Guatemala," *Social Science and Medicine* 37, no. 11 [1993]: 1303–1312). Thomas used household expenditure data from Brazil to show that unearned income—from pensions, social security, and income from fixed assets—"in the hands of a mother has a bigger effect on her family's health than income under the control of a father; for child survival probabilities the effect is almost twenty times bigger. ... Relative to men, women apparently direct more resources under their control toward improving household nutrition" (Duane Thomas, "Intra-household Resource Allocation: An Inferential Approach," *The Journal of Human Resources* 25, no. 4 [1990]: 637–647). See also F. C. Johnson and Bea L. Rogers, "Nutritional Status in Female-Headed Households in the Dominican Republic," paper prepared for the International Conference on Women, Development, and Health

(Michigan State University, October 21–23, 1988); I. S. Barbeau, J. Tiffany, C. V. Holland, D. W. T. Crompton, Katherine Tucker, D. Sanjur, and M. Nesheim, "The Impact of Women's Education on Traditional Gender Preferences, Allocation of Family Resources and Nutritional Status of Male and Female Children in Panama," paper prepared for the International Conference on Women, Development, and Health (Michigan State University, October 21–23, 1988).

6. Rae Lesser Blumberg, "Income Under Female Versus Male Control: Hypotheses from a Theory and Data from the Third World," *Journal of Family Issues* 9, no. 1 (1988): 51–84

7. Patrice L. Engle, "Intra-household Allocation: Perspectives from Psychology," in *Intra-household Allocation of Resources*, Bea L. Rogers and Nina Schlossman, eds. (Tokyo: United Nations University Press, 1990); Folbre, "The Black Four of Hearts."

8. See Engle, "Intra-household Allocation: Perspectives from Psychology," for a review.

9. John Hoddinott and Lawrence Haddad, "Household Expenditures, Child Anthropometric Status and the Intrahousehold Division of Income: Evidence from the Côte d'Ivoire," mimeo (Washington, DC: International Food Policy Research Institute, 1991).

10. Robert B. Tripp, "Farmers and Traders: Some Economic Determinants of Nutritional Status in Northern Ghana," *Journal of Tropical Pediatrics* 27 (1981): 15–22; Patrice L. Engle and Mary Pederson, "Maternal Work for Earnings and Children's Nutritional Status in Guatemala," *Ecology of Food and Nutrition* 22 (1989): 211–223; Patrice L. Engle, "Maternal Work and Child-care Strategies in Periurban Guatemala: Nutritional Effects," *Child Development* 62 (1991): 954–965; Katherine Tucker, "Maternal Employment Differentiation, and Child Health and Nutrition in Panama," in Joanne Leslie and Michael Paolisso, eds., *Women, Work, and Child Welfare in the Third World* (Boulder: Westview Press, 1989); see Joanne Leslie, "Women's Work and Child Nutrition in the Third World," *World Development* 16 (1988): 1341–1362, for a review.

11. Engle and Pederson, "Maternal Work for Earnings and Children's Nutritional Status in Guatemala"; Engle, "Maternal Work and Child-care Strategies in Periurban Guatemala."

12. Marian Zeitlin, Hossein Ghassemi, and Mohamed Mansour, *Positive Deviance in Nutrition* (Toyko: United Nations University, 1990) and Marian Zeitlin, "Nutritional Resilience in a Hostile Environment: Positive Deviance in Child Nutrition," *Nutrition Reviews* 49, no. 9 (1991): 259–268.

13. World Health Organization, *Measuring Change in Nutritional Status* (Geneva: World Health Organization, 1983).

14. Patrice L. Engle, Marian Zeitlin, Y. Medrano, and L. Garcia, "Growth Consequences of Low-Income Nicaraguan Mothers: Theories about Feeding One-Year Olds," in Sara Harkness and Charles Super, eds., *Parental Ethnotheories* (forthcoming).

15. All four testers were trained and standardized in anthropometry by a masters-level nutritionist. All measurements were made in the home. They were then converted into standardized z-scores using U.S. NCHS norms (M. Jordon

and N. Staehling, *Anthropometric Statistical Package, Version 3* (statistical program) (Atlanta: Centers for Disease Control, 1986).

16. Details of the selection procedure, validation of the instruments, procedures, and materials are in Engle, "Influences of Mothers' and Fathers' Income on Children's Nutritional Status in Guatemala."

17. Jordan and Staehling, *Anthropometric Statistical Package, Version 3*.

18. The amount per month divided by the number of members of the nuclear family.

19. The income measures used (per person, per month) were: total income earned, total money spent on food, mother's total income, amount of money mother spends on food, percent of her income she spends on food, and percent of husband-wife income earned by the wife. The last four were available only for women who work. The same four measures were calculated for men who were present. The strategy used here is the same as that reported in an earlier paper (see Engle, "Influences of Mothers' and Fathers' Income on Children's Nutritional Status in Guatemala."

20. The data for the entire sample are summarized here; tables are shown in Engle, "Influences of Mothers' and Fathers' Income on Children's Nutritional Status in Guatemala."

21. Engle, "Influences of Mothers' and Fathers' Income on Children's Nutritional Status in Guatemala."

22. Ibid.

23. First formulated in 1857, Engel's Law states that the lower the income, the higher the percent of it that goes toward survival (e.g., food). Hendrik S. Houthakker, "An International Comparison of Household Expenditure Patterns, Commemorating the Centenary of Engel's Law," *Econometrica* 25 (1957): 532–551.

24. Allen B. Wilson, "Longitudinal Analysis of Diet, Physical Growth, Verbal Development, and School Performance," in *Malnourished Children of the Rural Poor*, J. B. Balderston, eds. (Boston: Auburn House, 1981); Engle and Pederson, "Maternal Work for Earnings and Children's Nutritional Status in Guatemala"; Engle, "Maternal Work and Child-care Strategies in Periurban Guatemala: Nutritional Effects"; Johnson and Rogers, "Nutritional Status in Female-Headed Households in the Dominican Republic."

25. Engle, "Influences of Mothers' and Fathers' Income on Children's Nutritional Status in Guatemala."

26. Blumberg, "Income Under Female Versus Male Control."

27. This practice appears to be declining within the past decade. See Patrice L. Engle, "Is There a Father Instinct? Fathers' Responsibility for Children," Working Paper Series, Population Council, New York (1993).

28. Patrice L. Engle, "Consequences of Women's Family Status for Mothers and Daughters in Guatemala," final report to the Population Council, New York (1993).

29. Engle, "Is There a Father Instinct?"

30. O. Stavrakis and M. L. Marshall, "Women, Agriculture, and Development in the Maya Lowlands: Profit or Progress?" paper prepared for the International Conference on Women and Food (Tucson, Arizona, 1978). Martha Roldán, "Renegotiating the Marital Contract: Intra-household Patterns of Money Allocation and

Women's Subordination among Domestic Outworkers in Mexico City," in *A Home Divided: Women and Income in the Third World*, Daisy Dwyer and Judith Bruce, eds. (Stanford: Stanford University Press, 1988), 229.

31. Engle, "Is There a Father Instinct?"

32. Nsamenang, "Perceptions of Parenting Among the Nso of Cameroon."

33. Reuben Kaztman, "Why Are Men So Irresponsible?" *CEPAL Review* 46 (1992): 45–87.

34. Frank F. Furstenberg, "Good Dads–Bad Dads: Two Faces of Fatherhood" in A. J. Cherlin, ed., *The Changing American Family and Public Policy* (United Press of America, 1988).

35. F. A. Pedersen, M. Zaslow, R. L. Cain, J. T. Suwalsky, and B. Rabinovich, "Father-Infant Interaction among Men who had Contrasting Affective Responses during Early Infancy," in P. W. Berman and F. A. Pedersen, eds., *Men's Transitions to Parenthood: Longitudinal Studies of Early Family Experience* (Hillsdale, NJ: Lawrence Erlbaum Associates, Publishers, 1987).

CHAPTER NINE

———————— ■ ————————

Gender and Health in Nigerian Structural Adjustment: Locating Room to Maneuver

Kenna Owoh

FOR MANY AFRICANS, THE 1980s WERE A "LOST DECADE" during which living standards declined, previous gains in health care and education eroded, and social disruption and violence heightened. These events coincided with the influence exerted on African economies by the International Monetary Fund and the World Bank. Starting with Senegal in 1981, country after country has turned to these institutions for help with economic stabilization and the restructuring of their economies: By late 1993, thirty-five of forty-six African countries had adopted IMF and World Bank "structural adjustment programs."[1] Initially perceived as "short-term macro economic fixes," these IMF and World Bank policies are increasingly recognized as an internationally supported, long-range development agenda for Africa and other world regions. A gendered critique of these policies goes beyond considerations of the impact of structural adjustment policies on women to a deeper discussion of gender, neoliberal economics, and development in Africa.

This chapter presents a gendered analysis of the structural adjustment program in Nigeria, with particular reference to the health sector.[2] I begin with the premise that macroeconomic policies have gendered effects. The first section of this chapter examines the conceptualization of structural adjustment as a development strategy, the insertion of gender issues into adjustment policy discourse, and the framing of health-care issues within that discourse. The second section assesses the implementation and impact of SAPs at the household level and their different impacts on men and women. The third part deals with women's empowerment under adjustment and offers two cases of women's response to the privatization of health care in Nigeria. Finally, in the conclusion, I discuss grassroots political action as an integral part of an alternative strategy of development. □

STRUCTURAL ADJUSTMENT
AS A DEVELOPMENT STRATEGY

Structural adjustment must be understood as both more complex and more comprehensive than merely a short-term policy. Rather, it has emerged as a long-term development agenda undertaken by international financial institutions to ensure global financial stability. The agenda puts into play a privileged set of social and institutional practices and a set of shared assumptions. At its core it is neoconservative, and it remains only marginally open to challenges from alternative development strategies.[3]

With adjustment, a country seeks to remove internal (domestic budget) and external (balance of payments) financial disequilibriums in an attempt to provide a stable backdrop against which resource allocation can take place.[4] Markets are liberated, and resources are mustered into sectors according to world and domestic market prices. Adjustment typically entails two sets of policies: an initial IMF-led stabilization program concerned with demand-side adjustment (including devaluation, price liberalization, and fiscal austerity) and an accompanying expenditure-switching, World Bank–led structural program concerned with supply-side adjustment (removal of subsidies, introduction of user fees, and privatization of social programs).[5] These policies pull resources out of the nontradeables sector into the export and unprotected import sectors, in an attempt to take advantage of the country's comparative advantage on the world market. More recently, new policies have been added to the adjustment program to support long-term economic transformation. Prompted by the concern that the social costs of SAPs have been overlooked, adjustment programs have been widened to include investment in human capital, poverty alleviation, and compensatory programs. The structural adjustment program is the bundling together of the demand- and supply-side policy reforms with long-term economic transformation.[6]

The market is the key mechanism for organizing structural change within an SAP, and individual sovereignty is an essential condition for improving the process of resource allocation and for promoting dynamic and creative economies.[7] In the emergent development agenda, the state is viewed as both inefficient and obstructive. But to promote the efficacy of market forces as the best way to organize structural changes is to overlook the political and cultural nature of markets and their effects on structures of power and processes of development. Because gender is an important determinant of economic and social power, issues of gender differentiation inevitably need to be considered.

Gender Relations and Adjustment

Diane Elson critiques SAPs and gender in Africa.[8] Her work explores the linkages between macrolevel policies of adjustment and the impoverishment of women. As noted, adjustment programs seek to shift production from nontradeables, that is, goods and services (including public sector spending) that are produced and consumed only within national boundaries, to tradeables, or goods and services that are internationally tradeable. It is assumed that people, households, and the environment can survive the transitional costs of this switch or that the costs ultimately will be compensated. But Elson demonstrates that this switch entails a readjustment of production from the paid to the unpaid economy and, further, that the cost of this readjustment is bought with the labor, time, and health of women as they, not men, pick up the slack and perform the labor previously carried out in the public (nontradeable) sector. At the root of the problem is the undervaluation of the productive labor that women already perform and the inadequate appreciation of the burdens imposed by the sexual division of labor. There is an implicit assumption that women have time and effort to spare (in reality, most Third World time budget studies find that women worked longer hours than men, even before SAP). The flaw in this assumption is brought to light as social services are withdrawn, since women's labor is not "infinitely elastic." Elson argues that at some point there will be a "breaking-point ... and women's capacity to reproduce and maintain human resources may collapse."[9]

Adjustment policies are not inherently promale in intent, but they reflect an underlying male bias in society and the development process that operates in favor of men as a gender and against women as a gender. Male bias is not something that operates simply through social relations that are overtly gendered—the so-called women's work, which is demeaning for men to perform, and men's work which unsexes women. It operates through all social practices. My argument focuses not only on structures of inequality based in class and gender but also on the representation of gender differences within social practices, including those linked to structural adjustment.[10]

In adjustment programs gender differences are obscured through the assumed gender neutrality of macrolevel analysis. Cost, price, and markets seem to have no gender or power dimensions. In macrolevel analysis, men and women exercise individual sovereignty, enter liberalized markets, compete, and effect economic growth. Any consideration of the political structure of markets that promotes dominance and subordination between parties is absent.[11] For women, class and gender inequity intersect to constrain their participation. This nexus takes on particular resonance around issues of health.

Health in Adjustment

Pulling resources out of the nontradeable sectors and putting them into the export sectors reduces the public resources available for health services. To compensate, adjustment policies introduce fee-for-service arrangements in public institutions and encourage the privatization of health care. Health sector restructuring is spelled out clearly in a report by the World Bank entitled *Investing in Health.*[12] In the new vision, the public sector is responsible for health promotion and prevention, and curative care is left to the private sector. These factors have serious implications.

First, the introduction of the fee-for-service concept shifts the costs of health care from the broader citizenry base to the poor. In nearly all African countries, the largest source of government revenue is from traded commodities, especially exports. The citizenry pays health costs through direct and indirect taxes on production, rather than by direct income taxes. Imposing a fee-for-service system does not recover costs; rather, the portion paid by the sick increases, and, as a group, the sick are more likely to be poor.

Second, encouraging a greater role for the private sector ignores questions of distribution, both geographically and across social groups. In Nigeria, for instance, there is clear evidence showing the concentration of private services in urban centers.[13] Many health services for the poor are provided by traditional practitioners. For example, some traditional birth attendants and traditional healers have successfully entered a new arena as purveyors of a commodity, health care. When they do so, they abandon their community base and fill a niche at the lowest end of the urban health-delivery market.[14]

Third, the dichotomy between health promotion and curative care in the public and private sectors, respectively, means that a two-tiered system of health care is emerging. The second tier, the responsibility of the state, combines primary health care with some traditional services, and it serves the mass of urban poor and rural Africans. This approach breaks down the integration of prevention and cure that is necessary for comprehensive health care.

Last, the burden of compensating for lost social services falls unequally on women, as opposed to men. Because the sexual division of

labor assigns women the tasks of household reproduction and maintenance, women have a particular interest in access to health services. At
the same time, their responsibilities around health are frequently undermined by their lack of control of resources within households.[15] If a high
percent of the poorest of the poor are likely to be women, the expansion
of fee-for-service health care has an effect on women as women.[16] The
nexus of women and health care is incidental to the policy of privatization, but it is central to the welfare of women. The cost of health is an
adjustment burden for women, around which they must locate room to
maneuver. □

THE IMPACT OF ADJUSTMENT POLICIES

The SAP was introduced in Nigeria in July 1986, initially by the military
government. The precipitating cause was the fact that oil fell below
US$10 per barrel that year. Nigeria, the largest oil exporter in sub-
Saharan Africa and a member of OPEC, found itself in deep economic
crisis and heavily in debt. Following the outcome of a nationwide debate,
the conclusion of which was a rejection of the IMF structural adjustment
loan facility, the military regime of General Ibrahim Babangida introduced a homegrown economic structural adjustment program. In September 1986, the IMF issued a formal endorsement of the SAP, openly
signaling to Western creditors that agreement had been reached.

What are the issues arising from the impact of adjustment policy on
women? A starting point is the intersection of *micro*level households with
*macro*economics—unemployment and inflation, levels of government
expenditure, the changing balance between different sectors of the
economy, and monetary and exchange-rate policy. To round out the analysis, another level must be distinguished, linked to gender relations, and
drawn into the discussion: the *meso*level, which pertains to markets and
social and economic infrastructure.

Gender and Adjustment Policies:
Linking Micro-, Meso-, and Macroeconomics

Elson suggests that the process of adjustment affects households through
changes in: (1) income, including shifts in money wages and levels of
employment for employees, and product prices and product demand for
the self-employed; (2) prices of important purchases, especially food; (3)
working conditions, including hours of work, intensity of work, job security, fringe benefits, and legal status (for both paid and unpaid work);
and (4) levels and composition of public expenditure, particularly in the
social sector, including the possible introduction or increase of user

charges for services.[17] Applying this framework to Jos, Nigeria (a city of 500,000 located on a plateau in central Nigeria), the following picture emerges.[18]

Changes in Income

By the end of 1990, a combination of salary freezes; cancellation of minimum-wage legislation; currency devaluation; removal of food, fertilizer, and petrol subsidies; and regressive fiscal policies reduced real wages by 60 percent compared to the 1980 level. Rising unemployment, officially estimated at three million people, but affecting five million according to the Nigerian Labour Congress, pushed many Nigerians into a spiral of poverty. By the end of the 1980s, average incomes had fallen below US$300 a head, lower than in 1975, which dramatically increased the number of people living in absolute poverty.[19]

Disaggregated national figures on changes in income are not available in Nigeria, but researchers writing in the *Women in Nigeria Document* suggest that women in wage labor formed a small minority of all wage employment (8.6 percent) in the early 1980s. When Nigeria initiated economic restructuring, there were massive reductions in public sector employment—over 30 percent of public sector employees were retrenched, retired, or effectively laid off. Women were invariably the first to lose their jobs in all sectors, but the impact was most strongly felt in the health and education sectors. Nevertheless, the Jos research suggests a small increase in women's labor force participation was triggered through 1990 by the need to offset the drop in earnings by men. Women in wage labor are essentially confined to the service sector—cleaning, sales, clerical, cooking—with the more privileged employed as teachers and nurses.[20]

The informal economy presents another picture. With the retrenchment of labor in the formal economy, triggered by economic crisis in the 1980s and continuing into the 1990s, there has been an expansion of informal activities. The informal sector offers opportunities for women but under highly exploitative conditions.[21] Comparing participation rates from 1987 to those of 1992, the 1992 Jos sample showed that women's participation in the informal economy had increased from 72 percent to 97 percent of all women with work. In the rapidly expanding informal sector, women are clustered in jobs that are an extension of the domestic sexual division of labor: They are providers of services, snack-sellers, prostitutes, and so forth.

Changes in Prices

In Nigeria, inflation averaged more than 50 percent in the first half of 1989 and 200 percent by 1993; the price of kerosene, essential as a cooking fuel, rose 600 percent.[22] Devaluation greatly affected poor house-holds, which spend 60 to 80 percent of their income on food. Indicators show a decline in food intake for the bottom two quintiles of the popula-tion, an increase in malnutrition and child deathrates in this group and an increase in the number of people living below the poverty line. In addition, there are indications that the standard of living is lower for women than for men and lower for girls than for boys.[23] This reflects male bias in development.

Changes in Working Conditions

With adjustment women spent longer hours in both paid and unpaid work. In addition, they initiated a range of responses to buffer the impact of adjustment. For example, women produced and marketed outwork from their homes. They also devised strategies to improve existing resources, by bargain hunting, waiting in queues, and making resource-allocation choices, such as whether to forgo prenatal care or rely on the services of a traditional birth attendant for delivery.

These strategies have costs both in time and in health. Jos women consistently expressed that they were exhausted, and they pointed to an increase in violence in their homes and communities due to stress. Mothers indicated that their first choice for child-care assistance was an older female child, followed by an older male child, and the time women spent in child care has declined.

Changes in Public Expenditure

Under adjustment, cuts occurred across public services. Health-sector allocation as a percentage of total government expenditure declined from 3.0 percent in 1980 to 1.99 percent in 1987, with a further decline to 1.46 percent by 1990.[24] These declines were overlaid by rising health costs due to general inflationary trends and devaluation. Indeed, the Ministry of Health estimated that only 35 percent of the population had access to modern health care in 1990.[25]

Public expenditure cuts in health care have been accompanied by the promotion of private medical practice and the introduction of user fees. In Plateau State, Nigeria, in 1981, there were 23 registered, privately owned institutions; by 1983, this had increased to 54, and by 1987, the figure was 362. Reflecting the linkage between private interests and urban concentration of services, most of these facilities were located in Jos, the capital, which has only 13 percent of the state's population.[26]

The introduction of the fee-for-service system has changed utilization patterns. Data from the obstetrics sector show that delivery attendance at Jos University Teaching Hospital declined from 700 deliveries per month in 1982 to 160 in 1987. There was also a 52 percent increase in the number of home deliveries between 1980 and 1987, while private clinic deliveries rose somewhat, and private hospital deliveries increased only marginally.[27]

As privatization set in motion a particular dynamic in the health sector (that is, the expansion and proliferation of private clinics and hospitals), it also set up a particular dynamic in terms of what the private sector could offer. Clinics are poorly equipped since basic equipment must be imported. Without access to foreign exchange, clinics and hospitals lack medical technology, the preeminent symbol of Western-based, curative care. In the absence of these symbols, the shared assumptions that organize the health system along the lines of privatized curative care can be called into question. This opens up a space for possible maneuvering to construct alternative strategies within the dominant social practices and institutions of health. Such has been the case with women and health care in Nigeria. □

EMPOWERMENT OF WOMEN UNDER ADJUSTMENT

The following case studies present two instances of Nigerian women, who challenged power relations inherent in the adjustment agenda with at least some success. They reflect the commonalities and diversity involved in challenging health-care practices.

"If we pay, we get what we want . . ."

As noted previously, following the retrenchment of health workers in the public sector in 1983 and again in 1986, a number of private clinics were established in Jos. One clinic, owned by a private businessman, attracted a predominantly Hausa (Muslim) clientele, particularly for obstetrics. The clinic, staffed by three Hausa nurse-midwives, occupied a particular social niche in that it catered to women who wanted ethnically sensitive, Western-based care and who were able to prepay the 50 naira (approximately US$8) required for prenatal care and delivery in 1989.[28] The clinic was located in a high-density district, had access to clean water, and had an irregular supply of electricity, but it lacked telephone service. A certain doctor was said to be "on call," but because he was the owner of a private hospital in another part of town, there was no way he could have been reached in an emergency.[29] The women interviewed said that it would be very difficult for them to find additional money if an emergency occurred requiring the services of a doctor.

The women who attended the clinic represented various social groups: secluded women,[30] market-sellers, a small number of wage earners, and students from the nearby university. What brought these women together in the clinic was the intersection of ethnicity and class; what underlay the empowerment of the women was the alternative strategy they were able to construct within the adjustment agenda.

Social meanings and practices of privatization were played out in the clinic as was evidenced through the interviews. Women became consumers of health care, exercising individual sovereignty. They compared their experiences in this private clinic with that of the fee-for-service public hospital, noting that in the public sector, conditions are nonnegotiable; that is, one accedes to the conditions laid down by the staff, or one leaves. These conditions include a "disregard for privacy" and the likelihood that a man will see a woman in labor. The women were very uncomfortable with this, but in the public clinic, they had no choice: "You do as you are told. Even your husband must do as he is told, or you must leave the hospital." Non-negotiability is mediated in the private clinic. Although both public and private facilities work on a fee-for-service basis, in private clinics, because they compete to attract customers, a new meaning is introduced—the patient as customer, a purchaser of health care.

On the basis of this new meaning, some of the Hausa women came together as a group to renegotiate their relationship with the nursing staff at the clinic. This was facilitated by the SAP-imposed difficulty of acquiring imported equipment and technology for the poorly equipped clinic. Since the symbols of Western-based care were scarce, the Western, curative model itself began to break down. This breakdown coalesced around the issue of the delivery position. The women patients believed the Western horizontal delivery position did not serve their interests. As one said, "[The horizontal position] is easier for the midwives. It isn't easy for us. Everybody can see our private parts." Past experiences of easier births in the traditional, squatting position further confirmed some of the women's discomfort with the horizontal position. Drawing on their new power as consumers, the women confronted the Western-trained midwives, demanding that they be delivered in the squatting position.

When the group of women was able to renegotiate the delivery position on the basis of their role as consumers, they experienced a sense of empowerment that had not been attainable to them in the public sector, where negotiability was not on the agenda. Thus the privatization of health services and the introduction of the fee-for-service system both clearly marginalized and disadvantaged women but opened spaces for self-empowerment and greater control over their daily lives. The political challenge that remains is to move the agenda forward from this small space to develop alternative health models that offer people greater control than they can typically achieve under the adjustment agenda.

"We need to help ourselves.
We can't depend on the government . . ."

The second case study draws on the linkages between the social meaning of individual sovereignty and the obstructionist state in adjustment discourse. As conditions have deteriorated in Nigeria, the state has lost legitimacy and there has been a mushrooming of social movements and nongovernmental organizations (NGOs).[31] NGOs are deemed to be more effective than governments in extending social services to the poor.[32] The World Bank's health policy—in the context of economic transformation—defines clear roles for the private and public sectors. The private sector is primarily responsible for *individual cure*, and the state, in conjunction with the NGOs, is responsible for *collective prevention*. The implications of this dichotomy, however, have not been considered in World Bank literature. One NGO that emerged in this reconfiguration of state and civil society was the Country Women Association of Nigeria (COWAN), which assists women's groups in setting up and managing a revolving loan scheme. Among the groups that came together under COWAN guidance was Rishari COWAN, which built a maternity clinic in Mazah, Plateau State.

Mazah, a deep and inaccessible agricultural valley, is on the periphery of Jos Local Government Area. In the past four years, four women died in childbirth while being carried out of the valley to seek medical attention. This prompted a group of fourteen women to come together to do something about the need for health services, which spawned one of several women's groups in Plateau State that organized under the guidance of COWAN. After a year of building their common fund from the revolving loan scheme, the group applied to COWAN to borrow 5,000 naira for building materials needed to construct a small maternity clinic on land given to them by the village head. The women hired a builder but contributed their own time and labor to finishing the three-room clinic. The plan was to hire a nurse-midwife, apply to the Ministry of Health for basic supplies, and set up the clinic on a fee-for-service basis, offering primary health-care services. Plans were also made to sink a well and construct a house for the nurse. But the project faced numerous obstacles.

The group was unable to find a nurse-midwife willing to live in the valley. This increased the sense of urgency about building the nurse's house in order to attract someone, but the group did not have money to undertake the project. They could not return to COWAN until their first loan was paid back, and their attempts to secure another loan from other sources were not successful. Their clinic was rejected as collateral because it was collectively owned, and because the women did not own the land on which the clinic was constructed. As an alternative, the women turned to one of their members, a local traditional birth attendant who had taken an "upgrading course" offered by Jos University Teaching Hospital. This woman is now serving the clinic, but the group has been very disappointed that their original plans have not been realized. They have recognized that they must enter into discussions with the Ministry of Health and with credit organizations. It remains to be seen where this attempt to establish an alternative model will go. But it is ironic since this model of health care mirrors that promoted by the World Bank under the Bamako Initiative, adopted by African ministers of health in 1987 to promote the development of primary health care.

The basis of the Bamako Initiative is the implementation of self-financing mechanisms at the district level, as well as community participation and management of the primary health-care program. The initiative also aims at developing a comprehensive essential-drugs program that would be administered at the community level. Drugs would be supplied at a price significantly lower than that of the brand-name drugs sold by the private sector but high enough to plow profit back into the primary health-care program. Research findings on the effectiveness of the Bamako Initiative are mixed. What is clear, however, is that the success of the initiative depends not only on NGO and local-level initiatives but also on other factors, including the potential continuous budget support by the Ministry of Health, which may be too strapped to provide it. Thus, the efforts women made to empower themselves faced diverse obstacles outside the realm of the state or individual sovereignty. Poor women's control over health care was limited here even as both the state and private sector failed to respond to their health-care needs. □

CONCLUSION

These experiences suggest that the structural adjustment program has made little impact on poverty reduction in Africa. Moreover, women bear the cost of restructuring most heavily because of the underlying male bias in the development process, which is played out at the macrolevel, mesolevel, and the household level. The bias sets up a dynamic that ensures that the poorest of the poor are women. In the health sector, for instance, the intersection of macro- and mesolevel policies of adjustment with women's lack of control over societal resources has a direct impact on the health and well-being of households. African people experience more poverty and ill health today than ten years ago,[33] which raises the critical questions about the sustainability of the adjustment agenda.

The adjustment agenda has not only economic effects but also political and cultural effects. In the political sphere, adjustment policies contribute to the polarization of society and the disempowerment of the poor. In the cultural sphere, the agenda can shape the values and preferences of people, placing greater emphasis on individual sovereignty and competition and less on the building of community. But women are not just victims of this development agenda. The two Nigerian cases show that they cope with, challenge, and resist the process at several junctures. In the quest for an alternative development that would put the well-being of all people at the center of the agenda, we can learn from the two case studies. Both start from the premise that the restructuring of alternatives is essentially a political process, with self-definition a key ingredient to alternative political action.[34] In both case studies, self-definition was the starting point for the construction of alternatives. The Hausa women redefined individual sovereignty in a way that gained them control over one aspect of the privatized health-care system: the birth position. The Mazah valley women, on the other hand, began with the need to help themselves in the absence of government health service and constructed a clinic. They, together with COWAN, were able to construct a broader political agenda, although the long-term outcome was unclear. But to be effective, political action that reshapes microlevel power relations must be expanded and enlarged to address other levels in society.

There are several lessons to be learned from these experiences. First, private market-based initiatives only selectively fill the gap left by reduced public services. The market caters to those who can pay, thus concentrating services in urban areas while leaving the poor and rural communities to fend for themselves. Second, the economic and social processes of adjustment generate opportunities for people, at least at the microlevels. But the potential for empowerment that this represents can be undermined by the rules and regulations governing private and public initiatives. An example is the lack of opportunity for poor women to obtain credit. These constraints must be addressed at a broader policy level through democratic processes that include the interest of all social groups, especially the poor. Otherwise, microlevel initiatives and the potential empowerment they suggest remain illusory. □

NOTES

1. The chapter draws on my research in Jos Local Government Area, Plateau State, Nigeria during 1987 and again in 1992. The research was sponsored by the Canadian Society for International Health, to whom I am most grateful.

2. The terms *structural adjustment, structural adjustment program,* and *adjustment* will be used interchangeably to refer to the programmatic features of structural adjustment lending (SAL) on the part of the World Bank and the International Development Agency, as well as that of the IMF's structural adjustment facilities. Structural adjustment thus encompasses policies designed to produce both stabilization and adjustment. S. R. Weissman, "Structural Adjustment in Africa:

Insights from the Experiences of Ghana and Senegal," *World Development* 18, no. 12 (1990): 1623.

3. Kjell Havnevik, ed., *The IMF and the World Bank in Africa: Conditionality, Impact and Alternatives* (Uppsala: Scandinavian Institute of African Studies, 1987).

4. Lawrence Haddad, "Gender and Adjustment: Theory and Evidence to Date," paper prepared for the Workshop on the Effects of Policies and Programs on Women, IFPRI, Washington, DC, 1991.

5. When governments on their own implemented adjustment strategies, they have tended to follow this practice, too. For example, in Nigeria, fiscal and monetary aspects of stabilization were introduced in 1982 *prior* to the introduction of the IMF stabilization program of 1986.

6. Ingrid Palmer, *Gender and Population in the Adjustment of African Economies: Planning for Change* (Geneva: International Labor Organization, 1991), ix.

7. In Latin America this position is articulated most clearly in "Social Reform and Poverty," UNDP/IDB background paper, Inter-American Development Bank, Washington, DC, 1993.

8. Diane Elson, "Male Bias in Structural Adjustment," in Haleh Afshar and Carolyne Dennis, eds., *Women and Adjustment Policies in the Third World* (New York: St. Martin's Press, 1992), 49–51.

9. Ibid., 50.

10. Diane Elson, *Male Bias in the Development Process* (Manchester: Manchester University Press, 1991).

11. Isabella Bakker, "Engendering Macroeconomic Policy Reform in the Era of Adjustment and Restructuring" (Ottawa: North-South Institute, 1992), 28.

12. World Bank, *World Development Report 1993: Investing in Health* (Washington, DC: World Bank, 1993).

13. Dennis Ityavyar, "The Development of Health Services in Nigeria, 1960–85," Ph.D. diss., University of Toronto, 1985.

14. Kenna Owoh, "The Politics of Obstetrics," master's thesis, Political Science Department, University of Jos, 1987.

15. Rae Lesser Blumberg, "Income Under Female Versus Male Control," in Rae Lesser Blumberg, ed., *Gender, Family, and Economy* (London: Sage Publications, 1991), 104.

16. Commonwealth Expert Group on Women and Structural Adjustment, *Engendering Adjustment for the 1990s* (London: Commonwealth Expert Group, 1989).

17. Diane Elson, "The Impact of Structural Adjustment on Women: Concepts and Issues," in Bade Onimode, ed., *The IMF, the World Bank and the African Debt* (London: Zed Books, 1989), 64.

18. In the 1987 research, 132 low-income households were randomly selected. Households are defined as people who live and eat together on a regular basis and who contribute resources (income and labor) to meet the physical needs of the group as a unit. In 1992, 46 low-income households were selected from the 1987 group. In both samples, interviews were conducted with the dominant household manager, defined as the person, male or female, who is responsible for the daily management of household resources.

19. *Africa Recovery*, December 1989–February 1990, United Nations (1990); Digest of Statistics (Lagos, Nigeria: Lagos State Ministry of Economic Planning and Land Matters, 1989).

20. *The WIN Document: Conditions of Women in Nigeria and Policy Recommendations* (Zaria, Nigeria: Women in Nigeria [Organization], 1985).

21. Nanneke Redclift and Enzo Mingione, eds., *Beyond Employment: Household, Gender and Subsistence* (London: Basil Blackwell, 1985).

22. *The Guardian*, April 7, 1993.

23. UNICEF/Federal Government of Nigeria, "Children and Women in Nigeria: A Situational Analysis, 1990" (Lagos, Nigeria: UNICEF, 1990).

24. Ibid.

25. *Africa Recovery*, December 1989–February 1990, United Nations (1990); Digest of Statistics (Lagos, Nigeria: Lagos State Ministry of Economic Planning and Land Matters, 1989).

26. Disaggregating these figures according to type and location, the following picture emerges: 26 privately owned hospitals, of which 17 (65 percent) are located in Jos LGA; and 336 privately owned health clinics and maternity homes, of which 122 (40 percent) are located in Jos LGA. In addition, Jos LGA has 2 voluntary agency hospitals out of a total of 5 voluntary hospitals in Plateau State—all to serve a population of 500,000. Jos University Teaching Hospital is the largest public sector hospital in Plateau State. See also Ityavyar, "The Development of Health Services in Nigeria."

27. Owoh, "The Politics of Obstetrics."

28. The minimum monthly wage in 1989 was N150. By 1992 that same service cost N300 (about US$15). The GNP per capita in 1990 was US$300. See UNICEF/Federal Government of Nigeria, *Children and Women in Nigeria*.

29. In 1987, the Ministry of Health required private institutions to register and pay fees to the ministry. Apart from fulfilling initial registration requirements and paying annual fees, however, the growing private sector was de facto unregulated.

30. Seclusion, or *kulle*, is not a simple practice of confinement. Rather, it is a complex institution varying in degree of seclusion. See Barbara Callaway, *Muslim Women in Nigeria: Tradition and Change* (New York: Syracuse University Press, 1987), in particular chapter 3.

31. Julius Nyang'oro and Timothy Shaw, eds., *Beyond Structural Adjustment in Africa: The Political Economy of Sustained and Democratic Development* (New York: Praeger Press, 1992).

32. Housainou Taal, *Decentralization and Community Participation for Improving Access to Basic Services: An Empirical Approach* (Florence: UNICEF, 1993).

33. M. Ettema, G. Hansma, and L. Kloosterman, "SAP Does Not Fill the Gap," *A Literature Study of the Effects of Structural Adjustment on Health Care in the Third World* (Amsterdam: WEMOS, 1991).

34. Gita Sen and Caren Grown, *Development, Crises, and Alternative Visions* (New York: Monthly Review Press, 1987).

CHAPTER TEN

■

Gender Relations in Urban Middle-Class and Working-Class Households in Mexico

Brígida García
Orlandina de Oliveira

SINCE THE 1940s, MEXICO HAS UNDERGONE ECONOMIC and sociodemo-graphic transformations that have changed the relative position of women in society. Female economic participation has been stimulated by accelerated urbanization, the broadening of industrialization, and the expansion of the educational system. A decline in fertility, beginning in the 1970s, and changes in the legal status of women may also have created more favorable conditions for women to participate in the labor market while simultaneously fostering changes in the dynamics of family life and in the overall status of women. During the decade-long economic crisis of the 1980s, the Mexican government adopted an economic adjustment and restructuring program. Despite the increase in numbers of women in the labor market, there was a significant deterioration in the standard of living.[1] In response, women in different segments of society organized and demanded a more egalitarian status vis-à-vis that of men. Although achievements have been attained, however, it is clear that in Mexico, sharp inequalities persist between men and women and also among women from different social strata.

To understand changes in the status of women, it is crucial to undertake in-depth studies of gender relations within households in diverse social groups and at specific historical moments. This chapter presents one such study, conducted in 1990 at a time when women's labor force participation was rising, fertility was falling, and economic hardship was still widespread. The qualitative approach employed in this study helped illuminate aspects of family life—including power—that may be undergoing change. Gender relationships are asymmetrical and hierarchical but not immutable. Hence, an analysis of gender-based power relationships encompasses not only the issue of men's dominance over women but also the possibilities that women have for breaking such dominance. In this context, the daily resistance of women against their subordination takes on a role of crucial importance.[2]

This 1990 study involved seventy-nine in-depth interviews with mothers in stable marriages. These women were from urban middle-class and working-class households in three Mexican cities. When compared with earlier studies of Mexican women, our interviews provide insight into changes in family life and the possible effects of women's income-producing work on gender-based relationships. Given the nonprobabilistic nature of the sample, results must be considered as starting points for the discovery of relevant dimensions that could be explored in future research.

The women interviewed formed two cohorts, one consisting of those twenty to thirty-four years of age and the other of those between the ages of thirty-five and forty-nine. All the interviewees' partners regularly contributed money to household support. Sixty-one of the women performed different types of income-generating work, full-time or part-time, including salaried manual and nonmanual jobs and self-employment; eighteen women were not in the labor force.

Of the seventy-nine interviewees approximately half were over the age of thirty-four; approximately three-quarters were income earners and one-quarter were housewives; almost half had completed at least seven years of schooling; and all had partners and children (but not all unions were legalized). They were drawn equally from "poor" and from "better-off" neighborhoods (classified by type of housing and level of urban services). The interviewees were categorized as middle-class or working-class using the following criteria:

- middle-class—women who performed nonmanual salaried work or were self-employed, had middle to high educational levels, and lived in better-off neighborhoods;
- working-class—women who performed manual, salaried work, or were self-employed (manual or nonmanual), had low to middle educational levels, and lived in poorer neighborhoods.

To categorize housewives, the husband's work status was combined with the woman's educational level and neighborhood of residence. Class categories refer to the woman's status, not to the household, neighborhood, or husband's status.

The study was carried out in three urban areas characterized by different productive structures: Tijuana, a dynamic city on the border with the United States, widely known for the growth and diversification of its *maquiladora* (export-assembly) industry; Mérida, in the southeastern part of Mexico, a city that supplies a wide range of services to its region but is characterized by a much slower rate of growth; and Mexico City, the nation's center of economic and political power.[3] Place of residence, however, was not an important factor in the outcome of the study.[4]

This chapter focuses on two dimensions of gender relations in the household. The first dimension—division of income and labor—includes household income, control of the family budget, and domestic work. In our analysis, we examined the possible weakening of the traditional male role as exclusive economic provider and also considered the nature of the wife's contribution in covering essential domestic expenditures (rent and utilities, food, clothing, health care, and children's education). What is the woman's role in the control and management of the household budget? Is the man's contribution incorporated as a lump sum into the family budget, or is it doled out to the wife in installments? Is his contribution regular or sporadic? Does the woman know how much her husband earns and how he allocates his money? In general terms, what degree of control does the husband exert over the allocation and management of family expenditures? Concerning domestic work, to what degree do men participate in tasks such as cooking, cleaning, laundering of clothes, and transporting the children? Is there any change in the traditional pattern, whereby the wife is assigned chief responsibility for performing domestic work and reproductive tasks?

For the second dimension—patterns of power and authority—it is important to analyze fundamental changes in the traditional patterns of decision making concerning spouses and children. Do women, through active daily household decision making, achieve relative gains in sharing power? Does the woman call into question her husband's exclusive headship of the household? How are decisions about biological reproduction and the use of contraceptive methods made? Who makes decisions affecting the rearing of children? What are the perceptions about the person who assumes maximum authority in these and other important matters?

Many authors consider female control of the household budget or of economic resources, as well as shared decision making on household expenditures, as a key to obtaining more egalitarian relations in all other domains.[5] Our interviews and analysis stress women's *perceptions* of their lives and the meanings that they assign to their reality. We did not attempt to evaluate whether those perceptions were corroborated by facts or evidence. Hence, the analysis undertaken here first focuses on a deeper understanding of how women perceive their participation in the economic support of the household; only afterwards did we attempt to determine links between women's perceived support and other dimensions of family life. □

GENDERED DIVISION OF INCOME AND LABOR

Studies on the differential contributions of men and women to household income in Mexico indicate that it is no longer possible to consider a priori the woman's contribution as marginal. For example, a 1988 probabilistic survey on income and expenditure estimated that 44 percent of the working women contributed between 25 and 50 percent of the total household income and that about 30 percent contributed the majority of the household income.[6] In a 1982 study of women from low-income households who engaged in domestic outwork in Mexico City, Lourdes Benería and Marta Roldán found that 26.2 percent contributed more than 40 percent of the household budget. However, budget allocation patterns differed. In 62 percent of these households, both the husband's and wife's monetary contributions were placed in a common fund. In the remaining households the husband provided income to meet the family's basic needs and the woman spent her earnings on items beyond those necessary for a minimum standard of living. But in none of the cases did women have overall control of the household budget—all depended at least partially on the husband's contribution, and often they did not know how much he earned or what he withheld for his own personal expenses.[7] An important source of subordination at the familial level may arise from the practice of giving household money to wives piecemeal—in installments—thus keeping her insecure and in a state of dependency.[8]

Helen I. Safa has also emphasized control of the household budget in her studies of several Caribbean countries. In comparing women industrial workers in Puerto Rico and the Dominican Republic, she concludes that more changes are observed in Puerto Rico since women there are less dependent on male wages because of the availability of transfer payments (U.S. food stamps and other welfare benefits) to replace or supplement wages. In addition, in the sample studied by Safa, Dominican women were younger, had young children to support, were more likely to be in consensual unions, and had less job security, all of which heightened their fear of challenging male domination.[9]

In this study of Mexican women, we also looked at household budgeting, by examining the type of expenditure covered by a woman's economic contribution, including expenses considered basic to the household, personal items, and less indispensable purchases. Also noted was the allocation of the man's contribution, the way in which it was given to the woman, the overall control that she exerted in spending the family budget, and the meaning women attributed to this process of budget control.

Among *middle-class* women, 63 percent stated that their monetary contribution was spent on rent and utilities, food, and children's education—all essential aspects of the household. The remainder of these women reported spending earnings on personal needs or on less pressing children's needs, such as extra clothes and shoes (see Table 10.1). With respect to control of the household budget, the wife managed it in one-third of the cases, the husband in another one-third, and it was jointly controlled in the remaining third (see Table 10.2).

Women who considered their contribution to be crucial to the household were almost entirely those who felt a *commitment* to extradomestic income-generating activity. We have analyzed the meaning of work in the life of women by reconstructing the degree of commitment that they adopted toward economic activity in the course of their married lives or in consensual unions. We identified women whose attitude to work was one of individual commitment (work as a goal, as an element of self-realization) or one of familial commitment (work necessary to maintain social status or to guarantee children's well-being and education); in addition, we documented cases of women who did not assume a commitment (work as a secondary activity) and those who did not perform income-producing extradomestic activities.[10] Commitment may arise

TABLE 10.1   Middle-Class and Working-Class Women's Perceptions of the Importance of Their Monetary Contribution to Domestic Expenditures (in percentages)

	Middle-Class	Working-Class
Woman's monetary contribution is essential [a]	62.8	42.3
Woman's monetary contribution covers "extra" expenditures [b]	37.2	57.7
Total	100.0	100.0
	(N = 35)	(N = 26)

[a] The woman's contribution covers some of the essential domestic expenditures such as rent and utilities, food, clothing, health care, and children's education.

[b] The woman's contribution covers personal expenses or is spent on children's additional needs.

TABLE 10.2   Person in Charge of the Household Budget's Management in Middle-Class and Working-Class Households (in percentages)

	Middle-Class	Working-Class
Husband	32.3	28.0
Wife	35.4	56.0
Both	32.3	16.0
Total	100.0	100.0
	(N = 34)	(N = 25)

from the need for personal development or from the desire to strengthen the familial standard of living and to be a central part of the family's sustenance. The committed women of both classes worked in various types of occupation and were of different ages and levels of educational attainment. Moreover, women's perceptions of the centrality of their economic contribution were not necessarily linked either to their perception of economic need or to the type of work they performed; rather, these perceptions were tied to their greater commitment to work itself.

A notable point revealed in the study was the apparently unrestricted access that middle-class wives had to their husbands' income. The notion of a "housekeeping allowance" was not present in their discourse. Women from middle-class households who made significant contributions to the family economy felt satisfaction in acting together as a *team*, by pooling income in a common fund:

> I have never had the problem [that] this is mine and what is my husband's is his. We place my husband's earnings and my own ... in a small wooden box, and my husband may take what he wants and I may take what I want. ... If you make of your life a team, things are also bound to be better; for example, if you improve yourself, if you fulfill your obligations to your household, if you help out economically, the result is going to be much more ... more well-being, more happiness. (Delma of Tijuana, thirty-one years of age, with one daughter)

Only a minority of those interviewed considered their greater economic contribution to be the basis for enhanced personal autonomy. In fact, the link between income and autonomy was clearly expressed only among a few women with college-level education.

Among *working-class* women, the prevailing situation was qualitatively different. They more clearly expressed the idea that the man is the chief provider of the family's basic sustenance (understood essentially as food) and that he should contribute the housekeeping allowance. Two different situations were found regarding the women's perception of their contribution (see Table 10.1). More than half of the income-earning working-class women (57.7 percent) considered their earnings to be marginal, that is, for specific expenses or contingencies: "My husband is the one who takes care of the family's sustenance, as they say nowadays. In matters of taste, regarding the arrangement of the house or the kids' clothing, there is where my contribution enters ... for superfluous things ... those he could no longer take care of ... I help him" (María del Rosario of Mérida, forty-seven years of age, with five children). The remainder of the working-class group reported that their contribution to family income was, indeed, indispensable. As in the middle-class cases, the women who said their contribution was crucial were women who expressed an individual or familial commitment to extradomestic work. However, this did not prevent the working-class group from viewing the man as chiefly responsible for providing the housekeeping allowance. Wives' work was seen as helping the husband to significantly round-out the family budget. Compared to middle-class interviewees, fewer working-class women made a conspicuous reference to their own expenditures as "being on the same level" as those of their husbands. Working-class women also asserted fewer overt aspirations for a more egalitarian situation.

One very important dimension for working-class women was budget management. In 56 percent of the cases, women managed the household budget alone, and an additional 16 percent said they managed it jointly with the husband (see Table 10.2). To manage scarce money is a difficult task, and there was a note of pride present in some of these women's comments: "He has told me: 'I give you money because I know you need it, my children need it, and I know that it will not be ill spent'" (Laura of Mexico City, twenty-four years of age, with three children).

In summary, a higher proportion of income-earning middle-class women perceived their contribution to the family budget as essential and a source of personal satisfaction. In contrast, working-class women more frequently reported that they worked to supplement the housekeeping allowance, which was insufficient to meet essential or secondary expenditures.

Since the late 1970s, there have been a number of case studies on domestic labor in Mexico, both among less advantaged groups and in the middle class. Martha Judith Sánchez Gómez, in a review of these studies, states that "the majority of the investigations arrive at the conclusion that the participation of males in domestic housework is scant, variable, and on occasion nonexistent."[11] But, when a woman performs paid work, it is possible to expect some changes in the division of domestic labor. In her study of middle-class and working-class groups in Mexico City in the 1970s, Teresita De Barbieri notes that differences may occur in the general pattern that assigns women responsibility for domestic labor when both spouses are engaged in paid work, especially if they work in the same productive unit.[12] Sánchez Gómez finds, however, that women with paid work receive more support in domestic chores from household members *other* than their husbands (especially from daughters). She also observes that the sporadic chores performed by men are those related to the non-domestic domain, are the least routine and monotonous, and are also the least typified as "female activities."[13] Other recent studies in both developed and developing countries confirm that women's responsibility for domestic labor continues to be widely accepted and that systematic participation of spouses is rare.[14]

Our study also found no clear indication of husbands taking responsibility for the systematic performance of any domestic chore. The man's share of domestic chores almost always assumed the form of "help" or "collaboration." This meant that husbands undertook housework only intermittently, when they had free time or on weekends or vacations or whenever their wives were bedridden with illness. Therefore, it is not yet possible to speak of an important change in the gender-based division of intrafamilial domestic labor.

Despite the sporadic nature of men's participation in housework, important differences were encountered between the situation of women who worked for income and those who did not. In households where the woman did not earn income, participation of spouse and sons in domestic chores was nonexistent or scant, for both middle- and working-class women. In contrast, working women who assumed an individual or familial commitment to work often required the husband and children to take on a share of domestic tasks. This occurred with 49 percent of the middle-class women and 35 percent of the working-class women.[15] It is important to highlight that in our study, the domestic tasks performed by husbands or children, contrary to other studies' findings, were not necessarily the least routine or the least "feminine." On occasion, the interviewees reported that husbands laundered clothes, ironed, cooked (especially on weekends), swept and mopped the floors, tidied up and dusted, and cared for the children.

How did the women perceive the new pattern of sharing housework with husbands? The working-class women did not expect the man's contribution to housework to be systematic.[16] This aspect of the intrafamily division-of-labor roles was clearly fixed in their discourse. For example, one woman's husband "used to help her [in housework tasks], but he no longer does because he's out working all day, from 6 o'clock in the morning . .... He gets out at three P.M.; he works eight hours, [and] when he comes home, he's wiped out" (Natalia of Mérida, forty-seven years of age, with seven children).

In contrast, middle-class women relied on the help of domestic servants; they considered themselves responsible for the supervision—but not for the execution—of domestic housework. The presence of a domestic employee further distanced the men from assuming a share of housework. Many women reported that everyday conflicts in this particular arena had been solved by hiring an employee. As one woman reported, domestic chores "[are] my responsibility and he absolutely is in no way involved. He prefers to pay. We have two female servants. ... He can't bear the sight of a stain ... yet he is incapable of cleaning anything, well, not even of serving himself a glass of water. He prefers to pay. If possible, he would pay for twenty servants because he likes 'water, napkins'. ... In my case, I do nothing physically, because I have help, but I am the one who decides and gives orders if sweeping or whatever is to be done" (Evelyn of Mérida, thirty-four years of age, with three children). Given the absence of domestic servants in the homes of working-class women, it is other women or older sons or daughters who were charged with doing the housework. As noted earlier, some research studies found that daughters were expected to help out, but we found a more egalitarian pattern of domestic help among sons and daughters. This change was also reported by Rosa María Rubalcava and Vania Salles: In all, 81 percent of their respondents—both working women and housewives from working-class households—expressed the opinion that sons and daughters should help equally with household tasks. Such results may indicate that fundamental changes are possible in the future, as more and more women enter the labor market. □

DOMESTIC PATTERNS OF AUTHORITY AND POWER

Patterns of authority and decision making in the home traditionally have been areas of interest in the sociology of the family. Scholars in the field of women's studies have recently envisioned the domestic domain as a space of hierarchical relations between genders and generations. In the family, authority and power is still wielded predominantly by men, but emerging spaces for female power indicate that women's subordination may be changing.

In Mexico, both large-sample surveys and studies based on a small number of cases indicate that men and women have differentiated arenas with regard to decision making. De Barbieri's 1984 analysis of middle-class and working-class groups in Mexico City found that the feminine decision-making sphere included such things as daily meals, education, clothing, and nutrition of the family's children. For middle-class women, it also included the wages and characteristics of domestic workers. The male sphere included responsibility for important money disbursements, especially in working-class households. De Barbieri also observed that the clear-cut division in decision making between genders may vary when the woman works and among younger couples.[17]

Manuel Ribeiro, in a study of urban areas in the state of Nuevo León at the end of the 1980s, observed important changes in decision-making patterns, including a shift toward joint decisions in regard to having children.[18] This pattern also has been reported in other Latin American countries and may be influenced by family planning programs and the increasing proportion of women earning income. Nevertheless, other decisions may still be left to the husband alone. For example, Benería and Roldán found that although women from low-income households had decision-making power over child rearing, they expected husbands to discipline their progeny.[19]

Results of our study showed that for working-class women, decisions about education were made by wives in one-third of the cases, husbands in another third, and jointly by the couple in the remainder. By contrast, middle-class women have a somewhat greater say in children's education, and 42 percent have sole responsibility in this (see Table 10.3).

As for decisions about the number of children and the use of contraceptive methods, our results support the growing evidence that Mexican women from different social groups are increasingly active in fertility control. As reflected in Table 10.4, our interviews suggest that women from working-class and especially middle-class households have a significant voice in decisions concerning reproduction. In the case of working-class women, nearly 68 percent reported that they have a voice, either solely or jointly with the husband, in the final decision of whether to have more children. These women worked in manual, salaried jobs, and most were under thirty-five years of age. In the case of middle-class women, women's say in decisions about fertility—taken individually or jointly with the husband—were even more common, occurring in 73 percent of the cases. The middle-class women with the greatest voice generally had a college-level education or worked in nonmanual, salaried jobs.

These results about fertility do not mean that women have gained an indisputable space for taking control of their bodies, their sexuality, and their reproductive capacities.[20] In many cases, decisions on fertility control gave rise to serious conflicts in these households, conflicts that pressured women toward unwanted solutions, especially when husbands desired more children. Moreover, family planning for working-class women is difficult because women lack information and funds for

TABLE 10.3   Person Who Makes Household Decisions Concerning Children's Education in Middle-Class and Working-Class Households (in percentages)

	Middle-Class	Working-Class
Husband	22.3	32.3
Wife	42.2	32.4
Both	35.5	35.3
Total	100.0	100.0
	(N = 45)	(N = 34)

Source: Seventy-nine in-depth interviews of women workers and nonworkers (nonprobabilistic sample, 1990).

TABLE 10.4   Person Who Makes Household Decisions Concerning Fertility in Middle-Class and Working-Class Households (in percentages)

	Middle-Class	Working-Class
Husband	26.7	32.3
Wife	33.3	35.3
Both	40.0	32.4
Total	100.0	100.0
	(N = 45)	(N = 34)

Source: Seventy-nine in-depth interviews of women workers and nonworkers (nonprobabilistic sample, 1990).

the adequate use of available contraceptive methods. The following testimony reflects these difficulties:

> Right now, I have four [children], three boys and one girl; yet I only meant to have three. I had two, first two, and the last one I waited some six years to have; according to me, he was the last one. But no, they did not operate on me because I was too young and all that. Then came the other one, the fourth ... in other words, we did not "take care" [i.e., use contraceptives] ... and I became pregnant, so then I [had] the fourth, and right now I indeed already have been operated on, and I am left with four children. (Ana from Mexico City, twenty-seven years of age)

How is greater female control over procreation and the rearing of children related to patterns of authority in other domains of family life? In working-class households, women's say in fertility does not necessarily lead them to question their subordination to husbands in other dimensions. In fact, about 75 percent of the working-class women believed that men were the heads of households, that is, the ones who should have the last word in important decisions, such as granting permission for the wife to work, arranging for the family to construct a house, and planning and saving money for the future (see Table 10.5). This finding was most common among housewives over thirty-four and among the self-employed. On the other hand, the few working-class women who claimed that they participated in important family decisions were from the younger cohort, had at least seven years of schooling, worked in salaried employment, and had a commitment (individual or familial) to their work. This difference between age cohorts points to possible future changes in gender relationships.

For middle-class women, the "teamwork" theme reemerged, with 60 percent reporting that the couple shared headship, in comparison to only 23.5 percent of working-class women (see Table 10.5). In other words, middle-class women called into question the image of the husband as the exclusive head of the household. These women perceived that they also had authority in the home and that they participated actively with their spouses in important decisions that concerned the family. It is also relevant that the majority of the middle-class women had high levels of education (38 percent were college educated) and that they most frequently worked in salaried, nonmanual employment. □

CONCLUSION

In this chapter, we have explored domestic gender relations in two broad areas: the division of labor and income and the patterns of power and authority predominating in the household. Our purpose was to assess

TABLE 10.5   Women's Perception About Household Headship in Middle-Class and Working-Class Households (in percentages)

	Middle-Class	Working-Class
Husband is household head	40.0	76.5
Shared household headship	60.0	23.5
Total	100.0	100.0
	(N = 45)	(N = 34)

Source: Seventy-nine in-depth interviews of women workers and nonworkers (nonprobabilistic sample, 1990).

women's perceptions of change, along a series of dimensions that may point to new patterns of gender relations within Mexican urban households. Given the intentional or nonprobabilistic nature of the sample, findings must be considered as points of departure, which, in turn, should be reexamined and enriched in future investigations.

A key differentiating factor in our data is the social class of the woman. This was defined—in most cases—by women's work, education, and neighborhood characteristics. Thus, the study differed from the standard practice of classifying women according to the characteristics of their spouses or their neighborhoods or income level. Our findings indicate that women are perceiving a shift toward more egalitarian authority and power relations, coupled with a less dramatic change in attitudes regarding the domestic division of labor. These changes are most pronounced among middle-class, income-earning women. Surprisingly, *within* class groups, the same variables—age, educational level, and type of work—were associated with differentiated perceptions, commitment to work, and decision making. An important difference *between* class groups relates to the notion of "teamwork." Although about three-fourths of both the middle- and working-class women earned income, more middle-class women considered their monetary contribution to be essential to household support; they also expressed satisfaction and pride that they were in a team relationship. Teamwork was also reflected in their reports of shared decision making and budget management. Therefore, both intragroup differences and differences between groups may be important.

Although equal proportions of middle- and working-class women showed individual or familial commitment to remunerated work, working-class women were more likely than middle-class women to support men's role as household heads and to perceive their role as that of supporters and providers of income. This was true even for those women of the working class who managed the household budget. Thus middle-class women—who tend to have higher educational levels and engage in nonmanual work—reported intrahousehold patterns of authority and power that diverged from those found in earlier studies of Mexican women. Fewer working-class women, on the other hand, claimed their contribution to and management of budgets was critical to survival, even though, realistically, the economic situations of their households were more precarious than those of the middle class.

The perceptions of most working-class women supported the traditional notion that the husband is head of the household. This was strongest among working-class women over age thirty-four with lower educational levels. In contrast, younger, better educated, income-earning working-class women revealed perceptions that approach those of the middle-class women. They have succeeded in having their husbands help (albeit sporadically) with domestic tasks and have questioned the man's role as the exclusive domestic authority. This supports the idea that change is taking place in Mexican gender relations regardless of class. It should be remembered, however, that the study focused on women's perceptions and made no attempt to evaluate perceptions against information on household income or expenditures.

The information provided by women on their perception of the division of household labor reveals less change. The availability of maids in middle-class women's households makes a clear assessment difficult. In general, however, younger women and the better educated of both classes were more likely than older, less educated women to express support for a greater sharing of housework by husbands and sons. The most clear-cut differentiating factor, however, was income: Women who earned an income encouraged their husbands and children to lend a hand; housewives reported no or virtually no participation in domestic tasks by husbands or sons.

Another important conclusion of this analysis is that income-generating work introduced changes in a series of dimensions in family life, for both working-class and middle-class women. In various studies at the international level, it is argued that it is not work that gives rise to transformations but the control over income from work. We would add that the *commitment to work* is another factor to be taken into consideration.

In summary, households of women who earn income and who establish personal or familial commitment to their work generally featured the following characteristics: (1) the woman's monetary contribution was perceived as central to the support of the domestic unit, (2) there was more, if sporadic, male involvement in domestic chores, and (3) the patterns of male authority were questioned in a more systematic way.

In conclusion, this study provides a rare insight into a qualitative sample of urban Mexican women's relative commitment to work and their perceptions of intrahousehold power and authority and the division of domestic labor in their homes. What is surprising is the fact that women of both classes revealed virtually identical levels of commitment to work. Future studies on a larger probabilistic sample of women would do well to explore the issues of commitment to work, feelings of marital teamwork, and perception of the importance of wives' income. □

NOTES

Data reported on in this chapter were collected as part of a research project on fertility, work, and women's status funded by the Rockefeller Foundation. Our appreciation is expressed to María Teresa Ejea and María Waleska Vivas for their role in systematizing qualitative information and to Miguel Calderón for his assistance in preparing the references

1. John Sheahan, *Conflict and Change in Mexican Economic Strategy* (La Jolla: Center for U.S.-Mexican Studies, University of California, 1991); Mercedes González de la Rocha and Agustín Escobar Latapí, *Social Responses to Mexico's Economic Crisis of the 1980s* (La Jolla: Center for U.S.-Mexican Studies, University of California, 1991); Nora Lustig, "Mexico, the Social Impact of Adjustment," paper prepared for the Conference on the Demographic Consequences of Structural Adjustment in Latin America, Belo Horizonte, Brazil, September 29 to October 2, 1992.

2. Alejandra Massolo and Lucila Díaz Ronner, "Consumo y lucha urbana en la ciudad de México: Mujeres protagonistas," unpublished paper, 1985; Elizabeth Jelín, *Ciudadanía e identidad: La mujer en los movimientos sociales en América Latina* (Buenos Aires: CEDES, 1986); Teresita De Barbieri and Orlandina de Oliveira, *La presencia de las mujeres en América Latina en una década de crisis* (Santo Domingo: Centro de Investigación para la Acción Femenina [CIPAF], Editorial Búho, 1987); Orlandina de Oliveira and Liliana Gómez Montes, "Subordinación y resistencia femeninas: notas de lectura," in Orlandina de Oliveira, ed., *Trabajo, poder y sexualidad* (Mexico City: El Colegio de México, Programa Interdisciplinario de Estudios de la Mujer, 1987); María Luisa Tarrés, "Más allá de lo público y lo privado. Reflexiones sobre la participación social y política de las mujeres de clase media en Ciudad Satélite," in de Oliveira, ed., *Trabajo, poder y sexualidad*; María Luisa Tarrés, "Campo de acción social y política de la mujer de clase media," in Vania Salles and Elsie McPhail, eds., *Textos y pretextos: Once estudios sobre la mujer* (Mexico City: El Colegio de México, Programa Interdisciplinario de Estudios de la Mujer, 1991).

3. For a more detailed explanation of the selection of cases and of the interview guide used, see Brígida García and Orlandina de Oliveira, *Trabajo y vida familiar en México* (Mexico City: El Colegio de México, Centro de Estudios Demográficos y de Desarrollo Urbano y Centro de Estudios Sociológicos, 1994).

4. Although the sample size was too small to analyze each city separately, we did indeed find that changes toward somewhat less patriarchal marital relationships emerged among some couples in all three urban areas.

5. Rae Lesser Blumberg, "Introduction: The Triple Overlap of Gender Stratification, Economy and the Family," in Rae Lesser Blumberg, ed., *Gender, Family, and Economy: The Triple Overlap* (Newbury Park, CA: Sage Publications, 1991).

6. Hilda Dávila Ibañez, "Condiciones de trabajo de la población femenina. El caso de la Delegación Xochimilco," in Elia Ramírez and Hilda R. Dávila Ibañez, eds., *Trabajo femenino y crisis en México* (Mexico City: Universidad Autónoma Metropolitana, 1990).

7. This analysis was based on in-depth interviews in 1982 with fifty-three married women who were engaged in outwork manufacturing. They lived in different *delegaciones* of the Federal District. See Lourdes Benería and Marta Roldán, *The Crossroads of Class and Gender: Industrial Homework, Subcontracting and Household Dynamics in Mexico City* (Chicago: University of Chicago Press, 1987).

8. Teresita De Barbieri, *Mujeres y vida cotidiana* (Mexico City: Fondo de Cultura Económica-Instituto de Investigaciones Sociales, UNAM, 1984), and Benería and Roldán, *The Crossroads of Class and Gender.*

9. Helen Safa, "Women and Industrialization in the Caribbean" in Sharon Stichter and Jane L. Parpart, eds., *Women, Employment, and the Family on the International Division of Labour* (London: Macmillan Press, 1990). Safa analyzes a 1987 survey of 157 industrial female workers in the apparel industry in Puerto Rico. For the Dominican Republic, she analyzes information for 231 female workers in export assembly plants, interviewed in 1981.

10. See García and de Oliveira, *Trabajo y vida familiar en México.*

11. See Martha Judith Sánchez Gómez, "Consideraciones teórico-metodológicas en el estudio del trabajo doméstico en México" in de Oliveira, ed., *Trabajo, poder y sexualidad*, 70.

12. De Barbieri, *Mujeres y vida cotidiana.* Thirty-four women were interviewed, seventeen from middle-class households and seventeen from working-class households; eighteen were engaged in paid work, and sixteen were housewives.

13. In *The Crossroads of Class and Gender*, Benería and Roldán also report that in no case were the interviewees (who were performing outwork and were all from low-income households) able to reduce appreciably their responsibility for completing of household chores.

14. For Uruguay, see, for example, Cristina Torres, "El trabajo doméstico y las amas de casa. El rostro invisible de las mujeres," *Sociológica* (May–August, 1989): 145–176. In a 1991 study of owners of microenterprises in six capital cities in Central America, it is reported that women—although they may run their own businesses—assume responsibility for domestic chores in a much higher proportion than do their male counterparts. See R. Menjívar Larín and J. P. Pérez Sáinz, "Género e informalidad en Centroamérica: Una perspectiva regional," paper prepared for the Taller Género e Informalidad Urbana en Centroamérica, Costa Rica, September 3–4, 1992. For a review of results found in developed countries, see Blumberg, ed., *Gender, Family, and Economy.*

15. The corresponding percentages for sons who help out sporadically are 60 percent in working-class households and 75 percent in middle-class households.

16. Rosa María Rubalcava and Vania Salles, "Percepciones femeninas en hogares de trabajadoras en Matamoros," unpublished paper, El Colegio de México, Centro de Estudios Sociológicos, Mexico City, 1991. This study was carried out in Matamoros, Tamaulipas. In a subsample of ninety-one households that included both women who participated in the labor market and housewives, it was observed that 61 percent of working women and 67 percent of the nonemployed women believed that housework should be done by women. See also Benería and Roldán, *The Crossroads of Class and Gender.*

17. De Barbieri, *Mujeres y vida cotidiana.*

18. Manuel Ribeiro, *Familia y fecundidad* (Monterrey: Universidad Autónoma de Nuevo León, 1989).

19. Benería and Roldán, *The Crossroads of Class and Gender.*

20. Different studies lead us to conclude that sexuality is a domain of less change. In *The Crossroads of Class and Gender*, Benería and Roldán observe that the man almost always takes the initiative in this area.

PART FOUR

Paths to Power and Policy

In the preceding chapters, the contributors have looked at macro (societal, global) and micro (household, community) conditions under which women and men have striven for wealth or survival and welfare in different places and at different times. The authors in Part Four consider the ways in which women as well as men can be empowered to reinforce positive aspects of economic change (those that improve lives) and better cope with or resist negative aspects of change. All three chapters focus on the environment—natural or built. This is not coincidental. Environmental issues and the struggle to meet basic needs (including shelter) are critical issues for planners and policy makers concerned with economic change.

María Pilar García-Guadilla compares the political success of Venezuelan environmental organizations led by women to those led by men. Her analysis draws on social movement theory and Venezuela's recent history, particularly the style of democratization (centralized) and industrialization (grand projects). She identifies five factors critical to the success of organizations: access to resources, organizational structure and strategy, media attention, international relevance, and whether men or women propose them. In general, when posed by men, issues like water shortages or housing tend to be considered "political" by the media and politicians; when posed by women, the same issues tend to be relegated to the "domestic" domain. Yet there are cases where women have achieved political power. Of the three types of environmental organizations García-Guadilla analyzes—women-only, urban, and ecological—women-led ecological organizations were the most successful. She concludes that women's leadership style, nonconfrontational strategy, and use of the media are opening new paths to political power.

Bonnie Kettel's chapter focuses on Africa and Women, Environment and Development Network (WEDNET) that draws on the gender and development approach to women's participation in the development

211

process. Kettel documents African women's roles as active producers of nature, how they use their roles as wives and mothers to legitimate their leadership in environmental management, and how women's "landscapes" differ from those of men. Since both gender and environment are sociocultural constructions—that is, assigned meaning by people—whoever is able to impose concepts of women and nature has power. Women are empowered, then, when they control relevant discourse and when their landscapes and environmental interests and skills are granted rightful recognition in development agendas. Potentially, this approach will help eradicate the ethnocentrism and sexism of more traditional approaches to the environment that emphasize profits, technology, male control, and exploitation.

Irene Tinker provides a model for empowerment so logical that it is difficult to understand why it is not the norm: In designing programs and providing services, policy makers and planners should stop fragmenting women's lives into neat little sectors such as work, home, and shelter. The myth of gender-neutral policies cannot survive if work, family life, community, and other dimensions of "whole" women (and men) are taken into account. Tinker makes the case for the concept of "shelter" as a means to link home, the built environment, settlements, and livelihood—and to bring men back into the picture. Shelter issues include access to water and sanitation, home-based work, and urban food production not just housing. She provides examples of the ways in which women use space—inside and outside the home—as they fulfill their multiple roles and shows how women more than men are burdened by inadequate shelter. And she calls for assessments of the gendered impacts of past approaches and actions—for example, toward squatter settlements and food vendors—that made women's lives difficult and ignored the concerns around which they mobilize.

In sum, the three chapters in this section provide clues on how policies can be made more responsive to the needs of women and men, how gender impacts can be understood, how women and men approach power and policy-making, and how their efforts are seen by policymakers and development planners. Importantly, the chapters also present concrete examples of strategies for empowerment, including reuniting women's dual roles in the family and as citizens.

CHAPTER ELEVEN

—————— ■ ——————

Gender, Environment, and Empowerment in Venezuela

María Pilar García-Guadilla

ALTHOUGH WOMEN ARE ACTIVE IN SOCIAL MOVEMENTS in Latin America
(frequently more active than men), studies show that they have less
political power and less impact on government and public opinion than
do men.[1] Attempts to explain this difference have failed because they
have tended to focus on the links between women's participation in
social movements and their gender identities as wives and mothers. This
approach is too simplistic. It ignores the specificities of the context within
which women mobilize—household, barrio, city, region, or nation—and
how contexts influence the organizational structure and strategies of
social movements, factors that are important determinants of the political
power of movements. Furthermore, these factors have not been considered within a comparative framework that includes both men's and
women's organizations.

To understand the consequences of gender for women's power, it is
necessary to transcend a "women's movement" approach and adopt a
more general and gendered framework that considers both women and
men as political actors. Instead of assessing women's political power
within women's social movements, theory and empirical knowledge will
benefit from a comparison of political power *between* women's social
movement organizations and those in which both men and women participate.

Another relevant factor usually neglected in studies of Latin American women's political power is the influence of the mass media in creating *political facts*, defined as issues or problems with the intrinsic
potential to generate political power or public pressure regardless of who

is involved. Therefore, a study of gender and empowerment through social movements must consider organizational characteristics and strategies, context, and the role of the media.

In this chapter, I will use a comparative approach to evaluate gender and empowerment within the context of the environmental social movement in Venezuela—a movement composed of numerous groups and organizations that together provide the necessary heterogeneity to assess the relative importance of proposed determinants of women's political power. I will begin by laying out a framework informed by empirical and theoretical evidence on social movements in diverse settings. I will then discuss the ways in which environmental issues in Venezuela are reconstructed as "political facts" and assess the importance of gender in the process of construction. Finally, I will address the conditions under which women's demands have become politicized. □

A FRAMEWORK FOR STUDYING GENDER, SOCIAL MOVEMENTS, AND POLITICAL POWER

There is an abundant literature on women, politics, and power.[2] Contributors have found, among other things, that women are underrepresented in the formal leadership of social movements, that women's demands attract little attention from the media, and that women have limited access to decisionmaking processes.

But scholars have tended to ignore the question of gender in social movements by stressing that women's participation in political movements is a function of increasing feminism and political consciousness or women's traditional and reproductive roles. Even scholars of the "new social movements in Latin America" have evaded the question of gender by suggesting that women's participation originates in their domestic roles and collective consumption needs or, in a few cases, through their role in production.[3] Although each focus contributes to our understanding of women's mobilization, such approaches do not clarify the complexities of women's political participation as contrasted to that of men. One example, is the "practical-strategic" dichotomy that has become a popular analytical tool.

The "Practical-Strategic" Dichotomy

Some empirical research and theories have linked women's lack of political power to the prevalence of "practical gender interests"—classified as being in the domestic or private domain—over "strategic interests in women's demands—in the public domain."[4] Practical gender interests are concerned with daily survival needs or specific demands linked to women's ascribed domestic roles and the gender division of labor. Strategic gender interests concern empowerment, demands for legal or structural change, and women's struggles to overcome gender inequality.

This approach reveals that women, more than men, tend to mobilize around practical-domestic demands for such things as urban services (water supply, health care, food, schools, parks, garbage, sewage, and housing); it links women's mobilization to their deep ties to their communities as housewives and mothers. Motivation to mobilize rests in their self-definition as mothers and their commitment to implicit maternal responsibilities. For women in squatter neighborhoods, this includes responsibility for providing the basic necessities of life and leading "the day-to-day resistance strategies of Latin America's popular classes."[5] This is true in Venezuela, where more women than men traditionally have participated in organizations to demand individual and collective urban services.[6]

This dichotomous approach suggests that there is a unifying ideology of women's interests. Maxine Molyneux and Caroline O. N. Moser argue that it is necessary to take into account practical gender interests in the definition of strategic gender interests because the former are the basis of women's political participation in popular social movements. Moreover, the politicization of practical gender interests and their transformation into strategic interests become the core of feminist practice.[7] Thus, women's demands channeled through social movements cross the false divisions between domestic-strategic or domestic-public that emerged from the Western philosophical tradition. Both represent a struggle against "engendered everyday space, as well as a struggle against institutionalized forms of power inherent in traditional class-based political institutions and in the dominant Western practice of development."[8] Additionally, the dichotomy between practical-domestic interests, on the one hand, and public-strategic interests, on the other, does not permit an evolutionary view of women's political progress. Yet political identities are not fixed, and there are diverse spaces from which women mobilize. In Latin America, gender identities are also diverse, and there is a complex "multidimensionality of situations of power, subordination, and exploitation."[9] Studies of women's political power and social movements should address those issues.

Other approaches to the study of social movements provide conceptual tools that enrich and complement the practical-strategic dichotomy. For instance, the resource mobilization approach, though rarely applied specifically to studies of women or gender, considers the multiplicity of sites and identities from which men and women practice politics.

The "Resource Mobilization" Approach

Advocates of this approach focus on organizational structure, resources, and strategies as critical variables in the success or failure of pressure groups and social and political organizations.[10] In fact, researchers have revealed great differences among the environmental organizations studied in Latin America, often within the same country, with respect to structural characteristics, strategies, and resources.[11]

Moreover, some of their studies concluded that there are structural and strategic organizational differences according to the memberships' gender composition.[12] Women-only and women-led organizations are frequently less visible to the government because they often have more informal, amorphous, and casual structures than those whose memberships are predominantly male. The relative invisibility of leadership networks makes it more difficult for the government or political parties to co-opt them.[13] On the other hand, members also frequently maintain strong social ties that transcend formal links within the organization.[14] This contributes to the informal structure, greater consensus, and permanency of the organization. Some gender strategies of women-led and women-only organizations could even be related to greater success in achieving organizational goals because they represent new ways to do politics, pose new societal demands, and create new symbols or value codes through which domestic-practical interests can attain greater political recognition.[15] Although rarely studied within a comparative gender framework, the differences between men and women in terms of organizational characteristics and resources may facilitate or create obstacles to attaining political power and impact.

The practical-strategic dichotomy and the resource mobilization approaches significantly enhance possibilities of understanding why and how women organize. Yet they do not explain why certain issues, demands, and organizations become politicized. For this, the symbolic-cultural approach provides key tools for analysis.

The "Symbolic-Cultural" Approach

Some issues are associated with emerging value codes that, in turn, constitute a new political culture. These issues are likely to be appropriated by societies through the mass media and to be imbued with political power. This was the case with environmental problems identified by the industrialized countries (such as nuclear energy, acid rain, pollution, and other issues that fomented environmental movements). They were defined as strategic—political—issues while alternate environmental problems, such as community-based urban services and quality-of-life issues of concern to women, were relegated to the category of "domestic" issues.[16]

In the 1990s, strategic environmental issues and problems became a "new political fact" and were imbued with "symbolic" effectiveness.[17] That is, these issues have become effective symbols around which people mobilize; they are attached to new value codes (such as sustainable development) that often compete with previously existing codes (such as economic growth). The substitution of these value codes involves personal, cultural, and political change. In this case, it is not social mobilization per se that transforms the environmental issue into a new political fact but its diffusion through the mass media. However, social mobilization also can attract the attention of the media. In fact, mass media—whether TV, newspapers, or radio—have the highest potential for transforming strategic issues into "political facts" as they publicize environmental issues and heightening their importance in the public eye and in political arenas.[18]

Citizen organizations classified as "symbolic-cultural" alert society to the existence of problems whose solution requires decoding dominant models and searching for alternative meanings and orientations for social action. They fall within "new domains of the political." This is documented by the emergence of forms of social action that are independent of both the political parties and the state and that revolve around "new" themes and values. As in the case of environmental issues, these forms of social action tend to address problems that "can be acted upon and influenced, and around which a collective can be created without going through political parties or without their mediation, and without the need to validate proposals against the backdrop of a larger societal project or its corresponding strategy."[19]

Not all issues with environmental dimensions will command the same attention from politicians, the public, or the media. The symbolic-cultural approach argues that "domestic" issues receive less attention than issues identified as "strategic" by governments or public opinion—such as conservation of the Amazon or the Chernobyl disaster. Furthermore, when mobilized actors are low-income women, they will receive even less attention from the media than would women from the middle or upper classes or men of any class.[20] The explanation lies in questions of *who* demands *what*.

For instance, ongoing problems with public services such as water, disposal of garbage, or public health care traditionally have not attracted consistent or high levels of attention as political or media issues. However, widespread economic crises in Latin America since the early

1980s have led to a rapid deterioration of such services at the same time that purchasing power has fallen for middle- and low-income groups. The result is dramatic, sporadic mobilizations of low-income groups (such as food riots) and the sustained and increasing mobilization of middle-class women and men of all classes around such issues. These mobilizations have attracted—and leaders of some have sought to influence—media coverage and government and public opinion.[21] Widespread impoverishment also has attracted the attention of international financial and political agencies (such as the World Bank, the United Nations, and the Inter-American Development Bank), which has reinforced it as a strategic or political issue.

Demands defined as "environmental" by international agencies, the government, or public opinion also have a great potential to become politicized through the mass media. For example, in Third World countries, water shortages traditionally have not been considered an "environmental" problem. Providing water for domestic daily use is almost always the responsibility of women; low-income women use ever greater portions of their time to carry water from long distances, and a lack of clean water creates severe public health problems. But, when water shortages affect production in agriculture, industry, or commerce—particularly if those activities are the responsibility of men—then water shortage is defined as an environmental and a political problem.[22] This is related to global struggles to define "environmental problems." Before the United Nations Conference on Environment and Development (UNCED) held in Brazil in 1992, international development agencies stressed the environmental concerns identified by industrial countries, including pollution, climatic changes, and the ozone layer, while ignoring Third World issues of poverty and its environmental consequences.[23]

The Western-biased definition of "environmental problems" has it difficult to politicize the survival (i.e., practical-domestic) demands of the poor through the mass media. Since these are likely to be issues around which women from Latin America mobilize, gender also may play a role. The problem may be further exacerbated because production problems are often short-term and news of the moment, but domestic and community-based problems are endemic and thus viewed as commonplace and less newsworthy.

The preceding discussion shows that the symbolic-cultural approach can identify important obstacles to the politicization of issues. It could be argued that the political potential of issues is related to the gender and social class of those who mobilize. The discussion also reveals the ways in which issues are associated with men or women or with the "public" versus "private" (or "domestic") spheres.

An Integrated Approach

The three approaches described (practical-strategic, resource-mobilization, and symbolic-cultural) complement each other. Together, they provide the necessary conceptual tools for understanding gender, social movements, and political power. In this chapter, I apply these conceptual tools in an integrated and comparative approach to study gender, social movements, and political power in Venezuela. The focus is on organizations whose issues can be classified broadly as "environmental" because they address problems related to environmental-physical factors (such as water, soil, air, pollution), or to environmental-social factors (such as quality of life). Not all organizations explicitly apply the label *environmental* to the issues they address; some frame issues in terms of the needs of women or of poor communities. Some organizations use the political potential of the term *environment* as a mechanism to challenge existing political power structures; others have applied the label *environmental* to some dimension of issues addressed previously under other labels (such as *poverty, public health, women's issues*). My study focused on comparing the following variables: gender composition of membership, gender composition of leadership, use of a domestic or strategic approach to address issues of environment, resource mobilization by leaders, and whether mechanisms of symbolic effectiveness, particularly the media, were used. □

GENDER, ENVIRONMENT, AND SOCIAL MOVEMENTS IN VENEZUELA

Research Design and Questions

For about fifteen years, I have been involved in ongoing research, encompassing more than one hundred different organizations. The organizations selected for discussion in this chapter include some in which I have participated as well as studied. They can be classified into three distinct types of organizations within Venezuela's environmental movement: (1) women's environmental organizations, whose membership is exclusively women and whose focus is primarily on public services (water, garbage, sanitation, recreation) that affect the quality of life; (2) urban organizations (neighborhood associations) of mixed-gender membership and leadership that focus on a broad range of urban problems, including public services and quality-of-life issues similar to those of women's environmental organizations; and (3) ecological organizations that can be differentiated as politico-ideological (such as Habitat or Federación de

Organizaciones de Juntas Ambientales [FORJA]) or symbolic-cultural organizations (such as the Asociación de Amigos en Defensa de La Gran Sabana [AMIGRANSA]), both of which I will discuss below. In the case of the former groups, leaders are men and, in the latter, women. Organizations also differ in terms of their use of the media for symbolic effectiveness.

Methods employed to systematically study these organizations include participant observation; semistructured, in-depth interviews; document research; content analysis of issues as presented in the media; and self-evaluation sessions that I organized myself. (This last refers to strategic-planning and research-action exercises involving diagnostic and negotiation workshops.) Research addressed the following theoretical questions:

- Do organizational characteristics and strategies vary according to the gender composition of members and leaders?
- What characteristics of organizations are associated with political power: structure, strategies, resources, the use of mass media, gender composition, ideological homogeneity?
- How do organizations get power?
- What is the role of gender composition in gaining access to political power and the creation of an alternative political space (that is, an approach to political power that differs from that of political parties)?
- Do women-led, mixed-gender social movements have organizational characteristics and strategies that are similar to those of women-only organizations and different from men-led organizations?
- Are close social relationships found exclusively in women-only and women-led organizations? And do they contribute to a more informal, more permanent, less visible structure? Is there a relationship between visibility and co-optation?
- Do women-only and women-led organizations tend to use innovative strategies more frequently than men-led, mixed-gender organizations?
- Do such organizational characteristics and strategies facilitate the achievement of objectives (that is, do they contribute to greater organizational success)?
- What role do the mass media play in the politicization of environmental issues?
- What are the environmental issues most likely to get the attention of the mass media—practical or strategic, men's or women's—and why?

An Overview of Organizations and Issues

Ecological organizations in Venezuela have a Westernized view of the environment, and they stress the conservation of rich and unique ecosystems, the creation of national parks, the fight against pollution, and so forth. Women's environmental organizations and urban associations approach environmental issues from a Third World perspective of poverty, quality-of-life, and day-to-day domestic problems. Both ecological and women's organizations define themselves as environmental organizations, and urban associations have begun to redefine quality-of-life and poverty problems as environmental problems. It was the 1992 UNCED environmental conference that inspired these conceptual changes.

All four of the known women's environmental organizations in Venezuela are discussed: Los Círculos Femeninos (Women's Circles), La Red de Mujeres Todas Juntas (Network of Women Together), Grupo de Estudios Mujer y Ambiente (GEMA, Women and Environment Study Group), and the Asociación de Mujeres y Ambiente de Venezuela (AMAVEN, Venezuelan Association of Women and Environment). They vary in strategy—domestic or strategic—and degree of political success. Differences appear to be related to the degree of symbolic effectiveness.

No specific urban organizations were singled out for discussion. Rather, groups of organizations studied between 1976 and 1988—following passage of the Reglamento de Juntas de Vecinos (Neighborhood Association Regulations) and the Ley Orgánica de Régimen Municipal (Municipal Organic Law) in 1976—were compared with organizations studied following the passage of the reformed Municipal Organic Law of 1989 (which conferred political power on leaders of those associations). Both groups showed similarities in mixed-gender composition, structure, strategies, and demands, with one exception: After the 1989 law was passed, more men were attracted to leadership positions. The gender of leaders appears to be related to differences in strategy and degree of success.

Among the numerous ecological organizations in Venezuela, FORJA, a federation of environmental organizations that represents more than a hundred other organizations, was selected as representative of mixed-gender, men-led ecological organizations. FORJA is contrasted with AMIGRANSA, a women-led ecological organization. In both cases, group demands can be classified as strategic, but there are important differences between male and female leaderships' use of media and strategies to politicize these demands.

Thus, I will discuss organizations that vary by gender composition, ranging from women-only to mixed-gender memberships with varying levels of active participation by women and men. The organizations studied include both those that are women-founded and men-founded and those that are women-led and men-led. It should be noted that membership across organizations frequently overlaps for both men and women. For women, some members of environmental organizations also participate in urban or ecological organizations, some members of ecological organizations participate in urban organizations, and women from these organizations also participate in feminist groups and other women-only organizations.[24] All organizations have, at times, shown an ability to mobilize interest through the media (newspapers, local radio, TV) or through more traditional means of communication (personal interactions, bulletins, pamphlets, leaflets, telephone). The degree of success in generating widespread interest or the use of the media for political ends varies greatly across organizational types.

Age of the membership does not seem to be a significant discriminatory variable. The average age of most members is between thirty and fifty, and members of ecological organizations include a significant proportion of young adults. To understand gender, environment, and social movements in Venezuela is to understand that recent Venezuelan history has been critical in defining the political space open to social movements and the conditions under which movements acquire political power.

The Context for Social Movements

In Venezuela, until the arrival of democracy in 1958, there was no space for civil society or for social movements. The current national constitution, approved in 1961, fosters political stability through a "representative"—instead of participatory—democracy, with strong centralist, paternalist, populist, and clientelist features that do not encourage the growth of civil society.[25] From the 1960s to the 1980s, the state's industrialization and modernization strategies were based on an oil-export economy, and they generated a process of rapid urbanization, which made Venezuela one of the most urbanized countries of the world (91 percent urban according to the 1990 census). Venezuela also has heterogeneous social sectors with divergent interests. Most social sectors were co-opted under political pacts agreed on by key actors: the armed forces, the Catholic Church, political parties, the private sector, and the unions. This resulted in structural weakness for civil society—the social organizations excluded from such pacts.

The first groups to appear after the 1958 overthrow of Pérez Jiménez's dictatorship were the urban neighborhood associations (Juntas Pro Mejoras) in the squatter settlements (1959–1960). Highly politicized and co-opted by political parties, they had been created to distribute the "unemployment bonus" to squatters and migrants to Caracas. In the mid-1970s, reinforced by passage of the Municipal Organic Law of 1976, neighborhood associations also emerged in middle- and upper-middle-class neighborhoods whose residents were intent on defending their quality of life. In contrast to the Juntas Pro Mejoras, these operated independently of the government and political parties. They have been very active and created federations and networks that allowed them to articulate with other social movements to promote a more "participatory democracy" and "decentralization of the political system" as strategies for influencing local politics.[26] With passage of the Municipal Organic Law of 1989 and the subsequent Neighbors' Participation Regulation of 1990, neighborhood Juntas Pro Mejoras were recognized as the principal actors in local politics. This recognition paralleled a loss of legitimacy by political parties, which led them to attempt, unsuccessfully, to co-opt the movement. Ironically, the parties' formalization as political actors lowered the potential for the type of mobilization they had enjoyed as a social movement.

During 1976 and 1977, pioneer environmental legislation was passed—the Ley Orgánica del Ambiente (Organic Law of the Environment) and Reglamento de Juntas Ambientales (Regulation for Environmental Organizations)—and Venezuela's Ministry of the Environment encouraged *juntas de conservación* ("associations for the conservation and defense of the environment"). At the end of the 1960s, offers of "amnesty" and the end of the "guerrilla" struggle in Venezuela subsequently led some leftist university groups to shift their attention to environmental issues in the 1970s, creating an environmental movement that was independent of political parties, although it maintained close ties to the leftist parties that controlled the Legislative Commission on the Environment in the National Congress. From the early 1970s until the early 1980s, these groups focused on the expected negative environmental impacts of large-scale development projects in Venezuela, the creation of national parks, and other issues more in accord with the concerns of industrial countries than with the environmental concerns of Third World countries. In the 1980s, however, they did shift to Third World issues.

The consolidation of the ecology movement also dates from the 1970s. The first organizations—even those associated with leftist political parties—were dependent on the government. They acted as *juntas de conservación* and as part of the larger environmental social movement. Finally, by the mid-1980s, new environmental organizations, independent of government and political parties, emerged and showed great adroitness in using the media. All of these organizations together make up Venezuela's environmental movement.

Changes also were taking place in the arena of women's participation. Women's educational levels were increasing over the period, as was their labor force participation, especially at the professional level. Women also played a significant role in the organization and consolidation of all types of social movements, among them a number of women-only organizations; these included feminist groups and professional organizations that focused on strategic gender interests, such as the reform of the Civil Code (equal rights) and Labor Law. Most such organizations were composed primarily of middle-class university women or women born or educated abroad. Until the 1990s, women's organizations did not focus on environmental issues, such as recycling, solid-waste disposal, sanitary conditions, environmental education, or sustainable development.

Since the 1970s, women have been active in popular urban mobilizations, neighborhood associations, and cooperatives. Beginning in 1987, women have also created and led a growing number of mixed-gender ecological organizations.[27] Currently, Venezuelan women participate in social movements through a variety of organizational types:

- women-only organizations, such as feminist groups or women's circles;
- women's sections in labor unions, lawyers' or physicians' associations, political parties, and other groups;
- federations of nongovernmental organizations, such as the Coordinadora (Coordinator of Women's Nongovernmental Organizations)—an umbrella organization made up of women's groups with diverse demands and objectives;
- the mixed-gender, middle-class, and popular (working- and lower-class) urban movements, in which, in addition to participating with men, they frequently create their own splinter groups, such as the women's branch of the nongovernmental organization Centro de Formación a Servicio de la Acción Popular (CESAP)—a popular action advisory and research center;
- women-only environmental organizations (such as GEMA and AMAVEN); and
- other women-only or mixed-gender organizations (AMIGRANSA, for example) led by women that form part of the environmental movement in Venezuela.

In the 1990s, diverse women's groups and organizations articulated with other social movements. One of the most successful links was that between feminist and other women's groups, urban and environmental movements, and the cooperative movement. This articulation should have helped open the door to political power for women, but it failed to do so. This is probably because, in times of political and economic crisis, men tend to appropriate the power and resources that are becoming more scarce. However, there are conditions under which women are successful at obtaining political power. One way is through their participation in environmental organizations, which focus on strategic issues instead of domestic issues and use nontraditional political strategies.

Women's Environmental Organizations

The Women's Circles and the Network of Women Together are part of CESAP, one of the largest and better organized nongovernmental organizations in Venezuela, which was founded in the 1960s to help organize the poor and residents of squatter settlements. The Circles and the Network are organized and led by women and are part of the Coordinadora. They work with women only and aim to improve women's quality of life in squatter settlements by focusing on health problems, housing shortages, lack of employment, and the high cost of living and education. Since 1990, they have identified environmental problems with poverty.

The Circles and the Network are characterized by informal structures and strong bonds of solidarity and friendship. They have been very effective in proposing new ways of dealing with the economic crisis and defending the poor against macroeconomic structural adjustment policies. Nonetheless, their issues have not had symbolic value beyond women's domestic interests. With the exception of some independent financing from international sources, both depend on CESAP for financial support. Therefore, the transformation of women's everyday problems into political issues depends on the incorporation of such problems into the demands of CESAP—the larger, mixed-gender organization. But CESAP's male leadership has an ambivalent attitude toward women's domestic problems, which makes such an initiative unlikely.

GEMA, a group of professional women who were close friends, was founded in 1989. It has an informal horizontal structure that facilitates consensus, and it, too, is part of the Coordinadora. GEMA focuses on the deterioration or lack of public and social services. Its main projects focus on health and the environment in two squatter settlements in Caracas. The scale of these projects is small because the group maintains only four to five active members and relies on their donations of time and funding; efforts to get financial support from the Ministry of Women and other national and international agencies have not been successful. GEMA's impact on environmental and women's health problems has not been significant, and their issues do not transcend the interests of women's audiences, nor have their "domestic" environmental demands generated attention from the mass media.

AMAVEN was formally constituted at the end of 1991 and immediately joined the Coordinadora. Unlike other women's environmental organizations but like mixed-gender ecological organizations, the group has focused on strategic demands such as sustainable development. Its constitution defines AMAVEN as "an organization which professes that women should be protagonists in the conservation and defense of the environment, not mere tools."[28] AMAVEN's founders, through their roles as leaders and active members of political parties and as members of the Presidential Commission on Women, have links with center-left and right political parties—Movimiento al Socialismo (MAS, Movement to Socialism) and Acción Democrática (AD, Democratic Action)—and with the government. These links allowed them to participate in the 1992 UNCED conference held in Brazil and to get international funding. AMAVEN defined its objectives in terms general enough to transcend the practical-domestic (survival) realm to become political-strategic (empowering women and improving their status):

> To create an environmental consciousness among the population allowing them to participate and contribute to environmental conservation, increase the standard of living, and obtain common and equitable benefits. To promote and defend development, protection, and conservation of the environment through the dissemination of project information. To cooperate in the solution of environmental problems and stimulate sustainable development through the active participation of women ... to consolidate the democratic processes of social justice, the preservation of peace, and respect for human rights.[29]

The organizational structure of AMAVEN is vertical and more traditional, probably reflecting the political experience of its members, whereas GEMA and the Network tend to be politically independent and share a "consciousness-raising," feminist approach. This fact leaves AMAVEN more vulnerable to co-optation by the government and political parties, which frequently "silence" their demands for change. At the same time, the ideological heterogeneity of AMAVEN's executive committee, the vertical structure, and their connections to traditional party politics have made it difficult to transform the group's demands into new political facts. AMAVEN has had little influence on the government, public opinion, or the media.

In summary, women-only environmental organizations in Venezuela have been unable to politicize their environmental demands—demands that have lacked symbolic value and failed to appeal to the media.

Urban Organizations

In this section, I focus on neighborhood associations formally constituted since the enactment of the Municipal Organic Law of 1976. Although they differ in social base (some are middle-class and some working-class), they share demands, structure, and strategies. For this reason, the discussion will not differentiate by class. In recent years, membership in these associations has been mixed-gender. Women are somewhat more active than men, but men predominate among the formal leadership, especially since the passage of the revised Municipal Organic Law of 1989. Previously, some neighborhood associations had women presidents but men have always dominated the umbrella organizations, such as the Federación de Asociaciones de Comunidades Urbanas (FACUR, Federation of Urban Neighborhood Associations); La Escuela de Vecinos (the Neighbors' School), which was founded at the end of the 1970s and the Coordinadora Nacional de Federaciones de Vecinos (CONFEVECINOS, National Coordinator of Neighborhood Federations), created in the late 1980s. Membership overlaps, and the same men frequently rotate as leaders.

The issues raised by urban organizations were characterized in the past by the government, public opinion, and the media as "domestic" because of their focus on quality of life—lack of water, recreation, and sanitation.[30] In the 1990s, public services issues like water supply, garbage disposal, and sanitation have been redefined as "environmental" because of the potential to mobilize people from different socioeconomic levels around environmental issues. This is supported by the Municipal Organic Law's designation of neighborhood associations as the legal repositories of ecological concerns in the broadest sense of "quality of life."

Since the late 1970s, neighborhood associations have become the articulating axis of social mobilizations for political and economic democratization and decentralization. These umbrella organizations were successful at transcending the media and acquiring political power by creating participatory democracy as a symbolic fact. The neighborhood movement has succeeded in integrating cooperative, popular, environmental, and even women's organizations around the issue of "democratization"—which acquired the greatest symbolic value and mobilizing potential during the 1980s.[31] The 1980s witnessed numerous joint actions by neighbors and other social movements aimed at addressing not only participatory and social democracy but also environmental issues. Thus, urban organizations have combined domestic quality-of-life issues with strategic-symbolic issues, such as political reform, to create a more "participatory democracy." Both men and women actively took part in this process, but the leaders of the movement were primarily men.

Although Municipal Organic Laws mandated the separation of neighborhood associations and party politics, the increasing legal power allocated to them presented new opportunities to attain power through clientelism and populism—the realm of traditional party politics. Parties became more interested in controlling neighborhood associations after the 1989 Ley de Descentralización (Law of Decentralization) mandated greater control of decisionmaking and budgets to municipalities and locally elected officials, making neighborhood associations a vehicle for entering local and municipal politics. As a result, neighborhood associations became more vulnerable to co-optation by political parties, and they began to compete with each other for political and public attention. Male efforts to control leadership positions in these associations also increased.[32] Both trends—men permeating leadership positions of urban organizations and the rising importance of local politics—attracted the attention of the media, the government, and the public, and had the effect of making urban issues political. Undoubtedly, it is not merely coincidental that practical-domestic issues were picked up by the media and became identified as political-strategic (empowerment) issues when men were promoting them.

Ecological Organizations

Ecological organizations provide ample opportunities for an analysis of gender and political power. In Venezuela, ecological organizations can be traced back to the 1930s and more properly to the 1960s, although the environmental movement as such did not emerge until the late 1970s.[33] Members were primarily but not exclusively young men, some of them leftist university students or former guerrillas.[34] Thus, men and male-led organizations in the environmental movement have a long history of political activism, playing roles as the "opposition" to the state bureaucracy and parties in power.

From its inception, the movement was concerned primarily with the environmental impacts of government-sponsored and internationally funded development projects, such as the large-scale mining and industrial development projects (in oil, iron, steel, and aluminum) that were the basis of Venezuela's development pole economic strategy.[35] In the 1980s, the environmentalists established links with the neighborhood movement over local quality-of-life issues and the political reforms needed for greater democratization and the decentralization of the political system.

Like women's environmental organizations and most urban organizations, ecological organizations have been primarily middle-class. The pioneer organizations of the 1970s have become more gender heterogeneous in the 1990s, but their leaders continue to be primarily men. In the second half of the 1980s, some women created and led their own ecological organizations, which became mixed-gender groups focusing on strategic environmental issues.

The result of these processes is that Venezuela's environmental movement now encompasses six subtypes: pioneering scientific-conservationist societies, such as the Aragua Conservation Society (most active in the late 1960s); ecological rural and suburban communities from the 1970s and 1980s; environmental defense organizations or *juntas* created in the late 1970s; neighborhood organizations; leftist political-ideological environmental organizations founded at the end of the 1970s (confederated as FORJA); and AMIGRANSA, the symbolic-cultural organization founded in 1985.

The following discussion focuses on FORJA's member organizations and AMIGRANSA—that is, on the political-ideological and symbolic-cultural organizations. Both organizations have mixed-gender membership, and similar demands defined as strategic by the government, public opinion, and the media. These include eco-development, sustainable development, conservation and protection of rich biodiverse ecosystems like the Amazon or Venezuela's Great Savannah, the creation of national parks and protected areas, and so forth. There are two main differences in the organizations. First, the political-ideological organizations have male founders and leaders, the symbolic-cultural organization was founded and is led by women. Second, the political-ideological organizations also use political party or other traditional strategies of power, the symbolic-cultural organization, on the other hand, emphasizes alternative strategies of power, including deliberate use of the media to politicize issues.

Political-Ideological, Ecological Organizations Founded by Men

Political-ideological ecological organizations have not questioned the personalistic and *machista* practices associated with the political parties from which their leaders came. Instead, these practices were reproduced within the ecological organizations. This virtually precluded leadership by women and led to a style that supported male dominance.

These organizations share an ecosocialist view that criticizes the style of capitalist development in Venezuela as the cause of the gradual worsening of living conditions, the marginalization and impoverishment of large sectors of the population, and the growing deterioration of the physical and natural environment. The solutions they suggest are therefore aimed at transforming the economic and sociopolitical model into a more socially egalitarian and technologically rational one, as embodied in the notion of "ecodevelopment."[36] Some examples of this type of organization are Grupo de Ingeniería de Arborización (GIDA, Tree Engineering Group), HABITAT-Venezuela, and ECO XXI. They often assume a defensive position and oppose megaprojects, such as the exploitation of the Orinoco petroleum belt, and the petrochemical, coal, and gas industries—the core of Venezuela's economic development model. Although the organizations have mobilized people, they were unsuccessful in achieving their goal of transforming the economic model. On the other hand, their access to the mass media was somewhat restricted, and their demands did not transcend the type of environmental lobbying generated by the Ministry of the Environment, the state-owned oil company, Petroleos de Venezuela, or other environmental groups.

Some of these organizations were interested in acquiring political power, but their political style and strategy focused on penetrating the existing institutional system through traditional party politics. This "multiple militancy" did not create a new political space or garner media attention for the organizations' demands for structural changes, such as the transformation of neoliberal and capitalist models to a socialist model. Their major success—one of only a few—was the constitution of FORJA in the early 1980s. FORJA has struggled to implement a democratic, horizontal structure, but problems of personalistic relations, authoritarianism, ideological rigidity, and competition within and among member organizations eventually weakened the federation.[37] FORJA's major success was the infiltration, through technical advising, of the Congressional Committee on Environment, whose members and technical advisers are all men. Moreover, until 1994, almost all technical advisers belonged to MAS, the leftist political party, and to highly politicized and confrontational ecological organizations. These characteristics are an outcome of the situation in the 1970s when the leftist parties—MAS, the Communist Party, and the Socialist League—considered both environmental concerns and feminism to be petit bourgeois deviations and barred them from the leftist political agenda. As environmental problems became fashionable—especially with the UNCED Conference in Brazil, these issues were incorporated into the agenda of some of Venezuela's political parties. The traditional style of doing politics favored by males differs sharply from the style developed by symbolic-cultural organizations like AMIGRANSA.[38]

Symbolic-Cultural Organizations Founded by Women

AMIGRANSA is a mixed-gender organization led by women. It emerged in response to frustration with national environmental problems, a loss of credibility on the part of political parties and the government, a lack of space in male-led organizations, and the failure of political-ideological organizations to have a significant impact on environmental policy. It is a nonprofit civil association founded in 1985 by five women, who form its current executive committee and design the group's strategies through consensus. Most of AMIGRANSA's actions have focused, successfully, on the defense of Canaima National Park, the world's fifth largest park.[39]

AMIGRANSA's structure is flexible, horizontal, participatory, and less personalistic than that of political-ideological organizations, and it is characterized by close social relationships that facilitate consensus, organizational stability, and the use of alternative political strategies, such as the extended use of mass media. AMIGRANSA does not question the government's model of economic development; therefore, its demands can be legitimized within the existing economic and political system. When confronting government policy, AMIGRANSA proposes alternatives and approaches resolution through negotiation, devoid of party politics. Two of its proposals—the rejection of the Trans-Amazon Rally in 1987 and the declaration of the Tepuyes escarpments as protected "natural endowments"—were accepted by the government after they generated media attention, particularly among newspapers and through the efforts of the Congressional Committee on Environment.[40]

AMIGRANSA's lack of involvement in traditional politics has led to fruitful articulations with other ecological organizations and has reduced the possibility of political co-optation. This has reinforced a flexible and conciliatory approach to dealing with different political actors, including government institutions such as the Ministry of the Environment, the legislature, the Congressional Committee on Environment, and judiciary bodies. AMIGRANSA also has benefited from the use of the mass media to transform demands into political facts. Indeed, it is through the media that AMIGRANSA has reconstructed "the environment" in public space and has transformed environmental issues into new political facts. In general, it appears that the relative success of most ecological organizations has depended on their ability to use the media as a strategy to politicize their issues. But in Venezuela, the organization that has enjoyed the highest degree of success is the one that is led by women— AMIGRANSA.☐

CONCLUSION

The preceding discussion reveals that the three types of organizations share important similarities and differences in structure and strategies, and these appear to be related to the gender composition of membership and leadership. The organizations also differed in the nature of their

MARÍA PILAR GARCÍA-GUADILLA

ïeir efforts to politicize issues and attain greater political
their use of the mass media. For instance, women's envi-
ânizations make either domestic or strategic demands (as
ɼ GEMA and AMAVEN, respectively). Urban associations,
however, more frequently make domestic demands, that is, those that are
related to the quality of life and that are widely regarded as "Third World
environmental problems." Ecological organizations tend to focus on strategic, global environmental concerns, especially those defined as such by
industrialized countries. With respect to strategies, some women's environmental organizations (AMAVEN again provides an example), all
mixed-gender urban associations, and all mixed-gender ecological organizations led by men often use traditional political strategies; conversely,
other women's environmental organizations (GEMA) and all mixed-
gender ecological organizations led by women use alternative strategies.

The case studies confirm that gender identity alone is inadequate to
explain women's participation in social movements and their relative
access to power. If we may generalize from these case studies, achievement of political power depends, first and foremost on a combination of
gender and nature of the demand: When the issue is raised by women
only and is defined as domestic by the government, public opinion, and
the media, political power is weak regardless of strategy. If the issue is
domestic but raised by mixed-gender organizations or by men, political
power tends to be greater, and the issue is likely to attract the attention of
the government and the media. If the demand is defined as strategic, relative political power will depend on organizational characteristics and
the strategies used: Democratic and informal structures and the use of
alternative political strategies result in greater political power or success.
At the same time, the use of alternative strategies seems to depend on
gender: women use them more frequently than men. Therefore, the
highest political power and the greatest relative success can be expected
from those organizations whose issues are defined as strategic and that
use alternative political strategies. In Venezuela, those organizations tend
to be mixed-gender organizations led by women.

In summary, the main factors affecting the politicization of women's
environmental problems are: definition of demands, strategy employed,
and whether the demands attract media attention. Obstacles to this
politicization include: the persistent identification of women's environmental issues and women's movements in general with the practical-
domestic domain, the lack of political power assigned to practical-
domestic demands, and the increasing co-optation by political parties of
organizations with rigid, vertical, personalistic, and formal structures.

The identification or definition of demands as practical-domestic or
political-strategic depends less on the nature of the demands made than

on who appropriates them: men or women. In general, women's demands are often associated with practical-domestic interests by the sheer fact that they are appropriated by women. Unless also appropriated by men, they are unlikely to generate political power or recognition as political facts by the government, public opinion, or the mass media.

On the whole, women's strategies to deal with environmental problems differ from men's. Women tend to participate in organizations that have greater flexibility and are more democratic and more participatory. They also are more prone to create close social relationships that are difficult to co-opt. This contributes to a greater stability. These organizational characteristics and strategies are common not only among all-women organizations but also among women-led organizations. Women seem to bring these organizational styles with them.

However, the identification of women's interests with domestic roles creates obstacles to entering domains of traditional political power through social movements if those movements prioritize domestic demands. This is because governments do not recognize the domestic domain and derived demands as political and do not understand the political significance of those demands.

Another reason why some organizations are more successful than others is that their themes and values generate new, nationally or internationally relevant political facts, independent from traditional political actors. In this sense, it is not only strategy that warrants success (for example, defining demands as political-strategic), but also the symbolic value of the ecological message. Thus, if two organizations could share the same strategic demands, the one capable of using strategies to transform demands into new political facts via symbolic effectiveness will be more successful. Since practical-domestic demands attract less media attention than do political-strategic demands, to be successful—that is, to attract government attention and public opinion to the issues they promote—women need to abandon the practical-domestic approach.

Finally, women can become politicized by organizing around reproductive and other gendered issues; their women's organizations have shaped their visions of a more just society. But this does not change men's attitudes towards women's demands. The possibility of transforming women's environmental domestic demands into strategic or political demands requires rethinking such problems as global issues—as problems that affect the survival of both men and women alike. □

NOTES

I thank Cathy Rakowski for her comments on this and earlier drafts of this chapter and for her editorial assistance.

1. In this situation, political power is conceptualized as influential in power and decisionmaking. Maxine Molyneux, "Mobilization Without Emancipation? Women's Interests, the State and Revolution in Nicaragua," *Feminist Studies* 11, no. 2 (1985): 227–254; Susan Eckstein, ed., *Power and Popular Protest: Latin American Social Movements* (Berkeley: University of California Press, 1986); Jane Jaquette, ed., *The Women's Movement in Latin America: Feminism and the Transition to Democracy* (Boston: Unwin Hyman, 1989); Sonia Alvarez, *Engendering Democracy in Brazil* (Princeton: Princeton University Press, 1990).

2. Jaquette, ed., *The Women's Movement in Latin America*; Temma Kaplan, "Female Consciousness and Collective Action: The Case of Barcelona, 1910–1918," *Signs* 7 (1982): 545–566; Eli Bartra et al., *La revuelta* (Mexico City: Martin Casilla, 1983); Kathleen Logan, *Haciendo Pueblo: The Development of a Guadalajaran Suburb* (Tuscaloosa: University of Alabama Press, 1984); Kathleen Logan, "Women's Political Activity and Empowerment in Latin American Urban Movements," in George Gemelch and Walter P. Zenner, eds., *Urban Life* (Prospect Heights: Waveland, 1988); Kathleen Logan, "Women's Participation in Urban Protests," in Joe Foweraker and Ann L. Craig, eds., *Popular Movements and Political Change in Mexico* (La Jolla, CA: Center for U.S.-Mexican Studies, 1990); Molyneux, "Mobilization Without Emancipation?"; Dolores Lozano Pardinas and Cristina Padilla Tieste, "La participación de la mujer en los movimientos urbano-populares," in Luisa Gabayet et al., eds., *Mujeres y sociedad* (Guadalajada: El Colegio de Jalisco, 1988); Sonia Alvarez, "Women's Movements and Gender Politics in the Brazilian Transition," in Jaquette, ed., *The Women's Movement in Latin America*.

3. Tilman Evers, Clarita Muller-Plantenberg, and Stephanie Spessart, "Movimientos de Bairro e estado: Lutas na esfera da reproduçao na America Latina," in Jose Alvaro Moises et al., eds., *Cidade, Povo e Poder* (Rio de Janeiro: Cedec/Paz e Terra, 1982); David Slater, ed., *New Social Movements and the State in Latin America* (Amsterdam: CEDLA, 1985); Yvonne Corcoran-Nantes, "Women and Popular Urban Social Movements in Sao Paulo, Brazil," *Bulletin of Latin American Research* 9, no. 2 (1990): 249–264.

4. Maruja Barrig, "Democracia emergente y movimiento de mujeres," in Eduardo Bayon et al., eds., *Movimientos sociales y democracia: La fundación de un nuevo orden* (Lima: DESCO, 1986); Brinda Rao, "Struggling for Production Conditions, Producing Conditions for Emancipation: Women and Water in Rural Maharastra," *Capitalism, Nature and Socialism: A Journal of Socialist Ecology* 1, no. 2 (1989): 20–33; Molyneux, "Mobilization Without Emancipation?"; Caroline O. N. Moser, "The Impact of Recession and Structural Adjustment Policies at the Micro-Level: Low-Income Women and Their Households in Guayaquil, Ecuador," paper prepared for UNICEF, Ecuador, 1989; Logan, "Women's Participation in Urban Protests."

5. Nancy Sternbach, Marysa Navarro, Patricia Chuchryk, and Sonia Alvarez, "Feminism in Latin America: From Bogotá to San Bernardo" in Arturo Escobar and Sonia Alvarez, eds., *The Making of Social Movements in Latin America* (Boulder: Westview Press, 1992).

6. Talton F. Ray, *The Politics of the Barrios of Venezuela* (Berkeley: University of California Press, 1969); Lisa Peattie, *The View from the Barrio* (Ann Arbor: University of Michigan Press, 1972); Kenneth Karst, Murray Schwartz, and Audrey

Schwartz, *The Evolution of Law in the Barrios of Caracas* (Los Angeles: Latin American Center, University of California, 1973).

7. Molyneux, "Mobilization Without Emancipation?"; Moser, "The Impact of Recession and Structural Adjustment Policies at the Micro-Level."

8. Amy Conger Lind, "Power, Gender, and Development: Popular Women's Organizations and the Politics of Needs in Ecuador," in Escobar and Alvarez, eds., *The Making of Social Movements in Latin America*, 135.

9. Virginia Vargas, *¡Vota por tí, Mujer! Reflexiones en torno a una campaña electoral feminista* (Lima: Centro de la Mujer Flora Tristan, 1986), 9; Sarah A. Radcliffe and Sallie Westwood, eds., *VIVA: Women and Popular Protest in Latin America* (London: Routledge, 1993); Alvarez, *Engendering Democracy in Brazil*; Roy Boyne and Ali Rattansi, eds., *Postmodernism and Society* (London: Macmillan, 1990).

10. Edward Walsh, "Resource Mobilization and Citizen Protest in Communities Around Three Mile Island," *Social Problems* 29 (1981): 1–21; Edward Walsh and Rex Warland, "Social Movements in the Wake of a Nuclear Accident," *American Sociological Review* 48 (1983): 764–780; Russell J. Dalton and Manfred Kuechler, *Challenging the Political Order* (New York: Oxford University Press, 1990).

11. Slater, ed., *New Social Movements and the State in Latin America*; Eduardo Viola, "O movimiento ecológico no Brasil (1974–1986): Do ambientalismo a eco-política," *Revista Brasileira de Cienciais Sociais* 3 (1987); Gabriel Quadri, "Una breve crónica del ecologismo en México," Revista Ciencias UNAM 4 (1990); Juan Puig, "Larga marcha por la vida," *Revista Nuestro Ambiente* 15, no. 3 (1990); P. Gérez Fernández, "Movimientos y luchas ecológicas en México," unpublished paper, 1990; María Pilar García-Guadilla, "Venezuela: La red de organizaciones ambientalistas," in *El Nudo de la Red: Revista Cultural de Movimientos Sociales* 16.

12. See, for example, Jaquette, ed., *The Women's Movement in Latin America*; C. Andreas, *When Women Rebel: The Rise of Popular Feminism in Peru* (Westport, CT: Lawrence Hill, 1985); Marysa Navarro, "The Personal Is Political: Las Madres de la Plaza de Mayo," in Eckstein, ed., *Power and Popular Protest*; Elizabeth Jelín, ed., *Women and Social Change in Latin America* (London: UNRISD/Zed Books, 1990); Corcoran-Nantes, "Women and Popular Urban Social Movements in Sao Paulo, Brazil."

13. Eleanor Leacock, "Women, Power, and Authority," in L. Dube, E. Leacock and S. Ardener, eds., *Visibility and Power: Essays on Women in Society and Development* (New York: Oxford University Press, 1987).

14. Ray, *The Politics of the Barrios of Venezuela*; Peattie, *The View from the Barrio*; Larissa Lomnitz, *Cómo sobreviven los marginados* (Mexico City: Siglo Veintiuno Editores, 1975); Logan, "Women's Political Activity and Empowerment in Latin American Urban Movements"; Logan, "Women's Participation in Urban Protests."

15. María Pilar García-Guadilla, "Ecología: Women, Environment and Politics in Venezuela" in Radcliffe and Westwood, eds., *VIVA*.

16. UNCED, *United Nations Conference on Environment and Development, 1992* (New York: United Nations, 1992).

17. Alberto Melucci, "The Symbolic Challenge of Contemporary Social Movements," *Social Research* 52, no. 4 (1985); Alberto Melucci, "Social Movements

and the Democratization of Everyday Life" in John Keane, ed., *Civil Society and the State* (London: Verso, 1988); Alberto Melucci, *Nomads of the Present: Social Movements and Individual Needs in Contemporary Society* (Philadelphia: Temple University Press, 1989); Gabriela Uribe and Edgardo Lander, "Acción social, efectividad simbólica y nuevos ámbitos de lo político en Venezuela" in María Pilar García-Guadilla, ed., *Ambiente, estado y sociedad: Crisis y conflictos socio-ambientales en Venezuela y América Latina* (Caracas: Universidad Simón Bolívar/CENDES, 1991); María Pilar García-Guadilla, "The Venezuelan Ecology Movement: Symbolic Effectiveness, Social Practices, and Political Strategies," in Escobar and Alvarez, eds., *The Making of Social Movements in Latin America*.

18. Jürgen Habermas, "New Social Movements," *TELOS* 49 (1981): 33–37; Melucci, "The Symbolic Challenge of Contemporary Social Movements," 797.

19. Uribe and Lander, "Acción social, efectividad simbólica y nuevos ámbitos de lo político en Venezuela," 77.

20. Maria-Pilar García-Guadilla and Jutta Blauert, eds., *Environmental Social Movements in Latin America and Europe: Challenging Development and Democracy*, special issue of *International Journal of Sociology and Social Policy* 12, nos. 4–7 (1992); Melucci, "The Symbolic Challenge of Contemporary Social Movements."

21. Uribe and Lander, "Acción social, efectividad simbólica y nuevos ámbitos de lo político en Venezuela."

22. Vandana Shiva, *Forestry Crisis and Forestry Myths: A Critical Review of Tropical Forests, A Call for Action* (Malaysia: World Rainforest Movement, 1987); Vandana Shiva, *Staying Alive: Women, Ecology and Survival in India* (London: Zed Books, 1989); Rao, "Struggling for Production Conditions, Producing Conditions for Emancipation"; Brinda Rao, "Dominant Constructions of Women and Nature in Social Science Literature," *CES/Capitalism, Nature and Socialism*, Pamphlet #2 (1991); Melucci, "Social Movements and the Democratization of Everyday Life"; Melucci, *Nomads of the Present*; Uribe and Lander, "Acción social, efectividad simbólica y nuevos ámbitos de lo político en Venezuela"; García-Guadilla, "The Venezuelan Ecology Movement."

23. World Commission on Environment and Development, *Our Common Future* (London: Oxford University Press, 1987); Inter-American Development Bank, *Our Own Agenda* (Washington, DC: IDB, 1991).

24. García-Guadilla, "Ecología."

25. María Pilar García-Guadilla, "Crisis y conflictos socioeconómicos en la Venezuela post-Saudita: Hacia un redefinición de los actores, los roles y las demandas sociales," in F. Ebert, ed., *Consecuencias regionales de la restructuración de los mercados mundiales: Políticas alternativas relativas a la escala regional y local* (Buenos Aires: CEUR, 1990); Juan Carlos Rey, "El futuro de la democracia en Venezuela," in Juan Carlos Rey, ed., *Venezuela hacía el año 2000: Desafíos y opciones* (Caracas: Editorial Nueva Sociedad, 1987).

26. Nelson Lope-Bello, *La defensa de la ciudad* (Caracas: Universidad Simón Bolívar and Instituto de Estudios Regionales y Urbanos, 1979).

27. García-Guadilla, "The Venezuelan Ecology Movement."

28. AMAVEN, "Estatutos de la Asociación Mujer y Ambiente de Venezuela" (Caracas: AMAVEN, 1991).

29. Ibid.

30. O. Ovalles, "Movimientos de cuadro de vida en la Venezuela urbana actual" in Luis Gomez, ed., *Crisis y movimientos sociales en Venezuela* (Caracas: Trópicos, 1987).

31. Uribe and Lander, "Acción social, efectividad simbólica y nuevos ámbitos de lo político en Venezuela."

32. María Pilar García-Guadilla, "Crisis, Estado y sociedad civil: Conflictos socio-ambientales en Venezuela" in García-Guadilla, ed., *Ambiente, Estado y sociedad*.

33. Ibid.; García-Guadilla, "The Venezuelan Ecology Movement."

34. USB-ILDIS 1987; Viola, "O movimiento ecológico no Brasil (1974–1986)"; Slater, ed., *New Social Movements and the State in Latin America*; Quadri, "Una breve crónica del ecologismo en México."

35. María Pilar García-Guadilla, "La experiencia venezolana con los polos de desarrollo," *Cuadernos de la Sociedad Venezolana de Planificación*, no. 162 (1986); García-Guadilla, "Crisis, estado y sociedad civil."

36. García-Guadilla, "The Venezuelan Ecology Movement"; ECO XXI (Grupo Ambientalista) 1987, 1988.

37. USB-ILDIS, "Primeras jornadas de evaluación de las organizaciones ambientalistas."

38. Although AMIGRANSA is the only organization that can be properly classified as symbolic-cultural, ECO XXI, one of the political-ideological organizations, has been making the transition toward this type.

39. AMIGRANSA, *Renacuajo: Boletín de los grupos ambientalistas venezolanos*, no. 1 (1989) and no. 4 (1991); García-Guadilla, "The Venezuelan Ecology Movement"; García-Guadilla, "Ecología."

40. García-Guadilla, "The Venezuelan Ecology Movement"; García-Guadilla, "Ecología."

CHAPTER TWELVE

— ■ ———

Gender and Environments: Lessons from WEDNET

Bonnie Kettel

AFRICAN WOMEN'S ENVIRONMENTAL KNOWLEDGE offers a potentially significant contribution to the protection of the continent's natural habitats and to the improved well-being of its people. In examining the case of Africa in this chapter I will present a new paradigm for women, environment, and development research and for policy analysis. This new approach, which I refer to as "gender-and-environments analysis," addresses the promotion of secure livelihoods, the protection of biodiversity, and women's recognition and authority as environmental decision makers.[1]

In this chapter, I draw on the emerging results of WEDNET research to develop the gender-and-environments approach. After a brief introduction to the approach, I discuss the significance for the gender-and-environments paradigm of African women's involvement in the "production of life" and "nature." In addition, the central features of the WEDNET conceptual framework are presented, and the early results of the WEDNET research are outlined.

In its first iteration and especially in its initial use as a research paradigm, the WEDNET conceptual framework focused largely on women's environmental decision making. Women's relations with men and men's environmental decision making were not addressed as primary concerns.[2] The major features of gender and environment analysis are developed for the first time in this chapter, following the discussion of the WEDNET research. The final section outlines the implications of the new paradigm for research and policy formulation.

The gender and environments paradigm draws on the GAD approach to women's participation in the development process.[3] In this chapter, I use a GAD approach to reveal the importance of gender-based distinctions in the meaning and use of the natural environment. I also look at the implications of these differing perceptions for women's gender-based environmental interests and their empowerment as environmental decision makers.

The new paradigm focuses on women and women in relation to men, not because women are understood to be biologically more "in tune" with nature but because women's perceptions of the natural world—and of themselves in relation to nature—are most threatened and undermined by externally imposed development agendas.[4] Concomitantly, men's perceptions are more often recognized and validated by government and donor action. This focus on women's perceptions rather than on women simply as a target of development policy and action is central to gender and environments analysis, as is the nature advocacy that propels this new approach.

Two assertions constitute the essence of gender and environments analysis. The first is that *both* women and the natural environment must be understood as sociocultural constructions. Our appreciation of gender as a social construct that creates "women" out of female persons is long established. The gender and environments paradigm argues that the natural environment must be understood in the same manner, as a social construct that defines the natural world as a realm of human interaction and use. Further, gender and environments analysis suggests that these two constructs are, in fact, interdependent and that it is not possible to fully understand gender relations or relations between people and nature except as particular aspects of an underlying framework of interpretation that organizes both simultaneously. The new concept of the "landscape" is introduced here to illuminate the relationship between people, gender, and environment. Landscapes are perceptions of the natural environment that emerge from the culturally determined and socially derived links between women, men, and nature. The emphasis in this chapter is on women's landscapes, including their implications for women's environmental interests and their involvement in the use and protection of the natural environment.

The second assertion in gender and environments analysis is that nature must also be recognized as reacting (or having "interests") in relation to human use. Unlike the natural environment, which is a social construct, nature does exist apart from human perceptions. Rather, it is a synthesis of diverse econiches and species that react to human intervention in ways that are positive or negative for their continued existence and for the preservation of the biosphere. In this ecological and systemic sense, the species and econiches that constitute nature also have immediate and long-term interests. What is at issue here is the advocacy of nature—of "weeds, pests, and predators"—as legitimate and necessary components of the human life space.[5] The gender and environments paradigm draws on Maria Mies's conceptualization of women's significance in what she terms the "production of life." Here, I suggest that African women's gender-based involvements with nature are also important in the "production of the nature."[6] □

WOMEN, ENVIRONMENT, AND DEVELOPMENT: AN AFRICAN PERSPECTIVE

In *Our Common Future*, the World Commission on Environment and Development highlighted the potential contributions of women, particularly women in the nations of the South, who are users and managers of natural resources.[7] However, as Shimwaayi Muntemba, the WEDNET project leader, suggests: "Central to the issue of management ... are questions of who conceptualizes and designs patterns of management. ... As the major users and traditional resource managers, would more successes be recorded with longer-term implications if greater focus was turned on women? The answer is pointing to the loudest YES."[8]

This issue of conceptual authority over the meaning and use of the natural environment is fundamental to the empowerment of African women. Women scholars in Africa have made it very clear that their stand with regard to environment and development issues is shaped by their culturally defined position as *mothers of children*. The Nairobi Manifesto, adopted by the African participants at the NGO Forum at the end of the UN Decade for Women, attacks "the selective attribution of famine and the overall food crisis to population growth" and affirms "the right of African women to exercise their reproductive functions."[9] In this chapter I emphasize motherhood as a cultural metaphor, rather than a biological status, one that offers a powerful rationale for African women's increased participation and authority as environmental—and family—decision makers.[10]

Ifi Amadiume illuminates the traditional significance in Nigeria of motherhood as a gender-based ideology generated and manipulated by Nnobi women in their own interest. As producers of children and sustenance, Nnobi women acquired recognition, important social rewards, and a guaranteed position in political life. Amadiume points out that motherhood was also a basis for women's assertiveness ("traditional, positive female aggressiveness") in support of personal and public safety and order.[11] This is where a women, environment, and development approach that will respect and support African women's knowledge and environmental empowerment might begin—with women's "positive female aggressiveness" in their daily actions as mothers responsible for the production of life.[12]

In the daily production of life, women across rural Africa and in many urban neighborhoods act as primary agents of intersection between people and nature. By placing their hands on the raw ingredients of nature and by gathering and linking elements such as soils, water, and energy, African women create sustenance for human use. Women also create and nurture human life, thereby linking social issues such as fertility, health, and nutrition in the overall production of life in African communities. These activities are inadequately conceptualized as a series of *tasks*: Instead, the production of life is a comprehensive *process* within which women make decisions about their own time and energy, about the time and energy of others, and about the natural environment on which their sustenance depends.[13]

Through their decision making in the production of life, African women are also active producers of nature.[14] The diverse ecozones utilized by women across Africa are not a direct gift of nature. They are, in fact, *human habitats* created by generations of sustained use.[15] Women's decisions about the natural environment are central to the use and protection of these habitats, which include the extensive African rangelands and the forests—the source of a variety of useful fruits, herbs, game animals, and fuelwood. Ecozones are best distinguished, therefore, not by the simple presence or absence of human use but by the kind of use to which each zone has been consciously put and by the particular decision-making process that has supported its continued existence.

Western strategies for environmental management generally assume that the ultimate significance of nature rests in its exploitation and that the environment, the life space surrounding *us*, consists of a multiplicity of resources intended solely for human use.[16] Anything that is not recognizably useful is eligible to be defined as harmful and, therefore, as a legitimate target for "management" through eradication. Several authors have suggested that this Western outlook on nature results in an ethnocentric and sexist approach to development—one that focuses on profits, technology, and men's interests to the detriment of sustainability, resource conservation, and the well-being and interests of women and children.[17]

At the African Women's Assembly on Sustainable Development, held in Harare in 1989, women from rural Zimbabwe argued strongly that the problems of environmental degradation that confront them are a direct result of the imposition of inappropriate strategies for environmental use and management. The Zimbabwe National Report stated that "One of the strange and frustrating paradoxes of rural life is that as western technology and management techniques have increased, food surpluses in the rural areas have decreased and a pattern of sustained starvation ... has been ushered in. ... Unless the rural farmers (the women) are ... given their rightful recognition then what they are capable of will remain a mystery."[18]

As WEDNET results are beginning to reveal, women are involved in the production of life and nature across Africa. However, women's activities and interests in this regard, as with all human endeavors, are experienced in a specific cultural milieu and shaped, among other factors, by their particular gender—and class—affiliations. For this reason, we cannot universalize "women" or "African women," expecting that women's perceptions and interests in the use and protection of the environment are identical in every community or neighborhood. We also cannot assume that women's interests are always forged along gender lines. In some cultural contexts, class or caste boundaries or age may be as significant—perhaps more significant—than gender relations. Instead, we require a framework for research and policy analysis that will allow us to recognize the similarities and differences in women's interests and decisions in the production of life and nature. As a large-scale international research initiative addressed to women's knowledge and action vis-à-vis the sustainable use of the natural environment, the WEDNET initiative has some important lessons to offer. □

THE WEDNET CONCEPTUAL FRAMEWORK

With the publication of *Our Common Future*, women and environment suddenly became a significant focus for development research.[19] WEDNET developed ten projects in eight African countries, each concentrating—with some overlap—on a different resource sector or issue and each located—again with some overlap—in a different ecozone.[20] In the absence of an established research paradigm, the first necessity was to formulate a conceptual framework that would allow a diverse, multidisciplinary team to mobilize a complex research initiative centered on women's knowledge and action for the use and protection of the environment. We accomplished this through a new perspective on women's environmental decision making, one that provided a basis for detailed research as well as for comparison across cultures and regions and through various periods of time.

There are two necessary dimensions to a fruitful investigation of women's environmental decision making. The first dimension is sociocultural, and the second is historical. These two dimensions intersect to

establish a conceptual matrix within which women's changing perceptions and interests in the use and protection of the environment can be
understood and illustrated.

The WEDNET framework approached the *sociocultural* dimension
through three questions:

- What conceptualization do women have of the natural environment?
- What "styles" and strategies of decision making in the use of the
  natural environment do women recognize and employ?
- How do women interact with the natural environment as members
  of larger social networks and communities?

The first question leads us to ask about the cultural attributes and
meaning of the natural environment. The emphasis on women's knowledge of the environment has been largely technical to date, with a
detailed focus on women's use of specific natural resources, such as trees
and water. Although we need much more of this important research, it
fails to address the impact of women's perceptions on their knowledge
and use of the environment and the relevance of women's perceptions to
their gender-based responsibilities and interests. It also views women's
concrete interactions with nature as disparate issues, failing to perceive
the important symbolic and ecosystemic interconnections that may link
women's decisions in the use of specific resources in an overall style of
interaction with the environment.

The second question directs attention to women (particularly those
who use the natural environment for daily sustenance) as significant
environmental actors making day-to-day decisions about the production
of life and nature. As Patricia Stamp says: "The critical conceptual shift is
to focus on women as actors, rather than as passive recipients of change.
They are more or less successful [in the production of life and nature] ...
depending on the degree to which they are effectively empowered to
make constructive decisions."[21]

As the third question suggests, women do not interact with the
natural environment only as individuals; they also do so as participants
in family and neighborhood-based groups and networks. It is often
through social interaction, especially with other women, that they
acquire their environmental knowledge and skills, whether traditional or
innovative. We need to understand, therefore, the social context for
women's interactions with the environment and the impact of social participation on women's environmental decision making. A critical gap
involves the social units that form significant contexts for women's environmental decision making. Notwithstanding the apparent environmen-

tal importance of the household or of women's self-help groups, very little is known about the social organization of women's environmental decision making, particularly in the nations of the South.[22]

In addition, we know very little about the competition and cooperation that arises between women as they struggle in increasingly fragile and degraded environments. In many African communities, recognized contexts for cooperation between women have long existed, within which women supported each other through hard times. What has happened to these strategies for cooperation—in Africa and elsewhere—in the face of environmental degradation? What is the significance of female leadership and the accumulation of personal prestige to these networks of cooperation and competition among women? And, as Stamp asks, "What is the prognosis for the survival of women's cooperation" as women struggle to produce life in declining environmental circumstances?

In the African context, environmental change is a dominant aspect of contemporary life, and African women's perceptions of the natural environment reflect their immediate environmental circumstances. They also reflect the complex political, social, and environmental history of Africa. Thus, the second axis in the WEDNET framework dealt with the *historical* dimension of women's environmental decision making, and each of the three questions raised earlier was considered in a chronological sequence covering three periods: the precolonial era, the colonial and postcolonial nation-state era, and the future. □

LESSONS FROM THE WEDNET RESEARCH

The WEDNET research demonstrates clearly that women's technical environmental knowledge, which may have both traditional and modern elements, is best understood as an aspect of complex knowledge systems that are shaped by cultural and religious beliefs, and by the impact of formal education and contemporary innovation.

Ntombie Gata and A. L. Kathivu's research on "indigenous science and technology" in women's food production in Zimbabwe demonstrates that religious belief and ritual were important aspects of Shona women's perceptions and use of the environment in the precolonial period. They document Shona religious and cultural practices that contributed to women's conservation of trees and forests, soil and water resources, and wildlife and domestic animals. The most detailed aspect of their research involves Shona women's continuing knowledge of crop production, particularly their gender-based activities in the selection of seeds and management of soil and water in the production of eleven food crops. For example, a "sorghum discussion group" identified fourteen different varieties of sorghum, each with a Shona name, grown in Zimbabwe. All these varieties have different characteristics and potential uses; they require varying degrees of rainfall and soil of differing quality; and they can be grown through three different planting methods but are varyingly susceptible to birds, crickets, grasshoppers, and weevils.[23]

Gata and Kathivu argue that, in the precolonial period, "women farmers had an in-depth knowledge of plant taxonomy and systematic botany which they applied to identify and classify plants for the purposes of ... crop improvement and for sustainable utilization of natural resources."[24] They also document the attack that was launched on women's environmental perceptions and knowledge in the colonial period. Colonial authorities variously described traditional farming methods as "slovenly, ineffective and ruinous" and as "mixed with witchcraft, ancestral spirit worship, taboos, unsubstantial customs, and superstition."[25] And the attack on women's environmental perceptions and knowledge did not end with independence in Zimbabwe. As a result, "there has not been any development taking place whatsoever. If anything, what is happening could be construed as progressive environmental destruction characterized by a situation of great economic decadence. The soil is becoming more and more scanty, forests are declining at an alarming rate, while declining crop yields are the order of the day."[26]

Ruvimbo Chimedza also documents the importance of Shona women's environmental knowledge as a basis for food security and protection of the natural environment in Zimbabwe. Chimedza's study focused on food sources commonly identified in the Western resource management framework as "pests": caterpillars, termites, cicadas, and other insects. In the Shona area of Zimbabwe where Chimedza carried out her research, 88 percent of all households consume insects collected by women as a tasty, protein-rich, and inexpensive relish. As Chimedza reports: "It is essential that women know their environment and understand the kinds of things that it has to offer. Sound knowledge of forests and their products is crucial in their food security responsibilities. Other than identifying the edible resources, women also need to know the different ways of processing them into edible forms. ... These techniques are passed on to them by older women."[27]

In another WEDNET project, Elizabeth Ardayfio-Schandorf documents the complexity of women's knowledge of "forest resources management" in the northern region of Ghana. She reports that "local beliefs and practical applications have given women good ecological and biological knowledge which enable them to classify trees and the vegetation generally. In all the study areas the people have names for all trees, shrubs, and grasses ... but women tend to be more knowledgeable about certain classifications than adult men and boys, depending on task differentiation in the household."[28] Women's fuelwood choices are shaped by this gendered environmental knowledge system, and these choices, in turn, affect the way in which women perceive, classify, and organize the household economy. Ardayfio-Schandorf also comments that women are knowledgeable about ecological associations, including trees that characterize particular ecozones. Trees characteristic of sacred groves are protected (taboo) because of their religious associations.[29]

The importance of cultural and religious prohibitions on women's knowledge and use of the natural environment is also apparent in Suzanne Lankouande's research in Burkina Faso, a country that has experienced severe desertification. She reports that

> there existed ... rules governing the exploitation of these resources. ... The knowledge was handed down from mother to daughter during the nights of story-telling or informally through daily activities. These rules ... were respected because ... those who did not respect the taboos and restrictions were punished by deadly curses. ... Though it is true that today these rules are no longer obeyed ... consequences of their disobedience still haunts women. In effect, almost all the people contacted explained that the droughts were due to disobedience of taboos governing the management of natural resources.[30]

The destruction of the natural environment as a necessary basis for immediate survival is very clear in Lankouande's research on impoverished women migrants in Burkina Faso. These women are environmental refugees who have been forced to abandon the areas of the country that have undergone desertification and move to the city. "These migrant women," Lankouande reports, "must ... develop new strategies ... which inevitably are not beneficial to nature, so as to maintain their husbands and children." This, she reports, is what has led migrant women in Ouagadougou to sell sand from the riverbed in order to feed their households.[31]

Binta Sene Diouf found that women in the desertified Podor Province of Senegal discuss the environment with "nostalgia, bitterness, and hope."[32] She demonstrates that Toucouleur women in the region have detailed knowledge of the environment, including the plants and trees that they use for food, medicines, fuel, and forage. Desertification has forced women to replace food crops with foods gathered in the wild. To get along without fuelwood, women cook only one hot meal daily, and they replace foods that require long cooking with those that need less. They also replace fuelwood with cow dung or even goat droppings. Here, as in Burkina Faso, due to desertification and the massive departure of men, women are often forced to violate their own knowledge and beliefs about the proper use of the natural environment and "to adopt attitudes which can help them save more time and energy."[33]

In addition, as Sene Diouf points out, caste differentiation is clearly a factor affecting Toucouleur women's environmental knowledge. She comments that "fishing, especially of big fish, was exclusively reserved for the 'Subalbe' [subcaste]. ... Small fish were caught by women of mixed castes ... for home consumption."[34] On the other hand, it was women from the Peul subcaste who kept cows. Caste differentiation also affects women's ability to use and to protect the natural environment. The particular factor in this regard is access to land: The ruling castes own land; the professional, merchant, and serving castes do not. Especially for women of the serving castes, lack of direct access to land may be a hazard to survival and a further source of environmental degradation.

Only one WEDNET project was carried out by an individual male researcher, Joseph Ouma, who studied the role of women in the management of water resources in the Siaya area of Kenya. Ouma reports that this was "the most absorbing ... piece of research that I ever did in thirty years."[35] What so engaged his enthusiasm was his discovery that, in the area of Kenya where he himself was raised, the unrecognized factor in the organization of human settlements is women's knowledge and use of available water sources.

Local "water-stress zones" are determined by the availability of water in the dry season. Ouma discovered that "women know the water-scarcity conditions pertaining to all the stress zones ... conditions which play a great role in a young woman's preferences in the zones of her future marital home." They learn the essentials of water management in their natal areas through "the tutorial guidance of the elderly women." Through visits with relatives and friends, they learn "the problems and potentials of life systems ... especially those related to water stress." Then, after marriage, a "young woman is apprenticed to her mother-in-law ... or co-wife ... on the management of the local life systems, especially on harvesting the wilderness and management of the water resources."[36]

Finally, Ouma reports that

> to women ... the integrational dimension of water is fundamental. Water is not just the liquid resource; rather, the term *water* connotes both the liquid and essential resources, products and services which feature in the efficient management of their households. To them, water is life, through their life systems ... traditionally, through water resources, women are active participants in the management of most of the natural resources for the life systems—agro-pastoralism, fishing, hunting, handicraft, and

small-scale manufacture ... the efficient management of a homestead, the village and the wider community hinges upon the efficient management of households; and ... the efficient management of each household depends upon the woman and the management of water resources.[37]

This revealing paragraph on the significance of women's decision making with regard to the collection and use of water as the ultimate "life source" suggests the potential richness of future research on women's involvements in the production of life and nature in the African setting. The WEDNET initiative is making important contributions, but these are merely an indication that we have a great deal more to learn. Our future investigations will require a more fully elaborated paradigm for women, environment, and development research, as well as for gender-sensitive policy formulation. □

GENDER AND ENVIRONMENTS ANALYSIS

Bina Agarwahl describes "feminist environmentalism" as a struggle "both over *resources* and over *meanings*," wherein the forms of appropriation of nature—particularly the inequities of gender, class, and race that lead to environmental degradation—are identified and challenged.[38] She calls for a "transformational approach to development," involving "both how gender relations and relations between people and the non-human world are *conceptualized*, and how they are *concretized*." The translation of this approach into specific policies and programs is, as Agarwahl suggests, "*the* development challenge" for the future.[39]

The gender and environments approach emerges from the lessons of the WEDNET research, which has documented the importance of African women's perceptions of the natural environment, environmental interests, and styles for the use and protection of nature. Existing conceptual frameworks, which are based largely on the assumptions of a Western resource-management approach, offer little foundation for an unbiased appreciation of these environmental perceptions. They also make it difficult for us to recognize the impact of gender differences on women's and men's perceptions and use of the natural environment.

Ouma's experience as a WEDNET researcher offers evidence of our present conceptual difficulties and the important possibilities of an approach that recognizes the sociocultural interconnections between gender, people, and nature. Ouma is an experienced scholar with a geographer's understanding of the natural environment in his community of origin. Yet it was not until he embarked on his WEDNET project that he realized the local women see that environment very differently from the way he was raised and later trained to perceive it. It is also clear from his report that women's perceptions of the natural environment are central to the organization of social life in the community.

Henrietta Moore points out that "one of the widespread features of gender ideologies is that the distinction between what is male and what is female is also used to structure other cultural contrasts." These gender-based distinctions act as "models of intelligibility" through which various aspects of the natural world and social life are categorized and utilized.[40] One well-known example of such gender perceptions comes from early research on the Lele people of Zaire. The Lele divided the natural environment into male and female domains. Generally, they associated men with the forest and women with the grasslands.[41] Although the Lele actually divided the natural world into gendered domains, what gender and environment analysis suggests is that women and men may—even in the absence of such clearly differentiated distinctions—perceive and use the natural environment differently. □

THE CONCEPT OF LANDSCAPE

I use the term *landscape* to refer to the gender-based distinctions that people have of the natural environment. Landscapes are symbolic interpretations of the natural world, of the specific ecozones that people occupy, and of the network of social relations that locates people, collectively and individually, in relation to nature. Within these interpretations, women and men find their "sense of place."[42] Because they have an essentially symbolic aspect, landscapes are highly variable, with a diversity emerging out of the richness of the human imagination and lived out in varying social frameworks and in differing ecozones across the planet. Because they emerge in social contexts, landscapes are shaped by social relations based in significant forms of social differentiation, such as gender, class and caste, age, and race.

The WEDNET research makes it abundantly clear that African women's landscapes commonly arise from their gender-based responsibilities as mothers involved in the production of life and nature for the benefit of their families. Women's landscapes differ, often quite profoundly, from the gender-based perspectives recognized and furthered by African men as "fathers," and more recently, as increasingly autonomous individuals.[43]

The results emerging from the WEDNET initiative suggest that African women's landscapes act as a determining factor or as a language or grammar that underlies their styles of interaction with the natural world.[44] Environmental knowledge, such as awareness of ecosystemic interconnections, is an important component of these landscapes. However, this technical knowledge is contained in a symbolic framework that gives meaning to these interrelationships. Thus, an important aspect of the landscape is the creation of appropriateness in the combination of elements of the natural environment. This means not only ecosystemic appropriateness but aesthetic and moral appropriateness as well. The importance of moral appropriateness in the use and protection of nature is very clear in the WEDNET data. Women's complex sense of appropriateness—ecosystemic, aesthetic, and moral—in the use of the natural environment leads to particular styles of environmental decision making.

An important task for women, environment, and development research, I suggest, is to document women's landscapes, the differences between women's and men's landscapes in the same community or region, and the landscapes implicit in government and donor development agendas. We can use Moser's work on women's gender-based interests to show how women's environmental interests emerge out of landscapes that are shaped by relations of gender, caste and class, age, and race.[45] Moser argues that "gender interests" are those that develop as a result of women's "social positioning through gender attributes." Practical gender interests (or needs) are those "which are formulated from the concrete conditions women experience, in their *engendered* position within the sexual division of labour." These practical interests are directly related to human survival. Strategic gender interests (or needs) are those "which are formulated from the *analysis of women's subordination to men*." These strategic interests are addressed to "an alternative, more equal, and satisfactory organization of society."[46] □

WOMEN'S STRATEGIC AND PRACTICAL
ENVIRONMENTAL INTERESTS

Using these distinctions, we can articulate African women's gender- and class-based environmental interests at two important levels: the strategic and the practical. Women's strategic environmental interests emerge out of their landscapes and their involvements in the use and protection of nature. They relate to women's scope of autonomy and authority over environmental decision making, to the long-term production and protection of the natural environments on which women depend, and to their opportunity for a secure life, free from harm, in a peaceful community. Certain aspects of these strategic environmental interests are clearly shared by women everywhere; others relate to the specific context of women's lives in particular cultures and ecozones and in particular contexts of class and caste, age and race. Thus, African women's strategic environmental interests must be understood in relation to men's interests, to the interests of other categories of women in the same community and nation, and to the enduring ethnocentrism and sexism of national government policy and even the sustainable development agenda.[47]

In these relational contexts, women will have strategic environmental interests relating to their participation and authority as environmental decision makers, to their comparative rights in the natural environment (such as issues of property, control over the development and dissemination of technology, and access to information and skills), and also to networks of kinship and friendship that will support their successful involvement in the use and protection of nature.

Women's practical interests are, Moser says, "usually a response to an immediate perceived necessity which is identified by women within a specific context." Moser suggests that women's practical gender needs arise from the domestic arena, from income-earning activities, and from community-level needs such as housing and basic services.[48] To this list we may add women's practical *environmental* needs and interests, including access to basic environmental necessities such as fuelwood or energy, water, seeds, soil, and technical skills and information. Some of this technical information may have significant implications for the daily production of life and nature. And, clearly, when basic environmental necessities are not available, women will "fight against nature for survival," as Lankounade suggests, "to maintain their husbands and children."[49] Sene Diouf's research on Toucouleur women indicates that women will use every opportunity, especially "the principle of helping and sharing," to sustain the production of life and nature over the long term.[50] This tendency to help and share, which is relevant to women's lives in a number of African settings, is a critical asset in women's search for empowerment and environmental security.

Recognizing African women's practical environmental interests also has long-term strategic implications for the well-being of both people and the natural environment.[51] However, African women's strategic environmental interests are not limited to the solution of broad-based practical problems such as the impact of desertification and water pollution. Stamp comments that these "overt crises" have had "a dramatic claim upon public attention," but women also experience "hidden crises," arising out of the failure of nations and donors to meet their strategic environmental interests, "which have till now received little notice."[52]

We can draw an example of such a hidden crisis from research that I and others conducted on the lives of women in African herding communities. Women and men in these communities generally have very different goals in animal production.[53] Whereas men are primarily interested in producing animals, women's concerns center on the provision of milk. Although these objectives are related, they also differentiate women's and men's responses to issues such as the management of the herd for meat or milk. These differences involve significant choices about the use of milk for animal reproduction or human consumption, the location of herds in relation to human settlements, and the distribution of human labor in the care and herding of animals.

In these communities, women's landscapes for the use and management of the natural environment, including animals and rangeland, emerge from their role in the production and distribution of milk. Women's associations with milk extend beyond mere household responsibilities: They are important to their personal identity, prestige, and public authority. The symbolic association between women and milk is also recognized in myth and ritual, and milk acts as a cultural metaphor for women's lives and their relations with other women, men, and animals. In fact, this symbolic association is so strong that in some herding communities, men are actually prohibited from milking cows; the distribution of milk, which is socially more significant, is almost always assigned to women.

Recent donor interventions, which were intended to halt the spread of desertification by introducing meat production, have focused almost entirely on men's interests and ignored women's practical and strategic concerns in milk production. As a result, women's labor burden has been increased, while their property rights in animals and their participation in household decisions about animal and pasture management have been severely undermined. At the same time, household milk supplies have been reduced, with negative consequences for children's health. In addition, because production of animals for meat is more pasture-intensive than milk production, environmental degradation and destruction have spread even more rapidly. This example makes it clear that donors who ignore women's landscapes and environmental interests cannot hope to develop adequate policies and programs to halt and reverse accelerating environmental degradation in Africa or elsewhere. □

IMPLICATIONS FOR RESEARCH AND POLICY ANALYSIS

The potential significance of African women's environmental knowledge for the resolution of present-day environmental difficulties emerges clearly from the results of the WEDNET initiative. Women's everyday solutions to living in an endangered environment draw on their landscapes and styles of involvement with the natural environment, on their daily experiments in the use of nature, and on the ideas and skills they have acquired from other women. Their innovations in this regard are important for the sustainable use of African environments and deserve further documentation and dissemination. However, these innovations

are technical solutions to a broader set of problems that ultimately origi-
nate in international and national development agendas that ignore
women's landscapes and environmental interests. The *Zimbabwe
National Report* makes the message clear: African women will not be able
to sustain life and nature in the future unless their landscapes and their
environmental interests and skills are granted "their rightful recognition."[54] This rightful recognition includes scholarly documentation and
support for the conceptual authority of African women over their cultural and personal identification as mothers and for their landscapes and
styles for the production of life and nature.

Understanding women's landscapes from the precolonial and colonial periods presents special difficulties. These perceptions are buried
under the massive weight of colonial misinterpretation, both official and
scholarly; the ongoing reinterpretation of "tradition" in present-day
African nation-states; and the enduring ethnocentrism and sexism of
government policy and the donor development agenda.[55] In the contemporary setting, African women's gender-based landscapes and environmental interests and the many factors that have undermined women's
perceptions and production of nature are critical topics for new research.
Amadiume's work demonstrates the importance of indigenous insight
and the scholarly acumen that arises from a childhood spent in the midst
of sociocultural life in a particular environment. That work also suggests
that an appreciation of women's landscapes requires detailed field
research (combining oral history and the critical reading of earlier auto-
biographical and ethnographic accounts), as well as a careful investigation of women's knowledge and agency as environmental decision
makers in the contemporary setting. The conceptual framework developed for the WEDNET initiative and the more fully elaborated concepts
central to gender and environments analysis offer a significant new paradigm for such research.

Rightful recognition also entails government and donor policy
support for women's environmental perceptions, goals, and interests.
Without this official support for African women's empowerment as environmental decision makers and actors, they will be left, once more, to
struggle on their own, with help only from other women, and, far less
often, from men in their own communities. However, it must be pointed
out that in many regions and in countries such as Burkina Faso, women's
knowledge, talents, and solidarity have been undermined to the point
where they are no longer able to manage the natural environment in a
sustainable fashion, with devastating consequences for women, men,
and their children and for the natural environments on which they all
depend. The ultimate question for government and donor policy, therefore, is whether this travesty will be allowed to continue or whether

African women will finally begin to receive the support and encouragement that they so profoundly deserve.

There are resonant similarities between the involvement of African women in the production of life and nature and the landscapes and involvements of women in other regions of the South, as well as among aboriginal communities in the North. Most striking are the important spiritual and religious elements that shape the relation between women, men, and nature in each of these settings. This spiritual dimension—which brings people and nature together in a larger cosmological universe—is entirely missing from Western resource management agendas, which are narrowly focused on the use of nature for financial gain. This unity in diversity suggests that understanding women's landscapes and supporting their potential importance for both secure livelihoods and the protection of biodiversity will require a new outlook on women, environment, and development research and on policy analysis. This new outlook must be built on comparative research and global collaboration. The WEDNET initiative is an example of the kind of comparative international research that should be done. It is critical that research be undertaken by indigenous scholars, but as the WEDNET initiative demonstrates, there is also a need for comparative insight and for collaboration across cultures, regions, and continents, particularly in the formulation and analysis of this research. At a policy level, the need for collaboration—and shared commitment—is acute.

If we want to establish secure livelihoods and protect biodiversity, then we must begin with women's landscapes—especially the landscapes recognized by women who use and protect the natural environment as the source of human sustenance—and the implications of these landscapes for the production of life and nature. On that basis we can build a strong foundation for collaboration in research, policy formulation, and political action that will support the environmental goals and interests of women globally. As for the question that Muntemba posed in Harare in 1989—"would more successes be recorded ... if greater focus was turned on women?"—after considerable collective and individual work, the answer likely to emerge from future WEDNET research will be, more than ever, YES. □

NOTES

This chapter is the result of my involvement as the Canadian coordinator for the Women, Environment and Development Network. WEDNET is a large-scale research initiative that is documenting the importance of African women's environmental knowledge as a basis for the sustainable use of the continent's natural environmental heritage. The chapter benefited greatly from the comments of

David Bell, Rae Blumberg, Neil Evernden, Bill Found, Helen Hambly, Elinor Melville, and Eva Rathgeber.

1. In this chapter, my approach to gender and environments analysis is comparable to Robert Chambers's emphasis on "sustainable livelihood security" as a baseline for "sustainable development." Sustainable livelihood security involves meeting basic needs; ensuring access, particularly by the poor, to necessary resources and income; and maintaining (or enhancing) resource productivity over the long term. Indeed, Chambers's approach to sustainability underwrites the analysis in this chapter. See Chambers, "Sustainable Rural Livelihoods: A Key Strategy for People, Environment and Development," in C. Conroy and M. Litvinoff, eds., *The Greening of Aid: A Sustainable Livelihoods in Practice* (London: Earthscan, 1988), 1–17.

2. Patricia Stamp, Eva Rathgeber, and I developed the initial version of the WEDNET conceptual framework. See Patricia Stamp, "IDRC/York African Studies Programme Conference on Women and Natural Resources in Africa," York University, Toronto, 1988. This document, although informal and unpublished, has had widespread distribution through WEDNET, the Gender and Development Unit of the IDRC, and the ELCI.

3. Eva Rathgeber, "WID, WAD, GAD: Trends in Research and Practice," *Journal of Developing Areas* 27, no. 7 (1990): 489–502; Rae Lesser Blumberg, "Income Under Female Versus Male Control," in Rae Lesser Blumberg, ed., *Gender, Family, and Economy: The Triple Overlap* (Newbury Park, CA: Sage Publications, 1991), 97–127.

4. Irene Dankelman and Joan Davidson, *Women and Environment in the Third World: Alliance for the Future* (London: Earthscan, 1988).

5. Neil Evernden, "The Environmentalist's Dilemma," in Neil Evernden, ed., *The Paradox of Environmentalism* (Toronto: York University, 1984), 7–17.

6. Maria Mies, *Patriarchy and Accumulation on a World Scale: Women in the International Division of Labour* (London: Zed Books, 1986).

7. World Commission on Environment and Development (WCED), *Our Common Future* (Oxford: Oxford University Press, 1987).

8. Shimwaayi Muntemba, "By Our Own Bootstraps: Women, Resource Management and Sustainable Development," paper prepared for the African Women's Assembly on Sustainable Development, Harare, February 6–9, 1989, 4.

9. Association of African Women for Research and Development (AAWORD), *AAWORD in Nairobi '85: The Crisis in Africa and Its Impact on Women*, Occasional Paper no. 3 (Dakar: AAWORD, 1986), 4.

10. After marriage, adult men are similarly recognized and validated as "husbands" and "fathers" and not as autonomous individuals. However, in the postcolonial era, this gender-based identification has been significantly altered by government and donor policy and action. See Bonnie Kettel, "The Commoditization of Women in Tugen (Kenya) Social Organization," in Claire Robertson and Iris Berger, eds., *Women and Class in Africa* (New York: Holmes and Meier, 1986).

11. Ifi Amadiume, *Male Daughters, Female Husbands: Gender and Sex in an African Society* (London: Zed Books, 1987), 67, 69, 166. A similar analysis is presented in Jo-Anne Fiske, "Carrier Women and the Politics of Mothering," in Gillian Creese and Veronica Strong-Boag, eds., *From the Periphery: Essays on Women*

in British Columbia (Vancouver: Press Gang, 1992), 210–211. Fiske argues that Carrier women in British Columbia "integrate their diverse interventions into an ideology of 'mothering' and providing for future generations." Fiske also comments that "this mode of thinking makes no distinction between domestic authority and public leadership. The latter is seen to emerge from the former."

12. African women's decision making in the production of life also offers a culturally appropriate metaphor and arena for *improving* their access to the ingredients of a well-informed approach to family planning, including information for the prevention and promotion of conception, preventive and curative health care, and informal and formal education.

13. Bonnie Kettel, "Gender and Environments: Challenging the Myths," *Environments* 21, no. 1 (1991): 1–9.

14. As Plumwood says, "If 'reproduction' provides the conditions for 'production' to take place, then it must be thought of as including not only the production of the labour force and of society, but also the conditions of the natural world which make life, society and production possible"; see Val Plumwood, "Beyond the Dualistic Assumptions of Women, Men and Nature," *The Ecologist* 22, no. 1 (1992): 13.

15. In a preliminary report based on her WEDNET research, Suzanne Lankouande comments that there is no land anywhere in Burkina Faso that has not been under human influence: "Il ne possède pas de lopin de terre vierge, n'ayant jamais été sous l'empire humaine"; see *Lankouande, Project de Recherche sur 'Femme—Environnement—Emigration au Burkina Faso,'* WEDNET Preliminary Report (Nairobi: ELCI, 1991), 2.

16. Evernden, "The Environmentalist's Dilemma."

17. Gita Sen and Caren Grown, *Development Crises and Alternative Visions: Third World Women's Perspectives* (New York: Monthly Review Press, 1987); Vandana Shiva, *Staying Alive: Women, Ecology and Development* (London: Zed Books, 1988); Patricia Stamp, *Technology, Gender, and Power in Africa*, Technical Study 63e (Ottawa: International Development Research Centre, 1989); Bina Agarwahl, "Engendering the Environment Debate: Lessons from the Indian Subcontinent," CASID Distinguished Speaker Series no. 8 (East Lansing, MI: Center for Advanced Study of International Development, 1991).

18. African Women's Assembly on Sustainable Development, *Zimbabwe National Report on Women and Sustainable Development* (Harare: African Women's Assembly, 1989), 2.

19. Dankelman and Davidson, *Women and Environment in the Third World;* Agarwahl, *Engendering the Environment Debate;* Jane Collins, "Women and the Environment: Social Reproduction and Sustainable Development," in Rita S. Gallin and A. Ferguson, eds., *The Women and International Development Annual*, vol. 2 (Boulder: Westview Press, 1991), 33–58; Michael Paolisso and S. W. Yudelman, *Women, Poverty and the Environment in Latin America* (Washington, DC: International Center for Research on Women, 1991).

20. The following are the countries, researchers, and topics in WEDNET. Senegal: Binta Sene Diouf (Women's Knowledge of Technology and Production); Burkina Faso: Suzanne Lankouande (Women, Environment, and Migration); Zaire: Pascaline Kukwikila, Christine Tshiala, Germain Nzeba-Kazadi, and Rose

Ilibagiza (Women's Use of Indigenous Knowledge in Child Nutrition and Health as a Crisis Survival Strategy in Kinshasa); Ghana: Takyiwaa Manuh, Jacob Songsore, and Fiona Mackenzie (Gender and Access to Land: The Interface Between Recent Legislative Initiatives and Customary Tenure and Land Use Management); Ghana: Elizabeth Ardayfio-Schandorf (Women and Forest Resources Management in the Northern Region); Sudan: Asha Mustafa (The Role of Women in Food Security in Drought-Affected Environments); Kenya: Joseph Ouma (The Role of Women in the Management of Water Resources in the Lake Victoria Basin); Zambia: Elizabeth Kyewalabye and Monica Munachonga (Women and Livestock Management: Women Among the Ila and Tonga); and Zimbabwe: Ruvimbo Chimedza (Women, Household Food Security, and Wildlife Management); Zimbabwe: Ntombie Gata (Indigenous Science and Technology for Sustainable Agriculture and Food Systems).

21. See Stamp, "IDRC/York African Studies Programme Conference on Women and Natural Resources in Africa."

22. In a recent paper, I argued that women's relations with their co-wives and female neighbors were the actual context of women's work in milk production and indirectly with nature in indigenous African herding systems. Similar attention to the actual unit of environmental action is critical to understanding women's use and protection of the natural environment; see Bonnie Kettel, "Gender Distortions and Development Disasters: Women and Milk in African Herding Systems," *National Women's Studies Association Journal* 4, no. 1 (1992): 23–41.

23. Ntombie Gata and A. L. Kathivu, *Research and Documentation of Indigenous Science and Technology for Sustainable Agriculture, Food Systems and Natural Resource Management in Zimbabwe*: Proceedings of a Workshop (Chinhoyi, Zimbabwe: Chinhoyi Public Service Training Centre, 1991), 23–28, 54–59, 95–107.

24. Ibid., 103.

25. Ibid., 2, 5.

26. Ibid., 90–91.

27. Ruvimbo Chimedza, *Women, Household Food Security and Wildlife Resources,* WEDNET Preliminary Report (Nairobi: ELCI, 1991), 46–47.

28. Ibid., 14–15.

29. Elizabeth Ardayfio-Schandorf, *Women and Forest Resources Management in the Northern Region of Ghana*, WEDNET Preliminary Report (Nairobi: ELCI, 1991), 2–19.

30. Lankouande, *Project de Recherche sur 'Femme—Environnement—Emigration au Burkina Faso,'* 11–12, trans. R. Jommo.

31. Ibid., 12–13.

32. Binta Sene Diouf, *Natural Resources, Production and Women's Knowledge and Techniques in the Field of Nutrition and Health,* WEDNET Preliminary Report (Nairobi: ELCI, 1992), 20, trans. R. Jommo.

33. Ibid., 20–29.

34. Ibid., 24.

35. Joseph Ouma, *The Role of Women in the Management of Water Resources in Kenya,* WEDNET Preliminary Report (Nairobi: ELCI, 1991), 24.

36. Ibid., 14–20.

37. Ibid., 12–13.

38. Agarwahl, "Engendering the Environment Debate," 11, emphasis in original.

39. Ibid., 58, emphasis in original.

40. Henrietta Moore, *Space, Text and Gender: An Anthropological Study of the Marakwet of Kenya* (London: Cambridge University Press, 1986); Kettel, "Gender and Environments."

41. Mary Douglas, *The Lele of the Kasai* (London: Oxford University Press, 1963). This was a complex cultural phenomenon that restricted women's access to spiritual and political authority, while allowing them considerable autonomy and leisure.

42. Helen Hambly, "Agroforestry—A Gender and Environment Analysis: A Case Study of the CARE-Siaya (Kenya) Agroforestry Extension Project," master's thesis, York University, 1992. This sense of place arises from a cultural taxonomy that allows people to locate themselves in relation to the cosmos, nature, and other human beings. The landscape concept emphasizes the importance of perceptions of the natural environment in these cultural taxonomies.

43. See Kettel, "The Commoditization of Women in Tugen (Kenya) Social Organization," and Kettel, "Gender Distortion and Development Disasters."

44. Stamp, "IDRC/York African Studies Programme Conference on Women and Natural Resources in Africa."

45. Caroline O. N. Moser, "Gender Planning in the Third World: Meeting Practical and Strategic Gender Needs," *World Development* 17, no. 11 (1989): 1799–1825.

46. Ibid., 1803, emphasis in original.

47. Bonnie Kettel, "New Approaches to Sustainable Development," *Canadian Woman Studies* 13, no. 3 (1993): 11–14.

48. Moser, "Gender Planning in the Third World," 1803.

49. Lankouande, *Project de Recherche sur 'Femme–Environnement–Emigration au Burkina Faso,'* 12, 13.

50. Sene Diouf, *Natural Resources, Production and Women's Knowledge and Techniques in the Field of Nutrition and Health,* 28.

51. Hambly, "Agroforestry—A Gender and Environment Analysis," 32–33, argues that the distinction between women's practical interests (their condition) and their strategic interests (their position) is useful, "but it cannot be used as a 'chicken and egg' debate over whether women's life conditions must first be met before their position in society can be considered. ... Women themselves may not perceive any separation between their immediate and strategic needs."

52. Stamp, "IDRC/York African Studies Programme Conference on Women and Natural Resources in Africa," 3.

53. Kettel, "Gender Distortions and Development Disasters"; Gudrun Dahl, "Women in Pastoral Production: Some Theoretical Notes on Roles and Resources," *Ethnos* 52, nos. 1 and 2 (1987): 246–279.

54. African Women's Assembly on Sustainable Development, *Zimbabwe National Report on Women and Sustainable Development,* 2.

55. See Stamp, *Technology, Gender, and Power in Africa.*

CHAPTER THIRTEEN

■

Beyond Economics:
Sheltering the Whole Woman

Irene Tinker

WOMEN ARE NOT SOLELY HOMEMAKERS, nor do women live by work alone. Indeed, these two categories of housewife-reproducer and worker-producer do not exhaust the many roles women play in their daily lives: caretaker, community manager, teacher, nurse. A whole woman is all of these things. The ability of every woman to balance and perform her multifaceted roles is affected profoundly by the type of her shelter and the people who inhabit it. Whether her work takes place in or around the home, on the farm, or at some distance, her access to resources and control of surplus or income depends on the household composition and intrahousehold bargaining.

Perhaps because shelter is so central for survival, its existence was simply assumed—and ignored—by early development planners. Gradually, as urban migration crowded sidewalks and vacant lots throughout the developing world and produced periurban invasions of organized settlers, planners confronted the critical need for low-cost urban housing. To call attention to this need, the United Nations initiated the HABITAT Conference in Vancouver in 1976 and established the UN Centre for Human Settlements (UNCHS) to focus attention on shelter that "includes more than a roof over one's head ... but also involves a range of other supporting facilities that, together with a house, are necessary for a healthy living environment. This covers water and energy supplies, sanitation, drainage and access to transport networks. ... Shelter... includes the link between the home and the built environment of human settlements."[1]

Recent catastrophes have underscored the inadequacies of much rural housing. In October 1993, a devastating earthquake in central India killed thousands of farmers in homes made of piles of stone with little or no mortar, while wealthier citizens survived in reinforced-concrete houses. Yet, compared to its fundamental nature, housing and the broader shelter issues in which housing is embedded have been widely neglected both by development agencies and by women in development (WID) proponents.

Yet compared to its fundamental nature, housing concerns and the broader shelter issues in which housing is embedded have been widely neglected both by development agencies and by women in development (WID) proponents.[2] In this chapter, I will first discuss the reasons why WID focused so intensely on women's work, and I will review the implications of economic development policies in order to indicate why women's lives were fragmented for program purposes. In the next section, the evolution of housing policies, both urban and rural, is analyzed in terms of the differential impact of housing approaches on women and men. The third section considers the gender ramifications of two major aspects of shelter policy: provision of services and the use of space in and around the house for income activities or food production.

I will argue that because these issues encompass the many facets of women's lives, a focus on shelter provides an opportunity for the development community to recombine the fragmented perspectives of women's lives into a more holistic and realistic portrayal. A focus on shelter also allows men back into the private sphere of the family, from which they seemed excluded in the public-private debate. Shelter thus can be a focus for a human-centered development approach that reunites the affective and economic worldviews. □

DEVELOPMENT POLICIES

Shelter was listed as one of the primary basic human needs by development planners as they shifted their emphasis on infrastructure projects so dominant in the 1950s and 1960s. During those decades, roads or electricity were justified by their contribution to economic development; water projects were always designed for irrigation, not for household use. Economic activities were presumed to be done predominantly by men, largely outside the home. Too easily, the public-private and male-female dichotomies became the basis of policy making. Work at home, whether subsistence farming or small home-based industries—whether done by women or by men—went unrecorded in statistical data. The resulting inaccuracies strengthened stereotypes of distinct male and female roles and caused many development programs to fail.[3]

As women in development scholars began to document the differential impact of development on women in the 1970s, they utilized the same sectoral categories that framed the development debate because their policy objective was to ensure that women were integrated into development programs. They perceived their first challenge was to record women's economic activities in subsistence livelihoods so that those planning economic projects would not ignore or undercut women's contributions to the household. Hundreds of studies focused on women's unpaid work in gathering fuel, water, food, and forest products; in planting, weeding, and processing agricultural products; in weaving baskets or cloth; and in making pottery, batiks, or beer. Improved data on farming more accurately portrayed the roles of all family members by age and gender and demonstrated that men as well as women accomplish many off-farm tasks that are essential to their families' livelihood.

Women's work became the focal point for WID research in reaction to earlier programming that had considered women only in terms of their maternal or family planning activities. Gradually, even health and family planning programs began to recognize women's economic activities: Population programs combined pill distribution with income activities; health clinics scheduled hours when women were not weeding in the fields. But though the caring role that women play—nurturing children and ministering to the sick and the elderly—was acknowledged, particularly as structural adjustment policies reduced available health- and child-care services, such activities continued to be assumed and undervalued.

Research on the urban informal sector was initiated by the International Labor Organization in 1972, primarily to identify employment opportunities for men. Focusing on small (as opposed to family or self-employed) enterprises, ILO data generally ignored women. Once again, it was left to women scholars to study the women who were selling in both urban and rural markets or producing and vending street foods.[4] More recent scholarship on home-based work, both microenterprise and subcontracting, reiterates the concept of the home as the locus of much of women's work.[5] This literature also emphasizes the importance of women's income to the survival of poor families. The richness of data on women's economic and family roles, however, contrasts with the poverty of parallel studies on poor men and thus frustrates efforts to produce realistic gender analyses of family survival and livelihood techniques.

The accumulation of microlevel studies on women and work separated child care and household maintenance from subsistence tasks, such as farming, fuelwood and water collection, food processing, and craft production, which could be considered economic activities. This narrowed the concept of reproduction. Marxist economic theory honors the role of reproduction in the sense of reproducing the labor force and thereby permits some claim that Marxism is more sympathetic to feminism. But the liberal economic theory that dominates development planning has, for many years, ignored the household or considered it a site of consumption, not production. Only recently have economists disaggregated the household and provoked a debate on cooperation or contention among its members. But because nonmonetary activity is not esteemed in contemporary society, housework remains generally uncounted in economic statistics—provoking one international organization to demand wages for housewives.[6]

The emphasis on income also disadvantaged working women. Studies show that women make less money than men and spend less time in the market or on production because they have a second job—the "double day" that arises from women's responsibility for the household. The advantages of women's income are also easily undermined if women cannot control the money they earn or if their husbands reduce their own contribution to the household.[7] Clearly, work is only part of the whole woman.

Volunteer work also goes largely unrecorded and unappreciated.[8] Whether undertaken for charity purposes, as part of organizing efforts to affect policies, or to strengthen kin networks, women's work in volunteer activities is significant. To highlight the utility of social contacts to the welfare of the family, Hanna Papanek devised the term "family status production."[9] Men are also active in family, kin, and community networks, but their activities are interpreted in economic or political terms that reinforce the public-private dichotomy.

By fragmenting the activities of both women and men and by emphasizing sectoral programs, the development programs created unbalanced lives. Shelter—taken as home and community, work and play, wealth and well-being—brings the family into focus, reversing the prism of women's spectrum of roles so that these many strands join into the whole woman. □

HOUSING POLICIES

Housing concerns first surfaced as a development issue in response to pressures from developing countries whose cities were being inundated with migrants. By the year 2000, half the world's people will live in urban areas, up from one-tenth a century ago. But the distribution of these urban dwellers will not be evenly spread around the globe. Over three-quarters of the populations in Latin America and the industrialized countries will then be urban, while Africa and Asia will remain about 50 percent rural. The rate of urbanization is rapid even in these regions, however, and the percentage of urban dwellers will exceed 50 percent in both Asia and Africa by about 2015. Seventeen of the twenty-three urban agglomerations with over ten million inhabitants will be in the developing world. In Latin America and the Caribbean, where three-quarters of the population already lives in towns and cities, urban women outnumber men by a ratio of 108 to 100. Urban-rural ratios are rapidly changing elsewhere; the rate of urbanization is particularly high in west and north Africa and in Oceania, where about half the women live in urban settings today.[10] As governments struggle to absorb the new migrants, the experiences in Latin America—used as models and generalizations about both problems and policies—are too often projected on the rest of the world without adequate adaptation.

Urbanization promotes visions of high-rise offices and apartment buildings casting shadows on narrow canyonlike streets. In fact, few cities are as densely built as the archetypal Manhattan. Rather, quarries, swampy areas, or creekbeds are bypassed as commercial and middle-class residential areas sweep outward, following arterial roads; those "unbuildable" areas are then rapidly filled with low-income settlements. Existing villages are engulfed by city expansion, their open spaces filled with homes of rural kin.

Estimates indicate that as much as three-quarters of all newly built urban housing in developing countries is unauthorized.[11] This does not, however, automatically mean such houses are all shacks; the lack of authorization may arise from zoning limitations, building standards, or disputed land rights. These legal and regulatory issues affect all types of buildings: commercial or residential, mansion or hut. But for the urban poor, housing choices available to migrants or to expanding urban households are extremely limited—self-built housing in irregular communities or rented accommodations where facilities and even living space are often shared. Policies and programs relating to these categories have differential gender impact.

Self-built housing has received the most attention from both scholars and planners. The sight of shantytowns surrounding Westernized capitals, of straw shacks along rivers, or of hovels on steep hillsides is familiar throughout developing countries. On seacoasts, wooden walkways thrust out over tidal flats to link houses on stilts, an age-old technique that relies on water action to wash away refuse and excrement dropped from above. Frequently, too, rural kin descend on urban relatives and jam another shack into space meant for a garden. Parks and vacant land sprout settlements overnight; indeed, invasions by entire communities moving all at once into periurban areas created instant *suburbios* all over Latin America. Political parties in Peru and Mexico often promoted such invasions and protected the inhabitants; in Chile, similar efforts turned squatter settlements into a political battleground.

When squatters lack political support, they are attacked as they were in 1971 near Monterrey, Mexico. In Brazil, the government attempted to eradicate major *favelas* (squatter areas) in repeated bloody campaigns during the 1960s.[12] In Asia, the initial government response was to evict illegal squatters, trucking them out of town (though most were back the next day). A second response was to hide them; President Ferdinand Marcos had high fences erected along the highway leading from the airport to the center of metropolitan Manila in order to shield visitors from squatter areas. Today, when government planners wish to move squatters in order to beautify a beachfront for tourism or to clear streets of pavement dwellers or to build a shopping center at a central location, those who have built houses on public land are usually compensated or offered alternative housing. But, squatters on private land have no such protection, though governments may buy the land and sell to settlers in order to prevent rioting. Resettlement is often offered as part of a sites-and-services program, but where land is scarce, governments may build high-rise apartments. To avoid the high costs of such programs, many squatter settlements have become legitimized and upgraded through government schemes.

Sites-and-services programs require the government to acquire and clear available land throughout a city and install basic infrastructure. This might simply mean surrounding the area with a road, dividing the area into house plots reached only by pathways, providing water points for every ten or so plots, and building common latrines, bathing, and laundry facilities. More elaborate and expensive programs often provide a core unit on each site with water and electrical outlets and a bathroom connected to the city sewage system. Housing plots are then sold, usually through subsidized credit schemes; families build their own houses at their own pace. Sometimes, governments decree the standards and style or even provide materials at cost. Reflecting housing demand, the higher-cost core model in Karachi was often sold to lower-level civil servants or to speculators.[13]

To provide such housing to lower-income families, many nongovernmental organizations have adopted the sites-and-services concept but require citizen participation: Potential buyers are expected to contribute work toward preparing the area and providing infrastructure. NGOs eventually recognized that such labor was more difficult for women heads of households (who often constitute over half of all the squatters in many Latin American cities).[14] Because women household heads both work and care for their families, it was often impossible for them to work on project sites, and credit was hard to obtain because women are more likely than men to work at informal sector jobs and have uneven incomes. In San José, Costa Rica, the Comité Patriótico Nacional (COPAN), a local NGO, let child care or work in other COPAN projects (such as their pharmacy or library) count toward the requisite work points, enabling both women and the elderly to qualify for COPAN housing. Further, the organization staged demonstrations to make home loans easier to get and led efforts to introduce a law in 1990 that guaranteed women's ownership rights to any home subsidized by the government. To keep home building costs down, COPAN also trained work crews, mostly men, to lay foundations and erect much of the housing in order to meet seismic standards.[15] In contrast, Save the Children USA trained and then hired women of the community to lay foundations and build brick homes at their sites-and-services project in Colombo, Sri Lanka.[16]

In typical compartmentalized fashion, development agencies assigned housing programs to urban areas and have only recently realized the vast need in rural areas. Because attention to rural housing is generally the result of a major catastrophe, new housing must be built to a higher code to qualify for funding. In Bangladesh, floods regularly wash away traditional rural huts, with their bamboo poles and matting sides. UNCHS has encouraged NGOs to provide housing loans, and most have followed the lead of the Grameen Bank, which insists that each house it helps finance must have four reinforced concrete posts and a tin roof. Loans were made only to members, over 90 percent of whom are now women. Further, each woman had to own the land on which her hut would be built, and if her husband or male relatives would not give her land, she could first obtain a loan for buying land. Once the housing loan was granted, the householder would prepare the mud platform for the approximately 12-by-20 foot structure. A local male artisan, trained by Grameen Bank, would position the four posts in concrete, build wooden braces, and wire on the roof. The posts are made locally by teams trained and paid by the bank. The woman would also weave rush matting to serve as walls for her home. Floods might sweep the mats away, but the frame would withstand the waters and save the meager household goods tied to the cross-poles.[17]

Upgrading is the term used for programs that introduce minimal services for and infrastructure into existing spontaneous, or unplanned, communities. Upgrading emphasizes the creation of pathways and the provision of electricity, water standpipes, and common latrines. Early World Bank programs focused on squatter areas in India and on the *kampungs* in Indonesia. It is critical to distinguish between these two types of settlements. Squatters cluster primarily on unused and unbuildable public lands; in Calcutta, for example, where marshes constitute 21 percent of the municipal area and have been generally untouched by commercial development, squatters have burgeoned in places subjected to frequent monsoon floods.[18] In contrast, Indonesian *kampungs* are not illegal settlements. Rather, they are former villages with land rights governed by *adat*, or customary law. Under Dutch administration, urban *kampungs* were grouped with rural areas under provincial civil servants; European sections of the city were under a Dutch mayor, and land in those sections was regulated by European law. These two distinct systems of land rights have yet to be reconciled, and clearly, urban development is impeded until such reconciliation is achieved. What is critical to remember is the difference in security between squatters on public or private land and villagers with traditional land rights.

Kampung improvement projects were first introduced by the Dutch in the 1920s. Renewed emphasis began in the 1960s, utilizing funding provided by the Asian Development Bank and the World Bank plus numerous bilateral and NGO donors. Despite the rhetoric of encouraging citizen participation, most *kampung* improvement projects (KIPs) appear to involve the top-down imposition of designs originating in Jakarta for KIPs throughout the country. In interviews, *kampung* dwellers particularly appreciated the cemented footpaths and roads that allowed the use of motorcycles and bicycles inside the settlement; ease of transport encouraged residents to set up small shops within the *kampung*.[19] However, a study in Pune, India, found that realigning paths as part of the upgrading caused social as well as physical dislocation. The lack of consultation and the planners' preconceptions of order resulted in bisected neighborhoods that interfered with established patterns of social interaction.[20]

A 1992 survey of squatters in the Juhu area of Bombay City, India, found there were 93,000 people from fourteen states of India living on about 175 acres in seventeen different and not always continuous pockets of land along the ocean beaches and in nearby marshland. Settlement began over forty years ago, and because little space is left on government land, some families have pushed into neighboring private land. In 1974, the area was officially declared a slum by the municipality, a designation that provides residents a minimal degree of protection against eviction but only for those on government land. About half the families live in houses constructed of brick and cement with permanent fireproof roofs, but almost no houses include private latrines. Most have electricity illegally, but half of the families pay more for this illegal use than they would if they had legal connections. Party organizers, local NGOs, and an outreach project of the Women's University in Bombay have been able to pressure the city to improve toilet facilities, increase health and education services, and introduce training in income activities for the women.[21]

Squatters in many countries have been able to pressure governments to upgrade their areas by providing basic services and allocating land rights. The *pueblos jovenes*, or new towns, outside Lima are well-documented examples. These settlements begin as carefully planned invasions: Vacant land was mapped by the organizers as would be done for any housing development, and space was set aside for roads, schools, and clinics. Overnight, the entire community set up shacks on their assigned lots, and once people were in place, the community would agitate for electrical connections and water. Evicting an entire community is nearly impossible; community leaders would offer votes for land tenure, if not ownership rights. As squatters felt more secure, they would begin to construct well-built houses, usually hiring skilled workers from the informal sector. Over time, many of these "young towns" have become fully legalized, and they are difficult to distinguish visually from nearby suburbs.

Governments are also pressured to provide services to land that has been purchased. In Mexico, most cities are surrounded by land owned communally by *ejidos*, or Indian communities. Technically, such land could not be sold, but it was and at relatively low cost. In 1992, a law was passed that permits the sale of communal land, but because its implementation has not yet begun, the impact on land prices or on existing settlements is not known. Similarly, around Bogotá, land that was not zoned for housing nonetheless has been sold at low rates to poor people, who have erected substandard housing on steep slopes and then agitated for services. In both instances, the land may be legally held, but the housing is unauthorized. Yet it is unlikely that either government would try to evict the settlers. A distinct type of upgrading is being promoted in Bolivia to reduce the debilitating Chagas disease caused by a parasite that thrives in cracks in adobe houses and in thatched roofs throughout Latin America, even reaching as far north as Texas.

From the outset, most squatter settlements contain a wide range of housing types. Many houses emulate those traditional structures built in rural areas, but others are erected using modern materials. The two-story stucco houses of local merchants stood out among the shacks in Lima's new towns in the years before most residents could improve their dwellings, and *kampungs* are full of middle-level bureaucrats who prefer a crowded inner city to distant government flats. Recent evidence shows that after upgrading many families move out, renting their former homes. In Pune, India, 30 percent of the houses in a slum upgrading area were rented; landlords benefited from increased services and promptly raised rents, forcing poorer squatters out to the unimproved margins of the area.[22]

Removing squatters in order to construct new roads or buildings or to clean up public spaces such as sidewalks or parks is a difficult and expensive process for governments. Pavement dwellers in Bombay faced the threat of having their shacks demolished in 1985 when the Society for Promotion of Area Resource Centres (SPARC) began organizing the women pavement dwellers to resist being moved until a satisfactory resettlement site was allocated. SPARC was motivated by studies that indicated most low-cost housing and resettlement schemes rapidly became slums. Throughout India, half the families offered housing in the periphery move back into towns because they cannot afford the costs of their new shelter with their improved services and cannot spend either the money or the time required to commute to work. Further, relocation disrupts the community networks that spread news of job openings.[23]

Resettled families can often sell housing rights to somewhat wealthier people. When Indonesia provided walk-up apartment houses for families that were relocated so that a central boulevard in Jakarta could be widened, residents sold to middle-class families because they were not allowed to continue home-based work in the new apartments and therefore could not afford the higher costs of improved housing. The UNCHS is encouraging housing projects to link income programs for women with all resettlement schemes so that the families can afford the upgraded standard of living. To prevent resettled families from selling their newly acquired homes and returning to squatter areas, some NGOs also hold on to titles for five or more years. Other groups accept the idea that many poor may prefer to trade their stake in a house for cash that would allow them to start a trade or buy rural land.

Many governments subscribe to the idea that they must supply housing to those who cannot afford it, but the costs of such programs have overwhelmed low-income countries. Europe set this example by rebuilding cities and towns after World War II—from Norwegian fishing ports above the Arctic Circle to massive high-rise structures in Prague and Moscow. Postcolonial countries expanded housing stock for their employees at all levels, following on the colonial tradition. Rapid modernization and increased national income allowed both Singapore and Hong Kong to house their citizens in high-rise buildings of varying quality; in India, however, low-income housing with its modern services was quickly appropriated by the less poor.

Critics complain that the term *self-built housing* is misleading: As illustrated before, few poor men or women possess the skills to build structurally sound urban or rural housing from currently available materials. The term was widely adopted in the early 1970s to underscore the argument that the poor themselves designed shelters that were more appropriate to their incomes and lifestyles than most government-built public housing of the day. Originally meant to describe self-initiated as opposed to government-designed and government-built housing, the term has come to mean literally self-built. In fact, squatters save money to buy materials and hire skilled labor in order to upgrade their homes as long as their land rights are somewhat secure.[24]

In less developed countries such as Nepal, where some 80 percent of the people live in poorly built "temporary" housing, as much as half of the unskilled construction work in urban areas is supplied by poor rural women. A recent study in Nepal found that 61 percent of households interviewed used female family members in constructing their own houses, but as shelter became more formalized, fewer women were utilized.[25] This contrasts with the situation in south India, where women constituted nearly half of all laborers for house construction but seldom participated in the building of the mud huts that comprised 25 percent of all dwellings in Vellore; rather, they worked on more modern construction.[26]

Housing design often reflects the family's life cycle as well as income. Parents build second rooms—with outside entrances—for rental or for use by married children. In Lima, Peru, a problem arose with this type of arrangement when squatters were granted legal rights to land on which they had been living: Renters claimed equal rights with some squatters. Municipal authorities complained that these claims discouraged multiple dwellings in the new towns and thus pushed new migrants further into the desert; consolidation of existing squatter areas, they contended, would allow for improved and cheaper municipal services.

Critics of self-built housing also complain that emphasizing houses built by people allows a government to abdicate its responsibility for providing housing for its citizens.[27] Without government intervention, land markets soar in urban areas making land acquisition by the poor impossible and encouraging illegal squatting. Moreover, streambeds and marshes, clogged by houses and refuse, become environmental disasters endangering the health of both squatters and middle-class residents. A growing attachment to the free market ideology makes it more difficult for governments to address land-use planning, but the urban crisis demands governmental action. As such plans are formulated, gender aspects of self-built housing should also be acknowledged.

Rental housing has received less attention than self-built housing or upgrading, perhaps because it is not a new phenomenon. Although buildings erected for rent are recorded, the informal and often illegal nature of much rental accommodation in homes—found both in comfortable middle-class suburbs and in squatters' shacks—is difficult to monitor. Throughout the world, worker housing or walk-up apartments designed for the lower middle class are rapidly becoming slums through overcrowding and the subsequent deterioration of services. As cities grow, downtown slum areas are ripe for redevelopment, adding to the housing crisis for the poor.

Choices among rental units vary by family life cycle, income, and kin networks. Around the world, young women and men from rural areas move in with urban kin to attend school, helping with child care and cooking. Similarly, older relatives often come looking for work and help in the household until they are able to pay rent; related couples frequently share accommodations for years. Young men or women without kin seek hostel rooms, often so crowded that they are forced to share beds. The YWCA concept, so important for single women in the United States, is replicated in many parts of the world. However, in Dhaka, Bangladesh, young women with some secondary school education who hold clerical jobs in the city often stay for years instead of weeks since they literally have no other safe place to go. Village girls who come to work in the garment factories rent space in squatter areas and are often preyed on by pimps.

In Indonesia, circulatory male migrants find both shelter and assistance in earning money through the *pondok* system—boarding houses where the manager also runs an enterprise. *Pondok* residents tend to cluster with others from their own village or area. An entrepreneur selling products like ice cream or bread on commission will provide "his on-premise workers with board and lodging, and his vendors with equipment and shelter."[28] Other *pondok* bosses rent pedicabs or pushcarts to residents and may supply street food vendors with raw materials. In Surabaja, Joep Bijlmer found the relationship of the manager to the residents more like that of an uncle and his nephews than the often exploitative arrangements typical in Jakarta.

In Guadalajara, Mexico, Faranak Miraftab found that young, single mothers preferred the downtown slums, with shared facilities, to distant squatter settlements: Living in close proximity with other families provided company and reduced gossip, and closeness to shops and work allowed more time at home.[29] Male companions were tolerated as long as they contributed to household expenses, but they were told to leave if they drank too much or failed to help. To defray expenses and provide child care and companionship, three-fifths of the women in her sample of female-headed households had shared their homes for periods of three months or longer, compared with 43 percent in male-headed households. Self-built squatter homes in the periphery presented greater hardships for single mothers because distance, lack of shops, and poor services meant that domestic activities were more burdensome than they were downtown. As their children grew up, some older women overcame the gender bias in housing construction to acquire land and build or have others build their own houses.

Miriam Grant focused on accommodations available to women-headed households in Gweru, a medium-sized town in Zimbabwe.[30] Nearly half (42 percent) of these women lived alone, 50 percent lived only with their children, and the remaining 8 percent had other kin or nonrelatives living with them. Overall, a quarter of women household heads supported at least five people in their household; 80 percent of these women crowded into municipal rental housing, sharing rooms with other families and using common pit latrines and wash areas. Middle-income women household heads preferred to seek lodgings at double or triple the cost of municipal housing, and women with high incomes rented their own apartments. Poorer and high-income women had families of similar size, and lodgers had the fewest dependents living with them. Grant maintains that the lack of available accommodations led to family fragmentation, with young children left behind in the villages and older children sent back to rural areas to work. Lack of living space prevented women from bringing in alternative caretakers for their children, and the lack of garden space also raised food costs for the family.

A current study of the process by which individual families acquire housing and how they use it is being undertaken in informal and regularized settlements in eleven countries including low-income areas in Boston. Mona Serageldin's aggregate findings emphasize the critical nature of security: "Even when incomes rise, households will not spend more than 15 percent of their income on shelter without some assurance regarding security of occupancy as owners or renters."[31] Even with such guarantees, renters seldom spend more than 20 percent of their income to improve their homes, but property owners increase their expenditures to 30 percent of household income. Such findings sustain observations of the investment made in *kampungs* or squatments as residents feel more secure in their tenancy, and they underscore the policy imperatives that call for land-use rights in urban settlements.

These scattered studies suggest that women accept rental housing in crowded slum conditions because, with the community support that arises from shared space and with proximity to work, the daily demands of feeding and caring for their families are more easily met. The studies also found that household size and composition are constantly changing as male partners come and go and as children are farmed out to kin. Further, gender biases affect women's ability to acquire rental housing, but constructing "self-built" homes in the periphery is rejected as much because of isolation and lack of services as because of difficulties in obtaining assistance and funds. Finally, older women with grown children, or married couples where the wife does not work outside the home more frequently own homes and rent space to others. □

SHELTER ISSUES

The concept of shelter encompasses more than the structure of a house. Human habitat includes the built environment, the space surrounding buildings, and the access to services and transport. Because women continue to have primary responsibility for family maintenance, shelter issues have a differential impact on women and men that should be understood and incorporated in urban policies and planning. Three crucial issues—water and sanitation services, home-based work, and home food production—affect a woman's ability to provide a livelihood for herself and her dependents. These illustrate the centrality of a living space that encompasses more than a roof over one's head.

Access to water and sanitation services loom as critical ingredients for the quality of life and to a woman's ability to keep her family healthy, yet residents in most cities are grossly underserved. Whatever the housing type, the first service demand is for water supply. But burgeoning urban populations from California to Egypt must compete with agricultural users and demand may exceed supply. Beijing's projected demand by the year 2000, for example, will outstrip supply by 70 percent. Elsewhere, groundwater reserves are rapidly being exhausted: Mexico City exceeds its recharge rate by 50 to 80 percent, causing the city to sink. Moreover, available rivers are often badly polluted, and groundwater is becoming fouled by both domestic and industrial wastes. In Jakarta, less than half the urban residents are served by the municipal water system; yet more than half of the supply "disappears" through illegal connections or leakage, enough water to supply 800,000 people annually.[32]

Lack of water and sanitation are major causes of dangerous environmental health conditions in squatments, according to a review of over one hundred urban studies by a World Bank team.[33] Urban poor have a lower life expectancy and higher infant mortality rate than most rural poor or urban middle-class individuals. Particularly for children, private latrines and sewerage are critical for health. Poor nutritional status, accidents, respiratory diseases resulting from airborne pollution within and outside the home, and from occupational hazards connected to home-based work are among the issues that surface when talking about shelter activities in and around the house.

Moser argues that in Latin America women spend more time in community management than men because of their household obligations.[34] Cecilia Blondet elaborates on this model, showing how women establish mutual-aid networks and organize collective action to secure urban services during the first phases of settlement. Her longitudinal studies also show that working women cannot keep up the activism but that women with more resources continue their leadership by setting up community kitchens that introduce patron-client relationships into the settlement, which are cemented by parent-godparent reciprocal arrangements. Explaining why women's community activity does not seem to have political implications, Blondet observes that neither mode of organizing, whether through networks or through clientelism, goes "beyond the limits of family."[35]

Such activism among women is less marked in Asia, where upgrading is government policy and settlers are seldom consulted. NGOs with elite leadership are more likely to organize squatters than are the residents themselves. Moreover, government programs often impose technologies for upgrading that are inappropriate. For instance, squatter settlements may be supplied with water taps for each block, but given the distance to the taps and the weight of the water, residents often continue to buy from carriers who cart water down the narrow paths on shoulder poles or tricycles. In *kampungs*, municipal taps are frequently installed on donated land, meaning that the wealthier residents have the water nearby. In smaller Indonesian cities, Pauline Milone found that money was being put into the upgraded water and bathing facilities rather than into larger or better built homes, an investment with measurable impact on family health security.[36]

Toilets are usually communal in squatter areas, and the problem of keeping them clean is often solved by paying a custodian, sometimes by charging for each usage. The Juhu Beach squatment of Bombay, India, discussed earlier, has one latrine for every 134 people and one water tap for every 673 people.[37] *The Urban Edge* reports that "in 1987, less than 60 percent of the world's urban population had access to adequate sanitation, and only one-third was connected to sewer systems. Where sewage did exist, 90 percent of the wastewater was discharged without treatment."[38] Because conventional methods of treating water and sewerage are too expensive for services to keep up with population, services are usually confined to wealthier areas. Brazil has taken the lead in experimenting with low-cost technology that "ranges from simple pit latrines with hydraulic seals and pour flush toilets to simplified sewerage systems."[39]

Solid waste management is actually fairly efficient in most Asian squatments: Poverty encourages collection and recycling of almost everything by traditional scavengers. Efforts to modernize the waste pickers are often protested by workers themselves, who, despite their low social status, often earn incomes above other manual workers.[40] Many cities are seeking methods of improving trash collection while providing employment for displaced workers. For example, donkey carts have long been used by the traditional waste collectors, or *zabbaleen*, in old Cairo to negotiate the narrow alleys and carry the trash to the outskirts of the city, but the municipality is gradually helping them acquire small trucks. Meanwhile, an NGO is promoting the use of protective masks and clothing for the *zabbaleen* women and children, who sort waste in their settlement, and it has funded technology to recycle much of the waste, thus adding to household income.[41]

As caretakers and housekeepers, women more than men are burdened by insufficient water supply, unsanitary toilet and washing facilities, and inadequate waste collection. But though women are often leaders in demanding that the city improve these services, their community management seldom translates into political power. Further, upgraded services will reduce current jobs as water carriers and garbage pickers, which provide income for poor women and men, an impact that requires planning for alternative work.

Home-based work describes the norm of previous centuries: Weaving cloth or baskets, making furniture or pottery, building or repairing the house—work done by most families between subsistence farming tasks. Most craftsmen also worked at home, living over their workshops.[42] The Industrial Revolution moved workers to factories where unions flourished; to protect the factory workers, the unions then began to fight against the remnants of industrial homework, especially that related to textiles.

Two interrelated contemporary trends have reversed the concentration of industrial work outside the home and have enormous implications for gender relationships: The informalization of industry and the communication revolution. Rapid and accurate tracking of components has allowed the dispersal of manufacturing sites throughout the world, a trend that has created assembly plants around the globe but has also encouraged multiple layers of subcontracting for everything from garments to toys to television sets. The web of interrelationships among jobbers and subcontractors, from women to their sisters and friends, makes tracing homework—not to mention organizing the workers—nearly impossible. Studies show how the number of women increases at the edges of the web where payment rates are the lowest.[43] Yet this income from homework is critical for poor urban families. Indeed, in periods of high unemployment, women's income from homework may surpass that earned by husbands, and there are recorded instances of men joining their wives' enterprises on a part- or full-time basis. In her study of spatial aspects of homework, Miraftab argues that home-based work bridges the duality between women and men in Guadalajara, "bringing the domestic and public spheres together and ... bringing the possibilities of income generation and increased wealth into the home, which previously defined a site of economic confinement for women."[44]

The communication revolution has created the "electronic cottage," where women and men utilize computers and fax machines to interact with their offices. Such a use of the home contradicts the middle-class predilection to treat the home as a retreat from work and assign domesticity to women. Penny Gurstein provides a historical context, noting that although contemporary homes offer more privacy for individuals than medieval homes did, they are "still planned with minimal privacy between family members." She concludes that "home-based work could potentially have an impact on the way homes and neighborhoods are structured, precipitating a change from the segregation of single use zoning to a natural integration of housing, work places, and services."[45]

Although unions look with dismay on the increase of home-based industrial work, the development community is promoting microenterprise around the world. Because microenterprise means entrepreneurial activity carried out by an individual alone or with family members, most microenterprises are also home-based. Street food vendors will prepare foods at home; some sell these foods in front of their houses or in the market, but others may be ambulatory. Service activities such as hairdressing, barbering, making herbal medicines, or sewing also fluctuate between home and community. Craft work such as dyeing or printing cloth, creating batik, and weaving baskets or rattan chairs continues to be done primarily in the home. These activities, like subcontracting, provide essential income for poor families.

Around the world, NGOs are offering credit, largely to women in groups, so that they may set up their own microenterprises. Following the Grameen Bank model that was pioneered in Bangladesh, credit is secured only by the group; social pressure from the group has resulted in an astounding 98 percent repayment rate. Loans are used to start enterprises that range from producing special spices to raising goats to catering services. In the United States, such groups are spreading, supported by their own magazine, *Equal Means*. Ideologically, microentrepreneurs are perceived as independent businesspeople, but industrial homeworkers are perceived as exploited workers. These oppositional standpoints set the trade union movement against nongovernmental groups, with trade unions resisting and NGOs supporting work for women at home. It is often impossible to categorize a particular economic activity as microenterprise or industrial homework because the functions and relationships with larger enterprises merge.[46]

Urban food production is another extension of traditional home-based work that not only has survived the industrial transition but is becoming more important in the contemporary world.[47] Guinea pigs, long a staple of Andean diets, are now raised in downtown Oakland, California; vines twine over squatter shacks in Cebu, Philippines, providing essential vitamins and minerals for a rice diet; corn is grown using recycled water from domestic tasks in the new towns outside Lima, Peru. Upward mobility in African cities is marked by a move from food production to flower gardens, a process encouraged if not forced by colonial regulations still on the books.

Urban food is also produced commercially: As much as 70 percent of all poultry eaten in Kampala, Uganda, for example, is raised in the city. Creating fishponds along urban rivers or in vacant lots is a lucrative economic enterprise throughout Asia. Trees are cultivated for fruits and nuts as well as firewood in the cities of Burkino Faso or Indonesia. And throughout Africa, the greening of cities reflects urban migration and failing rural infrastructure. UNICEF reported that food production in Kampala, Uganda, contributed enough nutrients to prevent malnutrition among children despite the disruption in farm production caused by the civil war.

The actual contributions to food security of households or urban areas are unknown; research has been paltry in this area. Women, however, are expected to feed their families, and food production is an indispensable alternative to earning income for fulfilling this obligation. The urban commercial food production that has been recorded is largely done by women, but urban fish ponding in Asia is usually a man's work. As with home-based work, home-based food production requires new social arrangements and new planning guidelines to accommodate the changing lifestyles and needs of urban residents.

The critical role that nonwaged income plays in family survival was underscored by a recent eleven-country study that found households relying on microenterprises for 30 percent of their income and on rental payments for another 10 percent; only 60 percent of household income was from wages and salaries.[48] Income constraints on households may cause worsening nutrition if the costs of resettlement or upgrading are too high, unless opportunities for urban food production are available. □

CONCLUSION

Shelter for the urban poor will become an even more critical issue as increases in natural population and continued rural-urban migration strain urban areas further. Most of the land that is available for informal settlement within municipal boundaries or in adjacent areas has already been occupied, forcing new self-built homes further to the periphery. Distances to towns and lagging transport systems complicate formal employment outside the home and thereby encourage the use of the home as a base for work and food production. Furthermore, downtown slums will be replaced by more valuable buildings unless there is government intervention in land markets. Meanwhile, suburban families may add rooms or floors to accommodate kin or renters, and green space around the homes will be filled with shacks or utilized for food production.

As housing shortages increase in the central cities, governments should set up temporary housing centers and consider building shared housing units so that single women and men as well as women household heads can find safe accommodations near their work. Such housing would particularly benefit the most vulnerable group of new migrants: young, single women. Too often today, the kin with whom many live may reduce them to servant status; non-kin may force them into prostitution. Poor single men migrating to the city also need receiving centers that provide entry into employment as well as decent food and sleeping space; little is known about such institutions as the Indonesian *pondok* in other countries.

Informal kin and village networks have aided migrants for years, and client-patron relationships—whether based on political parties, religious groups, or clientelism—have provided some direction and support for long-term residents. More recently, NGOs have begun to work among the urban poor, focusing on *shelter* issues of housing, water, sanitation, and microenterprise, as well as *community* issues of environment, education, and health. All these institutions—the traditional ones based on kin and village or the newer, sectorally focused NGOs—deal with reality and try to moderate it. But the situation in most cities is deteriorating as services are strained: Transport corridors are clogged, raising the cost of food and complicating existing employment patterns; rivers and canals are polluted, making water scarce and unsafe; and schools and clinics cannot meet the demand.

Needed first is more information on how urban dwellers in fact survive today. To date, research has been concentrated in a few areas, such as informal sector activity or self-built housing. Differential gender roles in the informal sector have been explored, but the impact of housing choices on gender has only begun to be studied. More attention to the intersection of jobs, services, housing, and food—to shelter issues—is needed in order to develop urban space for the next century. New approaches, new designs, and new interventions are critical if cities, as well as their inhabitants, are to survive. □

NOTES

1. UN Centre for Human Settlements, "Shelter for Sustainable Development," news release, Nairobi, October 5, 1992.

2. Important sources for the limited material available on these issues include: "Women and Shelter," *Bibliographic Notes* #7, produced for the 1985 UN Conference on Women in Nairobi by UNCHS (four pages); Marianne Schminck, Judith Bruce, and Marilyn Kohn, eds., *Learning About Women and Urban Services in Latin America and the Caribbean* (New York: Population Council, 1986); Caroline O. N. Moser and Linda Peake, eds., *Women, Human Settlements, and Housing* (London:

Tavistock, 1987); and Irene Tinker, "Women and Shelter: Combining Women's Roles," in Gay Young, Vidjamali Samarasinghe, and Ken Kusterer, eds., *Women at the Center: Gender Issues for the 1990s* (West Hartford, CT: Kumarian Press, 1993).

3. For a history of these issues, see Irene Tinker, "The Making of a Field: Advocates, Practitioners, and Scholars," in Irene Tinker, ed., *Persistent Inequalities: Women and World Development* (New York: Oxford University Press, 1990).

4. For home-based workers, see: Andrea Menefee Singh and Anita Killes-Viitanen, eds., *Invisible Hands: Women in Home-Based Production* (New Delhi: Manchar Publishers, 1987); Florence Babb, "Women, Informal Economies, and the State in Peru and Nicaragua," *Latin American Anthropology Review* (forthcoming); Lilian Traeger, "A Re-Examination of the Urban Informal Sector in West Africa," *Canadian Journal of African Studies* 21, no. 2 (1987): 238–255. On street food vendors, see: Tole O. Pearce, Olufemi O. Kujore, and V. Aina Agboh-Bankole, "Generating Income in the Urban Environment: The Experience of Street Food Vendors in Ile-Ife, Nigeria," *Africa* 50, no. 4 (1988): 385–400; and, on Egypt, Irene Tinker, "The Street Food Project: Using Research for Planning," *Berkeley Planning Journal* 7 (1992): 1–19.

5. A comprehensive set of case studies appears in Eileen Boris and Elizabeth Prügl, eds., *Invisible No More: Homeworkers in Global Perspective* (New York: Routledge, forthcoming); Lourdes Benería and Martha Roldán reveal the interconnections and layers of home-based work in their *Crossroads of Class and Gender: Industrial Homework, Subcontracting, and Household Dynamics in Mexico City* (Chicago: University of Chicago Press, 1987).

6. Delegates to the 1985 UN Women's Conference in Nairobi included an item in the official conference document entitled *Forward-Looking Strategies for the Advancement of Women to the Year 2000* calling for governments to include housework in their national accounts.

7. Rae Lesser Blumberg, "Income Under Female Versus Male Control: Hypotheses from a Theory of Gender Stratification and Data from the Third World," in Rae Lesser Blumberg, ed., *Gender, Family, and Economy: The Triple Overlap* (Newbury Park, CA: Sage Publications, 1991); Daisy Dwyer and Judith Bruce, eds., *A Home Divided: Women and Income in the Third World* (Stanford: Stanford University Press, 1988).

8. Lourdes Benería, "Accounting for Women's Work: The Progress of Two Decades," *World Development* 20, no. 11 (1992): 1547–1560.

9. Hanna Papanek, "Family Status-Production Work: Women's Contributions to Class Differentiation and Social Mobility," paper prepared for Regional Conference on Women and the Household in Asia, New Delhi, January, 1985.

10. For data on women, see two United Nations publications, *World Urbanization Prospects 1990* (New York: UN/DIESA, 1991) and *The World's Women: Trends and Statistics 1970–1990* (New York: United Nations, 1991).

11. Marcia D. Lowe, *Shaping Cities: The Environmental and Human Dimensions* (Washington, DC: Worldwatch Institute, 1991), 41.

12. For differing views, see Manuel Castells, *The City and the Grassroots: A Cross-Cultural Theory of Urban Social Movements* (Berkeley: University of California Press, 1983), and Alan Gilbert and Josef Gugler, *Cities, Poverty, and Development: Urbanization in the Third World* (New York: Oxford University Press, 1987).

13. David Dowall and Giles Clark, "A Framework for Reforming Urban Land Policies in Developing Countries," Urban Management Program Policy Paper, World Bank, 1991.

14. Ana Falu and Mirina Curutchet, "Rehousing the Urban Poor: Looking at Women First," *Environment and Urbanization* 3, no. 2 (1991): 23–38.

15. Site visit in January 1992. See also Monserrat Sagot, "Women, Political Activism and the Struggle for Housing: The Case of Costa Rica," in Esther Nganling Chow and Catherine White Berheide, eds., *Women, the State and the Family* (Albany, NY: SUNY Press, 1994).

16. Site visit in June 1988. For a critique of the program, see Marina Fernando, "New Skills for Women: A Community Development Project in Colombo, Sri Lanka," in Moser and Peake, eds., *Women, Human Settlements, and Housing,* 88–112.

17. Irene Tinker, "Women's Access to Housing and Work: An Evaluation of UNCHS Programs in Indonesia, Bangladesh, and Nepal," an evaluation for the United Nations Fund for Women (UNIFEM) and the United Nations Centre for Human Settlements (HABITAT), March 1991. Summaries of these case studies appear in Irene Tinker, "Global Policies Regarding Shelter for Women: Experiences of the UN Centre for Human Settlements," in Hemalata Dandekar, ed., *Shelter, Women and Development: First and Third World Perspectives* (Ann Arbor, MI: George Wiley, 1993).

18. B. Misra, "Public Intervention and Urban Land Management: The Experience of Three Metro-Cities of India," *HABITAT International* 10, no. 1–2 (1986): 59–78.

19. Pauline Milone, "Kampung Improvement in the Small and Medium Size Cities of Central Java," *RURDS: Review of Urban and Rural Development Studies* (Winter 1992).

20. Wil Glover, "Transformation of an Urban Squatter Settlement in India: Modernism in the Margins," in Nezar Alsayyad, ed., *Traditional Dwelling and Settlement,* Working Paper Series no. 51 (Berkeley: Center for Environmental Design Research, University of California, 1992).

21. Mariamma A. Varghese, "Improving Health and Nutrition of Urban Slums Through Community Participation," report of an IDRC/UNICEF-sponsored project, Women's University, Bombay, 1993.

22. Glover, "Transformation of an Urban Squatter Settlement in India."

23. Meera Bapat, "Women and Housing: A Training Manual," mimeo, Society for Promotion of Area Resource Centres, Bombay, 1987.

24. Debates over the origin and meaning of "self-built" housing have continued ever since John Turner wrote his classic critique of government-built housing in 1967. The arguments are reviewed in Gilbert and Gugler, *Cities, Poverty, and Development,* chapter 5.

25. Emma Hooper and Kanta Singh, "Women and Shelter in Nepal," report to the Ministry of Housing and Physical Planning, Government of Nepal, Khatmandu, 1991.

26. Theo van der Loop, "Labour Recruitment and Subcontracting in the Building Sector of the Medium-Sized City Vellore (Tamil Nadu, India)," in Paul van Felder and Joep Bijlmer, eds., *About Fringes, Margins and Lucky Dips—The Informal*

Sector in Third World Countries: Recent Developments in Research and Policy (Amsterdam: Free University Press, 1989).

27. Nientied and van der Linden, "Approaches to Low-Income Housing in the Third World," in Josef Gugler, ed., *The Urbanization of the Third World* (New York: Oxford University Press, 1988), 138–156; Caroline O. N. Moser, "Introduction" and "Women, Human Settlements, and Housing: A Conceptual Framework for Analysis and Policy-making," in Moser and Peake, eds., *Women, Human Settlements, and Housing*, 1–32.

28. Joep Bijlmer, "The Informal Sector as a 'Lucky Dip': Concepts and Research Strategies," in van Felder and Bijlmer, eds., *About Fringes, Margins and Lucky Dips*, 153–154.

29. Faranak Miraftab, "Issues of Class, Gender, and Household Composition: The Search for Housing by Female-Headed Households in Guadalajara, Mexico," paper prepared for the Sixth Conference of the Association for Women in Development, Washington, DC, October 21–24, 1993.

30. Miriam Grant, "On Their Own: Women Tenants in Gweru, Zimbabwe," paper prepared for the Canadian Association for African Studies, Toronto, May 12–15, 1993.

31. Mona Serageldin, *The Use of Land and Infrastructure in the Self-Improvement Strategies of Urban Lower Income Families*, U.S. Agency for International Development Working Paper (Washington, DC: USAID, 1993), 4.

32. Sandra Postel, "Facing Water Scarcity," in Lester Brown et al., eds., *State of the World: 1993* (New York: W. W. Norton, 1993).

33. David Bradley, Sandy Cairncross, Trudy Harpham, and Carolyn Stephens, *A Review of Environmental Health Impacts in Developing Countries*, Urban Management Program Policy Paper (Washington, DC: World Bank, 1991).

34. Moser, "Women, Human Settlements, and Housing."

35. Cecelia Blondet, "Establishing an Identity: Women Settlers in a Poor Lima Neighborhood," in Elizabeth Jelín, ed., *Women and Social Change in Latin America* (London: Zed Books, 1990), 45.

36. Milone, "Kampung Improvement in the Small and Medium Size Cities of Central Java."

37. Varghese, "Improving Health and Nutrition of Urban Slums through Community Participation."

38. *Urban Edge* (Washington, DC: World Bank, August 1991).

39. Tim Campbell, "Applying Lessons from Housing to Meeting the Challenge of Water and Sanitation for the Urban Poor," *APA Journal* (1987): 190.

40. Christine Furedy, "Social Aspects of Solid Waste Recovery in Asian Cities," *Environmental Sanitation Reviews* 30 (Bangkok: Asian Institute of Technology, December 1990).

41. Marie Assaad and Nadra Garas, *The Mokkattam Garbage Collector's (Zabbaleen) Settlement: Lessons Drawn from a Massive Up-Grading Program in the Eighties* (Cairo: UNICEF, 1992).

42. Ken Kusterer and Louise Vitt, "Workspace at Home: A Comparative Perspective of First and Third World Environments," in *Traditional Dwellings and Settlements*, Working Paper Series no. 26 (Berkeley: Center for Environmental Design Research, University of California, 1991).

43. Benería and Roldán, eds., *Crossroads of Class and Gender*; Boris and Prügl, eds., *Invisible No More*.

44. Faranak Miraftab, "Space, Gender, and Work: Home-based Workers in Guadalajara, Mexico," in Boris and Prügl, eds., *Invisible No More*.

45. Penny Gurstein, "The Electronic Cottage: Implications for the Meaning of Home," in *Traditional Dwellings and Settlements*, Working Paper Series no. 26 (Berkeley: Center for Environmental Design Research, University of California, 1991), 14–15.

46. Elizabeth Prügl and Irene Tinker, "Home-Based Work: Exploitation or Opportunity?" manuscript, 1993.

47. These paragraphs summarize information in Hunger Notes 18-2 (1992) on "Urban Food Production: Neglected Resource for Food and Jobs," for which I was guest editor. See also *Urban Agriculture in Africa* (Ottawa: IDRC, 1994).

48. Serageldin, "The Use of Land and Infrastructure in the Self-Improvement Strategies of Urban Lower-Income Families."

———————— ■ ————————

CHAPTER FOURTEEN

Conclusion: Engendering Wealth and Well-Being — Lessons Learned

Cathy A. Rakowski

THE CONTRIBUTORS TO THIS BOOK SEEK TO PROMOTE cross-national and comparative research on the gendered outcomes of economic change broadly defined—not limited to economic crisis—and on related social and political change. They weave a richly textured tapestry of the issues and manifestations of change in diverse settings. This tapestry depicts the complexity and dynamics of macro- and microlevel dimensions of change and the linkages between them; of wealth, survival strategies, well-being, and their intersection; of power and powerlessness. Gender—and the gendered nature of change and its impacts—is the common thread that ties together these chapters on economic crisis, structural adjustment, marketization, social movements, housing, environment, health and nutrition, trading, agriculture, industrialization, and division of labor and decision making in the family.

These chapters are not meant to be read merely as interesting but unconnected case studies. Those studies are the details that illustrate the macro- and the microdimensions of gendered change and illuminate the links between wealth, survival, well-being, and empowerment. It is, therefore, important to identify common themes across chapters, to highlight diversity of experiences, and to draw explicit lessons from these comparative and cross-national studies. This is the task of this conclusion. □

AN OVERVIEW OF ECONOMIC CHANGE AND ITS CONSEQUENCES

Many of the chapters present a process of economic change that is unyieldingly capitalist and linked to privatization and marketization. This is the case of economic restructuring, industrialization, agricultural development policies, and marketization in Eastern Europe, the Caribbean, Taiwan, and Turkey, among others. It is also evident in manifestations of economic crisis and in the implementation of structural adjustment policies designed to deal with that crisis—regardless of the region in which they arise.

These diverse manifestations of processes of economic change, added to population pressures, have imposed conditions of great hardship on workers, families, and communities. Men and women in places as far apart as Guatemala, Turkey, the Dominican Republic, and Kenya find it increasingly difficult to meet their needs and those of their children. Traditional support systems and forms of subsistence production have broken down. (These are not to be romanticized, however, since they frequently failed to provide adequate material support or opportunities for self-fulfillment.)

Cash work, which now replaces declining forms of production, has been depicted as insufficient to meet the demand for foodstuffs, goods, and services. We saw how people could create their own income opportunities through trading, street vending, migration, home-based workshops, and diverse self-employment or subcontracting ventures. As was the case for the households of Taiwan and Turkey, some income opportunities lead one group (in this case, men) to confirm or increase control over the labor of women. In other places, including the Caribbean and Kenya, wage opportunities for women displace men's economic importance in the household. But everywhere, women's burden significantly increases, and gender relations in the household change. Some changes may be positive for women (for example, among middle- and working-class couples in urban Mexico) or negative (in farming households of Turkey and the farm-trader households of Nairobi). The authors in this volume have shown clearly that the outcomes of economic change are complex and conditional and not always quantifiable.

Many of the case studies provide evidence that the typical process of planned economic (and frequently social) change in the 1980s subordinated social welfare to accumulation and alternately ignored or romanticized household units and families. Contradictorily, as political and economic policies and programs articulated with or transformed preexisting structures of privilege and opportunity based on class, ethnicity, and gender, among other variables, they gave rise to patterns of economic behavior that are not strictly capitalist (mostly self-employment). They also led to the expansion of poverty, built on or transformed gender relations in households, and frequently increased violence and protest (both within and outside the household unit). We know this not only from the discussions of macro-level policies and their microlevel incarnations but also from the descriptions of the actions of real people as they cope with economic and social conditions thrust on them and as they determine which aspects of economic and social transformation they will embrace and which they will resist.

This book provides numerous examples of people's actions and reactions. They include a wide variety of seemingly distinct phenomena: Islamist movements; Nigerian women's re-appropriation of childbirth through privatization of health care; working- and middle-class Mexican women's shared commitment to work and different perceptions of appropriate gender relations; the increase in female household heads among Nairobi traders and Caribbean assembly workers; Turkish men's refusal to do "women's" agricultural tasks, even when their own cash crops depend on it, and—in one village—young women's resistance to an increased workload; Taiwanese women's complaints over working long hours as unpaid family workers even as they increase productive activities over which they have control; variations in patterns of paternal and maternal involvement in child support in Guatemala and Nicaragua; Venezuelan women's creation of new political spaces and strategies; African women's linking of gender interests to long-term environmental well-being; women's resistance to housing projects that isolate them or distance them from urban services, and markets for their goods and services; and Latin American women's ongoing struggle for political and social change. By contrasting and comparing the case studies in this volume, lessons can be learned about the gendered nature of economic and social change. □

LESSONS LEARNED

The most conspicuous conclusion in this book is that economic change and gender intersect in diverse ways. Economic change may be linked—under certain conditions and through women's increasing incomes relative to men's—to greater autonomy and decision-making power within the household and community. But under other conditions—especially the appropriation of women's unpaid labor or declining standards of living in general—economic change may contribute to greater inequality and subordination. These patterns confirm that the household and the family cannot be assumed to be a "unit" of members with mutual interests whose individual actions have as an implicit goal the welfare of the group.[1]

Differences in the gendered impact of economic crisis suggest that women's responsibilities and obligations to the support of others typically increase while those of men decline—voluntarily or involuntarily. The case studies and numerous research projects that preceded this volume vividly illustrate the division of responsibilities and rights and the conflicts and negotiations that take place in the household as a result of the intersection of patriarchal forms of household and community organization, local forms of production, public policies, religious teachings, and pressures to restructure.

For instance, men in many settings find it increasingly difficult to maintain traditional bases of control and privilege—the breadwinner role, access to stable and well-paid employment, and so forth. Their responses may include acknowledgment of women's importance and a shift toward greater partnership in decision making, or they may include the use of violence or declining contributions to support women and children. In general, men and children appear to have increased their dependence on women's often meager incomes, even as women's health and well-being have declined.

Where women's incomes and crucial roles as budget managers increase their importance for household survival, women's relative power in the household seems most likely to improve. But even the limited historical analyses available on the complex gender impacts of crises and restructuring suggest that, at the very least, crises should not be thought of as transforming experiences for women. Thus, the outcomes of the intersection of economic change, crisis, household, and gender cover a full range of possibilities for women: increased status and power,[2] greater vulnerability and exploitation, sometimes a little of both, and sometimes little or no significant change in their relative power or well-being. Outcomes depend on a myriad of factors, including both supply variables—the characteristics of women and of the household division of labor—and demand variables—the nature of employment and production. This explains why, in the case of Puerto Rico and the Dominican Republic and among the middle- and working-class women of Mexico, restructuring coincided with or followed on improvements in education or new social mechanisms of support for women (welfare, family planning programs, and so on) and relative power was not solely explained by declining real incomes for men or the nature of industrial restructuring (which created a demand for women's labor).

On the other hand, as we saw in the studies of Turkey and Taiwan, restructuring took place in ways that circumvented social factors that might have supported greater choice and freedom for women (e.g., legislative reform and expansion of education). Instead, it intersected directly with households under male authority. As a result, industrialization and agricultural change both incorporated and were incorporated into the existing pattern of gender relations and obligations at the household level. In Poland and Algeria, among other areas, restructuring provoked a revival of traditional gender norms.

It follows, then, that we can conclude that economic policies and programs are not "neutral." That is, they are value laden and privilege some groups (ethnic, class, gender, age, and so forth) at the expense of others. Failure to recognize and address the biases in policies camouflages exploitive agendas—whether intentional or unintentional, whether based on traditional or emerging systems. Several contributors here document how these agendas are made explicit when women or certain class or religious groups mobilize in response to policies or programs. In other cases, ethnic differences intersected with gender relations in ways that undermine potentially exploitive policies or forms of production.

We can also conclude that human life and social organization cannot be fragmented or broken down into discrete sectors (agriculture versus trade), spaces (shelter, workplace), or interests (domestic versus strategic). These dimensions have little meaning for whole individuals and the activities in which they engage, and moreover, policies that attempt to regulate fragments of human life are doomed to fail because they cannot possibly consider all the factors that come into play. Examples include the overlap between domestic tasks and income-generating tasks that share a space in the household; African women whose roles as mothers give them a different view of environment than men or women may have as workers; cost-efficient agricultural and microenterprise programs that depend on the gender division of labor in the home; links between women's decision-making power over fertility and the relative importance of their incomes to household survival; the policy distinctions made between so-called domestic issues and political-strategic issues or between shelter and work; and the overlap of domestic and strategic concerns.

Another important conclusion is that although the application of almost uniform economic reforms and policies to diverse political, economic, cultural, and ecological contexts may be the norm, it is unrealistic. Furthermore, crises with similar origins or causes do not necessarily lead to similar social or economic outcomes. Ignorance of the ways in which policies intersect with gender, class, ethnicity, age, and other variables reduces the likelihood that objectives will be achieved, it also increases the likelihood of resistance and negative outcomes and exacerbates the vulnerability and poverty of disadvantaged groups. In some cases, social movements may arise to combat negative effects. At other times, smaller-scale, seemingly personalized strategies emerge. And in still other cases, macroeconomic policies can be made or broken at the microlevel—in households and communities or by widespread social movements.

The gendered impacts of economic change can be evaluated through many methods and approaches, but those that assess people's perceptions of their circumstances are especially revealing. For instance, in-depth interviews with even small numbers of women can revise our notions of gender or class differences and of "progress." Such interviews revealed that women of different classes express similarly strong commitments to work, showed pride in their contributions to the household, and reported having important domestic decision-making roles; a few women even voiced an ideology of partnership with or independence from the male household heads.

Interestingly, women's words show that their commitment to family is expressed in children's education and nutrition, in the high value they place on ethnic traditions and values, and in their struggles to defend communities and the natural environment.[3]

On the other hand, some women expressed an acceptance of male entitlement and authority, although the contributors who interviewed them believed that ideological pressures and social norms inhibited open manifestations of discontent. Research suggested that in some cases, gender relations may have been more egalitarian in the past and, that in others, women as well as men will go to great lengths to increase their autonomy and control over income and productive resources. Women, however, seem more likely than men to sacrifice their own interests for those of children.

The preceding chapters also revealed that women's overall empowerment relative to men is multidimensional, complex, and conditional and varies markedly across space and time. Factors to consider include income, control over resources, degree of patriarchy, organization of production, division of labor, and political context. Yet the most persistent argument is that access to income and control over productive resources are positively associated with women's relative power and autonomy. Evidence in this volume also supports the probability that this relationship is weaker in more patriarchal settings.

Some evidence is contradictory. For instance, does linking women's gender identity or roles to their interests and demands support politicization of those demands (as the evidence from Africa suggests), or does it hinder politicization? Do movements to defend ethnic and religious tradition hurt women (as some would argue happened in Catholic Poland and some Islamist countries), or can they improve women's status relative to men? A determining factor appears to be the degree to which control of ethnic revival movements and political movements are promoted and led by men. Movements led by men may be more likely to disadvantage women; conversely, movements promoted and led by women may be more likely to validate women's importance as political actors.

Although the point is never explicitly discussed in the volume, I would argue that the previous chapters suggest that women's potential power—be it economic, political, or personal-familial—is highest in circumstances where new, nontraditional opportunities arise (or are created by women) than in settings where women are included in or are integrated into traditional forms of production, reproduction, and politics. These new opportunities may displace or coexist with traditional opportunities. The difference is that traditional opportunities tend to be gendered already—in most cases controlled by men. Thus, with a few exceptions, traditional forms of production or provision of services intersect with patriarchal gender relations or state authority to reinforce male control and give greater attention to men and "men's issues." The same applies to party politics, where a confrontational political style and competition over power devalue what women bring to politics or organizing and where "domestic" issues only garner attention when, appropriated by men, they are redefined as "public" issues.

When looked at as a set, the case studies also seem to suggest that women are most successful when they take advantage of (or appropriate, if need be) new political facts, introduce alternative symbolic discourses, and address policy-making or programs in a practical and nonconfrontational manner. In fact, some political discourses and issues that have emerged through planned change appear to be more amenable to women's appropriation than others. These include health and nutrition, housing and community services, and environmental issues—probably because of their relevance for and overlap with women's traditional roles as nurturers and food producers.

The news, in summary, is not uniformly positive. On the one hand, gender-sensitive policy-making and development programs can encourage recognition of women's contributions to households and the economy. But they also can justify measures that take advantage of women's labor at the household level and encourage men to exploit women. Nonetheless, promoting the recognition of women's knowledge and roles can support their access to legitimate power in the political arena. □

WHERE TO FROM HERE?

We have observed that people are most likely to resist aspects of economic and social change that impoverish, insult, and disempower them. For women, these include policies and programs that reinforce patriarchal control. Negative change is confronted not only through survival strategies but also through collective struggles for self-determination and defense of tradition, family, and the land.

To paraphrase Kettel's use of women and men's "landscapes" as a means of understanding gendered relations to the environment, I would argue that researchers and policymakers alike could benefit by broadening their "humanscapes." This can be done by studying and acknowledging the multidimensionality of gendered human life and experience. Important components of an appropriate humanscape would be a reconsideration of the gendered nature of planned change experiences from the past, abandonment of the myth of neutral economic policies and programs, and an assessment of the gendered and ethnocentric nature of politics and economic restructuring. An important advance would be the promotion of a range of "alternative" political and decision-making strategies with potential for humanizing planned economic change and social policies. This is a daunting task, but the contributors in this book have established some guidelines. In general, three research strategies show great promise.

First, cross-regional, multidisciplinary, longitudinal, and stratified comparisons are critical. As Moghadam and Monteón reveal, there is little hope that we will understand change processes or global linkages if we focus on one geographic region, are locked into a narrow research problem or perspective, or ignore the importance of historical and other contextual factors. It also should be unthinkable for social scientists to ignore ethnic, environmental, and gender issues in studies of policy-making and change processes. It is not mere coincidence that the three "policy" chapters in this book share the underlying theme of "environment" (whether built or natural) or that several contributors considered the intersection of gender with class or ethnicity and spatial factors. Reality is both complex and unruly. Scholars producing successful accounts of economic and social transformation give careful consideration to unruly details.

Comparative analyses can be used to search for trends and commonalities and can reveal the variability and conditionality of change. They also challenge researchers to explain why, how, and under what conditions very different change processes (revolution, environmentalism, marketization, industrial restructuring, legal reform, and employment of women, among others) occur together, precede, or follow one another. Just as human life is not fragmented, so processes of change are multidimensional.

Second, the case studies confirm both the advantages of linking macro- and microlevel processes and the impossibility of separating them. How can research and policy-making focus on the "whole individual" if the "whole context" within which people act and react is not understood? How can policy be successfully implemented (in nonexploitive ways, of course) if economic policy does not take into account gendered divisions of labor or if social and political policies do not take into account the way in which access to and control over productive resources intersect with gender roles to produce specific survival strategies? How can infrastructural policies contribute to human welfare if they do not confront gendered notions of male and female "space" and uses of public services? Every author in this book found it necessary to look at the economic and political context in order to understand gender relations and household dynamics. They provide us with diverse models of how to go about making those links.

Third, the contributors have revealed both the benefits and the obstacles to "bringing men back into" gender research and analysis. The numerous examples of analyses that benefited from disaggregation of data by class and ethnicity, religion, place, and age also point to the importance of the gender identity and roles and of gender composition of mixed activities. Men's and women's interests, actions, and reactions are understood accurately only through identifying and understanding their social positions. Social positioning, in turn, affects not only experiences but also worldviews.

Although each author deals with the issue of gender (e.g., comparison of men and women, identification of gendered roles and differences), most give far greater attention to women than to men. This is not an oversight nor does it belie the importance of gender comparisons. However, it does reveal the irony following two decades of correcting women's statistical invisibility and absence in policy documents. For some issues, we now find comparisons made difficult by the absence of equally rich and reliable information on men.

The gender and development approach outlined in Blumberg's introduction and Kettel's chapter is useful for showing how gender is socially constructed via men's and women's productive and reproductive activities. Many of the authors who have been successful at using a GAD approach have produced their own empirical data (for instance, Gallin, Engle, García-Guadilla, Morvaridi, and Robertson). Some deliberately emphasized women's experiences and reality in their work as a mechanism to achieve GAD research objectives (as did Kettel, Owoh, Robertson, and García and de Oliveira); in so doing, they were able to contrast women's reality with gendered expectations and stereotypical notions. But a few authors found it difficult to assess women's condition relative to men. More information on men's activities that are taken for granted and their responses to economic and social dimensions of change would improve opportunities for comparisons (as pointed out by Engle, Safa, and Tinker).

As Blumberg notes, there has been a shift in the field of women/ gender and development from "women as victims" to "women needed to save the world." But there is a danger in the romanticization of women's courage and resourcefulness at the expense of acknowledging their burdens and obstacles, and there is a risk of overlooking men's burdens and obstacles as well. Romanticization can lead to reduced demands for institutional or legal reform because women manage to cope or circumvent obstacles. It also can lead to excessive reliance on women's resourcefulness in compensating for cutbacks in services, to inattention to mechanisms that encourage greater contributions by men to family and economic life, and to subordination of women's labor in the name of development. Proper gender analyses should look at the gender division of labor, the gender division of resources and income, the gender division of time, and the gender division of other opportunities or constraints, such as mobility and institutional-regulatory context. A more holistic approach to the study of human life can facilitate efforts to bring men back into the picture and bridge the diverse dimensions of women's lives. Failure to use a holistic, gendered approach will limit our understanding of how to improve men's contributions without undermining women. Alternately, an exclusive focus on women's contributions may encourage policies that increase women's workload as a mechanism for improving the well-being of families. These are the unavoidable conclusions to be drawn from the case studies in this book. □

NOTES

1. Many planners and policy makers and the development economists who advise them seem to find it difficult to accept that the values and processes of capitalism do not stop at the front door of the household. Contradictorily, they may construct economic policies and programs that implicitly depend on the division of labor in the household.

2. Status can include legal equality as well as the more generalized respect and importance accorded to women in the home, the workplace, and politics. Higher status usually implies greater relative power—autonomy and influence over others.

3. Few authors raised questions regarding men's commitment to family and children. But their initial findings suggest that individual factors (marital status, educational level, number of children, and work status of children's mothers) and societal factors of entitlement, opportunity, and need operate together to influence variations in men's commitment to children.

About the Book

The new international division of labor and the imposition of structural adjustment on Third World countries has necessitated a reexamination of development policies and a reevaluation of the role of gender in their success or failure. Although women often bear the heaviest burden under structural adjustment, there is also considerable evidence of women being empowered through their responses to the challenges of economic restructuring.

Based on case study material from Eastern Europe, the Islamic nations, Africa, China, and Latin America, this volume explores the significant contributions women make to the wealth and well-being of their families and nations. The contributors argue persuasively that women may hold the key to *sustainable* development, an increasingly critical issue at a time when policymakers are reconsidering the full costs and benefits of a growth-fixated development model.

One of the first to embody the new "gender and development" paradigm, this book reports on research at the frontiers of knowledge and theory about the gendered outcomes of economic transformation, restructuring, and social change. By incorporating "voices from the South," it makes a provocative addition to our understanding of the political economy of development and of the relationship between world ecology and the world economy.

About the Editors and Contributors

Rae Lesser Blumberg received her M.A. and Ph.D. from Northwestern University and is professor of sociology, University of California, San Diego. She is the editor of *Gender, Family, and Economy: The Triple Overlap* (1991) and has authored various books and numerous essays and articles on gender, power, and Third World development. She has researched gender and development in over twenty countries and has served as a consultant to the World Bank and the United States Agency for International Development.

Orlandina de Oliveira is research professor at the Center for Sociological Studies, El Colegio de México. She received her Ph.D. in sociology from the University of Texas at Austin. She has published widely on migration and the Mexican labor force; her works include *Hogares y trabajadores en la Ciudad de México* (1982). She is also the coauthor of *Trabajo feminino y vida familiar en México* (1994).

Patrice L. Engle, professor and department chair of psychology and human development, California Polytechnic State University, San Luis Obispo, is the author of numerous journal articles on nutrition, women's work, and child well-being in developing countries. She has served as a consultant to more than twenty-five programs.

Rita S. Gallin is director of the Women and International Development Program and associate professor of sociology at Michigan State University. She is the editor of the *Women in International Development Working Paper Series* and chief editor of the *Women and International Development Annual*, published by Westview Press. She has published numerous articles on women, development, and Taiwan.

Brígida García is a researcher in demography and urban studies at El Colegio de México. She received her Ph.D. from the Universidad Autónoma Nacional de México and has published extensively in the field of fertility, family, and the labor force in Mexico. Her publications include *Desarrollo económico y absorción de fuerza de trabajo en México* (1988), and she is coauthor of *Trabajo feminino y vida familiar en México* (1994).

María Pilar García-Guadilla is a Venezuelan sociologist, environmentalist, and urban planner. She holds an M.A. in demography and human ecology and a Ph.D. in urban sociology from the University of Chicago and is a professor at the

Universidad Simón Bolívar, Caracas, Venezuela. She has written extensively on environmental issues and movements in Latin America and is editor of *Estado, ambiente y sociedad: Crisis y conflictos ambientales en América Latina y Venezuela.*

Bonnie Kettel is assistant professor of environmental studies at York University in Toronto, Canada. She received her Ph.D. in social anthropology from the University of Illinois at Urbana-Champaign. Since 1988, she has been the Canadian coordinator for the Women, Environment, and Development Network (WEDNET), a large-scale research initiative funded by the International Development Research Centre. Her recent efforts have involved policy formulation for women, environment, and development for several organizations, including the Women's Environment and Development Organization in New York and the Gender Programme of the UN Commission on Science and Technology.

Valentine M. Moghadam is senior research fellow and coordinator of the Research Programme on Women and Development at the United Nations University's World Institute for Development Economics Research in Helsinki, Finland. Born in Iran, she studied in Canada and the United States, earning a Ph.D. in sociology with a concentration in development from the American University in 1986. She is the author of *Modernizing Women: Gender and Social Change in the Middle East* (1993) and the editor of *Identity Politics and Women: Cultural Reassertions and Feminisms in International Perspective* (1994).

Michael Monteón is associate professor of history at the University of California, San Diego. He was educated at the University of Denver (B.A.) and Harvard University (M.A. and Ph.D.). He is the author of *Chile in the Nitrate Era: The Evolution of Economic Dependence, 1880–1930* (1982) and of articles on labor history and the political economies of Argentina and Chile. Since the early 1980s, he has been working on a study of Latin America during the Great Depression.

Behrooz Morvaridi teaches and conducts several research projects at the Development and Project Planning Centre, Bradford University, England. His research is on gender relations, development, and the environment, as well as on agrarian change in both Asia and Africa.

Kenna Owoh is an adjunct lecturer at York University, Toronto, Canada. She is currently completing her doctoral dissertation in political science on the gender implications of structural adjustment in Nigeria. Prior to beginning her doctoral studies, Ms. Owoh worked extensively as a medical professional in Africa.

Cathy A. Rakowski is assistant professor of women's studies and rural sociology at The Ohio State University. She received a Ph.D. in sociology from the University of Texas at Austin. Between 1979 and 1986, she worked as a research consultant in Venezuela for the Corporación Venezolana de Guayana (Guayana Development Corporation), the national planning agency, and the UN Development Programme, among other organizations. She is editor of *Contrapunto: The Informal Sector Debate in Latin America* (1994) and has published on gender and class issues in social and cultural change in rural and urban Venezuela.

Claire Robertson received her Ph.D. from the University of Wisconsin and has done fieldwork in Ghana and Kenya. She has published several dozen articles and three books, one of which, *Sharing the Same Bowl?* (1984), won the African Studies Association's Herskovits Book Award. She is presently working on another book, *"Healing Together Gave Us Strength": Women, Men, and Trade in the Nairobi Area, 1890–1990.*

Helen I. Safa is author of *The Urban Poor of Puerto Rico* (1974) and coauthor of *In the Shadows of the Sun: Caribbean Development Alternatives and U.S. Policy* (1990), as well as several other books and articles on migration, urbanization, and women and development. Safa is currently professor of anthropology and Latin American studies at the University of Florida. A past president of the Latin American Studies Association, she received her Ph.D. in anthropology from Columbia University. Her chapter in this volume is drawn from her forthcoming book, *The Myth of the Male Breadwinner: Women and Industrialization in the Caribbean.*

Irene Tinker is professor of city and regional planning and of women's studies, University of California, Berkeley. A pioneer in the field of women in development, she organized the first international conference on the topic in conjunction with the UN World Conference for Women in Mexico City in 1975. She cofounded the Wellesley Center for Research on Women (1974), the International Center for Research on Women (1976), and the Equity Policy Center (1978). She was also the first director of the Office of International Science at the American Association for the Advancement of Science and an assistant director of ACTION under President Jimmy Carter.

Index